OXFORD HISTORICAL MONOGRAPHS

Editors
BARBARA HARVEY   A.D. MACINTYRE
R.W. SOUTHERN   A.F. THOMPSON
H.R. TREVOR-ROPER

The First Rockingham Administration 1765–1766

BY

P. LANGFORD

OXFORD UNIVERSITY PRESS
1973

Oxford University Press, Ely House, London W. 1

GLASGOW NEW YORK TORONTO MELBOURNE WELLINGTON
CAPE TOWN IBADAN NAIROBI DAR ES SALAAM LUSAKA ADDIS ABABA
DELHI BOMBAY CALCUTTA MADRAS KARACHI LAHORE DACCA
KUALA LUMPUR SINGAPORE HONG KONG TOKYO

Printed in Great Britain by
Pitman Press, Bath

TO
MY PARENTS

PREFACE

No study of this kind can be carried out without incurring a great many debts of gratitude. I should therefore like to express my appreciation of the assistance rendered by the staffs of the following institutions: the British Museum; the Public Record Office; the House of Lords Record Office; Berkshire, Bury St. Edmunds and West Suffolk, Essex, Hertfordshire, Ipswich and East Suffolk, Northamptonshire, Staffordshire, Warwickshire, and Wigan Record Offices; the Bodleian Library; Nottingham University Library; Sheffield City Library; the History of Parliament Trust. In addition I must acknowledge the kindness of the following owners of manuscripts in granting me access to their collections and permission to publish quotations: the Controller of H.M. Stationery Office, the Trustees of the British Museum, the Trustees of the Bedford Settled Estates, the Duke of Buccleuch and Queensberry, K.T., G.C.V.O., the Duke of Grafton, the Duke of Portland, K.G., the Marquess of Bute, the Earl of Albemarle, the Earl of Dartmouth, Earl Fitzwilliam and his trustees, Lord Rayleigh, Lord Henley, Victor Montagu, Esq., and F.H.M. Fitzroy Newdegate, Esq.

I cannot sufficiently stress the extent of my obligation to those who have borne the burden of supervising my work; both Professor J.B. Owen and Dame Lucy Sutherland have given unstintingly of time and trouble in advising and assisting me in my studies. I must also record my gratitude to the Principal and Fellows of Hertford College, and the Rector and Fellows of Lincoln College, who have done so much to finance and facilitate my work, and finally to all those who have, in the course of the past three years, helped with their comments and suggestions.

PAUL LANGFORD

Lincoln College,
Oxford.

CONTENTS

LIST OF ABBREVIATIONS
FOR PRINCIPAL SOURCES USED

Add.MSS.	British Museum, Additional Manuscripts.
Am. Hist.Rev.	*American Historical Review.*
Bedford Correspondence	*The Correspondence of John, Fourth Duke of Bedford*, ed. Lord J. Russell London, 1846.
Burke Correspondence	*The Correspondence of Edmund Burke*, ed. T.W. Copeland (Cambridge, 1958–).
Burke's Works	*The Works of the Right Honourable Edmund Burke* (London, 1886).
Can.Hist.Rev.	*Canadian Historical Review.*
Chatham Correspondence	*Correspondence of William Pitt, Earl of Chatham*, ed. W.S. Taylor and J.H. Pringle (London, 1839).
Correspondence of George III	*The Correspondence of King George III from 1760 to December 1783*, ed. Sir J. Fortescue (London, 1927).
also *(Additions and Corrections)*	L.B. Namier, *Additions and Corrections to Sir John Fortescue's Edition of the Correspondence of George III* (Volume I) (Manchester, 1937).
E.H.R.	*English Historical Review.*
Econ.Hist.Rev.	*Economic History Review.*
Grafton Autobiography	*Autobiography and Political Correspondence of Augustus Henry, Third Duke of Grafton, K.G.*, ed. W.R.Anson (London, 1898).
Grenville Papers	*The Grenville Papers*, ed. W.J. Smith (London, 1852).
H.M.C.	Historical Manuscripts Commission.
Jenkinson Papers	*The Jenkinson Papers: 1760-66*, ed. N.S. Jucker (London, 1949).
Letters from George III to Lord Bute	*Letters from George III to Lord Bute, 1756-65*, ed. R.Sedgwick (London, 1939).
Newcastle's Narrative	*A Narrative of the Changes in the Ministry: 1765-67*, ed. M. Bateson (London, 1898)

P.R.O.   Public Record Office.

Rockingham Memoirs   *Memoirs of the Marquis of Rockingham and his Contemporaries,* ed. Earl of Albemarle (London, 1852).

Walpole Correspondence   *Horace Walpole's Correspondence,* ed. W.S. Lewis (London, 1937–).

Walpole's Memoirs   Walpole, Horace, *Memoirs of the Reign of King George III,* ed. G.F.R. Barker (London, 1894).

WWM   Sheffield City Library, Wentworth Woodhouse Muniments (Fitzwilliam Papers).

NOTE

Extended footnotes giving full details of a biographical nature are not generally given in the following pages, though adequate relevant information is normally supplied in the text. Brief details are to be found in the index, and fuller information is of course available in Sir L. Namier and J. Brooke, *The History of Parliament, The House of Commons 1754-1790,* G.E.C.'s *Complete Peerage,* the *Dictionary of National Biography,* etc.

INTRODUCTION

IT IS one of the paradoxes of eighteenth-century history that a ministry as seemingly insignificant as the first Rockingham Administration should have cast its shadows so far. To contemporaries it was merely one of the many short-lived administrations which reflected the intense political instability of the times. The ten years between the accession of George III in 1760 and the establishment of Lord North's regime in 1770 saw a rapid succession of governments, most of which were forgotten almost as soon as they had fallen. The fourth of these ministries, remembered by the name of the second Marquess of Rockingham, was actually one of the shortest of the entire century, lasting as it did barely twelve months. Yet it was to have a substantial impact on the history of the following years, and still greater influence on the historiography of the next century. The fact that the men who formed and directed it had previously been identified with the Whig élite of George II's reign, and were in future to create a party of opposition recognized as the direct ancestor to the Whig party of Fox, Grey, and Russell, gives to the events of the years 1765-6 a significance which they would otherwise scarcely possess. The 'old Whig' party of the 1770s and 1780s, the party first of the Rockinghams and later of the Foxites, was strongly influenced by its brief period of office in the mid-sixties, and drew heavily on that experience for its propaganda. Moreover the generalizations with which nineteenth-century Whig historians like Macaulay and Trevelyan sought to depict this age—so important to their own because of its proximity—were taken largely from the highly partisan effusions of Edmund Burke, himself deeply affected by the events of 1765-6. Those events were thus doubly distorted and misrepresented until they bore little resemblance to reality. In particular George III's difficulties with the Rockingham Ministers, intrinsically no more significant than any other year in the history of relations between the eighteenth-century monarchy and its ministers, were turned to good account by Whig politicians at the time and Whig historians later, both intent on destroying the character of the King.

Similarly the Stamp Act crisis of 1765-6, in retrospect an important episode but by no means the only one of significance in the tortured history of imperial relations at this time, became first the inspiration of the policy which the Rockingham party adopted in the period of the American War, and subsequently the evidence with which their nineteenth-century admirers both in England and America were able to prove their consistent liberalism. If any single episode can be said to contain the seeds both of the Whig programmes of the 1770s and 1780s and the Whig mythology of the nineteenth century, it is that of the First Rockingham Ministry.

Today of course the Whig myth of history has been largely dismantled. Layer after layer of distortion and misrepresentation has been stripped away from the years of the mid-eighteenth century, and what follows is not intended to expatiate still further on the grosser crudities of Victorian historiography. On the other hand if the simple outlines of the old picture have been erased, the detailed composition beneath has been revealed only in patches. In particular, no full account of the First Rockingham Administration has been written, and while the supporting mythology is in ruins, many of the misconceptions remain. The Rockinghams are still frequently treated on the one hand as the unhappy victims of George III's personal government and on the other as the far-seeing champions of American rights and liberties. Necessarily these topics are major features of the narrative of the years 1765-6, and in each case the reality is a good deal more complicated than the legend. In the story of the King's relations with his Ministers there were many misconceptions and misapprehensions, but few rights and wrongs; in the erratic evolution of the policy which culminated in the repeal of the Stamp Act, there were many vacillations and hesitations, but few predispositions and preconceptions.

If these are inevitably the outstanding aspects of the history of the first Rockingham Administration, secondary themes and subjects are by no means lacking. For Ministers as little inclined to vigorous political activity as those led by Rockingham, their year in office was a suprisingly busy and eventful one. Many significant themes not merely of the 1760s but also of the period as a whole crop up in the story of their

activities. The growing ineffectiveness of British foreign policy
in the years before the American Revolution, the emergence
of new imperial options in the inauguration of the Free Ports,
the equivocal role of party in the appearance of the King's
Friends, the rising tide of radicalism in the strange career of
John Wilkes, the regional politics of the counties in the repeal
of the Cider Excise, the constitutional role of the House of
Lords in the divisions on the Repeal of the Stamp Act, the
swelling voice of nascent industrialism in the economics of the
Stamp Act crisis, all these emerge clearly in the varied events
of the years 1765-6. Above and beyond these themes, however,
is the dominant role of personality. In defiance of the modern
fashion for detecting the sway of impersonal forces, the politics of England in the 1760s are not reducible to simple formu-
las or straightforward generalizations; the critical factor at
every turn is the role of personality. Some of the *dramatis
personae* are indeed of particular interest and importance;
the significant, not to say unique, position of the Duke of
Cumberland, the controversial conduct of George III and Lord
Bute, the declining influence of the old Duke of Newcastle,
and the rising star of the young Edmund Burke, all naturally
demand attention. But even without these special points of
interest, the story is primarily one of human personality. What
follows is the study of an important and controversial period,
of the rise and fall of an administration, of the emergence of
a new and unconventional opposition party; it is also the tale
of a group of men whose policies and politics were dictated
first and foremost by their own characteristic attitudes and
ideas.

I

THE RETURN OF THE 'OLD WHIGS' (JULY 1765)

'AFTER all the Variety of Political Bustles', wrote the Marquess of Rockingham on 8 July 1765, 'I now hope that an Administration is formed.'[1] The First Rockingham Ministry was formally inaugurated two days later on Wednesday 10 July, when Rockingham and his more important colleagues kissed hands for their respective offices. Few Administrations could have begun less auspiciously, at least in the view of contemporaries. Charles Townshend's celebrated epithet—'a Lutestring ministry; fit only for the summer'[2]—with its implication that the Ministers were incapable of facing a Parliamentary session in the winter, was wholly representative of current opinion, and was indeed widely imitated. It was to be expected of course that the enemies of the new Ministers would loudly claim to 'have no idea of a man of a serious turn of mind embarking in such a bottom'.[3] However the fact was, as Sandwich fairly pointed out, that 'the general language seems turned to ridicule the new ministry, and to pronounce their existence to be of a very short duration.'[4] Even their supposed supporters were not optimistic. Northington, a member of the new Cabinet as of the old, described the new Government as 'a damn'd silly system', while Horace Walpole had 'never heard a more wild proposal, nor one fraught with greater improbability of success'.[5]

In retrospect the chorus of disapproval which greeted the formation of the Rockingham Ministry was to be forgotten. Whig historiography in the nineteenth century treated the return to power of the 'Old Whigs' in 1765 as a great triumph for a party purified and strengthened by the stresses of the

[1] Staffordshire Record Office, Dartmouth MSS, Rockingham to Dartmouth, 8 July 1765.
[2] *The Letters of Philip Dormer Stanhope, Fourth Earl of Chesterfield*, ed. B. Dobrée (1932), vi. 2661: Chesterfield to P. Stanhope, 17 Aug. 1765.
[3] History of Parliament Trust transcripts, Sandwich MSS., Sandwich to Hervey, 4 July 1765.
[4] *Bedford Correspondence*, iii. 316: Sandwich to Bedford, 26 Aug. 1765.
[5] Add.MS. 51341 (Holland House Papers), f. 129: W. Digby to Lord Ilchester, 20 July 1765; *Walpole's Memoirs*, ii. 135.

early years of George III's reign. In fact the reality was less
flattering, for Rockingham and his friends owed their elevation
not at all to their own endeavours or merits. 'It is not their
own Strength w[hi]ch has brought Them into Play again',
the Earl of Hardwicke remarked to his brother.[6] Indeed the
performance of the 'Old Whigs' in Parliament in the session
before their return to office had been such as to cast the
gravest doubts on their continued existence as a credible
party of opposition. Only once in the winter of 1765 (on
29 January) had the Government been in any danger of defeat,
and then on the exceptional issue of General Warrants. Even
so the hopes of the Opposition were disappointed. 'We are
beat, 224 to 185', George Onslow reported to Newcastle;
'to be so on such a Question is too serious.'[7] As the session
advanced it became increasingly plain that the opponents of
the Ministry commanded no prospect of success in the everyday business of the House of Commons. Richard Rigby was
emphatic that 'the Opposition is reduced as low as I wish it
to be' while his colleague Sandwich later remarked 'We have
had the quietest and most expeditious sessions of Parliament
that ever I remember; the opposition is so low that it scarcely
deserves the name of a party.'[8]

If the total ineffectiveness of the Minority was so obvious,
its corollary, the growing strength and reputation of the
Grenville Ministry, was no less marked. Grenville, indeed, was
carving out for himself a Parliamentary position comparable
to that of Walpole and Pelham before him. The view of one
of his followers, Hans Stanley, was most percipient.

Mr. Grenville establishes himself upon very solid foundations every day,
and gains credit both by his Parliamentary abilities, and by the improve-
ments he is gradually making in the Revenue . . . I think that with
sober and substantial people, Government begins to be more settled,
than I have yet seen it since the death of Mr. Pelham: the minority are
much divided, many individuals softened and would I believe quit their
Colours on the smallest encouragement.[9]

Certainly the political pundits had no doubts as to the security
and permanence of the regime. 'For politics', Horace Walpole

[6] Add.MS. 35361 (Hardwicke Papers), f. 207: 9 Aug. 1765.
[7] Add.MS. 32965 (Newcastle Papers), f. 318: 29 Jan. 1765.
[8] J.H. Jesse, George Selwyn and his Contemporaries, (London, 1843), i. 365:
Rigby to Selwyn, 12 Mar. 1765; H.M.C. Denbigh MSS., v. 294: Sandwich to
Denbigh, 18 Mar. 1765.
[9] Add.MS. 22359 (Buckinghamshire Papers), f. 44: Stanley to Buckinghamshire,
24 Feb. 1765.

confidently forecast in February 1765, 'unless the ministers
wantonly thrust their hands into some fire, I think there will
not even be a smoke.'[10] It is against this background that the
developments leading to the accession of the 'Old Whigs' must
be seen. The essential fact was that by the spring of 1765 the
Grenville Administration was to all appearances immensely
strong and secure, while the Opposition, by contrast, was
weak, disunited and demoralized. It was with some reason
that a hostile pamphleteer later informed Grenville's
successors in office,

> you have not . . . the claim of conquest to urge on the behalf of your
> acceptance. The forts of Government were put into your hands when
> you had not even so much as summoned them to surrender, nor made
> a sally from your trenches for some weeks before; nay, the garrison was
> actually marching out, before you could collect a sufficient force to
> take possession of the several batteries and strong-holds which were to
> be delivered up.[11]

Ironically the 'Old Whigs' owed their return to place and
power solely to a revolution at Court, since Grenville and his
colleagues had, in the course of the previous two years,
steadily eroded their credit in the Closet. Fundamentally, the
problem was that Grenville aspired to supplant Lord Bute as
the King's favourite, whereas George III regarded him merely
as the Minister deputed to carry out the business of
government. Nothing did more to alienate the King than
Grenville's interminable suspicions of Bute's influence, his
unending efforts to keep him as far from Court as possible,
and his repeated attempts to extort formal guarantees of his
political retirement. In 1764 the consequent friction all but
precipitated a change of Ministry. When Grenville complained
of the access obtained to the Closet by Thomas Worsley, the
Surveyor of the Works, the King reacted with fury:

> had I follow'd my own inclinations [he wrote later], I certainly should
> have dismiss'd him the moment I heard this, but I knew the great detri-
> ment it would have been to the public affairs had any change taken
> place during the time that the National business was transacting I there-
> fore stifl'd my sensations.[12]

[10] *Letters of Horace Walpole*, ed. P. Toynbee (Oxford, 1904), vi. 189: Walpole
to Hertford, 12 Feb. 1765.
[11] *Universal Magazine*, xxxvii. 214: 'Abstract of the Political Apology, or,
Candid Reasons for not taking Part with the present Public System'.
[12] *Correspondence of George III*, i. 164–5: Memorandum by the King, [Nov. -
Dec. 1765]; (*Additions and Corrections*, p.38).

Worsley, of course, was considered by Grenville to be a tool of the 'Favourite', and there were similar incidents in 1765 over the appointment of a new Irish primate and a Secretary to the Order of the Thistle, when Grenville felt that his own just demands were over-ridden by agents of Bute, in the former case by Northumberland, Bute's relation by marriage, in the latter by Mackenzie, his brother.[13]

In addition to these difficulties there was the fact that Grenville was personally offensive to the King. There is no reason to doubt the veracity of Horace Walpole's well-known anecdotes—of Grenville's petty refusal to gratify the King's desire to buy land near Green Park, and of the way in which,

as if non-compliance with even his innocent pleasures was not sufficiently offensive, that awkward man of ways and means, whom nature had fitted for no employment less than a courtier's, fatigued the King with such nauseous and endless harangues, that, lamenting being daily exposed to such a political pedant, the King said to Lord Bute of Grenville, 'When he has wearied me for two hours, he looks at his watch to see if he may not tire me for an hour more.'[14]

Evidently Grenville, a thoroughly competent manager of the Commons, was totally incapable of mastering the Closet, and it is scarcely surprising that by May 1765 George III was desperate to the point of distraction in his anxiety to rid himself of his Ministry. Thus he informed Bute towards the end of that month,

every day I meet with some insult from these people; I have been for near a week as it were in a feaver my very sleep is not free from thinking of the men I daily see; patience cannot last I encline much to putting everything to a quick upshot, that I may know who are friends and who secret foes; indecision is the ruin of all things; excuse the incoherency of my letter; but a mind ulcer'd by the treatment it meets with from all around is the true cause of it.[15]

This was the reality behind the accession of Rockingham and his friends; they were required not to rescue George III from 'the resentment of his subjects, at home and across the seas',[16]

[13] *Grenville Papers*, ii. 533–5; iii. 112–13, 124, 126–7.
[14] *Walpole's Memoirs*, ii. 115; these anecdotes appear to have come from Lord Holland (see Add.MS. 51406, f. 99: Holland to J. Campbell, 22 Sept. 1765) and doubtless in the first instance from Bute or Mackenzie.
[15] *Letters from George III to Lord Bute*, p.241: [soon after 23 May 1765].
[16] G.O. Trevelyan, *The Early History of Charles James Fox* (London, 1881), p.125. In fact news of the Stamp Act disturbances in America had not even reached England at this time, while the political issue of general warrants was all but dead.

but to replace Ministers who had become intolerably odious
to their master.

If the change of Ministry in 1765 was a natural result of
the deterioration in relations between the Crown and its
servants, the actual circumstances in which the 'Old Whigs'
took office were extraordinarily complicated. Samuel Touchet
for example later remarked that 'such a scene of political
confusion were we in for a month or 6 weeks as I believe was
never known in this country.'[17] As early as 7 April the Duke
of Cumberland was summoned to Court with a view to clearing
the ground for negotiations between the King and the Opposition, but this initiative was overtaken by a complex series
of events. The touchstone for the latter was the introduction
at Westminster of a Regency Bill, a measure plainly justified
by the gravity of the King's illness a month or so earlier,[18] yet
a source of intense anxiety in the Cabinet. Grenville and his
colleagues seriously believed that the provisions of the bill,
and in particular the clause leaving the nomination of any
future regent to the discretion of the King, were designed to
ensure the joint rule of Bute and the Princess-Dowager of
Wales in the event of George III's death. As a result they
proved uncooperative and obstructive from the inception of
the scheme, and their resentment culminated in an act of
extreme stupidity—the deliberate exclusion of the Princess-
Dowager from the bill's schedule of those among whom the
King was to seek a Regent. The circumstances in which this
excision was made still remain obscure. Though Grenville and
his friends afterwards insisted that it had actually originated
with Bute and been fully endorsed by the King himself,[19] it
was universally construed as a gross insult to the mother of
the reigning monarch. Moreover, when the House of Commons
reversed the Ministry's decision of its own accord and thus
demonstrated that the proscription of the Princess-Dowager
had by no means been required by the state of opinion at

[17] Add.MS. 51425, f. 119: Touchet to Holland, 18 July 1765; in general for the
circumstances preceding and accompanying the formation of the new Ministry,
see A. Hardy, 'The Duke of Newcastle and His Friends in Opposition, 1762—
65' (Manchester Univ. M.A. thesis 1956), chapters vii and viii.

[18] For the nature and significance of the illness, see I. Macalpine and R. Hunter,
George III and the Mad-Business (London, 1969), chapter xi.

[19] It is suggested by D. Jarrett, 'The Regency Crisis of 1765', E.H.R. lxxxv (1970),
282—316, that Grenville was the victim of an elaborate conspiracy by George
III and the Opposition; no hard evidence is presented for this view, nor can it
be regarded as a plausible one.

Westminster, George III took the view that he had been
maliciously deceived by his Ministers, and reacted with understandable anger. The Regency Bill, though not responsible
for the King's decision to rid himself of Grenville's loathsome
presence, undoubtedly added to his anxiety to do so as quickly
as possible.

However the sequel was not quite as straightforward as
George III could have wished. Though the friction over the
Regency Bill developed in the first fortnight of May and led
the King to hasten his search for a new Ministry, it was not
until two months later that his efforts were rewarded with
success. The intervening period saw an unavailing appeal to
William Pitt through Cumberland, the reinstatement of
Grenville on terms which were utterly repugnant to the King,
a violent clash between the Crown and its Ministers over the
issue of royal confidence, a renewed approach—this time by
the King himself—to Pitt, who again mysteriously declined
to form a government, and finally, after much doubt and
vacillation, an announcement that the Dukes of Cumberland
and Newcastle would form a Ministry themselves. This period
of confusion, which reduced George III himself to a state of
intense despair and anxiety, was dominated by the figures of
Pitt and Grenville. The latter seemed to have brought the
Crown to a degree of subjection scarcely paralleled even by
the Pelhams in the 1740s. 'George the Third', Horace Walpole
pointed out at the end of May, 'is the true successor of
George the Second, and inherits all his grandfather's humiliations—indeed they are attended with circumstances a little
more cutting.'[20] Grenville's terms on his reinstatement after
the failure of the May negotiations exploited his advantage
to the hilt, extorting a new assurance from George III that
Bute would have no influence in political matters, as well as
dismissing Bute's brother Mackenzie from the office of
Scottish Privy Seal and his ally Lord Holland from that of
Paymaster-General. This was generally thought to have put
Grenville in a position of unprecedented supremacy, though
its real effect was to reinforce in the strongest possible fashion
the King's utter detestation of his Ministers, and to advance
their ultimate downfall. The conduct of Pitt was no less
spectacular than Grenville's. Twice he refused to accept office,
once when Cumberland acted as intermediary in May, and

[20] *Walpole Correspondence*, x. 153: Walpole to Montagu, 26 May 1765.

again when summoned to the Closet in June. In the former
case he appeared unenthusiastic at the prospect of power and
laid down conditions, notably the revival of the Anglo-
Prussian alliance, which did not wholly please the King; in the
latter he showed himself seemingly anxious to form a
Government, yet dramatically changed his mind when his
brother-in-law and ally, Temple, proved unwilling to join him.
Pitt's reluctance was as perplexing as Grenville's ruthlessness
was predictable.

In historical perspective the conduct of Grenville and Pitt
is overshadowed by the curious role of the men who eventually
emerged as the new Ministers. Throughout this period the
latter showed an extraordinary disinclination even to consider
the possibility of forming an Administration themselves. A
whole series of unavailing attempts were made to get Newcastle
and his friends to serve. Thus after Pitt and Temple had
initially refused to negotiate on 19 May, Cumberland immediately sought 'to establish some third system'.[21] Lyttelton, to
whom he appealed to act as First Lord of the Treasury,
declined 'tho' greatly prest',[22] and on 21 May it was agreed
'that the Duke of Cumberland should pass all the Remainder
of the Day in seeing the duke of Newcastle, his Friends, etc.
to try whether they could be brought upon a second Recol-
lection knowing the Crisis to Join with the King'.[23] However,
'he c[ou]ld make no Impression upon any one Man of the
d[uke] of Newcastles,' and on 22 May a 'third Trial' proved
equally futile.[24] On the following day George III submitted
once again to Grenville and the negotiations with the Minority
were abandoned.

A month later, after Pitt had proved uncooperative a
second time, Newcastle and his friends were no keener to
take office without him, despite George III's desperate plea
to Cumberland that 'the World will see that this Country is
not at that low Ebb that no Administration can be form'd
without the Grenville family'.[25] Richard Rigby's conviction

[21] P.R.O., Chatham MSS., lvi. f. 46: Shelburne to Pitt [May 1765].
[22] R.M. Davis, *The Good Lord Lyttelton* (Bethlehem, 1939), p.348: Lyttelton
to Mrs. Montagu, [21 May 1765].
[23] *Correspondence of George III*, i. 108: Egmont's Notes, 21 May 1765. (*Additions
and Corrections*, p.29).
[24] Ibid. i. 110, 111: Egmont's Notes, 22 May 1765.
[25] *Correspondence of George III*, i. 118: 12 June 1765.

that 'they would give the matter entirely up',[26] was
apparently confirmed by a critical meeting held at Newcastle's
Surrey seat at Claremont on 30 June. Of the seventeen friends
of the Duke present, six, including the most considerable
young men in the Commons, 'were of opinion that, in the
present circumstances, no new administration should be
undertaken'.[27] The remainder favoured the formation of a
new Ministry, though only on certain conditions—notably
the hounding out of all traces of Bute's influence, direct and
indirect, in government. After this Cumberland, the principal
mediator in all these negotiations, was inclined to give up; it
was Newcastle, backed by Rockingham and Conway, who
persuaded Cumberland to persevere and was thus responsible
'for having set on Foot *again* This Negotiation; When It was
determined to drop it'.[28] Though his intervention decided the
day, Newcastle himself remained in an agony of doubts,
declaring 'I have been blamed for my Backwardness, and
Timorousness; I hope, I shall not now be blamed, for My
Rashness, and Forwardness.'[29]

The state of indecision in which George III's appeals had
found the 'Old Whigs' aroused the surprise and derision of
contemporaries. Thus Holland, an arch realist in politics,
taunted Horace Walpole on 11 June:

What have you been doing, dear Hori, these two years? Acting with
men, or rather children, in the eager pursuit of what was not very likely
to be attained. *Volvenda dies en attulit ultro.* And then they won't take
what they had been so long looking for.[30]

This was perfectly fair comment. Newcastle himself was
moved to remark on 1 June, 'One would naturally ask, what
The Opposition had been doing for These Three Years', and
certainly there was little injustice in his opponents' jibes that
'we have got a Ministry *in spite of itself.*'[31] However, in
retrospect this phenomenon is not altogether surprising, for
it was a logical consequence of the composition and circumstances of the Opposition to the Bute and Grenville Admin-

[26] Bedford Estate Office, Bedford MSS., li. f. 238: Rigby to Bedford, 29 June
1766; not included in the version printed as *Bedford Correspondence*, iii. 303–4.
[27] *Rockingham Memoirs*, i. 218–20: Newcastle's account of the meeting.
[28] Add.MS. 32967, f. 214: Newcastle to Albemarle, 3 July 1765.
[29] Ibid., f. 192: Newcastle to Albemarle, 2 July 1765.
[30] *Walpole Correspondence*, xxx. 189.
[31] Add.MS. 32967, f. 1: Newcastle to Bishop of Oxford, 1 June 1765; *The
Principles of the late Changes Impartially Examined* (2nd edn., London, 1765),
p.50.

strations. The Rockinghams are sometimes treated as a
clearly defined political party which emerged with the
resignation of Newcastle and his friends in 1762-3.[32] In
reality the so-called Whig Opposition of the years 1762-5
was an incoherent and incohesive amalgam of various elements,
united by little more than the obvious fact that they were all
in some sense the victims of a new reign and a new regime.
The Duke of Cumberland, nominal head of the Minority and
an able, experienced, and resolute politician, doubtless performed a valuable role for the Opposition, lending it the kind
of prestige and respectability which only royalty could bestow,
and in some measure fulfilling the function of a reversionary
interest. However his views had little in common with those
of most of the old corps Whigs, ill health prevented him from
taking a very active part in day-to-day politics, and in general
his contribution was more that of the influential adviser than
that of effective director. Pitt and Newcastle were of course
the obvious leaders of the Minority, but neither succeeded in
welding it into an effective tool of opposition. Newcastle,
ageing and irresolute, himself felt the need to defer to Pitt,
and indeed though many of the young men who had left
office with him in 1762-3 claimed to be his followers, most
of them flocked naturally to Pitt's banner. 'Many of the party',
Richmond noted in June 1765, 'are now quite Pitt's men.'[33]
It was most noticeable that the chief opponents of forming
a Ministry without Pitt were not the ineffectual and much
despised great Lords, but the young and ambitious politicians
who were expected to be the main props of the new
Government in the Commons, men like George Onslow, Lord
Villiers, Thomas Townshend junior, Charles Townshend of
Honingham, and Thomas Walpole, all of whom were among
the dissenters at Claremont on 30 June. Of course had their
idol chosen to come to an amicable agreement with the other
leaders of the Opposition and played a prominent part in
their activities, all would have been well. But this was precisely
what Pitt, the most difficult of men to work with, would not
do. His constant failure to cooperate with those who were
desperately, even pathetically anxious to follow his lead,
inevitably disrupted the Opposition. By 1765, 'in the same

---

[32] A.S. Foord, *His Majesty's Opposition, 1714-1830* (Oxford, 1964), p.311.
[33] *Letters to Henry Fox, Lord Holland*, ed. Lord Ilchester (London, 1915), p.223:
Richmond to Holland, 8 June 1765.

isolated, unconcerting State', [34] he was publicly contemptuous
not merely of Newcastle and his aristocratic colleagues, but
even of the young men who longed to serve under him.
George Onslow, for example, felt bound to confess that there
was little prospect of 'a general Opposition in which he will
never join with People who, (in essentials and in Principle I
do believe) he does not agree, [sic] nor mean the same as
we do'.[35]

Unfortunately there were no really effective secondary
leaders to deputize for Pitt. The obvious man for the role, the
eminently sensible and highly respected Duke of Devonshire,
had died in 1764, a mortality which, with those of Hardwicke
and Legge in the same year, left a marked gap in the ranks of
the Minority. Holland rightly lamented 'the death of the late
Duke of Devonshire, whose temper was not bitter and who
could have done much: that Opposition resorted to Mr. Pitt,
who would have nothing to do with them.'[36] The leaders who
remained were in the main ineffectual and inexperienced.
Some, like Grafton and Portland, were extremely young.
Rockingham, despite his growing stature after the death of
Devonshire and despite his success in helping to hold together
the disparate elements among the 'Old Whigs'[37] scarcely had
the drive and abilities requisite at this stage. Pitt's brother-in-
law and comrade-in-arms, Earl Temple, had little liking for
the Whig lords and their friends, and by 1765 was near to
deserting the Opposition for the Administration headed of
course by his brother Grenville. He did his utmost to discourage
Pitt from negotiating with Cumberland in May, and immediately afterwards agreed to a complete and public reconciliation
with his brother. It surprised no one that when Pitt again
appealed to him for assistance in the June negotiations he
preferred to maintain his new connection with Grenville.

Division and disunity were thus the hallmarks of the
Opposition during the early years of the new reign, though
Newcastle maintained a rather pathetic hope that the divisions
could be bridged.

---

[34] Add.MS. 35361, f. 138: Hardwicke to C. Yorke [? Feb. 1765].

[35] Add.MS. 32966, f. 70: Onslow to Newcastle, 19 Mar. 1765.

[36] *Walpole's Memoirs*, ii. 70–1.

[37] L.S. Sutherland, 'Edmund Burke and the First Rockingham Ministry', *E.H.R.*
xlvii (1932), 53.

All that I wish, [he told Rockingham on 19 June,] with Regard to
Publick Affairs, is, To see Such an Administration settled, as may support
The Whigs, and carry on The King's Business, and That of The Public,
with Ease, Honor, and Success; Which, I think, cannot be done, without
Mr. Pitt, and the Great, and Little Whigs; I mean the Whole Whig Party,
There is My Heart; and There shall be my Wish. The Duke of Cumberland
is, and ought to be at our Head.[38]

In fact the much desired 'Union amongst ourselves'[39] was not
practicable. Given the divisions which racked the Minority,
the extreme reluctance of the 'Old Whigs' to take office on
their own is understandable enough. Their dependence on
Pitt, by virtue of the reliance which the 'young friends'
placed on him, was all but total. As Grafton later pointed out,

the Opposition had so little expectation of being called upon to take a
part in administration, unless under, and by the recommendation of
Mr. Pitt, that even when the coolness between the King and his servants
was apparent to all mankind, to act under Mr. Pitt became the general
voice and was our principal wish.[40]

If it was true that Rockingham and his friends accepted
office only 'after having twice acknowledged themselves
incapable of so arduous a task',[41] it was also the case that
they were anything but well equipped for it. 'Chiefs who
could not conduct a party with sense', as Horace Walpole
remarked, 'seemed little qualified to govern a nation.'[42] Most
of the specific criticisms levelled at the newcomers by contemporaries were not easily rebutted. For example the Opposition
was predictably savage about a 'Ministry composed of the
Extravagancies of Youth, and of the Infirmities of Age'.[43]
The deaths of Devonshire and Legge in the previous year had
effectively destroyed a generation in the 'Old Whig' leadership, and the consequent lacuna was strongly reflected in the
new Cabinet. Newcastle was seventy-two and Winchilsea
seventy-six, while at the other end of the scale Grafton was
not thirty and Rockingham a mere five years older. Only
Conway, at forty-six, was in his prime. Moreover the new
Ministers had little experience of the business of Government.

[38] Add.MS. 32967, f. 70.
[39] Add.MS. 32967, f. 46: Onslow to Newcastle, 16 June 1765.
[40] *Grafton Autobiography*, p.32.
[41] *Grenville Papers*, iii. 72: Temple to Grenville, 14 July 1765.
[42] *Walpole's Memoirs*, ii. 148.
[43] C. Lloyd, *An Honest Man's Reasons for Declining to take any Part in the New
Administration, in a Letter to the Marquis of* —— (London, 1765), p.11.

Thus the young Edward Gibbon reported to his friend Porten, 'We stare with astonishment at seeing a first Lord of the treasury, Chancellor of the Exchequer, and both Secretaries of State who were never in any publick office before. I believe the case is unparalleled in our history. It is to be hope[d] that genius will supply the place of experience.'[44]

The three key positions in the Administration were held by young men none of whom had any significant experience. Rockingham had formerly been a Lord of the Bedchamber, as had Grafton, while Conway, apart from his military appointments, had held only the post of Secretary to the Lord Lieutenant of Ireland. Though Newcastle and Winchilsea had both been active members of Government in the past, neither was in a position to utilize his expertise.

The Opposition naturally made great play with the supposed inadequacies of the new Ministers. It was claimed, for example, that this was an unusually aristocratic regime, though neither its predecessor nor successor was markedly less so. Thus Humphrey Cotes called it 'this Oligarchy, formed upon Aristocracy', and remarked to his friend Wilkes, 'you will observe that there is not a Commoner concerned at the head of any of these negotiations.'[45] More just, if still less charitable, was the derision with which the new Ministers met on account of their social habits. Anti-Sejanus[46] was merciless about 'Persons called from the *Stud* to the *State*, and transformed miraculously out of Jockies into Ministers', while one pamphleteer sarcastically descried 'Arthur's and Newmarket become the seminaries of administration'.[47] The Turf has never been better represented in the effective Cabinet than it was by Cumberland, Grafton, and Rockingham, in that of 1765. It was singularly appropriate that much of the negotiating for the formation of a new Ministry in the summer of 1765 had been conducted by Cumberland at Newmarket in May, and at Ascot in June.

---

[44] *The Letters of Edward Gibbon*, ed. J.E. Norton (London, 1956), i. 198: 21 July 1765.

[45] Add.MS. 30868 (Wilkes Papers), f. 178: 4 July 1765.

[46] Anti-Sejanus: the Revd. James Scott, (1733-1814), Fellow of Trinity College, Cambridge, and Sandwich's hack journalist. His diatribes in the *Public Advertiser* between July 1765 and March 1766 rank him second only to Junius in this period.

[47] *Public Advertiser*, 21 Sept. 1765; *The Principles of the Late Changes Impartially Examined*, p.50.

However, the most palpable hit of all was made by Grenville's pamphleteer Charles Lloyd in his *Critical Review of the New Administration*. The Ministers, he argued, had previously

> put themselves, (and few People undervalue their own Abilities), upon that Rank of common Court Lords, who form as constant a part of the Furniture of a Drawing-Room as the Figures in the Tapestry of it. There are in all Courts, as well as in all Theatres, certain uninteresting well drest Figures in waiting, ready to perform any Part which is cast for them; they carry Messages, copy Letters, repeat Orders, or bear Staves with equal Propriety; when the principal Actor chuses a Part of less apparent Dignity, these People are dressed in Blue Ribbands, and with white Wands, and in a grave and well-measured Pace, walking before the King, and represent the great Officers of the State. But call such People what you will, you cannot increase their Importance.[48]

There was a good deal of truth in this sketch. Fundamentally Rockingham and his friends were, in the public mind at least, 'second-rate politicians'[49] who had stumbled reluctantly and accidentally into office, 'a sett of men incapable of filling the employments they are now in'.[50] Neither as a group nor as individuals were they such as to impress the political world by their talents.

No appointment was more surprising than that of Rockingham as First Lord of the Treasury. Walpole's observation that he was 'only known to the public by his passion for horse-races',[51] was by no means an exaggeration. At thirty-five he was a public figure only in his native county of Yorkshire, where his political influence, largely inherited from his father the first Marquess, was immense. Before the accession of George III his career had shown little indication of talent or distinction.[52] At fifteen he had created something of a sensation by riding to Carlisle to join the Duke of Cumberland's army against the Jacobites, but apart from this there was nothing unusual in a perfectly conventional education and upbringing. In politics he had found no difficulty in befriending the Pelham establishment, though like his father he had maintained a degree of independence proper in a great north-country magnate. As a Lord of the Bedchamber

[48] (London, 1765), pp.29–30.
[49] H.M.C. *Lothian MSS.*, p.258: Buckinghamshire to Nugent, Oct. 1765.
[50] Add.MS. 51408, f. 251: Lord Bateman to Holland, 6 Oct. 1765.
[51] *Walpole's Memoirs*, ii. 140.
[52] The only biographical study of Rockingham, apart from the unfortunate attempt of Albemarle, is G.H. Guttridge, *The Early Career of Lord Rockingham: 1730-65* (Univ. of Calif. Pubs. in Hist., xliv (1952)).

to both George II and George III he seemed to have found his natural role in public life. In the normal course of events, he could doubtless have looked forward to a lifetime of Court office free of the burdens of political decision and Government business. However the violence of political conflict in the first years of George III's reign, and Rockingham's personal attachment to the Newcastle-Cavendish group guided his career into new and unfamiliar paths. Once the 'Old Whigs' found themselves in opposition Rockingham's importance grew steadily as he came to play a leading part in the affairs of the Minority, associating with the young men of Wildman's, placating Newcastle and the older Whig Lords, and in general contributing to such unity and confidence as the Opposition possessed. Even so his emergence as a political leader and first Minister was still very much a matter of chance—the elimination in one way or another of every rival. The deaths of Devonshire, Hardwicke, and Legge in 1764, the desertion of Temple, Pitt, and Lyttelton at the critical moment in 1765, and also the general unacceptability of Newcastle all cleared the way for Rockingham's success. Even then he was not the only possibility. Grafton was equally useful to the Minority, since like Rockingham he was able to command the sympathies of the 'young friends'. However he was still younger than the Marquess, seemed to find little time for politics in 1765, and above all had not Rockingham's intimacy with Cumberland. This was most important. Rockingham's adolescent escapade, his obsession with the Turf, his natural good humour, and his rising reputation in the Minority in 1764 and 1765 all helped to establish him with the Duke. In the last analysis, he was Cumberland's personal choice.

None the less Rockingham accepted the trust only with the utmost regret and reluctance. Dartmouth recorded that he 'was pitched upon to be *first* L[or]d of the T[reasury], w[hi]ch he strenuously refused, for some time, but being told that the scheme must be abandoned, he unwillingly consented to take that part and the other management ensued.'[53] This was certainly the case. Cumberland himself noted that

only the Marquis objected to any employment for himself, believing he might be of more use as an independent man, than personally engaged

[53] Dartmouth MSS., Dartmouth's Notebook.

in the service; . . . yet when he saw the shyness of our friends he shook
off his natural dislike and was ready to kiss the King's hand in whatever
shape was most for the service in general. To this resolution I flatter
myself his personal friendship for me had some share, seeing the
distressed situation my friends had left me in, from their fears of stirring
hand or foot without Mr. Pitt at their head.[54]

Rockingham's own account was no less emphatic.

The necessity here, [he told Sir William Meredith], made it necessary
that something should be done, and therefore howsoever unsuitable I
might be for that office from my health and inexperience in the sort of
business, yet I thought it incumbent on me to acquiesce in the attempting
it, rather than throw any fresh confusion into the negociation, w[hic]h
had but too many difficulties without my adding to them by a refusal
w[hic]h my own private ease and comfort w[oul]d no doubt strongly
have inclined me to.[55]

Rockingham must indeed have been greatly surprised to find
himself in the limelight. The offices which it was generally
imagined he would be offered were those of Lord Lieutenant
of Ireland and Lord Chamberlain,[56] and the Treasury was as
far beyond his aspirations as it was beyond his abilities. On
the other hand, once he had accepted this position and
especially after the death of Cumberland three months later,
his attitude underwent a change. The attractions of the most
powerful and prestigious office in the land were such as to
affect even a politician as reluctant and unsuited as Rockingham.
In 1765 he was only brought to accept the Treasury with the
greatest difficulty; thereafter he was to find it impossible to
accept anything less.

In his favour Rockingham had little but one or two natural
advantages of character. Thus Edmund Burke announced his
recruitment by 'Lord Rockingham, who has the reputation of
a man of honour and integrity; and with whom, they say, it is
not difficult to live'.[57] This would have been a generally
acceptable assessment, though Burke's friend O'Hara was not
entirely admiring. 'You have pride to deal with', he opined,
'but much softend by manner: and exceeding good sense, but
you must feed it, for it cant feed itself.'[58] On the debit side

---

[54] *Rockingham Memoirs*, i. 192, 197–8: Cumberland's Statement.
[55] WWM.R1–473: Rockingham to Meredith, [14 July 1765].
[56] See for example WWM.R1–454: Meredith to Rockingham, 29 June 1765;
Correspondence of George III, i. 92.
[57] *Burke Correspondence*, i. 211: Burke to O'Hara, 11 July 1765.
[58] Ibid. i. 214: O'Hara to Edmund and William Burke, 30 July [1765].

there was indeed much with which to be dissatisfied.
Naturally indolent as he was, Rockingham's habits were
notoriously unbusinesslike, even by the leisured standards of
the time. 'I already see that L[or]d Rockingham does not
dispatch business quite so quick as I could wish', Richmond
complained in September 1765.[59] Almost invariably unpunc-
tual, he on one occasion failed to attend one of his own
Cabinet meetings. 'I have been guilty of a Strange Forgetfulness
tonight', he informed Newcastle, 'in having totally forgot that
there was to be a Meeting by appointment, at the D[uke] of
Grafton's. I did not recollect it till I came home and heard
that they had just sent here for me.'[60] When it came to
decision-making he tended to be rather timid and irresolute;
George III found, for example, that he 'never appeared to
him to have a decided opinion about things'.[61] Nor was his
health such as to sustain his cares with ease. Within three
days of accepting the Treasury, he was grumbling 'My
Complaints suffer much—by all the Agitation, I am forced
constantly to be in',[62] and to the end of his life he remained
something of a valetudinarian.

However these handicaps were trivial by comparison with
the central problem of Rockingham's almost total and
apparently insurmountable incapacity to speak in Parliament.
The last word on this subject was Hardwicke's. 'His Lordship
himself who should have been the mouth of the administration
of which he was the Head, never rose without affording
matter of mortification to his Friends, and of Triumph to his
Enemies, as he was incapable of exerting the good sense which
he was really Master of.'[63]

The difficulty was apparently merely one of nervousness,
though the standard of debate in the House of Lords was not
comparable to that in the Commons. Moreover when
Rockingham addressed his compatriots in Yorkshire and his
friends among the 'Old Whigs' he seemed able to make himself
perfectly clear. Indeed on one of the rare occasions when he

---

[59] Add.MS. 51424, f. 265: Richmond to Holland, 27 Sept. 1765.
[60] Add.MS. 32972, f. 94: 1 Dec. 1765.
[61] Lord E. Fitzmaurice, *Life of William, Earl of Shelburne* (London, 1875-6),
i. 373.
[62] Add.MS. 32967, f. 375: Rockingham to Newcastle, 13 July 1765.
[63] Add.MS. 35428, f. 27: Hardwicke, 'Private Memoirs'. Though Albemarle
printed much of this document in his *Rockingham Memoirs*, he carefully
omitted all references which might discredit Rockingham.

spoke in the Lords in 1766, at least one not particularly well-disposed onlooker was favourably impressed.

The Marquiss of Rockingham opened his mouth at last upon the second reading of the window tax; spoke in general very well; apologised for his silence, which he owned was a natural infirmity proceeding from his great respect for their Lordships.[64]

Unfortunately Rockingham spoke only twice during the session. On 20 January the Opposition pointed out that certain papers delivered to the Lords were incorrectly endorsed. 'L[or]d Rockingham was obliged to answer,' he himself wrote to the King that night, 'and in which he rather shewed his desire of giving all further Information which might be wanted than the Perfect Knowledge of what had occasioned the omission on the Papers. L[or]d R[ockingha]m never wished more for the Power of any degree of Oratory than then.'[65] Though George III responded with the assurance that he was 'much pleased that Opposition has forced you to hear your own voice, which I hope will encourage you to stand forth in other debates',[66] Rockingham did not rise again until the Window Tax debate of 28 May, when he was apparently compelled to speak by a chorus of taunts and jeers from Bedford and his friends. 'Lord R[ockingham] spoke in such a tremor', it was reported; 'but it is a benediction he has found the use of his tongue in any way.'[67] But by this time it was far too late. Rockingham's failure to take his part in the everyday debate of the Lords was most damaging; a source of endless mockery and ridicule for the Opposition, it severely marred his standing in the public eye, and inevitably affected the credit of his Administration.

One of Rockingham's undoubted assets was his wife. The former Mary Bright, a great Yorkshire heiress in her own right, was an invaluable political aid to her husband. In addition to acting, to use her own term, as a secretary,[68] she was an astute and trusted adviser. It is clear from the letters which she wrote when apart from her husband, as when she was at Bath in the autumn of 1765, that she was accustomed

---

[64] *Selection from the Family Papers Preserved at Caldwell* (Glasgow, 1854), part ii, vol. ii, p.85: W. Rouet to Baron Mure, 5 June 1766.

[65] *Correspondence of George III*, i. 239–40 (*Additions and Corrections*, p.49).

[66] *Rockingham Memoirs*, i. 271.

[67] H.M.C. *Various Collections*, viii. 184: Duchess of Grafton to Viscountess Irwin, 29 May 1766.

[68] Add.MS. 32973, f. 224: Lady Rockingham to Newcastle, 21 Jan. 1766.

to give detailed counsel, though it was always accompanied
by diplomatic assurances of the kind which Rockingham
received with a lengthy missive on the death of Cumberland—
'If you happen'd to have had the same Idea it would flatter
me much more than y[ou]r taking it from me.'[69] Newcastle
had good reason to urge his own wife, also in Bath at this
time, to cultivate Lady Rockingham. 'The Little Woman', he
assured her, 'Has *Her Influency*.'[70]

Another of Rockingham's assets was undoubtedly his new
Private Secretary, Edmund Burke. For some years Burke had
hovered expectantly on the fringe of the literary and political
establishments, but without finding the vital opening for his
talents. 'In all this time', he afterwards wrote to his friend
Hutchinson, 'you may easily conceive, how much I felt at
seeing myself left behind by almost all my cotemporaries.
There never was a Season more favourable for any man who
chose to enter into the Carrier of publick Life.'[71] In the
spring of 1765 he had severed his long association with William
'Single-Speech' Hamilton—'an eternal rupture' he declared,
'. . . on my side, neither sought nor provoked',[72] though it is
difficult not to sympathize a little with Hamilton, the victim
of an extraordinarily bitter and emotional attack from Burke.[73]
This was followed by a rather injudicious connection with
Charles Townshend, although Burke himself was well aware
of Townshend's unreliability.[74] However in the midst of these
developments he had also become associated with William
Fitzherbert, and through him with the Cavendish brothers
and the other young men of the Minority. Between them
Fitzherbert and Lord John Cavendish managed to place both
Burke and his 'cousin' William Burke, the former as Private
Secretary to Rockingham, the latter as Under-Secretary of
State to Conway. 'This little gleam of prosperity which has
at length fallen on my fortune', as Burke called it,[75] was of
the utmost significance for his own career. Until then he had
merely been a shadowy figure in the background of the
political scene, more honest no doubt than some of his

---

[69] WWM.R168—177: Lady Rockingham to Rockingham, 2 Nov. 1765.
[70] Add.MS. 33078, f. 35: 31 Oct. 1765.
[71] *Burke Correspondence*, i. 200: [May 1765].
[72] Ibid. i. 192: Burke to Flood, 18 May [1765].
[73] See T.W. Copeland, 'Burke's First Patron', *History Today*, ii (1952), 394—9.
[74] *Burke Correspondence*, i. 209.
[75] *Burke Correspondence*, i. 211: Burke to Garrick, 16 July 1765.

unscrupulous friends, like Lauchlin Macleane and William
Burke, but certainly no more distinguished. Thus one of his
friends had written, 'I long to hear that you are fixt in some
employment, I don't care how troublesome, that will give
you an opportunity of displaying your abilities.'[76] The
appointment to Rockingham's household was just what was
needed—in Burke's own words, 'an employment of a kind
humble enough; but which may be worked into some sort of
consideration, or at least advantage'.[77] Henceforth the way
was open to a seat in Parliament and to public recognition of
Burke's immense gifts.

The precise circumstances of the appointment, which
appears to have taken place on or about 10 July,[78] remain
rather obscure. Rockingham obviously felt the need of some
personal assistance when he took over the Treasury. His
employee George Quarme, though described by John
Milbanke as a private secretary, did not for the most part
concern himself with political business.[79] At this time
Rockingham was apparently consulting John Roberts, an
experienced Treasury man from the days of Henry Pelham,
about the technical and procedural problems of his new
office.[80] However, if there was ever any formality to this
arrangement, it was very short-lived. Roberts, though always
ready to give gratuitous advice to Rockingham,[81] soon
accepted a seat at the Board of Trade. In consequence, Lord
John Cavendish's suggestion of Burke was doubtless opportune.
It was also a means of fending off the interference of Newcastle.
The latter characteristically had his own candidate for the post
of Private Secretary to Rockingham, one James Royer, a
connection of the Grafton family whom Rockingham later
rewarded with promotion in the Lottery Office. 'He was My
private Secretary, many years', Newcastle later assured his
colleague, 'and was trusted with the most secret Affairs; And,
I was so convinced of His Integrity, that I recommended Him

---

[76] WWM. Bk. 1—28: J.M. Mason to Burke, 28 June [1765].
[77] *Burke Correspondence*, i. 211: Burke to O'Hara, 11 July 1765.
[78] Ibid. i. 211 and footnotes.
[79] Add.MS. 33095 (Pelham Papers), f. 140: Milbanke to Pelham, 19 Aug. 1765.
Milbanke was Rockingham's brother-in-law.
[80] J.E. Tyler, 'John Roberts, M.P. and the First Rockingham Administration',
E.H.R. lxvii (1952), 547—60.
[81] WWM.R35—18h: Roberts to Rockingham, 14, 29 Nov. 1765.

to your Lordship, To serve you in the same capacity.'[82]
According to Lord Charlemont's account, Newcastle accused
Burke of being 'by birth and education a Papist, and a Jacobite',
whereupon Burke offered to resign his hard-won employment,
on the grounds that 'no earthly consideration should induce
him to stand in that relation, with a man who did not place
entire confidence in him', though Rockingham, apparently
impressed by this declaration, suitably reassured him.[83] While
there is no evidence to confirm this story, Burke's hints at the
'designs of my Enemies, who not long since made a desperate
Stroke at my Fortune, my Liberty, and my Reputation', as
well as Newcastle's later anxiety that Rockingham's *'private*
Secretary One Burk, an Irish Man, and of a popish Family',
would 'prevent My having any Credit with Him', are certainly
corroborative.[84]

The degree of Burke's influence in the year following
his appointment is far from certain, though there can
be no doubt that he performed an important role in the
liaison between the commercial interests and the Ministry.
The money which he received at regular intervals from
Rockingham was avowedly 'for obtaining various informations
and materials relative to the Trade and Manufactures',[85] and
the organization and coordination of the evidence given to
the House of Commons American Committee in 1766 owed
not a little to his labours. All Burke's close friends were
impressed by the ardour with which he flung himself into
his new pursuits, 'as much as if he was to receive twenty per
cent from the commerce of the empire, which he labours to
improve and extend'.[86] It has not always been recognized
that Burke's spectacular début on the Parliamentary scene,
after his election in December 1765 for Lord Verney's
borough of Wendover, was as much the product of intense
industry as of sheer oratorical genius. 'I have heard', Sir
Joseph Yorke remarked to his brother Hardwicke, 'from Sir
Ja[me]s Porter several times that L[or]d R[ockingham]'s
Sec[reta]ry Mr. Burke knew more of American affairs than

[82] Add.MS. 32974, f. 183: 15 Mar. 1766.
[83] F. Hardy, *Memoirs of the Political and Private Life of James Caulfield, Earl of Charlemont* (2nd edn., London, 1812), ii. 281–2.
[84] *Burke Correspondence*, i. 211: Burke to Garrick, 16 July 1765; Add.MS. 33078, f. 35: Newcastle to Duchess of Newcastle, 31 Oct. 1765.
[85] WWM.R15–1, 2, 3, 4: Cash Account Books: payments made to Burke on 25 Nov. 1765, 21 Jan. 1766, 19 Apr. 1766.
[86] *Burke Correspondence*, i. 245: W. Burke to J. Barry, 23 Mar. 1766.

anybody, and therefore was not surprised to find him a
great actor in this interesting Scene.'[87]

None the less historians have tended to read back into the
earliest stages of Burke's career an authority and eminence
which he only attained later. By contrast, few contemporaries,
despite his brilliant success at Westminster, rated his influence
highly in 1765-6. One of those who did was the Earl of
Buckinghamshire, who described Burke as 'the name not of
L[or] d Rockingham's Right hand but of both his hands,'
... 'descended from a Garret to the Head of our administration',
though it is not easy to endorse his view.[88] Indeed the debt
was largely on Burke's side in the early stages of his relationship with Rockingham. He joined his patron as a minor
politician of great ambitions but few achievements, equipped
only with the most conventional of convictions and principles.
A year later he had acquired the leader, the friends, and above
all the cause, for which his nature craved. Almost overnight,
a mere grubbing adventurer, 'tagging', as he himself reflected,
'at the heels of factions',[89] was transformed into a mature
and respected man of affairs. His friend Vesey must have had
good cause in retrospect to reiterate his comment of 27 July.
'I rejoice to think that your new Connection is so very
different from y[ou] r former one.'[90]

Public attention, however, at the time of the Rockingham
Ministry's formation was concentrated not on the chief
Minister's Private Secretary but on his Cabinet colleagues.
Unfortunately the two most important offices outside the
Treasury—those of the Secretaries of State—were held by
men barely superior to their leader in point of experience
and ability. It is admittedly true that one of them, the Duke
of Grafton, was highly regarded in some quarters. 'I think
the only man among them likely to stand in the Ministerial
class is the Duke of Grafton', Burke's friend O'Hara
declared.[91] Yet his reputation was based upon the slenderest
foundations. As the ever acute Hardwicke pointed out, he
'had only distinguished himself by one or two smart opposition speeches in the House of Lords'; furthermore, he

[87] Add.MS. 35368, f. 40: 15 Apr. 1766.
[88] Add.MS. 22358, f. 35: Buckinghamshire to Grenville, 11 June 1766.
[89] *Burke Correspondence*, i. 210: Burke to O'Hara, 9 July 1765.
[90] WWM.Bk. 1—29 + 2.
[91] R.J.S. Hoffman, *Edmund Burke, New York Agent* (Philadelphia, 1956), p.323:
O'Hara to Burke, 30 July 1765.

asked 'who can answer for the D[uke] of Grafton's
Sufficiency in any tolerable Degree?'[92] Moreover Grafton,
despite his earlier exertions in the Wilkes controversies, was
but little disposed to political activity in the summer of 1765.
His domestic affairs were acutely absorbing and in the early
months of the new Ministry he did little to sustain the general
expectation entertained of him. 'The Duke of Grafton is
silent, does little, but seems thoroughly pleased with being
Secretary of State', was Newcastle's observation at the end of
August.[93] On the whole Grafton was actually less industrious
as a Minister than Rockingham, and his habits, which included
that of sleeping at Cabinet meetings,[94] were certainly not
notably more business-like. Indeed most of his energy in the
autumn of 1765 was devoted to a furious contest with the
Earl of Albemarle for a vacant Garter,[95] a struggle which led
to an open quarrel with Albemarle's patron Cumberland and
came near to dividing the Ministry. Moreover Grafton had a
personal commitment to Pitt which went far beyond that of
the other Ministers and which in time was to create considerable
problems for them. All things considered, the young Duke
was less of an asset to the new Administration than his
colleagues initially imagined.

Henry Conway, Grafton's colleague as Secretary of State
for the Southern Department, was not much better suited to
high office. Despite his long-standing connection with the
Cavendish family, he had emerged as one of the leading figures
of the Opposition only with his rebellion against the Government on the issue of General Warrants. Though regarded by
his friends as an obvious candidate for office in a new Administration, he was most unwilling to play his allotted part,
'refusing any of the great emploiments' in May,[96] protesting
his wish to decline the Exchequer in June, and agreeing to
become a Secretary of State only after much hesitation. His
personal ambitions lay very much in the military line, and
the prediction that 'Conway will return to his profession' was

---

[92] Add.MSS. 35428, f. 23: Hardwicke, 'Private Memoirs'; 35361, f. 172:
Hardwicke to C. Yorke, 4 July 1765.
[93] Add.MS. 32969, f. 247: Newcastle to Ashburnham, 31 Aug. 1765.
[94] Add.MS. 33078, f. 63: Newcastle to Duchess of Newcastle, 14 Nov. 1765.
[95] This quarrel became a matter of public comment. See for example, *Jenkinson Papers*, p.391; *Grenville Papers*, iii. 101.
[96] Add.MS. 23218 (Conway Papers), f. 206: Hertford to Walpole, 30 May 1765.

indeed ultimately to be borne out.[97] As a result, though
Newcastle was certain that he would 'be a considerable Man
of Business',[98] he was too discontented with his position to
be a very effective Minister. The November after his appointment he was to cause near-panic among his colleagues by
attempting to retire, assuring his brother Hertford, 'You know
how I hate this life, and it raises my spirits much to think I
see a hole to creep out at.'[99] Though this scheme fell through
because Charles Townshend declined to succeed him as
Secretary of State, he was only prevented by his chronic and
characteristic irresolution, together with his conscience-stricken
sense of loyalty to his friends, from resigning thereafter.

Had Conway been restricted to the duties of Secretary of
State, he might have proved adequate. Unfortunately he was
also responsible for the management of the House of
Commons. Though this was not a formal office, it was none
the less important, especially at a time when the chief
Minister was a peer—when, as Charles Yorke put it, 'the
H[ouse] of C[ommons] is to be led (as the D[uke] of
N[ewcastle] weakly thought of managing it after his Brother's
death in 1754) by *sub-ministers*'.[100] It had to be confessed
that Conway, in one commentator's words, 'so unable, so
weak and indecisive for a Minister in the House of Commons',
was a less than satisfactory candidate for this role, and even
his devoted friend Walpole felt bound to admit to doubts.[101]
Not a little of the pessimism of contemporaries about the
prospects of the new Administration was based on its plain
inadequacy in the lower House. With Pitt either non-combatant
or indifferent, and Grenville in opposition, it was of the utmost
consequence to find a suitable leader in the Commons. Burke's
friend Vesey clearly had some justification for asking him to
explain 'why you think this Administration likely to Continue, when I see no person who is fit to conduct Gov[ern-
men]t Affairs thro' the house of Commons'.[102]

[97] R.J.S. Hoffman, op.cit., p. 323: O'Hara to Burke, 30 July 1765.
[98] Add.MS. 32972, f. 186: Newcastle, 'Mem[orandum]s for the King', 10 Dec.
1765.
[99] *Companion to the Newspaper and Journal of Facts in Politics, Statistics, and
Public Economy* (London, 1834-7), 1835, p.365: 7 Nov. 1765.
[100] Add.MS. 35428, f. 73: Yorke to Sir Joseph Yorke, 7 Sept. 1765.
[101] *Letters to Lord Holland*, ed. Ilchester, p.238: Digby to Holland, 16 July
1765; *Walpole Memoirs*, ii. 139.
[102] WWM. Bk. 1—29 + 2: 27 July 1765.

The new Ministers had sought to remedy their evident
weakness in the Commons by appealing to two prominent
political figures of the day, sometimes bracketed in popular
parlance as the 'two Charles's',—Yorke and Townshend. It had
been hoped at first that the latter would accept the positions
ultimately bestowed upon Conway. There was a dramatic
mission by Rockingham to his country seat at Adderbury, a
journey by Townshend and his brother to London, and a
series of interviews by Cumberland, Rockingham, and even
the King—'what does not these horrid times make me stoop
to', enquired George III.[103] The chief result was a state of
doubt and confusion frequently produced by Townshend in
the politics of the 1760s. In the end it emerged that he
'desir'd to be excus'd stand[in]g forth as the responsible
minister in the house of Commons and to stay where he is
under an assurance of his endeavour to support the measures
of government and of attend[ance]',[104] and it was agreed
that Conway should be appointed in his place. There was
general mystification as to Townshend's failure to seize this
opportunity for promotion, though he himself did his best to
throw the responsibility for his refusal on to his elder
brother, Lord Townshend, with whom he had recently been
reconciled after a lengthy estrangement. None the less, the
decision was undoubtedly Townshend's own. Various motives
were attributed to him, ranging from simple pique to a distaste for the policies supposedly to be adopted by the 'Old
Whigs' in office.[105] The plain truth was his conviction that
'the plan opened to me has not the show of much stability
nor of necessary strength in it.'[106] For the moment he was
quite content with the lucrative office of Paymaster-General,
which he had long sought and finally obtained after deserting
the Minority for the Grenville Administration at the start of
the 1765 session. As he told Burke in June, 'I had rather
remain as I am, than pass to any station of power, until things
have taken some settlement.'[107] His attitude towards the new
Ministry remained one of rather ambivalent neutrality. Both
he and his brother were allowed to retain their offices,[108] and

[103] *Correspondence of George III*, i. 148: King to Egmont, [9 July 1765].
[104] Add.MS. 51425, ff. 119–20: Touchet to Holland, 18 July 1765.
[105] *Letters to Lord Holland*, ed. Ilchester, pp. 236, 242.
[106] *Grenville Papers*, iii. 68: C. Townshend to Lord Townshend, 4 July 1765.
[107] *Burke Correspondence*, i. 204: 23 June 1765.
[108] Lord Townshend was Lieutenant-General of the Ordnance.

while this did not prevent Lord Townshend consistently opposing his new masters, Charles was more cautious. Though he refused the renewed offers made him in November 1765 and May 1766, he avoided overt opposition, and on the major issue of the ensuing session, the Stamp Act, adopted a rather equivocal attitude.[109] Given the right occasion, of course, his eloquence in debate could be devastating, but for the most part Rockingham and his colleagues escaped its lash. Paradoxically, yet characteristically, Townshend did the succeeding Administration, of which he was a leading member, far more damage than that which he had been so reluctant to join.

The 'other Charles' was ultimately brought into the Government, though only with considerable difficulty. Like Townshend, Yorke had over estimated Grenville's security in the Parliamentary session of 1765; like Townshend he had deserted the Minority, though with less thoroughness, merely accepting a patent of precedence as Crown lawyer between the Attorney- and Solicitor-Generals; and like Townshend he had been taken unawares by the surprising developments of the spring and summer. None the less all concerned were anxious to obtain his services. Cumberland was informed by George III, for example, that

I look on my service in the Law as but on a very weak foundation if a Man of Mr. Yorke's great worth and capacity is not in Office, I beg therefore that all those who are coming into Ministry may be convinc'd of the necessity of some inclination being shewn to him that may still gain him; for I repeat it again if Mrs. [*sic*] Greenville, Townshend and L[or]d George Sackville should oppose in the House of Commons Administration would not go on there pleasantly unless Mr. Yorke was hearty in their cause.[110]

Yorke was undoubtedly a useful ally. A sound and constructive lawyer, he was also an able and respected speaker in the Commons; his accession could only assist the public standing of the Ministry.

Unfortunately, Yorke took a remarkably long time to come to his decision. He was repeatedly interviewed by Cumberland, Rockingham, Egmont, and George III throughout July, and not until 9 August was Rockingham's hope that 'at last he will

---

[109] See Sir L. Namier and J. Brooke, *Charles Townshend* (London, 1964), pp. 138–9.
[110] *Correspondence of George III*, i. 145: [8 July 1765].

take the office' realized.[111] In part this delay reflected Yorke's
well-known and characteristic irresolution. His brother was
emphatic 'that he must finally concur; and tho' it may be
right to pause a little, and seem as if he was not quite
determin'd, yet I hope he won't carry that matter too far,
for all sorts of reasons'.[112] The objections Yorke himself
advanced were, as Newcastle insisted, 'ridiculous Scruples',[113]
amounting chiefly to a desire not to accept an office which
would have to be vacated by Sir Fletcher Norton. In view of
the fact that Norton was the epitome of the unscrupulous,
brutal, and vulgar in eighteenth-century politics, this
excessive concern for his sensibilities was more than a little
absurd, though it was seemingly sincere. Only after Rockingham
had made it clear that Grenville's Attorney-General would be
dismissed regardless, only after Yorke had made several visits
to a much-amused Norton to express his anxiety, and only
after the Archbishop of Canterbury had been called in for
'the sattisfying Mr. Yorke' on the score of conscience, was
this objection obviated or at least quieted.[114] However there
were perhaps more fundamental difficulties. Yorke's over-
riding ambition was the Lord Chancellorship, and his greatest
rival for it, Lord Chief Justice Pratt. Unfortunately Rockingham
chose this moment, for quite unconnected reasons, to bestow
a peerage upon Pratt, an action which Yorke regarded 'as a
most humiliating Circumstance to himself', despite the efforts
of his friends to reassure him that it would 'not interfere in
The least with you, in the great Point of The Law'.[115] There
could be no question, of course, of compensating him with
either the Lord Chancellorship or a peerage, since it was the
earnest wish both of the King and his Ministers to utilize him,
in Yorke's own words, 'as a sub-minister in the H[ouse] of
C[ommons]'.[116] In the end he submitted to the wishes of his
friends, partly because he had little real alternative, partly
because he received what Hardwicke correctly described as
'an express Promise from the King's own mouth that he should

[111] Add.MS. 32968, f. 241: Rockingham to Newcastle, 25 July 1765.
[112] Add.MS. 35374, f. 244: J. Yorke to Hardwicke, 20 July 1765.
[113] Add.MS. 32967, f. 354: Newcastle to Grafton, 12 July 1765.
[114] Add.MS. 35430, f. 14: Rockingham to Yorke, 19 July 1765; 32967, f. 40:
  Cumberland to Newcastle, 15 July 1765.
[115] *Correspondence of George III*, i. 159: Egmont to King, 13 July 1765;
  Add.MS. 32967, f. 336: Newcastle to Yorke, 11 July 1765.
[116] Add.MS. 35428, f. 104: Yorke to Hardwicke, 10 Aug. 1765.

be Lord Chancellor by the end of next Session'.[117]

Even so the Ministry's position in the Commons was not strong. Conway was less than satisfactory, Townshend had withheld his assistance, and Yorke was far from happy in his situation. To some extent the consequent deficiency was offset by a new and surprising acquisition. The choice of the Tory William Dowdeswell as Chancellor the Exchequer by an avowedly 'Whig' Administration, aroused much derision in the press, but was none the less fortunate.[118] Though Dowdeswell had played a prominent part in the Opposition to the Bute and Grenville Ministries, he had never been closely associated with the Minority. Even when appointed to the new Government, he seemed curiously detached from his colleagues.

I remain [he wrote to Townshend on 24 July] equally uninformed and unadvised with upon the removals and the arrangements which are making, as I was when I last saw you. You know, that I do not mention this with regret. Far from it. It teaches me that I am called to the office I hold, only because I am supposed to have some talents for the execution of it. To the business of that office I shall set myself down. If either inability in me, or the disposition of the times shall put it out of my power to do good, I know what I have then to do. In the meanwhile I shall ask no question who is to be in or out; nor give any opinion upon a measure in which I have not previously taken any part.[119]

This of course did not endure long. During the ensuing year, Dowdeswell quickly established himself as Rockingham's most dependable lieutenant, a position which he was not to lose until his death in 1774.

No one has suffered more in historical retrospect by Horace Walpole's ferocious prejudice in favour of Conway than has Dowdeswell—'a duller edition of Mr. Grenville, though without his malignity', . . . 'who was so suited to the drudgery of his office, as far as it depends on arithmetic, that he was fit for nothing else. Heavy, slow, methodical without clearness, a butt for ridicule, unversed in every graceful art, and a stranger to men and courts, he was only esteemed by the few to whom he was personally known'.[120]

[117] Ibid., f. 10: Hardwicke, 'A Memorial of Family Occurrences from 1760 to 70 inclusive', Jan. 1771.
[118] Dowdeswell was first proposed as a junior Treasury Lord but was moved to the Exchequer when Conway opted for the Secretaryship of State. (Correspondence of George III, i. 130, 136, 142).
[119] History of Parliament Trust transcripts, Buccleuch MSS.
[120] Walpole's Memoirs, ii. 219, 139.

This was a monstrous distortion of the truth; in reality
Dowdeswell was a respected and effective Minister and House
of Commons man. Almost every comment on his performance
in the Commons during the session preceding his elevation,
for example, had been laudatory, and though the emphasis
was on command of subject rather than power of oratory,
this in no way detracted from his reputation.[121] If the
eighteenth-century Commons delighted in the eloquence of
a Pitt, a Townshend, or a Burke, it also demanded, at least on
the critical subject of finance, solid and unspectacular argument, it is a measure of Dowdeswell's prowess that in this
respect he fell only a little behind the acknowledged masters.
Thus Onslow assured James West in October 1765, 'I have
already seen enough of his Abilities, Application, and steadiness in Business to be quite sure you will be pleased with him
when you hear him on the Treasury Bench. He will be our
great Stay there, and I am the most mistaken in the world if
he does not give general Satisfaction'.[122] Though he was
best known for his concern with the Cider Excise—the '*Apple
Chancellor*' one journalist christened him[123] —Dowdeswell
was permitted to play a major role in all the important business of the 1765-6 session, particularly that concerned with
commercial affairs. By the spring of 1766 he was, in Conway's
absence, not merely leading the Government in the Commons,
but regularly attending the Cabinet and drafting royal messages
to the Commons.[124] Burke was by no means the only valuable
acquisition made by Rockingham and his friends in 1765.

However in July 1765 Dowdeswell was an untried and
unimportant member of the Government. To all intents and
purposes it was a small group composed of Rockingham,
Grafton, and Conway, which, subject to the supervision of
the Duke of Cumberland, made the significant decisions.[125]
Beyond this inner circle, even the other members of the
conciliabulum or 'effective' Cabinet had little real influence.

[121] Hertfordshire Record Office, Baker MSS., 10: W. Baker to Revd. W. Talbot,
    4 Feb. 1765; Add.MS. 32966, f. 47: Newcastle to Conway, 12 Mar. 1765;
    f. 115: Onslow to Newcastle, 28 Mar. 1765.
[122] Add.MS. 34728 (West Papers), f. 106: 12 Oct. 1765.
[123] *St. James's Chronicle*, 8-10 Apr. 1766: 'A Constitutionalist'.
[124] Bury St. Edmunds and West Suffolk Record Office, Grafton MSS. 295:
    Conway to Grafton, 7 Apr. 1766; Add.MS. 32974, f. 349: Rockingham to
    Newcastle, 11 Apr. 1766; History of Parliament Trust transcripts,
    Dowdeswell MSS., Dowdeswell to Rockingham, 30 May 1766.
[125] Sir L. Namier, *Crossroads of Power* (London, 1962), pp. 105 et seq.

Winchilsea, the new Lord President, appointed partly because
he was 'very zealous',[126] partly because he was related by
marriage to Rockingham, but most of all as a makeweight in
a poorly staffed Administration, played virtually no part in
the events of the following year. His elevation at the age of
seventy-six caused general surprise, and even the King
'wondered at Lord Winch[ilsea]'s accepting that office, at
his time of Life'.[127] Hardwicke was frankly contemptuous.
'Is that a great Acquisition', he asked his brother Charles
Yorke, 'He has not opened his Mouth in Parl[iame]nt these
12 Years, and was Violent ag[ain]st the Peace.'[128] Winchilsea
had indeed held no office since giving up the Admiralty in
1744, apart from a brief period in 1757, and as far as his
impact on public affairs was concerned, he need scarcely have
occupied one in 1765-6.

Two further seats in the Cabinet belonged to Lord Egmont
as First Lord of the Admiralty, and Lord Northington as
Lord Chancellor, both continued from the Grenville Administration. Neither was much consulted by Rockingham and
his friends in practice. Indeed one of Newcastle's most consistent complaints was that he did not recieve 'different
Confidence, and different, and previous Communication,
from That which is made to My Lord Chancellor, or My Lord
Egmont, who had never, at any Time, been in The Secret of
Affairs; or, admitted to such Confidence, or Communication'.[129]
Both Egmont and Northington were in some sense the King's
agents in the Cabinet. Egmont was a sensible and experienced
politician. As an old member of the Leicester House connection
and friend of Bute, he had benefited appropriately by the new
order of the 1760s, and spoke quite consciously as the representative of those, who in his own words, were 'The King's
faithful servants'.[130] His 'evident favour at Court', the fact
that in 1765 he 'was frequently with the King', was much
noted, and there can be no doubt that he was George III's
most trusted confidant in the negotiations of the spring and
summer, consulting for instance with Cumberland in the

[126] Add.MS. 32967, f. 194: Albemarle to Newcastle, 2 July 1765.
[127] Add.MS. 35428, f. 96: Yorke, Notes of Audience with the King, 4 July 1765.
[128] Add.MS. 35361, f. 176: Hardwicke to Yorke, 4 July 1765.
[129] Add.MS. 32971, f. 320: Newcastle, 'Considerations To be laid before My
    Lord Rockingham only', 9 Nov. 1765.
[130] Ipswich and East Suffolk Record Office, Albemarle MSS.: Egmont to
    Albemarle, 27 May 1765.

Closet, undertaking interviews on the King's behalf, and in general doing the latter's bidding.[131] Though it was reported that 'he declares very openly his wishes that this scheme may not take effect, from his unwillingness to engage in it and his apprehensions of its success',[132] he was on the whole very friendly to the new Government, and if he remained a personal associate of the King over and above the other Ministers, he never gave them cause to complain of his position.

Northington too owed a special allegiance to the King, and early in his quarrel with Grenville, George III had made it clear that he did not wish to lose the Lord Chancellor.[133] He was however a very doubtful asset to the new Ministry, thoroughly unmanageable and unreliable as a colleague, and a source of endless friction and disruption in the Cabinet. According to one typical story of July 1765, his attitude towards Rockingham and his friends was one of total indifference.

The Chancellor said lately at his table, Here's a Political Toast Gentlemen, 'Damn all those that are gone out'. Some of the Company startled. If that does not please you, here is another, 'Damn all those that are come in'.[134]

In fact Northington never acquired any liking for his new colleagues, and almost from the inception of the Administration, he was to be a thorn in its side.

The last member of the Cabinet was the new Lord Privy Seal, the Duke of Newcastle, the most experienced, yet also the most ridiculed, figure in the political world of the sixties. Newcastle has generally fared as badly at the hands of historians as at those of contemporaries, though for all his eccentricities and absurdities, he remains one of the more endearing of eighteenth-century statesmen.[135] In terms of rank, experience, and authority, he had an overwhelming

---

[131] H.M.C. *Stopford-Sackville MSS.*, i. 65: Townshend to Sackville, [12 July 1765]; Add.MS. 51423, f. 187: Digby to Holland, 23 May 1765; *Correspondence of George III*, i. 102 et seq.

[132] *Additional Grenville Papers*, ed. J.R.G. Tomlinson (Manchester, 1962), p. 292: Grenville to Temple, 6 July 1765.

[133] *Grenville Papers*, iii. 177; *Correspondence of George III*, i. 124.

[134] Add.MS. 51433, f. 56: W. Digby to Holland, 18 July 1765.

[135] For relatively favourable modern appraisals, see Sir L. Namier, *England in the Age of the American Revolution* (2nd edn., London, 1961), pp. 67–83; J.B. Owen, *The Rise of the Pelhams* (London, 1957), pp. 127–9.

claim to the Treasury in 1765, especially after Pitt's refusal
to take the lead. However, he had, ever since his resignation
in 1762, protested his determination not to return to his old
office. 'As to myself,' he assured Dartmouth, 'My Age, and
other circumstances, have made me long declare, both pub-
lickly and privately, That I could never accept any Ministerial
Office, or Office of Business.'[136] There is no evidence that
his friends urged him to change his mind, despite public
reports that 'The D[uke] of Newcastle was much pressd, but
w[oul]d not take the Treasury.'[137] Neither the King, nor
Cumberland, nor the great majority of the 'Old Whigs' themselves would have been willing to tolerate his installation as
chief Minister, and there was general relief that he had put
himself out of the question so completely. He was however
offered the Lord Presidency, which he declined 'as being an
Office of Business',[138] and accepted instead the Privy Seal in
accordance with an intention first expressed to the Bishop of
Oxford on 18 May:

I am most disposed, for The Ease and Comfort of my Life, To accept
no Office at all; The Privy Seal is The only One I would take, on any
Account: But, I think, It would be most for my Honor, and Comfort,
To have no *Office* at all; But, To take Care of my Friends; and To have
Satisfaction for all Those poor Unhappy Men, who have suffer'd upon
my Account. The Dear Dutchess of Newcastle is mighty desirous, That
I should have The Privy Seal; or otherwise, I should now be determined
To have Nothing.[139]

None the less, Newcastle did not quite limit himself to the
Privy Seal. He was also given 'The Department', in his own
words, 'of Ecclesiastical Preferments',[140] —complete control,
with the collaboration of his old friend Archbishop Secker,
of Church patronage, an unprecedented but judicious provision on the part of Cumberland and his friends. Newcastle
was delighted, as Walpole waspishly remarked, to find himself 'patronizing the clergy again, not being yet cured by their
behaviour, of loving to make bishops'.[141] From the point of
view of his colleagues his being 'a Sort of Church Minister'[142]
would doubtless help to divert his attention from matters of

[136] Add.MS. 32967, f. 366: 12 July 1765.
[137] Add.MS. 51433, f. 44: W. Digby to Holland, 12 July 1765.
[138] Add.MS. 32968, f. 214: Newcastle to Sir E. Wilmot, 24 July 1765.
[139] Add.MS. 32966, f. 426.
[140] Add.MS. 32968, f. 428: Newcastle to Albemarle, 2 Aug. 1765.
[141] *Walpole Correspondence*, xxii. 323: Walpole to Mann, 12 Aug. 1765.
[142] Add.MS. 32973, f. 228: Newcastle to Dr. Caryl, 21 Jan. 1766.

greater moment.

It soon became clear that Newcastle's object in declining a major office was less to renounce power than to shirk responsibility, as he perhaps revealed when he declared to Lord Ashburnham, 'For my own Part, I never will be a Responsible Minister Myself, or be in any Responsible Office Whatever.'[143] He was of course an incorrigible politician. Throughout his life politics had been his obsession, at times a torment no doubt, but a self-inflicted one. Lacking both family and interests—not even the Turf or the Chase could claim his enthusiasm—he had grown into a rather pathetic old man, quite incapable of abandoning the habits of a lifetime. Not surprisingly his colleagues in the new Administration were less than well-inclined to his attempts at interference. From first to last Newcastle complained bitterly of neglect and inattention at their hands. Even during the years of Opposition he had become increasingly remote from the younger members of the Minority; but in office the friction, as he sought to make his influence felt and they struggled to resist it, was multiplied greatly. Throughout his tenure of the Lord Privy Seal's office, a steady stream of complaints issued forth to Newcastle's oldest and dearest friends. The Archbishop of Canterbury, the Bishop of Oxford, the Earls of Bessborough and Albemarle, Thomas Townshend senior, and especially John White—all were kept informed of the old Duke's grievances. As early as July he was indignant that 'These young Men go on so fast, without consulting any Body', but by October this annoyance had grown to open fury at 'The Total Want of Confidence, and Communication', and henceforth there was no let-up.[144] Some of Newcastle's attacks were levelled in general at a whole

list of ungrateful men of which I am sorry to say I find more *now*, since the establishment of an *administration of friends*, than ever I did before, during the Opposition, when it might have been thought by lookers-out that I should have more weight with the next administration than appears now to be the case.[145]

For the rest the emphasis was varied. Sometimes it was the ruling trio of Rockingham, Grafton and Conway who thought

---

[143] Add.MS. 32967, f. 143: 27 June 1765
[144] Add.MSS. 32968, f. 303: Newcastle to Sondes, 27 July 1765; 32971, f. 177: Newcastle to Albemarle, 28 Oct. 1765.
[145] *Newcastle's Narrative*, pp. 34–5.

'no other opinion necessary, but that of themselves',[146] and
sometimes Rockingham alone, 'To whom I have been a Slave,
for some Years', who was severely castigated.[147] Even the
Duke of Cumberland was not placed beyond reproach by his
rank or authority.[148]

On the whole it must be conceded that Newcastle's conviction that he was neglected by his colleagues was largely
justified, though the outside world had a quite different
impression. Charles Townshend thought he discerned 'the
ascendant of the Duke of Newcastle,' and there were those
who were convinced that the Ministry was divided into two
great camps of 'Cumberlanders and Newcastleites'.[149] The
truth was that Newcastle's political importance from July
1765 was minimal. His role in the decision to form a
Government at the end of June was his last of any real significance in the political history of his times. Almost before the
new Administration was settled, he was forced to a confrontation with Rockingham which clarified his position.
With the return of the 'Old Whigs' to office Newcastle was
understandably anxious to ensure the re-employment of his
own followers and friends dismissed in 1762-3. For the most
part Rockingham was amenable to his desires, since they
coincided with his own, but at certain points he became
uncooperative. The consequent disputes came to a head over
the position of James West, Newcastle's old Secretary of the
Treasury and the Duke's candidate for office under Rockingham.
The principal victim of this quarrel was undoubtedly West
himself who, after much vacillation on Rockingham's part,
was refused a place for himself or his son,[150] and who, while
remaining loyal to the Ministry, was justifiably indignant,

If you can, safely [he wrote to George Onslow in October], Do advise
the first Com[missione]r of the Treasury not to humbugg, poor honest

---

[146] Ibid., p. 41.
[147] Add.MS. 32969, f. 201: Newcastle to Sondes, 27 Aug. 1765.
[148] Add.MS. 32968, f. 88: Albemarle to Newcastle, 19 July 1765.
[149] *Sir Henry Cavendish's Debates of the House of Commons in the Thirteenth
    Parliament of Great Britain, 1768-74*, ed. J. Wrighte (London, 1840-3),
    i. 576: Townshend to Dowdeswell, 6 Aug. 1765; H.M.C. *Weston Underwood
    MSS.*, p. 396; Bury St. Edmunds and West Suffolk Record Office, Hervey
    MSS., 50/5, f. 360: a list made out by Augustus Hervey.
[150] See Add.MSS. 32967, ff. 234, 286, 303, 316, 338, 347; 32968, ff. 264, 299;
    32972, f. 145. A comparable case was that of John Offley, the first of
    Newcastle's followers to resign in 1762, who was disregarded by Rockingham
    in 1765.

Country Gentlemen by ordering them more than once to attend the K[ing's] Levees to kiss H[is] M[ajesty's] hands by his orders and send them back again; It may be wise not to promote them, It never can be so to disoblige them, and to endeavour to render them ridiculous.[151]

Yet as West well knew, he was sacrificed to Rockingham's determination not even to appear to be directed by Newcastle;

the case must be very Extraordinary, [he remarked to his patron] that leaves one only person unprovided for, who was honoured with your confidence served you and your family with fidelity and Integrity and is I believe now used in this manner, on no other account but the having so done and the fear, he should so continue to do.[152]

This incident set the tone for relations between the old and new leaders of the 'Old Whigs' in the coming year. Despite his repeated protests and unremitting pressure, Newcastle was never admitted to the inner circle of the Administration. To all intents and purposes his effective political career was over.

But if Newcastle had ample evidence on which to ground his complaints, he had little real claim to sympathy. He had after all stipulated that he wished for no position of business or responsibility, 'no Ministerial Office, or any *Share* in Administration'.[153] Yet all his grievances were founded on the assumption that he was entitled to play a prominent role in affairs of state. Thus he remarked to Rockingham in December 1765, 'as Mr. Pitt told me, when we were *Ministers*, or Something like it together—My Lord, I must be in The first *Concoction* of Things.'[154] His sentiments were made transparently clear in a letter which he despatched to John White on 3 December.

The office of Privy Seal [he declared] is the only one I would take, as I thought it answer'd all my purposes and those of my friends; I thought it gave me an opportunity of serving in some measure that cause which I had and ever will support, without subjecting me either to the trouble, fatigue or responsibility of a Minister: but little did I think that these young men, and particularly my Lord Rockingham would take any one material step in government either with regard to measures or men, without previously consulting me and knowing my thoughts, and *that* they would not do, if they either had that regard for my opinion, which, from vanity, I may think they should have, or in their situation thought they wanted my assistance.[155]

[151] Add.MS. 34728, f. 104: 7 Oct. 1765.
[152] Add.MS. 32968, f. 273: 26 July 1765.
[153] Add.MS. 32966, f. 465: Newcastle to Bishop of Oxford, 25 May 1765.
[154] Add.MS. 32972, f. 96: Newcastle to Rockingham, 1 Dec. 1765.
[155] *Newcastle's Narrative*, p. 36.

What Newcastle would not recognize was that his demands were neither reasonable nor practicable. Conway's logic, 'That', in Newcastle's words, 'as I would not be *Minister* Myself; and it was forced upon Them; They must act, as They thought best for The Service', was unanswerable.[156] It would have been best, both for Newcastle and his colleagues, if he had made a graceful retreat from the public stage, like his old friend Kinnoull, who when asked to join the new Ministry in 1765, proved 'fully resolved not to break into his plan of retirement'.[157] Regrettably this was not in his nature.

Outside the Cabinet there was no obvious abundance of talent with which to reassure the doubtful observer. Dartmouth, who claimed 'to have never entertained a serious thought of taking a part in administration',[158] but accepted the Board of the Trade, turned out to be a conscientious and not ungifted Minister. The Lord Lieutenancy of Ireland was given to Lord Hertford, a mediocrity who had long been pressing for promotion from the embassy in Paris to the Castle in Dublin, and was now successful as a result of his brother Henry Conway's elevation. Portland, a young and amiable member of the Minority, was awarded a Household plum, the Lord Chamberlainship, while two lords of the old Pelham regime, Grantham and Bessborough, shared the Post Office. Among the lower ranks the newcomers were almost frighteningly untried. The Treasury Board was staffed by young men with little or no experience of public business—Lord John Cavendish, Thomas Townshend junior, and George Onslow, while at the other Boards (Admiralty and Trade) only the two admirals, Keppel and Saunders, and John Roberts, could lay claim to any expertise. Perversely, two of the more experienced of the 'young men', Lord Villiers and Thomas Pelham, were awarded sinecures at Court.

Moreover one or two friends of the 'Old Whigs' declined to take office in the Ministry. 'It was impossible to persuade our friend S[i]r George Savile to take a part in Office', Rockingham wrote to Meredith, 'out of it, I am sure he will be a very warm one.'[159] The Earl of Hardwicke, though 'not Insensible to the being thought not quite a Cypher in the Country', also turned

[156] Add.MS. 32968, f. 266: Newcastle to Rockingham, 26 July 1765.
[157] WWM.R1–475: Archbishop of York to Rockingham, 3 Aug. 1765.
[158] Dartmouth MSS., Dartmouth to Rockingham, 9 July 1765.
[159] WWM.R1–473: [? 14 July 1765].

down an offer of the Board of Trade.[160] Neither was a great
loss in terms of administrative ability, though Savile enjoyed
immense public regard and respect and Hardwicke was
intellectually the most formidable of the 'Old Whigs'; his
advice from the sidelines was always eminently sensible.
Perhaps more seriously, Sir William Baker, a respected, useful,
and experienced man of business, was unavailingly offered
the posts of Chancellor of the Exchequer and Leader of the
House, which were eventually given respectively to Dowdeswell
and Conway.[161]

All in all the new Ministry was not such as to inspire great
confidence in its ability to survive. Every circumstance of its
formation seemed to militate against its chances of success.
The 'Old Whigs' had been invited to take office through no
merits or efforts of their own, and had accepted it only with
the utmost reluctance and doubt; in almost all respects they
seemed ludicrously unsuited for the task of government, and
there appeared to be every justification for the general scepti-
cism and disapproval which greeted their return to place and
power. John Yorke's comment on the Administration--'It
was patch'd up in haste, to serve some unintelligble turn, and
made up of the *rawest* materials'[162] —was all too apt. None
the less most of the factors which weakened the new Ministry
were essentially negative. Few Governments in the eighteenth
century were absolutely foredoomed to failure, and in the
last analysis the Ministerial future of Rockingham and his
colleagues lay in their own hands, in their positive response
to the new situation in which they found themselves and to
the many problems which beset them.

[160] Add.MS. 35361, f. 189: Hardwicke to Yorke, 18 July 1765.
[161] *Grenville Papers*, iii. 205.
[162] Add.MS. 35374, f. 302: J. Yorke to Hardwicke, 15 July 1766.

II

PROBLEMS AND PROSPECTS (JULY 1765)

THERE were those who considered that the obvious inadequacies of the new Ministers in no way affected their prospects. Thus Lord Holland assured his friend George Selwyn on 9 July, 'Stability they may well promise themselves. There is no mystery in the thing. Make whom they will ministers, the Parliament will follow; and what has happened these last six weeks is (if I mistake not) a very strong security against more unnecessary changes at Court.'[1] Of course Holland held an unduly cynical view of the political realities of his day and this sometimes clouded his judgement. None the less there can be no doubt that the future of the new Administration depended first and foremost on its standing at Court. Few Ministries in the eighteenth century—and none at all during George III's reign—endured long in the face of the Crown's hostility, while several which were secure in Parliamentary terms were destroyed simply by weakness in the Closet. It must be admitted that the 'Old Whigs' were not viewed with great favour at Court. As leaders of the old corps in the 1750s and of the Opposition to the Bute regime in the sixties, their credit with the King was inevitably low. But so great was George III's loathing for Grenville by the summer of 1765 that he was only too glad to bury or at least repress this particular prejudice. As Mackenzie remarked, 'His Majesty, offended in the highest degree with the insolencies offered him by his present Ministers, would have put any mortal in their place that could have carried on business.'[2]

Moreover the King fully accepted the implications of his determination to be rid of Grenville at any cost. It was to be expected that when he first made overtures to Cumberland on 7 April, he would express his desire 'to see people of consequence behave in such a manner as might justify me in giving them a share of the Crown favours, which might be the easier

---

[1] J.H. Jesse, *George Selwyn and his Contemporaries*, i. 380.
[2] *Selection from the Family Papers preserved at Caldwell*, Part ii, vol. ii, p. 37: Mackenzie to Mure, 4 June 1765.

done as I have not reason to be satisfy'd with some of the
people I employ'.[3] Yet even after a large section of the 'Old
Whigs' in the Commons, disobeying their leaders, had opposed
the Regency Bill, and even after they had failed, with or
without Pitt, to respond to the opportunity of May, he persisted in demonstrating his new-found trust in them. Thus he
went out of his way to assure Cumberland of his respect for
'those worthy Men, L[or]d Rockingham, the Dukes of
Grafton, Newcastle and others; for they are men who have
principles and therefore cannot approve of seeing the Crown
dictated to by low men'.[4] It is a measure of George III's
alienation from Grenville and his colleagues that he was prepared to talk in such terms of those whom he had found
utterly repugnant a few years before. In the lull between the
negotiations of May and June, after the King had been compelled to restore Grenville to office on his own terms, the
'Old Whigs' were welcomed at Court with open arms. On
25 May Onslow reported how he and his friends were 'all of
us received with such distinguishing Civility yesterday at
St. James's,'[5] and even the family which had borne the brunt
of George III's enmity in 1762 was now rehabilitated. 'The
Lord Cavendishes', the King informed Cumberland on 12
June, 'brought the D[uke] of Devonshire to day, who seems
a pretty behav'd Young Man.'[6] The scenes at Court in June
were indeed quite extraordinary, and astonished the Ministers,
who had briefly imagined that they had achieved a total
victory in May, not a little. On the one hand Walpole could
write to Holland, 'You call the Opposition, the late Opposition,
very apropos, for they declare they lay down their arms, and
are attached to the King.'[7] On the other, William Rouet
could comment drily: 'We now say that the King is at the head
of the minority, and therefore, under such a leader, great
achievements may be expected.'[8]

Naturally when a new Administration was at last constructed
in July, the royal favour continued unabated, Holland, for
example, noting that George III 'seems satisfy'd with his
deliverance from Gr[enville], etc. He speaks of and to his new

[3] *Correspondence of George III*, i. 125. (*Additions and Corrections*, pp. 31–2)
[4] Ibid. i. 118: 12 June 1765.   [5] Add.MS. 32966, f. 467: Onslow to Newcastle.
[6] *Correspondence of George III*, i. 119.
[7] *Walpole Correspondence*, xxx. 185: 29 May 1765.
[8] *Caldwell Papers*, Part ii. vol. ii, pp. 40–1: W. Rouet to Mure, 11 June 1765.

Ministers as his deliverers'.[9] Whether this was sufficient for
the future was another matter. While the memory of his
humiliations at the hands of Grenville, and indeed Pitt,
remained fresh in the King's mind, he would doubtless continue to look favourably upon his new servants. But this was
more a useful foundation for the future than a cast-iron
guarantee of unlimited support. Charles Yorke's word of
warning was most apposite.

As the whole of this change arises from *Internal* causes in the Court
itself, the permanency of it must depend on being respected there;
otherwise it will *end* as it *began*; and some new scene of intrigue, of
Faction, of arrangement, and of Power, will arise, not *precisely* corresponding with the Ideas of the K[ing], the Public, or any one Man
living.[10]

One factor likely to assist the 'Old Whigs' in riveting the
goodwill of the King was their connection with the Duke of
Cumberland. It is a curious yet undeniable fact that
Cumberland's role in the events of 1765 has rarely received
full recognition at the hands of historians.[11] Doubtless, both
for the Rockinghams themselves in their later years, and for
their nineteenth-century admirers, there were embarrassments
in their close association with Cumberland. Obviously it was
awkward to have to admit that the 'men worthy to have
charged by the side of Hampden'[12] rode into the great
constitutional battle of George III's reign with the King's
own uncle and confidant, not merely at their side but at their
head, not just their comrade but their recognized leader. None
the less there is more to the obscurity of Cumberland's later
political career than mere historical prejudice. Cumberland
died barely three months after the ministerial changes of
July 1765—before the new Administration faced Parliament
or took action on the burgeoning American crisis. Those
three months were traditionally the quietest of the political
calendar, relatively undisturbed by serious business. Had
Cumberland lived through the deliberations and decisions of
the winter of 1765-6 it would have been impossible to evade
the questions raised by his association with the Ministry. As

[9] Earl of Ilchester, *Henry Fox, First Lord Holland* (London, 1920), ii. 300:
Holland to J. Campbell, 26 Aug. 1765.
[10] Add.MS. 35428, f. 74: Yorke to Sir Joseph Yorke, 7 Sept. 1765.
[11] Namier was the first to concede such recognition. See Sir L. Namier, *Crossroads
of Power*, pp. 105 et seq.
[12] Lord Macaulay, *Essay on the Earl of Chatham* (London, 1887), p. 151.

it was, his brief return to the forefront of the political stage
faded into insignificance, a minor episode at the close of a
long and chequered career. Moreover it is an extremely ill-
documented episode. Those of Cumberland's papers which
survive at Windsor cast no light whatsoever on the politics of
his last years. Cumberland himself took the precaution of
burning his private papers at regular intervals, and little
remains beyond the few documents which found their way
into the custody of Albemarle, his trusted aide and closest
associate.[13]

Contrary to the belief of his biographers,[14] Cumberland
held no office himself. He was indeed required by the King,
at the height of the Silk Riots of May 1765, to act as Captain-
General of the Army, a post which he had previously occupied
before his disgrace in 1757.[15] But no formal appointment was
ever made, partly because the riots were short-lived, partly
because it was Cumberland's own desire to avoid heightening
political tension by such a blatant provocation of Grenville,
who had his own candidate, Granby, for the army command.
The fact that the military honours which attended Cumberland's
funeral in November were those appropriate to the rank of
Captain-General was misleading, for as Rockingham informed
his wife, 'tho' his R[oyal] H[ighness] did not die Captain
General', the funeral honours were particularly requested by
George III, in consideration of his 'having been so—and upon
a late occasion His Majesty having desired him to act as such'.[16]

Cumberland had no need of office however. It was sufficient
that he was the King's uncle, a celebrated general and formidable politician. A bitter enemy of Leicester House in earlier
days, he had been closely associated with the Parliamentary
Opposition in the new reign. But the King's volte-face in the
spring of 1765 found him quite amenable to the situation
once one or two personal demands—notably his inclusion in
the board of Regency provided for by the Regency Bill—had
been satisfied. 'I am ingaged from dutty [sic] and inclination',
he assured the King at the end of June; 'and as long as the

13 Add.MS. 32971, f. 244: Albemarle to Newcastle, 3 Nov. 1765.
14 For example, the *Dictionary of National Biography*, and B.W. Kelly, *The Conqueror of Culloden* (London, 1903), p. 161.
15 *Rockingham Memoirs*, i. 209–10.
16 WWM.R156–3: 2 Nov. 1765.

rope will hold I'll draw.'[17] George III himself was nothing if
not thorough in his new attachment. Onslow pointed out that
he had 'offer'd Carte Blanche to the Duke of Cum[berland]
(the only one I believe that was really offer'd by or to any
body)',[18] while Northumberland, who was at one stage
employed to carry messages between George III and his
uncle, told Albemarle in words much imitated thereafter,
that 'the King was determined to fling himself into the Duke's
hands.'[19] In any event there can be no doubt that Cumberland
was the dominant figure in the negotiations of 1765. In May
he was in direct control of his nephew's affairs, personally
travelling to Hayes to see Pitt and carrying out all interviews
and consultations himself. With the failure of his efforts and
the reinstatement of the old Ministry, he none the less made
himself prominent at St. James's, so much so indeed that
Grenville complained to the King that 'he did not understand
why his Royal Highness was so often at Court.'[20] Though he
retired to Windsor in June in order to avoid irritating Pitt
when the latter was again asked to form a Government, he
quickly re-emerged when negotiations broke down. Once
Newcastle and Rockingham had indicated their readiness to
rescue the King themselves, Cumberland's was the key role.
Grafton's later statement that 'the principal line of ministerial
departments was settled between His Majesty and H[is] R[oyal]
H[ighness]',[21] is entirely sustained by the evidence of the
time. It was Cumberland who planned the distribution of the
principal offices, he who personally interviewed the more
important candidates for them, prevailing upon some of those
reluctant to accept, and he who supervised the arrangements
preparatory to the dismissal of Grenville and his colleagues.[22]
Quite clearly there was every justification for the general view
of contemporaries that he was the guiding light of the new
Ministry.

It was natural enough that Cumberland's position at Court
should continue to be a commanding one once the Adminis-

[17] *Correspondence of George III*, i. 140: [30 June 1765] (*Additions and Corrections*, p. 35).
[18] Add.MS. 34728, f. 95: Onslow to West, 24 (misdated 22) May 1765.
[19] *Newcastle's Narrative*, p. 4.   [20] *Walpole's Memoirs*, ii. 125.
[21] *Grafton Autobiography*, p. 54.
[22] Add.MS. 32967, f. 349: Newcastle to Rockingham, 12 July 1765; Albemarle MSS., Cumberland to Albemarle, 28 June 1765; *Correspondence of George III*, i. 134–5, 145, 155–7.

tration of his friends had been inaugurated. Despite Horace
Walpole's opinion to the contrary, there is little reason to
doubt the extent or reality of the reconciliation in the royal
family.[23] Desperate for assistance, in a state of intense
emotional anxiety, George III had appealed to Cumberland
for the aid which Bute, long his 'dearest friend', either would
not or could not supply, and indeed in some sense the Duke
replaced Bute as the confidant of the King, provoking the
latter to remark that 'if He had been his Father He could not
have behaved with more Tenderness and Affection to Him.'[24]
In any event this newly forged bond was of the utmost value
to Rockingham and his colleagues. Newcastle, for example,
was delighted to find that 'The Duke of Cumberland has
certainly removed all the Prejudices to The Whigs; and That
is a great Point gained; and for which we *All* ought to shew our
Gratitude.'[25] Though this probably exaggerated the influence
of Cumberland—the initial decision to approach the Opposition
was after all the King's own—there could be no denying its
importance. Even Walpole had to concede Cumberland's
utility from the Ministerial vantage-point.

The personal character of his Royal Highness was in such estimation,
his behaviour was so full of dignity, he was so attached to the Crown,
and understood the Court so much better than the Ministers, and could
dare to hazard language in the closet which their want of authority and
favour forbade them to use, that he could have interposed in their
behalf, or could have bent them to necessary submission to the Crown,
which no other man in England was capable of doing.[26]

Important though it was, the allegiance of the Closet alone,
even sustained by the influence of the redoubtable Cumberland,
was scarcely sufficient to assure a secure future for the Ministry.
Despite Holland's belief that 'Whoever has the Places, the
Parliament will follow',[27] the amenability of Parliament and
particularly of the Lower House, was not something to be
taken for granted. In the House of Commons there were
many Independents who were not to be won over by the
loaves and fishes at the command of the Government. A fair
estimate of their strength would be roughly two hundred,

[23] *Walpole's Memoirs*, ii. 156; *Walpole Correspondence*, xxii. 364: Walpole to
Mann, 15 Nov. 1765.
[24] Add.MS. 51425, f. 20: Bishop of Ferns to Holland, 28 May 1765.
[25] Add.MS. 32967, f. 4: Newcastle to Rockingham, 1 June 1765.
[26] *Walpole's Memoirs*, ii. 157.
[27] Add.MS. 51387, f. 145: Holland to Ellis, 12 July 1765.

a number quite sufficient to affect the fortunes of Ministers.
The degree of their independence, like their political convictions, varied a good deal, but most would have liked to
consider themselves country gentlemen untrammelled by
interested views and personal ambitions.[28] In general, policy
rather than patronage was the instrument with which eighteenth
century Ministers were compelled to woo them. Rockingham
and his colleagues made generous promises in this respect, and
went out of their way to boost themselves as men 'who, if
their Offices had been elective, would, upon Mr. Pitt's
Declension, have been chosen by the independent Part of the
Nation'.[29] Unfortunately many of the Independents were not
disposed to favour the newcomers. From the country gentleman's point of view, Grenville had been a most satisfactory
Minister; his business-like economies at the Treasury seemed
worth more than all the pledges of the 'Old Whigs' on the
score of cider tax and general warrants. Moreover one large
section of the Independents, those who still delighted in the
name of Tory, were frankly hostile to the new Administration.
Throughout the crisis of the spring their sympathies had lain
very much with the existing regime, and at the end of May
there were even rumours of 'a meeting of 36 Cocoa Tories
who sent to Lord Litchfield and Denbigh to tell them they
designed to support and be connected with the Duke of
Bedford'.[30] Though the new Chancellor of the Exchequer,
Dowdeswell, was himself a Tory, the incoming Ministers
declared themselves to be the champions of Whiggism so
vociferously that their doctrinal enemies were unlikely to be
conciliated. In addition the effective head of the incoming
Government was extremely unpopular with the old Tory
party.

I hope [Richard Rigby urged Sandwich] , neither Grenville nor you will
fail to write proper letters to our dear friends the Tories upon this
occasion, and blazon forth their happy prospect under the Duke of
Cumberland's abomination of them; I won't meet a Tory gentleman
in his coach and four this whole summer, without stopping to remind
him how well the Court is disposed to reward their services and zeal to

---

[28] On the Independents, see Sir. L. Namier, *Crossroads of Power*, pp. 30—45,
and Sir L. Namier and J. Brooke, *History of Parliament: House of Commons;
1754—90* (London, 1964), i. 145—9, 190—7.

[29] G. Cooper, *The Merits of the New Administration Truly Stated* (London,
1765), p. 2.

[30] Add.MS. 51408, f. 238: Lord Bateman to Holland, 28 May 1765.

the present Government, by placing their avowed and mortal enemy at the head of it.[31]

If the attitude of the Independents towards the new Ministry was at best unpredictable, at worst hostile, that of the outgoing Ministers was crystal clear. It was of course inevitable that Grenville would take a number of friends and followers into opposition with him. In type they varied considerably; there was a group of personal friends in the Lords—notably Hyde, Suffolk, and Buckinghamshire—a few personal assistants such as Thomas Whately and Charles Lloyd, and a number of latter-day Tories and country gentlemen, like Bamber Gascoyne, George Hay, and Edward Kynaston. In July 1765 Grenville's rather inchoate party may have numbered as many as fifty or sixty; during the ensuing few years it was gradually to diminish as less loyal friends, men like Hans Stanley, Augustus Hervey, and Robert Nugent, returned to Court, until only a small band led by Whately and Suffolk remained to await Grenville's death before themselves resuming the pleasures and profits of office. The other section of the outgoing office-holders, led nominally by the Duke of Bedford, was quite different in character;[32] though the Bedford party was at this time smaller than Grenville's, commanding twenty or thirty votes in the Commons and a dozen or so in the Lords, it was far better disciplined and organized. Cumberland and the King did indeed endeavour to obtain the support of part of this group, with offers to the Duke of Marlborough and his brother Lord Charles Spencer, respectively Lord Privy Seal and Treasurer of the Household under Grenville.[33] However this manoeuvre failed; Marlborough decided that he 'could not think of leaving all my Friends without Rhyme or reason, merely for the sake of having His Majesty's arms upon my Chariot—for that seems to have been the bait I was to have gorg'd', and Bedford thanked him for 'this fresh instance of your friendship'.[34] For the rest the Bedfords, accompanied by a few stragglers such as Sandwich, Halifax, and North, left

[31] Sandwich MSS., Rigby to Sandwich, 11 July 1765.
[32] For analyses of the Grenville and Bedford Parties in 1767, see J. Brooke, *The Chatham Administration, 1766–68* (London, 1956), pp. 255–75.
[33] *Grenville Papers*, iii. 210; Bedford MSS., lii. f. 46: Marlborough to Gower, 11 July 1765.
[34] Bedford MSS. lii. f. 10: Marlborough to Bedford, 15 July 1765; *Bedford Correspondence*, iii. 306: 5 July 1765.

in excellent order, marshalled as they were by Rigby and the
Duchess.

There could be no doubt of course that the Grenville and
Bedford blocks would go immediately into open opposition.
On 10 July Sandwich assured Bedford that Grenville had
given 'the King to understand, I think pretty plainly, that he
meant to lose no opportunity of exposing the misconduct of
the new administration'.[35] Moreover the union of the two
component parts of this new Opposition, if rather dubious in
the long term, was temporarily secure. Grenville, despite his
frequent disagreements with his colleagues in office was
naturally anxious for cooperation against his successors, and
Bedford, who was personally ready to retire from public life,
was at this time 'extremely warm and cordial in his
expressions'.[36] More importantly, the Duchess of Bedford
and Richard Rigby, the dominant forces in the Bedford party,
had no high opinion of the new Administration's prospects,
and out of sheer expediency were content, for the moment
at least, to follow Grenville's lead. Whether as Rigby claimed,
it was true that 'upon an inspection into the red-book, we
have all the reason in the world to be satisfied with our
numbers', is open to question.[37] But that there would be a
vociferous and uncompromising Opposition for Rockingham
and his colleagues to contend with, regardless of their
measures, was certain.

If there was relatively little which the incoming Ministry
could do to secure the loyalty of the Independents or the
forbearance of the Opposition, there was ample scope for
thought and action in relation to the Court's following at
Westminster. Naturally a sizeable section of the Government's
committed supporters in both Houses consisted of those
entering office with Rockingham. Indeed one of the more
remarkable features of the change of Ministry in 1765 was a
massive upheaval among office-holders, unprecedented in
scope at least since the Hanoverian Accession, and explained
only by an almost wholesale migration of Opposition into
Government. 'There has been pretty clean sweeping already;'

[35] *Bedford Correspondence*, iii. 310.
[36] *Grenville Papers*, iii. 218: Grenville Diary, 17 July 1765; it is now clear that
this diary was written by Mrs. Grenville (see *Additional Grenville Papers, 1763-
65*, ed. J.R.G. Tomlinson (Manchester, 1962), pp. 4–11), though this by no
means reduces its value.
[37] *Bedford Correspondence*, iii. 314: Rigby to Bedford, 5 Aug. 1765.

Chesterfield noted on 15 July, 'and I do not remember, in my time, to have seen so much at once, as an entire new Board of Treasury, and two new Secretaries of State, *cum multis aliis*, etc.'[38] It was natural enough, as Shelburne pointed out, that 'these Old Whigs were very hungery and would want many places for themselves.'[39] But it was also the case that there was something of a principle involved. In a very real sense July 1765 was intended to see the return of the Pelhamite Innocents, those victimized in 1762-3 for their loyalty to Newcastle. Thus in later life George Onslow recalled 'how in 1765 all things were set to rights again and every person who had been turned out of their office restored to it or promoted to better'.[40] At the time the new Ministers were agreed that '*Restitution is no Obligation*; That was The Principle, and Foundation of This Administration', and there was much talk of 'the General Rule of restoring all those who were turn'd out', and of 'rules of strict justice in favour of former sufferers'.[41]

Great efforts were certainly made to ensure that all those who had been victimized received adequate compensation if not restoration. The batch of Lords Lieutenancies forfeited in 1762 were once again distributed among Rockingham, the Cavendishes, Grafton, and Newcastle.[42] Moreover, most of Newcastle's friends and followers were given appropriate rewards for their loyalty. John Yorke and John Roberts actually returned to the seats at the Board of Trade which they had left in 1763; the two George Onslows, the Townshend cousins, Lord Villiers, and Thomas Pelham, even contractors like 'Tommy' Walpole, all shared in the great windfall. The strategy of restitution and compensation also extended a good deal lower thanks to the joint efforts of Rockingham and Newcastle. One of the more notorious aspects of the activities of Bute and Holland in 1763 had been the wholesale dismissals even of the small fry of public life, men who in the years of plenty had profited nobly from their association with the

---

[38] *Letters of Chesterfield*, ed. B. Dobrée, vi. 2658: Chesterfield to P. Stanhope, 15 July 1765.

[39] Add.MS. 51405, f. 172: C. Upton to Holland, 30 July 1765.

[40] H.M.C. *Onslow MSS.*, p. 521.

[41] Add.MS. 32968, f. 242: Newcastle to Rockingham, 25 July 1765; H.M.C. *Weston Underwood MSS.*, p. 393: E. Sedgwick to E. Weston, 6 Aug. 1765; *Burke Correspondence*, i. 215: Burke to C. Lloyd, 1 Oct. 1765.

[42] For a full list, see *E.H.R.* lxvii. 552–3 (a paper written by John Roberts).

Pelhams, men who could cast no vote at Westminster but could perform useful service in more lowly and more local spheres, 'the small wares of Power', as John Yorke called them.[43] Vast lists of those to be favoured were drawn up at Claremont and Newcastle House, ranging from those in the Alienation Office, 'being all deserving Men, and dismiss'd purely for being Friends to the D[uke] of Newcastle', through Mr. Thomas Perry, former Comptroller of Hawkers and Pedlars, 'an Old, most Faithful Servant to The Dutchess of Newcastle', to the large squadron of the 'Sussex Friends' who had staffed the Government's posts in the county which Newcastle regarded as his personal, ducal preserve.[44]

On the whole, Rockingham, who was subjected to an endless stream of lists and memoranda from Newcastle, proved cooperative. By 27 July Newcastle could report to John Page, 'The Restitution of all our Sussex Friends is near over; and I own, It will give me the greatest pleasure, To see Them Reinstated, Gay, and Happy, after all Their Sufferings *on my Account.*'[45] However there were limits to Rockingham's forbearance.

I must say My Dear Lord [he wrote to Newcastle on 8 October] If Your Grace expects me to Act upon a Spirit of Retaliation—not of Restitution—I can neither justify it to my own feelings—nor to what I think in the End—will prove politically right . . . I am satisfied If a Stand is not made to the Warmth of Friends in different Parts of England—who would desire dismissions in low offices, in order to make Room for Persons to serve their Interests—I doubt not but that all who have been put in for the last Two or Three years would be turned out— and we might suffer the Vindictive Spirit of Retaliation to prevail so far—that we should surpass in Severity the Example of 1763—and be equally deservedly odious.[46]

There followed a minor tussle over one or two of Newcastle's claims in Sussex, in which Rockingham's attitude was not altogether unaffected by the fact that one of those involved was a racing friend; this demonstrated to the Duke that he was not to expect automatic compliance with his demands. As it was, the extent of the changes imposed by the accession of the 'Old Whigs' was huge, but if Newcastle had had his way they would scarcely have ended where they did.

[43] Add.MS. 35374, f. 245: J. Yorke to Hardwicke, 20 July 1765.
[44] WWM.R14—10: 17 July 1765; WWM.R14—3: 'Observations upon a Paper', 26 July 1765; Add.MS. 32968, f. 185: Newcastle to Rockingham, 23 July 1765.
[45] Add.MS. 32968, f. 309.   [46] Add.MS. 32970, ff. 227—8.

However the principal task in the organizing of a dependable
Court majority at Westminster lay less in the marshalling of
the 'Old Whigs' and their supporters than in the handling of
that portion of the previous Administration which was permitted to retain office by the newcomers, that portion which
in popular parlance owed allegiance to the Earl of Bute. It
cannot be sufficiently stressed that it was the universal
belief in 1765-6, not merely among the press and public, but
also among serious and knowledgeable politicians of every
party and persuasion, that Bute was in the fullest sense 'The
Favourite', master of the Closet and director of the Crown's
activities, though he had held no office in form since giving
up the Treasury in 1763. Every significant development in the
early months of 1765 for example, was attributed to Bute's
baleful 'influence behind the curtain'. When the King was ill
in February it was reported that 'to secrete him from all
intercourse with his Court, Lord Bute had placed the King
at Buckingham House, a damp unwholesome spot, and
rendered more perilous by the neighbourhood of two
infectious hospitals.'[47] Again, during the Crown's disputes
with the Grenville Administration and the subsequent train
of negotiations for the introduction of a new Government,
Grenville noted 'that there was but one voice on this subject,
that all the world saw it to be Lord Bute's doing, and contrary
to the express declarations made to his present Administration'.[48]
On the other side of the political fence John Roberts was
similarly persuaded.

It is evident, from the first commencement of the negotiation to its
present stage, that it principally *owes its rise* to Lord Bute's hatred of
Mr. Grenville and the D[uke] of Bedford's party . . . We must therefore
reason always upon this *datum* that the negotiation is with his lordship
and not with any other greater person.[49]

The true significance of Bute's influence in the Closet
remains obscure even today, the only fixed point being the
violent quarrel which shattered it for good in the summer of
1766.[50] Before this all that is clear is that Bute retained some
hold on the personal affections of the King, but exercised

[47] *Walpole's Memoirs*, ii. 59.
[48] *Grenville Papers*, iii. 179–80: Grenville Diary, 21 May 1765.
[49] *E.H.R.* lxvii. 554: 'Account of the real Springs which moved Lord *Bute* with
regard to the new Administration 1765'.
[50] See R. Pares, *King George III and the Politicians* (Oxford, 1953), pp. 105
et seq., and *Letters from George III to Lord Bute*, pp. 255–8.

only a very limited degree of political control. In 1765 he rarely saw or heard from his master, though Chesterfield believed in the King's 'nocturnal conferences with the Princess of Wales and Lord Bute', and Charles Jenkinson 'owned to Mr. Grenville that the intercourse in writing between His Majesty and Lord Bute always continued, telling him that he knew that the King wrote him a journal everyday of what passed, and as minute a one as if, said he, "your boy at school was directed by you to write his journal to you." '[51] By the spring of 1765 George III had come to recognize that his 'dearest friend' was a broken reed when it came to helping him in his difficulties, and accordingly appealed instead to his uncle. In consequence Bute had very little to do with the political developments of the summer. He himself protested in June 1766 'I have not been at Court these 9 months, nor seen H[is] M[ajesty] for this year past, nor know when I shall. Ignorant to the last degree of what is going forward, the papers are my only intelligence.'[52]

This was perhaps a little disingenuous. Especially after Cumberland's death at the end of October 1765, Bute did receive some long and very confidential missives from the King, and also transmitted some advice of his own, despite the repeated promises and protestations of both George III and Bute to the contrary.[53] However such consultation as there was bore no relation to the wild notions current among contemporaries. Lord Holland was astonished to hear Bute's own version of his relations with the King in November 1765, and wrote to him soon after, 'I believe firmly whatever you tell me on your Word; but 'till Thursday, I thought with the whole world, that you saw the King in private, at Leicester House, and at Kew 3 or 4 times in a Week. Now I know the Contrary.'[54]

Bute's relative inactivity in the politics of this period was no doubt by his own desire. He had thrown himself with gusto into the struggles of the early sixties, and yet, disil-

---

[51] *Letters of Chesterfield*, ed. B. Dobrée, vi. 2657: Chesterfield to P. Stanhope, 2 July 1765; *Grenville Papers*, iii. 220: Grenville Diary, Nov. 1765.

[52] Sir W. Fraser, *Memorials of the Family of Wemyss of Wemyss* (Edinburgh, 1888), iii. 223: Bute to J. Wemyss, [17 June 1766].

[53] For the King's anxiety as to the possibility of their correspondence being discovered, see *Letters from George III to Lord Bute*, pp. 249–50.

[54] Add.MS. 51379, f. 175: 9 Nov. 1765.

lusioned by the frustrations and anxieties of his new career, had clearly lost his nerve. Apparently glad to escape from what had been chastening experience of power and responsibility, he claimed to have abandoned all political ambitions.

Whatever I may think, [he remarked to Holland in November 1765] is of little consequence indeed; happy had it been for me If I had never left . . . that private philosophick line, for which nature intended me, and in which I trodd for so many years unknown, unenvy'd, and content; but that is over and cannot be recall'd, t'is then the business of a man of sense; to look forward and to shape His future course, by all the experience he has dearly bought in a most unpleasant voyage; I have left the Political world for ever.[55]

Understandably enough there were a few glimmers of renewed interest and activity before Bute finally faded from the public scene. He still had relatives and friends very much concerned in politics, he still liked to speak in Parliament on matters of outstanding national importance, and he was still somewhat reluctant to give up his personal credit in the Closet. However these lapses were not very significant. Whereas Newcastle had renounced high office merely to reinforce his own political influence, Bute was quite clearly set on a course for retirement. Not the least of George III's misfortunes in the first years of his reign was the fact that the man in whom he had been led to put all his trust and faith was wholly unworthy of his confidence, a man whose courage had failed him in a battle provoked largely by his own attitudes and activities, and a man who had failed to fulfil his duties to a ward whose opinions and affections he had infiltrated without scruple.

Unfortunately the fact of Bute's virtual retirement from public life did not preclude the existence of a party which regarded him as its leader, and which in the eyes of others seemed at times to dominate both the Court and the Government. This was doubtless inevitable. Bute had demonstrably been the King's Favourite and for a period had also been his chief Minister. He naturally acquired his own circle of friends and followers, notably Scots like Eglinton and Marchmont in the Lords, and James Oswald and Gilbert Elliot in the Commons, but also some Tories, such as Samuel Martin and Lords Despenser and Botetourt, and miscellaneous politicians and men of business, a Charles Jenkinson, a Lord Egmont, a Sir Fletcher Norton. In addition there were many others who

[55] Add.MS. 51379, f. 177: [10 Nov. 1765].

felt no personal loyalty to Bute himself, but who were very anxious to remain in the Government of the day. As long as Bute was universally thought to retain his command of the Closet, such men, like Lord Northington in the Upper House or Lords Barrington and Strange in the Lower, were apt to be associated with his name and party. Once Bute had resigned and passed his official mantle to Grenville, it was to be expected that both these groups would gradually lose their independent identity. They were after all cast very much in the Court and Treasury mould; some of them had been obedient supporters of the Pelham regime in the forties and fifties, and many were to fall in behind North in the seventies. However Bute's apparently continuing connection with George III, and above all the growing evidence that the Ministers had ceased to be his friends on the one hand, or the King's on the other, ensured that the Bute party would retain some degree of cohesion. From the beginning of 1765 a basic division in the forces of Government, between those who opted for Grenville and Bedford on the one hand and those who declared their allegiance to the King and Bute on the other, became increasingly marked. In January Grenville complained strongly of 'the independency avowed by the Gentlemen of the Army, and that of those lukewarm friends to Government who professed attachment to His Majesty, but at the same time thought themselves at liberty to oppose his measures and ministers.'[56] At the pre-session meeting of the Court's supporters in the Lords on 9 January, two of the most prominent of Bute's friends, Lichfield and Pomfret, were ostentatiously uncooperative, and two others, Despenser and Denbigh, absented themselves.[57] Bute apparently apologized for their conduct,[58] but the incident was not quickly forgotten, and a few months later more serious conflict arose. A new Poor Bill, proposed by Thomas Gilbert, a friend of the Bedford connection, was defeated by a combination of Bute's friends on the one hand and the Opposition on the other.[59] Though this measure was not one to which the Administration had committed itself as such, it was certainly one championed by the Bedfords, being 'the personal point of The Duke of

[56] *Grenville Papers*, iii. 116: Grenville Diary, 25 Jan. 1765.
[57] Ibid. iii. 114.   [58] Ibid. iii. 115.
[59] In the Commons the bill had been carried against a tiny minority of nine; in the Lords it was the subject of some close divisions and was effectively destroyed by that of 2 Apr. 1765 (the voting was 58-44).

Bedford, the Duke of Bridgewater, and Lord Gower'.[60] The
result was a minor sensation in the papers, and a serious
worsening of the tension at Court. However worse was to
come in May and June.

The Regency Bill split the Administration down the middle.
Grenville's success in inducing George III to agree to the
exclusion of his mother from its provisions caused horror and
surprise among Bute's friends, and led directly to the motion
to repair the omission carried by 'people well affected to
Government, and who formerly had been attached to the late
Prince of Wales'.[61] George III's subsequent efforts, albeit
initially unavailing, to call in the help of Pitt and the 'Old
Whigs' made plain the extent of his alienation from his
Ministers, and this lesson was driven home still further by
the terms which Grenville extorted before returning to office
on 23 May. Henceforward the unity of the Court and
Treasury party under the leadership of Grenville and Bedford
was shattered beyond repair. Throughout June 1765 the
King, determined to give 'the Ministers no difficulty in
carrying on his Government but at the same time to shew
the world that they were not in his favour', made a habit of
publicly ignoring and slighting them.[62] Not surprisingly this
policy produced a strong remonstration from Bedford (on
12 June) against the separation of the Crown's confidence
and authority, which George III in his turn construed as a
declaration that his Ministers intended to resign and used as
a pretext to make a new appeal to Pitt.[63] By this time Bute's
friends were perfectly aware of the need to avoid involvement
in the fortunes of a doomed Administration. 'I was informed
yesterday,' one of Temple's minions reported on 30 May,
'that Sir James Lowther and Mr. Wedderburn particularly
have now set up something like a standard of declared
opposition, and, with others of the same connection, are
beating up for members to join it.'[64]

From this moment the existence of the King's Friends as a
distinct problem with which the incoming Administration

---

[60] Add.MS. 33077, f. 147: Newcastle to Duchess of Newcastle, 5 Apr. 1765.
[61] *Grenville Papers*, iii. 158: Grenville Diary, 8 May 1765.
[62] *Jenkinson Papers*, p. 373: Giblert Elliot's Memorandum, 29 May 1765.
[63] *Grenville Papers*, iii. 57–9; *Jenkinson Papers*, p. 374; *Bedford Correspondence*,
iii. 286–90; *Correspondence of George III*, i. 124.
[64] History of Parliament Trust transcripts, Grenville (Murray) MSS., R. Mackintosh
to Temple.

would have to contend, was inevitable. A few months later
Sir Joseph Yorke, the British Ambassador at the Hague, was
to write home 'in one letter I saw, an expression is made use
of which is a little unintelligible, the writer talks of *le Parti
du Roi* as something distinct from the old or the present
administration; I am sure I am thoroughly of that Party, for
after all what can anybody propose in the place of it.'[65]

This was the authentic voice of the Pelhamite old corps
man, astonished that it should be necessary to state so obvious
a principle as loyalty to the Crown, yet incapable of disputing
its validity. Indeed most of the King's Friends were just such
men as Yorke, career politicians whose interests and convictions naturally predisposed them in favour of the Court. What
was remarkable about the party and political developments
of 1765-6 was not the fact that there existed those whose
primary allegiance was to the Crown, but that the exceptional
conditions obtaining in the 1760s compelled them to proclaim
this allegiance not merely against factious Opposition, but
even against the King's Ministers.

Prudence dictated that Rockingham and his friends should
do something to win over these men. 'No solid or firm
Administration', Hardwicke pointed out, 'can be formed on
the narrow Bottom of one particular Set of Men',[66] and
certainly the 'Old Whigs' needed auxiliaries. Their new recruit,
Edmund Burke, as yet untouched by their prejudices, had no
doubt of the proper course to be pursued. 'It is certain', he
wrote to O'Hara, 'that if they act wisely, they cannot fail to
make up a lasting administration. I call taking in Lord Bute,
or at least not quarrelling with him, and enlarging their
Bottom by taking in the Tories, and all the men of Business
of the house of commons not listed against them, acting
wisely.'[67] To the merits of such advice the Newcastle-
Rockingham group remained regrettably blind. Ever since
their retreat into opposition in 1762 their most constant cry
had been against Bute and Bute's friends. Naturally every
politician in opposition in the sixties utilized the Bute bogey;
however the 'Old Whigs' persisted in this tactic even when it
was plainly to their disadvantage. In the matter of the
Regency Bill they had vehemently objected to the inclusion

[65] Add.MS. 35385, f. 186: Sir J. Yorke to C. Yorke, 1 Nov. 1765.
[66] Add.MS. 35361, f. 171: Hardwicke to C. Yorke, 4 July 1765.
[67] *Burke Correspondence*, i. 208: 4 [July 1765].

of the Princess of Wales in its schedule, and 'had given all the
trouble they could', though as Walpole pointed out, 'they
were doing the business of the Ministers, who wished for
nothing so much as a vigorous opposition to the bill'.[68] Again
in May, when Grenville's regime was restored on its own terms,
all of which were intended to humiliate and proscribe Bute and
his friends, the 'Old Whigs' were openly delighted. The dismissal
of Mackenzie and Holland particularly met with their admiring
applause; Newcastle's comment—'I am glad, The Two great
Strokes are struck, whoever struck Them'—was typical.[69]
Moreover throughout the negotiations of May and June they
were intent on extracting similar conditions themselves. As
early as 21 May Newcastle set out the terms which he and
his friends regarded as essential prerequisites to their taking
office, terms, it may be added, which were fully endorsed by
the representatives of the party who assembled at Claremont
on 30 June.

It is . . . proposed, That some Effectual Means should be taken, To
convince The Publick, That neither His Majesty, nor His intended
Ministers, should have anything to do with My Lord Bute, directly or
indirectly, in The Conduct of The Administration, and The Management
of Publick Affairs. And That, neither My Lord Bute, nor His Brother
Mr. Mackenzy, should concern Themselves, or have anyThing to do, in
The Administration of Affairs in Scotland.
And as a Proof of This, That some Persons, known to depend entirely
upon My Lord Bute, and To be in His Lordship's Confidence, should,
with others of The present Administration, be immediately removed
from Their Employments.[70]

These demands can only be explained as part of a wider
problem, for the attack on the King's Friends was merely one
aspect, if the most important, of a general preoccupation with
popularity. The chief objection which the 'Old Whigs' felt to
forming a Ministry themselves, was that 'The Opposition
would be said to join Lord Bute, and would suffer in their
reputation.'[71] Thus Lord Digby reported Egmont's apprehensions on the score of the new Ministers' susceptibilities to
Holland, 'I told him you thought this would go on; that the

---

[68] Warwickshire Record Office, Newdigate MSS., A.7: Newdigate Diary, 13 May
1765; *Walpole's Memoirs*, ii. 76.
[69] Add.MS. 32966, f. 475: Newcastle to Albemarle, 26 May 1765.
[70] Ibid., ff. 436–7: 'For His Royal Highness's Consideration', 21 May 1765 [not
delivered].
[71] *Walpole's Memoirs*, ii. 122.

Power of the Crown would carry the House of Commons. He agreed with you in general, but not If the Government don't trust to that strength, and are courting popularity.'[72] Certainly there can be no question but that the 'Old Whigs' pursued public approval with an intensity which went far beyond the lip-service politicians customarily paid it, and which both surprised and mystified contemporaries.

In retrospect this obsession is easily indicted as at best injudicious and at worst suicidal. In an age when the Court held most if not all the tactical cards, when opinion 'out-of-doors' could only have significant consequences in very exceptional times of crisis and war, popularity was hardly an object to be sought at the expense of credit at Court and in the Closet. But by 1765 Newcastle and his friends had some excuse for their attitude. Their experiences in the ten years or so since Henry Pelham's death had been confusing, if not traumatic. They had seen unprecedented popular reactions to the causes of Pitt and Wilkes. They had themselves striven awkwardly to harness this force to their own opposition to the Bute and Grenville Ministries on a series of issues—in particular the Peace, cider tax, and general warrants. In their anxiety to enlist popular support and enthusiasm, they tended to lose sight of the tactical considerations vital for success in the restricted political world of St. James's and Westminster. As to the power of the Crown, they had some reason to be sceptical. George II had more than once been compelled to accept Ministers whom he regarded with indifference or dislike and to abandon those of his own choice. His grandson was utterly humiliated by Grenville in May 1765 and was saved from still greater subjection only by the intervention of Cumberland and the 'Old Whigs' themselves. Two most important elements in Opposition thinking— the quest for popularity 'out-of-doors' and the avowed need to bind the Closet by sheer force—which have generally been associated with the views of Burke and Fox, were in reality embedded deep in the experience of the 'Old Whigs' before 1765 and transmitted to the Opposition of the 1770s by Rockingham and those who stood by him in 1766.

None the less the arguments against these attitudes are, in retrospect at least, overwhelming. The metropolitan radicalism which flared up in the fifties and sixties was only of

[72] *Letters to Lord Holland*, ed. Ilchester, p. 239: 18 July 1765.

relatively long-term significance, as, for that matter, were the
petitioning movements of the decade after. It was not until
the country's entire economic and social structure had been
drastically altered by the Industrial Revolution, that appeals
to extra-Parliamentary opinion as against the exploitation of
the Crown's prestige and influence could be used as part of
the everyday armoury of politicians. Moreover George III's
circumstances were not such as to assist the 'Old Whigs' in
their strategy. The Closet could only be successfully and
lastingly forced when an indispensable majority of the
political establishment was sufficiently united. Yet in the
1760s the world of politics was more fragmented than at
almost any other moment between the Hanoverian Accession
and the end of the century, and the circumstances of 1744 and
1746 could hardly be repeated. To anyone capable of political
realism and sound judgement it must have been apparent that
the Newcastle-Rockingham group were set on a futile if not
dangerous course. But by 1765 among the remnants of the
old corps who regarded themselves as the true repositories
of the Whig tradition, realism and judgement were among the
last qualities to be found. Moreover their foolish anxiety to
concentrate all on a campaign for public support was much
intensified by their generally poor reception as Ministers. In
some quarters they were anything but popular. Grenville's
most vaunted boast had been his success in making fiscal
economies in general, and in satisfying the financial and
commercial interests of the City of London in particular,
to say nothing of his growing reputation with the country
gentlemen for his conduct at the Treasury. Indeed one of
George III's avowed complaints against Grenville had been
his neglect of all measures 'except those which Mr. Grenville
thought tended to his acquiring Popularity' and his
determination to 'have the popularity of raising but small
supplys'.[73] Grenville's public standing did not bode well for
the incoming Ministers. One of Lord Holland's friends, for
example, was certain that 'The City of London I mean the
merchants and least Factious part, don't like the Exchange of
G[renville] for L[or]d Rockingham.'[74] His impression was
confirmed by an extraordinarily insolent address which the

[73] *Correspondence of George III*, i. 172: Memorandum by the King [Nov.-Dec.
1765] (*Additions and Corrections*, pp. 38–9).
[74] Add.MS. 51433, f. 64: W. Digby to Holland, 19 [July 1765].

City presented to the King in August on the birth of a new son. Though it attacked George III's choice of Ministers, and was much condemned for 'the monstrous impropriety of tacking a palpable affront to an address of congratulation',[75] it could only add to the determination of Rockingham and his colleagues to raise their credit in the public estimation, whatever the cost.

'To talk to Conway against public opinion', remarked Horace Walpole, in words which were equally applicable to Conway's friends, 'was preaching to the winds.'[76] Fortunately there was one voice to which even the new Ministers were bound to listen. The Duke of Cumberland possessed considerabl more political acumen than his subordinates and by no means shared their prejudices. That he was particularly wary of endorsing their attitude to Bute's friends he had twice demonstrated in May 1765. He had then done his best, though not with conspicuous success, to prevent his friends exposing themselves by a campaign against Bute during the debates on the Regency Bill,[77] and in the ensuing negotiations with Pitt had strongly supported the proposal to make Northumberland First Lord of the Treasury.[78] One of the Oppositions's charges against the new Administration was that it was dominated by a 'double Favouritism', which redounded to the joint benefit of the friends of Cumberland on the one hand and Bute on the other.[79] Cumberland, of course, like his former ally Holland, was a supreme realist, and recognized that secure tenure for the new Ministry could not be guaranteed unless his colleagues abandoned their prejudices and cooperated with the King's Friends. Though the latter perversely regarded him as an implacable enemy,[80] Cumberland was their most effective—and indeed virtually sole—advocate among the newcomers. As such he was surprisingly successful.

One of the critical 'Conditions *Sine qua non*', as Newcastle informed Albemarle, 'without which, We All Unanimously

[75] *A Letter to the Common-Council of London, on their late very extraordinary Address to His Majesty* (2nd edn., London, 1765), p. 36.
[76] *Walpole's Memoirs*, ii. 146.
[77] See Add.MSS. 32966, ff. 275–6, 300, 351, 363–4; 33077, f. 153.
[78] According to Northumberland himself, it was actually Cumberland who proposed this arrangement (*Jenkinson Papers*, p. 400).
[79] C. Lloyd, *An Honest Man's Reasons for Declining to take any Part in the New Administration*, p. 8.
[80] Add.MS. 51433, f. 64: W. Digby to Holland, 19 [July 1765].

thought, We could not enter into The King's Service, consistently with His Majesty's Interest, and our own Honor', was
the wholesale proscription of Bute's friends.[81] On one point
particularly the 'Old Whigs' were immovable. When Mackenzie
had been dismissed by Grenville in May, George III had
objected very strongly, since he had earlier promised Mackenzie
life-tenure of his office. 'You will make me', he informed
Grenville, 'do, *as King* [that] which I should *be a scoundrel
to do, as a private man*',[82] and though Bute and his brother
released their master from his promise, this episode was not
to be forgotten or forgiven. During the following year the
question of Mackenzie's restoration to office came to
epitomize the whole problem of the posture to be adopted
towards the King's Friends, and while it would have been
wise in the 'Old Whigs' to reinstate Bute's brother at once,
they declined to do so, though as it happened they had considerable difficulty in finding anyone else to serve at the
Scottish Privy Seal Office.[83] But with this exception Cumberland
was relatively successful in restraining the ardour of his
colleagues. Only two of Bute's friends were actually dismissed
by the incoming Administration, Lord Despenser from the
Great Wardrobe and Sir Fletcher Norton from the post of
Attorney-General. The Bute group's chief representatives in
the Commons, James Oswald and Gilbert Elliot, were permitted to remain in office after giving appropriate assurances
in response to the King's declaring 'how necessary it is for
them if they have any Duty and attachment to me to support
that Administration that I have been able to form'.[84] The
Earl of Lichfield, a former Tory, and like Despenser a prominent friend of Bute's, was surprised to find himself retained,
'as He is within the Circle laid down by *them*, and openly
acknowledges it', while Denbigh, Master of the Harriers, was
'very happy', as John Yorke recorded, 'that he is not to be
remov'd, that his *Bow wows* (as he calls them) are safe; of
wh[i]ch, my good L[or]d Northington had the K[ing]'s
permission to acquaint him'.[85] Newcastle, of course, struggled

[81] WWM.R1—455 (b): 3 July 1765.   [82] *Newcastle's Narrative*, p. 18.

[83] The Earls of Kinnoull and Hopetoun, and Lord President Dundas, all refused
this post, and it was finally given to the Earl of Breadalbane, a connection
of the Yorkes by marriage.

[84] *Correspondence of George III*, i. 146: King to Egmont, [8 July 1765].

[85] Add.MS. 51405, f. 163: C. Upton to Holland, 15 July 1765; Add.MS. 35374,
f. 245: J. Yorke to Hardwicke, 20 July 1765.

hard to resist Cumberland's tactics. His ambitious scheme for
a formal promise by the King never to consult Bute, and for
sweeping dismissals of all those associated with the Bute
connection,[86] was strongly discountenanced by Cumberland,
and doubtless by his nephew. Though Newcastle grumbled
incessantly about 'The Keeping some in, who, I wish, were
out',[87] it was made clear yet again that his voice was not to
be heard in the inner councils of the new Administration.

Unfortunately the good effects of this conciliatory policy
in the Closet, in Parliament, and in the political world in
general, were nullified by other factors. In the first place,
while it was quite true that the new Ministers removed very
few of Bute's own friends, they dismissed many who in the
public mind were associated with the Court. The expulsion of
men such as Lord Hillsborough at the Board of Trade, Welbore
Ellis as Secretary at War, and George Hay and Hans Stanley
at the Admiralty Board, seemed to penalize those whose only
offence was loyalty to the Crown and who would scarcely
have followed Grenville and Bedford into opposition volun-
tarily. There were constant reports that 'they everday turn
out some of the ablest and best friends of the King', and that
'they seem [to] be for turning out almost all the men of business in the house of commons.'[88] These reports were exaggerated, for some of the most valuable placemen in the
Commons who left office at this time, like Lord North of the
Treasury Board, Robert Nugent, a Joint Vice-Treasurer of
Ireland, and Thomas Pitt of the Admiralty Board, resigned
without being compelled to do so. None the less the impression
on the public of these losses, with whatever justice, was less
than fortunate.

It was rendered considerably worse by another circumstance.
If Cumberland had had some degree of success in preventing
his friends from executing their more extreme intentions, he
could not stop them delcaring them. Quite apart from the

[86] Newcastle envisaged the dismissal of the Earls of Darlington, Ilchester,
Lichfield, Pomfret, Denbigh, Talbot; Viscount Falmouth; Gilbert Elliot,
James Oswald, John Mackye, Humphrey Morice, W.R. Earle, and John
Tucker. (Add.MSS. 32967, f. 170; 32968, f. 386; 32969, f. 239; for
Newcastle's draft of the King's written promise concerning Bute, see Add.MS.
32968, f. 381).
[87] Add.MS. 32968, f. 118: Newcastle to Fetherstonhaugh, 20 July 1765.
[88] Letters to Lord Holland, ed. Ilchester, p. 236: C. Upton to Holland, 16 July
1765; Add.MS. 51425, f. 120: Touchet to Holland, 18 July 1765.

inevitable in-fighting at Westminster and Whitehall, the press saw a violent controversy from which it emerged that the 'Old Whigs' were by no means disposed to abandon their loathing for Bute and his friends. Report after report emphasised that 'the present M[inistr] y seem as hostile to L[or] d Bute, as the last', and 'that these new people talk more offensively of my Lord Bute than the late ministers did'.[89] Rockingham and his colleagues were indeed absurdly sensitive in this respect. When, for instance, Lord Hertford tried to obtain a favour for his celebrated friend and assistant, David Hume, he was informed that 'it could not be done at this time though it may hereafter because it would now open a scene of political writing or suspicion against him which he could not risk.'[90] Hume himself commented 'The Cry is loud against the Scots, and the present Ministry are unwilling to support any of our Countrymen, lest they hear the Reproach of being connected with Lord Bute.'[91]

This loudly proclaimed detestation of Bute and his party by the 'Old Whigs' was exceedingly foolish. It neutralized the genuine concessions they had made at the instance of Cumberland, and in every quarter, except that of their own inflamed supporters, did them material harm. Bute himself, limited though his power was, was astonished by their attitude.

The conduct of the present Ministers seems, [he later remarked to Oswald] whether out of fear of the newspapers, or disinclination to me, or both, to be all pointed in having nothing to do with me. This is so singular, that I cannot help thinking they mean some day or other to resign, and then lay the cause on me, though I shall know no more of it than you do; a situation not the most pleasant for a man, who, at present estranged from all business, from the King, am as ignorant of what passes as if I was shut in Bute.[92]

Inevitably both Bute's own friends and the wider grouping of the King's Friends were disturbed and disillusioned by the new Ministers' violent and imprudent hatred of the King's Favourite and his connections. Some of them indeed could only be induced to retain their places in such an unpromising

[89] Add.MS. 51433, f. 44: W. Digby to Holland, 12 July 1765; *Letters to Lord Holland*, ed. Ilchester, p. 228: Lord Digby to Holland, 10 July 1765.
[90] *Letters of David Hume*, ed. J.Y.T. Greig (Oxford, 1932), i. 517: Hertford to Hume, 16 Aug. 1765.
[91] Ibid. i. 519: Hume to J. Home [Aug. 1765].
[92] *Memorials of the Public Life and Character of the Right Hon. James Oswald* (Edinburgh, 1825), pp. 418–19: Bute to Oswald, n.d.

venture, on condition, like Granby, that 'he should be at full liberty to act as he pleased, and unconnected with the new system'.[93] As early as August it was reported to Temple,

Some, I can say, that are personally attached to the [King] , and do not chuse to take their mark from any other gnomon, avow their having no liking for, no confidence in, our present steersmen, and so much so that they have abstained going near them, though they have received broad hints.[94]

Still more serious was the King's own reaction to the suspicion and hostility with which his rescuers regarded men whom it would have been prudent to conciliate. He was always solicitous of the welfare of 'those', as he assured Bute, 'who have invariably stood by you, and those few besides whose personal conduct to me have made them dear to you'.[95] The prejudices of his new Ministers against his friends surprised and alarmed him. 'I know too well', he later informed Bute, 'from the many cruel scenes I underwent during the formation of them how very personal they are against the men they got remov'd, and their diffidence of those that remain'd.'[96] He even went to the extraordinary lengths of sending personal messages of reassurance to some of those dismissed. Thus Lord Hillsborough had a 'message from the King, thro' Lord Barrington, telling him that nothing had ever given him more concern than being obliged to consent to his removal, but such was the present necessity of his affairs that he could not refuse, but that he might depend upon being brought in the first favourable occasion.'[97]

Of course George III had no option but to suppress his irritation. As he remarked to Charles Yorke, 'in changes of this sort, Those who *undertook* were to be gratified, in many things not otherwise eligible'.[98] None the less such conduct was most injudicious on the part of the 'Old Whigs'. The folly

[93] Sandwich MSS., Grenville to Sandwich, 7 July 1765. Lord Townshend, the Earl of Suffolk, and Lord Strange made similar stipulations. *Grenville Papers*, iii. 209; Nottingham University Library, Portland MSS., PwF 7922: C. Price to Portland, 18 July 1765; Bedford MSS., lii. ff. 19, 24: Grenville to Bedford, 7, 8 July 1765.

[94] *Grenville Papers*, iii. 82: Mackintosh to Temple, [30 Aug. 1765].

[95] *Letters from George III to Lord Bute*, p. 241: [10 Jan. 1766].   [96] Ibid.

[97] H.M.C. *Various Collections*, vi. 263: 'Lord Hillsborough', 12 May 1779; for another example, see Bodleian Library, Dashwood MSS., B.3/2/la: Egmont to Despenser, 10 July 1765.

[98] Add.MS. 35428, f. 103: Yorke to Hardwicke, 10 Aug. 1765.

of 'disobliging Behavior to L[or]d Bute worse than the last, when their whole dependance must be on the King's Steadiness in supporting them', should have been obvious.[99] Unfortunately they wilfully ignored it. 'Nothing', Horace Walpole later wrote, 'could induce them to take the smallest step that might secure favour in the closet, by even civility to the Favourite.'[100]

The assistance which the new Ministers failed to seek among the King's Friends, they sought to obtain from William Pitt. It was perhaps inevitable that they should continue in power to feel the dependence which they had placed on him in Opposition. After the failure of the May negotiation, Newcastle had insisted that,

if this plan could ever have been proper to undertake, in any way, it should have been so formed, as to appear only as a summer suit, till Mr. Pitt could come with his winter's dress. In short, it should have been, in my opinion, such a one, as should shew Mr. Pitt, that it was meant to subsist only till he should come, and take the administration upon himself.[101]

This view was much strengthened by the insistence of 'the younger part of the Ministry',[102] articulated, for example, by Sir George Colebrooke,[103] on the need not merely to conciliate Pitt by every means possible, but to demonstrate to the public that the new Administration had Pitt's full support. 'I see, Every Day', Newcastle remarked to Grafton on 11 July, 'by the Temper of our best Friends, That, If Mr. Pitt is not kept in good Humour, Nothing will go on well.'[104] In any event the consequence was a general agreement that 'The Plan of Administration should, in General, be made as palatable to Mr. Pitt; and as agreable, as possible, to His Notions, and Ideas.'[105] In terms of measures this meant a much publicized determination to adopt all the points which Pitt had announced his intention of carrying in the preceding negotiations—the reorientation of foreign policy in favour of a Prussian alliance, the repeal of the Cider Excise, the compensation of army officers dismissed from their regiments for their oppo-

---

[99] Add.MS. 51408, ff. 250–1: Lord Bateman to Holland, 6 Oct. 1765.
[100] *Walpole's Memoirs*, ii. 146.   [101] *Newcastle's Narrative*, p. 15.
[102] *Letters of David Hume*, ed. J.Y.T. Greig, ii. 21–2.
[103] Add.MS. 32967, f. 226: Colebrooke to Newcastle, 4 July 1765.
[104] Ibid., f. 332.
[105] Add.MS. 32967, f. 178: Newcastle, 'Measures', 1 July 1765.

sition to the Grenville Ministry in 1764, and a Parliamentary declaration against the employment of general warrants. In terms of men, it meant a readiness to favour all who could claim some slight association with Pitt. Thus Lord Chief Justice Pratt, one of Pitt's closest friends and hero of the campaign against warrants, was awarded a peerage by the Ministers, 'on account', as Charles Yorke remarked, 'of giving themselves some *air of false popularity* and courting Mr. P[itt]'.[106] Thomas Nuthall and George Cooke, both followers of Pitt, were made Solicitor to the Treasury and Joint Paymaster-General respectively.[107] George Dempster, a connection of Pitt's lieutenant, Shelburne, was given the office of Secretary to the Order of the Thistle, while Sir John Griffin Griffin, another of Pitt's friends, also found himself the recipient of Ministerial favours.[108] Shelburne was offered the Board of Trade, and his associate Barré, a Vice-Treasurership of Ireland, though both, like Pitt's brother-in-law, James Grenville, declined to serve.[109]

On the basis of this conduct Rockingham and his friends made such extravagant claim of Pitt's countenance and support that outsiders might have been forgiven for believing that he was far more effectively the 'Minister behind the Curtain' than Bute had ever been. 'Woud to God', Henry Flood wrote to Burke, 'that Pit were in *actual* office.'[110] In the press a huge battle developed between Government and Opposition, both sides striving for the accolade of Pitt's good opinion, as they fought to avoid the stigma of Bute's. Neither side had a very secure foundation for its claims. Though Grenville made much of a personal meeting with Pitt, the latter clearly had no intention of joining his politics to those of his brother-in-law. Similarly, while there was a general impression that the 'Old Whigs' had been 'pressed and encouraged by Mr. Pitt' to take office,[111] the reality was less propitious. On 4 July

[106] Add.MS. 35428, f. 73: Yorke to Sir J. Yorke, 7 Sept. 1765.
[107] Nuthall wrote to Lady Chatham for permission to accept (Chatham MSS., li. f. 247: 11 July 1765).
[108] Essex Record Office, Braybrooke MSS., C. 8/50 to 56: correspondence of Rockingham, Conway, and Griffin, Sept. 1765.
[109] *Rockingham Memoirs*, i. 234–6; Fitzmaurice, *Life of Shelburne*, i. 332–40; Add.MS. 32968, f. 5: Grafton to Newcastle, 16 July 1765.
[110] WWM.Bk. 1–29 + 3: 27 July 1765.
[111] *Walpole Correspondence*, xxii. 310: Walpole to Mann, 12 July 1765.

Keppel and Saunders, the two naval friends of the Newcastle-Rockingham group, visited Pitt at Hayes, and as Rockingham reported to his colleagues, were 'much satisfied with Mr. Pitt—who declared that *we ought* to undertake—and that he would shew his approbation'.[112] Whether the Admirals misunderstood their host or whether Pitt was playing a subtle game of his own is not clear, but in any event, when Grafton paid a visit to Hayes not long afterwards, he found his idol less enthusiastic than he had expected. Though the reports which Grenville mischieviously circulated were greatly exaggerated,[113] there can be no doubt that Pitt did not express himself in his admirers' favour. By the beginning of August Pitt's friends, and particularly those who had accepted favours from the new Ministers, were publicly declaring that their master was in no way committed to supporting the Administration.[114] A few weeks later Pitt himself, in a letter to Grafton intended for public consumption, made his own views perfectly clear.

Let me now, my Lord, be as explicit in declaring what I have said, with regard to rumours industriously propagated, and which I could not acquiesce in, namely, that the present ministry was formed by my advice and approbation. To men under such impressions I have constantly averred, that this ministry was not formed by my advice, but by the counsel of others; that, from experiences of different ways of thinking and of acting, Claremont could not be to me an object of confidence or expectation of a solid system for the public good, according to my notions of it; and as the authority I most wished to refer myself to, upon this subject, I have appealed to the conversation I had the honour to hold with the Duke of Grafton at Hayes.[115]

This attitude was a considerable blow to Rockingham and his friends. Their reliance on Pitt's name, their dependence on his ultimate readiness to emerge as their leader, their paralysing incapacity to act without the assistance of his approval, were all so complete that the public declaration of his indifference, if not enmity towards them, did much to destroy their credibility as a Government.

Though the 'Old Whigs' were indeed not a little disconcerted by their failure to obtain the approval of the 'Great

---

[112] Add.MS. 32967, f. 234: Rockingham to Newcastle, 4 July 1765.

[113] See *Chatham Correspondence*, ii. 318–24; *Grafton Autobiography*, p. 56.

[114] Add.MS. 51425, f. 123: Touchet to Holland, 27 July 1765; Grenville (Murray) MSS., Grenville to Whately, 4 Aug. 1765. Nuthall and Camden were the culprits.

[115] *Chatham Correspondence*, ii. 321–2: 24 Aug. 1766.

Commoner', they had only themselves to thank for it, for
they had a fundamental misapprehension of Pitt's political
attitudes and ambitions. Pitt, of course, loved to make his
own position as 'various and full of mystery' as possible,[116]
and never more so than in the summer of 1765 when he
retired to his newly-acquired seat at Burton Pynsent to
become a 'Somersetshire bystander'.[117] Yet through all his
conduct in 1765 and 1766 there ran a consistent and coherent
strategy. He was above all else a natural autocrat and had not
grown less so with the passing years—'He will be Master',
Welbore Ellis rightly remarked to Holland in November 1765.[118]
A long career in politics, and in particular his fall in 1761, had
led him to stipulate two conditions as essential prerequisites
of his return to office—the complete confidence of the Crown,
and the absence of any significant rival either in Cabinet or
Closet—'There could be *but One Minister*' he declared in
January 1766.[119] In 1761 Bute's influence with the King, to
say nothing of George III's own detestation of him, combined
with Newcastle's power in Administration, had put him in a
position which he was determined never to accept again.

   This emphasis on the need for total authority in every
sphere explains all Pitt's apparent eccentricities in the summer
of 1765. His unwillingness to participate in the negotiations
of May 1765 was simply a result of the fact that they were
conducted not by the King but by his uncle. Cumberland
himself 'told the king that he was convinced his interposition
had prevented Mr. Pitt from closing with His Majesty's
propositions, and he advised him to see that gentleman personally'.[120] In June the situation was slightly more complex.
Then, indeed, he was summoned directly by the King; but
Cumberland's influence raised special problems. The Duke
himself assured Pitt that there was no question of his continuing to play a part at Court. 'The King called me to this business, and the moment it is over, I shall retire to Windsor.'[121]
None the less Pitt plainly feared having 'to discuss business
with Princes of the Blood', and talked of his 'despair of
transacting with the K[in]g as he had done in the late Reign,

[116] *Walpole's Memoirs*, ii. 142.   [117] *Grafton Autobiography*, p. 59.
[118] Add.MS. 51387, f. 180: 17 Nov. 1765.
[119] Add.MS. 32973, f. 237: 'Lord Rockingham's Account of His Conversation
   with Mr. Pitt, on Tuesday last The 21st Inst.' 23 Jan. 1766.
[120] *Jenkinson Papers*, p. 375: Gilbert Elliot's Memorandum, 18 June 1765.
[121] *Walpole's Memoirs*, ii. 123.

by L[ad]y Yarmouth etc.'[122] Temple's refusal to take the
Treasury clinched the matter, for it compelled Pitt to depend
entirely on the friends of Cumberland and Newcastle for
assistance. With so flimsy a power-base for his authority, he
not surprisingly declined to serve.

Cumberland's death in October was of course to remove a
major obstacle; as Lord Holland remarked after that event,
'the generall Voice is, that he was one obstruction to Mr. Pitts
acceeding, and that he will now come in.'[123] However by this
time, Pitt's other condition—that he would negotiate only
with the King—was unlikely to be fulfilled. Not until the
summer of 1766, after a year of intense anxiety and distress,
of ministerial instability and crisis, did George III bring himself to succumb to Pitt's dictatorship. In the meantime
Rockingham and his friends completely failed to perceive the
nature of Pitt's strategy. Despite Pitt's rejection of their conciliatory gestures they declined to be deflected from the course
they were pursuing, just as they refused to amend their
attitude towards Bute and his friends despite the pressing need
to unite the forces of the Court and the Administration in
Parliament. The quest for Pitt's approval and favour, and the
refusal to contemplate an alliance with the King's Friends
were to remain the hallmarks of their political strategy until
their dismissal in July 1766. Fundamentally the error of
Rockingham and his colleagues was that they acted in power
as they had in Opposition. George III was struck by their
'still imbibing those strange ideas in government, that they
addopted whilst in opposition',[124] a most perceptive remark
which went to the root of the problems raised in 1765-66,
and which goes far to explain the ultimate unsuitability of
the 'Old Whigs' as a party of power. However at the beginning
of their Administration in July 1765 this was very much in the
future. For the moment at least the political world was prepared to wait and see.

[122] Add.MS. 35428, f. 72: C. Yorke to Sir J. Yorke, 7 Sept. 1765; f. 76:
C. Yorke to Hardwicke, 3 July 1765.
[123] Add.MS. 51387, f. 172: Holland to Ellis, 5 Nov. 1765.
[124] Letters from George III to Lord Bute, p. 242: [10 Jan. 1766].

III

THE CUMBERLAND ADMINISTRATION
(JULY TO OCTOBER 1765)

To A considerable extent the future of the new Ministry lay in the hands of Cumberland. The elevation of Rockingham did not conceal the essential fact that it was the King's uncle who was the new power to be reckoned with. 'The Duke's Ministry', 'The duke of Cumberland's administration', 'The Duke's Administration, with Lord Rockingham at the Treasury'—such were the terms in which contemporaries described the new ministry of 1765.[1] These descriptions merely reflected the strength of Cumberland's political position. He was, after all, the 'Former and Protector of that Ministry'.[2] He had negotiated its formation, dictated its composition and, by his control of the Closet, held the key to its continuance. In July 1765 all the important political cards were in his hands, though later on there was to be some difference of opinion as to the way in which he played them. The Ministers, putting on a brave front, maintained in public that his death was 'an event of no consequence, for that he took no part in the conduct of affairs'.[3] Opposition opinion naturally differed, Charles Jenkinson, for example, claiming that 'without him they can do nothing; for as I am told they dare not take a step, but as he directs.'[4] In July this problem had puzzled Newcastle and his friends. There was no precedent for Cumberland's position in 1765, and it was a matter for conjecture whether he would gracefully withdraw into seclusion or take the lead in the everyday direction of business.[5]

Quite apart from his natural authority as a prince of the

[1] Bedford MSS. li. f. 234: Rigby to Bedford, 28 June 1765; Add.MS. 51350, f. 15: R. Bateman to Ilchester, 28 [June 1765]; Fitzmaurice, *Life of Shelburne*, i. 335: Shelburne to Barré, 7 July 1765.
[2] Add.MS. 35428, f. 25: Hardwicke, 'Private Memoirs'.
[3] *Grenville Papers*, iii. 107: Whately to Grenville, 8 Nov. 1765.
[4] *Jenkinson Papers*, p. 388: Jenkinson to Lowther, 3 Oct. 1765.
[5] Add.MS. 32968, f. 140: Newcastle, 'Mem[orandum]s for My Lord Rockingham,' 21 July 1765.

blood and the King's uncle, Cumberland was in many ways
well fitted to play a leading role. In point of experience and
capacity he was far better qualified than his young colleagues.
Though his career had been severely marred by his disgrace
after the Convention of Klosterseven in 1757, he had previously been at the centre of affairs all his adult life. As
befitted a son of Queen Caroline he had always shown himself
an intelligent and realistic politician, and for long periods
had exerted a powerful influence on government. Though his
political activities and military associations had made him
many enemies under George II, especially among the country
gentlemen, he was by the 1760s a highly regarded and
respected figure. He was also genuinely popular; Culloden
and its sequel, which were later to bestow such odium on his
name, were at this time still cause for adulation rather than
recrimination. This was amply demonstrated after his death
at the end of October 1765. Though it was to be expected
that the demise of a prince would be accompanied by
appropriate panegyrics,[6] there can be no question that his
loss was felt in the public mind.

His R[oyal] Highness memory [wrote Mrs. Montagu,] is so popular in
the City that the mob insult all the people who appear out of mourning,
if they seem of a decent condition, and they calld out to the King at
the play to know why he had not weepers on his coat, tho no one wears
them for an Uncle. The good people of England are very foolish in their
idolatry.[7]

If there were any doubts about Cumberland's suitability
for a prominent role in government in 1765 they concerned
not his qualifications, but rather his medical condition. A
lifetime of dissipation, a war wound in the leg, and a severe
stroke in the autumn of 1764 had combined to undermine
his health, and in the winter of 1765 his death was almost
daily expected. Lord Holland, who had once been Cumberland's
closest political associate but was now estranged from him,
seriously considered that the Duke's illness had broken his mind
as well as his body.[8] In fact, however, Cumberland made a

[6] For example, See *Critical Review*, xx. 394–7, for reviews of a 'Book of
Lamentations', 'A Pastoral Elegy', 'A Monody', and three 'Sermons', all on the
death of Cumberland, one of them declaring 'in one day this great man (the
duke) appeared in Court, both on earth and in heaven.'
[7] *Mrs. Montagu, the "Queen of the Blues"*, ed. R. Blunt (London, 1923), i. 134:
Mrs. Montagu to E. Montagu, 30 Nov. 1765.
[8] Add.MS. 51379, f. 125: Holland to Bute, 9 Nov. 1765.

remarkable, if superficial, recovery in the spring of 1765. Though his underlying condition remained very grave and was indeed to carry him off a few months later, at the critical point in the summer his mental and physical health gave every appearance of revival. In July 1765 when the so-called Rockingham Ministry was inaugurated, there was nothing whatever to prevent Cumberland from continuing to play the dominant part which he had assumed in the preceding negotiations and consultations.

In fact it was soon made apparent that Cumberland had no intention of retiring from the scene of action. He had already presided at meetings held to arrange the instalment of the new Ministers and to decide the composition of the 'conciliabulum' or 'effective Cabinet', though it had not been made clear whether he was to attend Cabinet deliberations in person.[9] Grafton later stated that 'The Duke of Cumberland was present at all our councils, on a general request made to H[is] R[oyal] H[ighness], approved by the King.'[10] In fact it was the determination of Cumberland and the King that the Duke should participate in ministerial consultations. Though the initial Cabinet meeting—of 22 July—was held in Cumberland's absence, a minute of the proceedings was despatched to the Duke for his approval. In his accompanying letter, Conway revealed:

I have at the same time the honour to acquaint your R[oyal] H[ighness] that it is his Majestys pleasure when we cannot have that of attending you in person that we shou'd not fail to make your R[oyal] H[ighness] acquainted with anything that is propos'd material to his M[ajesty']s service in order to have your R[oyal] H[ighness']s opinion therein; And your approbation before any Step is taken.[11]

Cumberland's reply ensured that thereafter he was not excluded from such meetings. 'I am highly sensible', he wrote, 'of the great Honour and Attention H[is] M[ajesty] is pleased to have to my poor opinion: but shall never think it any Trouble when the Lords judge it worth while to have me attend in Person.'[12]

Fourteen meetings were apparently held or scheduled

[9] *Correspondence of George III*, i. 156–7, (*Additions and Corrections*, pp. 36–7); Add.MS. 32968, f. 34: Rockingham to Newcastle, 17 July 1765.
[10] *Grafton Autobiography*, p. 55.
[11] Albemarle MSS., Conway to Cumberland, 23 July 1765.
[12] Albemarle MSS., Cumberland to Conway, 23 July 1765.

before Cumberland's death on 31 October, and nine of these actually took place at the Duke's house. Though the remaining five were convened at Grafton's house, Cumberland also seems to have been present at these.[13] Moreover he was accustomed to take the lead in arranging meetings. When the Cabinet appointed for 18 September was found to clash with a royal christening and a diplomatic function, and consequently postponed 'in form', Ministers were none the less asked to call on the Duke informally between the two engagements 'as his R[oyal] H[ighness] will be in Town and has s[ai]d he wou'd be glad to See us'.[14] Again, when Newcastle requested details of the agenda for the meeting of 31 October, Conway confessed his ignorance—'I acted chiefly in obedience to H[is] R[oyal] H[ighness]'s Intimation, and can only add I think these Meetings tend to advance business.'[15] In short, Cumberland was by no means a figurehead. As a matter of routine, he certainly attended and probably presided at ministerial meetings, though he held no office or departmental brief himself, a constitutional phenomenon without precedent or parallel.

There is ample evidence that Cumberland was personally consulted on all ministerial decisions of any importance. For example he customarily vetted the disposal of patronage. When a Regiment of Foot fell vacant in August, Rockingham suggested a complicated arrangement which would provide for a series of military promotions and declared: 'But in the whole of this matter your Royal Highness's Judgement will be our Safest direction and what we shall with the most pleasure adopt.'[16] The express, offering the Marquess of Lorne the vacant regiment, was not despatched until Cumberland had given his consent; all such military matters in the next two months were referred to the Duke.[17] Simi-

---

[13] The dates of the meetings, obtained from references in the papers of Rockingham, Grafton, Newcastle and Albemarle, are as follows:
At Cumberland's house: 15, 30 Aug., 18, 19, 22, 25 Sept., 3, 13, 31 Oct.
At Grafton's house: 29, 31 July, 6 Sept., 16, 18 Oct.
Of these meetings, two (18 Sept. and 3 Oct.) were apparently cancelled, and one (31 Oct.) was prevented by Cumberland's death. Namier (*Crossroads of Power*, p. 107) appears to have underestimated both the number of meetings and the number of Cumberland's attendances.
[14] Add.MS. 32969, f. 429: Conway to Newcastle, 18 Sept. 1765.
[15] Add.MS. 32971, f. 197: Conway to Newcastle, 30 Oct. 1765.
[16] WWM.R2–27: [9 Aug. 1765].
[17] See for instance, Add.MSS. 32968, ff. 359, 392; 32969, ff. 64–5, 74, 76, 78, 82; Braybrooke (Essex) MSS. C8/53, 55.

larly, when Lord Holland requested a favour for a dependent it was natural for Rockingham to refer the application to the prince who had been Holland's patron until three years before.[18] But Cumberland was by no means restricted to topics which so obviously concerned his own interests and connections. The disposal of civil honours, the preferment of bishops, requests for offices in the Administration, even, it seems, the distribution of colonial land grants, all required his opinion.[19] Only in matters of purely departmental or local concern did he take no part, and even then Newcastle was not above mis-using his remarks to pressurize Rockingham into satisfying the most extreme of his Sussex demands.[20]

The resulting situation was more than a little strange. The control which the First Lord of the Treasury normally exer-cised over the great bulk of patronage was severely restricted in the early months of the Rockingham Administration, partly no doubt by Rockingham's inexperience, but more especially by Cumberland's recognized hegemony. This is well illustrated by the consultations over the disposal of the vacant Governorship of Carisbrooke Castle, in August 1765. The recommendation to this post, which was a military sinecure of some importance in the electoral politics of the Isle of Wight, would in normal times have been settled by the First Lord of the Treasury, subject to the approval of the Crown. But in 1765 this was not the case. Though Rockingham personally approved the application of Harcourt Powell (the leader of the Isle of Wight borough-mongers) on behalf of a follower, he could give no assurances until he had sent an express to Cumberland at Windsor, recommending Powell as a '*Very good Man*' and hoping to 'hear his R[oyal] H[ighness's] determination before I go to Court tomorrow . . . [I] shall be very glad if Mr. Harcourt Powel's friend gets the Govern-ment'.[21] However Cumberland's written approval was not the end of the matter. Newcastle also found it necessary to inter-vene, writing to Cumberland himself on behalf of Powell and asking Barrington, the Secretary at War, to take no action

[18] WWM.R1–506, 521: Holland to Rockingham, 17 Oct. and 4 Nov. 1765; *Rockingham Memoirs*, i. 240–3.
[19] Add.MSS. 32967, f. 432; 32968, f. 244; 32969, f. 109; 32970, ff. 39, 312.
[20] Add.MS. 32968, f. 242: Newcastle to Rockingham, 25 July 1765.
[21] Add.MS. 32969, ff. 64–5: Rockingham to Newcastle, 17 Aug. 1765. Also ff. 60–1, 76, 78, 81, 82, 85, 135.

until he had received a reply.[22] When Conway characterisically developed scruples at the political manipulation of theoretically military appointments, Newcastle refused to discuss the relative arguments and appealed simply and solely to the authority of Cumberland. 'I had not troubled you, or any Body, about The little Government in The Isle of Wight, If I had not had The Duke of Cumberland's *Permit*.'[23] There was nothing unique about this case. Every such decision of any political interest was settled with the Duke before being presented to the King. Thus an important characteristic of the eighteenth-century chief Minister—the last word, apart from the King's, on the disposal of Government patronage—belonged to Cumberland rather than to the responsible ministers.

However, Cumberland was to influence far more serious decisions than those involved in the distribution of patronage. The imperial problem, which was to dominate and disrupt the political history of the next two decades, presented itself almost as soon as the new Administration had been formed. Precisely what lay behind the sudden outburst of American resistance to imperial authority in the 1760s remains one of the most formidable of eighteenth-century problems. What is certain is that the series of measures[24] affecting North America, carried out by the Bute and Grenville Ministries, proved unacceptable to colonies which had already attained a high degree of social and political maturity, and that the last of these measures, the Stamp Act, unleashed a flood of violence which was not to be exceeded until Lexington and the outbreak of war.[25] The American Stamp Act, which had

[22] Add.MS. 32969, ff. 66, 74: Barrington to Newcastle, 17 Aug. 1765; Newcastle to Cumberland, 18 Aug. 1765.
[23] Add.MS. 32969, f. 137: Newcastle to Conway, 21 Aug. 1765.
[24] These measures fall into three groups:
  1. The Proclamation of 1763 and later schemes devised by the Board of Trade for the regulation of the Indian trade and western frontier, together with the retention of some 10,000 troops in North America after the Seven Years War.
  2. The commercial measures of Grenville: principally the Sugar Act of 1764 and an amending statute of 1765, as well as customs regulations directed by the Treasury.
  3. Three unconnected measures which all affected the internal state of the colonies: the Currency Act of 1764, the American Mutiny Act of 1765, and the Stamp Act itself.
[25] There is of course a vast literature on the subject of the Stamp Act. One of the most useful recent accounts is in E.S. and H.M. Morgan, *The Stamp Act Crisis* (rev. edn., New York, 1963).

been formally proposed in the spring of 1764 and enacted in
that of 1765, though it merely extended to the colonies
duties long tolerated in the mother country, covered a multi-
tude of evils for the Americans. The encouragement it gave
to Vice-Admiralty Courts, the demands it made on increasingly
scarce specie, and the irksome penalties it inflicted on the
most influential and articulate classes in colonial society (the
lawyers, printers, and merchants), all aggravated the essential
fact that it represented the first systematic attempt to draw
a significant revenue from North America. Yet the storm
aroused by its enactment was utterly unexpected in England.
At Westminster the measure had been overwhelmingly
endorsed by the legislature. As Augustus Hervey remarked,
it 'went thro for two sessions almost without a Negative,
quite without a difficulty',[26] meeting no opposition at all in
the Lords and very little in the Commons, where the decisive
division had been in its favour by 245 votes to 49. Even
Americans in England, including two who had only recently
arrived in Europe (Benjamin Franklin and Jared Ingersoll),
had bowed to the apparently inevitable and had hastened to
recommend their friends as stamp distributors. Only Grenville
himself foresaw at his fall that 'every day would produce
Difficulties in the Colonies.'[27] Yet the reaction of the
Americans to the news that they were at last to be taxed
from England was unequivocal. At the end of May the
Virginian House of Burgesses flatly denied the British right
to tax the colonies, and in mid-August protest turned to
violence in New England. By 1 November when the Stamp
Act was due to come into force, the offices, courts, and ports,
in which it was to be administered, were in the control of
the Sons of Liberty, and the royal administration in the
colonies reduced to a state of total impotence. News of these
events, which tended to cross the Atlantic in about six weeks,
reached England in three distinct waves. The first overt act
of opposition, the Virginia Resolves, was known of in London
by the end of July; the first outbreak of violence at Boston
in early October, and the most serious disturbances of all,

---

[26] Hervey MSS. 50/5, ff. 431–2: Hervey: 'My Speech for enforcing the Stamp
Act'.
[27] Add.MS. 35428, ff. 99–100: Charles Yorke's Notes recording a conversation
with Grenville on 19 July 1765.

those at New York, in December.[28] For the rest the pattern
was one of repetition and imitation, as propaganda and protest
swept through the thirteen colonies until the Stamp Act was
effectually nullified from New Hampshire in the north to
Georgia in the south.

These developments took Cumberland's new administration
completely by surprise. The Cider Excise, general warrants,
and foreign policy had loomed far larger than imperial problems in their consideration of measures, and there is not the
least substance to the traditional view that Rockingham and
his friends came to power pledged to repeal the Stamp Act,
and committed to supporting colonial aspirations. It is true
that great hopes were entertained of the new Ministers,
especially by Americans. Joseph Sherwood, for example, the
Rhode Island agent in London, wrote home to Governor
Ward, 'I give you Joy on the Revolution in the Ministry, . . .
It is confidently Asserted these Changes will produce great
Ease to the Inhabitants of America', while the American newspapers were quick to 'declare their expectations'.[29] In part
these hopes rested on the simple assumption that 'the new
State Physicians will naturally find fault with the Prescriptions
of the Old Doctors',[30] and certainly Rockingham and his
colleagues were determined to discredit and undo much of
Grenville's work. But there appeared more solid grounds for
expecting relief in the fact that some of those newly in
office had opposed the Stamp Act at Westminster in the
previous spring. Conway had been one of the only two M.P.s
prepared to deny the legality of taxing the Americans, and
several of his colleagues and associates had at least objected
to the expediency of the tax.[31] But the significance of this

[28] In each case the following despatches gave the first information of these
events: Fauquier (Virginia) to Board of Trade, 5 June 1765, received 27 July;
Bernard (Massachusetts Bay) to Halifax, 31 Aug. 1765, received 5 Oct.;
Colden (New York) to Conway, 5 Nov. 1765, received 10 Dec. (P.R.O.,
Colonial Office Papers, Series 5, vol. 1331, ff. 29–31; 755, ff. 287–300;
1097, ff. 177–8.)

[29] *The Correspondence of the Colonial Governors of Rhode Island: 1723-1775*,
ed. G.S. Kimball (Boston and New York, 1902-3), ii. 367: 16 July 1765;
Dartmouth MSS., J. Smith to Dartmouth, 5 Nov. 1765.

[30] WWM.R1–522: copy of a letter from America, 8 Nov. 1765.

[31] The fullest information about speakers in the debates of 6 Feb. and 15 Feb.
1765 on the Stamp Act is in *Camden Miscellany*, xxiii (Camden Soc., 4th Ser.,

opposition was limited. As Jared Ingersoll pointed out, it was the opposition of a 'few of the heads of the minority who are sure to athwart and oppose the Ministry in every measure of what Nature or kind soever'.[32] Moreover it had been far from unanimous. 'We had a *sad* division on adjourning', George Onslow had reported to Newcastle on 6 February; '49 to 245. Many of our People with them'.[33] Perhaps Franklin's assessment of the significance of the change of ministry was the fairest. 'Some we had reason to Doubt of are removed', he wrote, 'and some particular Friends are put in place.'[34] There was, from the colonial point of view, reason for hope, but not necessarily for confidence.

None the less, this hope seemed at first capable of realization. Though the Board of Trade flatly declared that the Virginia Resolves amounted to an 'absolute Disavowal of the Right of the Parliament of Great Britain to impose Taxes upon her Colonies, and a daring Attack upon the Constitution of this Country', and strongly advised vigorous measures,[35] the Ministers showed no anxiety to act precipitately. The Cabinet did not discuss the Virginia Resolves until 30 August,[36] and

vii, 1969), 'Ryder Diaries', ed. P.D.G. Thomas, pp.253−61, and in *The Fitch Papers* (Collections of Connecticut Hist. Soc. vols. xvii and xviii, 1918 and 1920), ii. 332−5: Ingersoll to Fitch, 6 Mar. 1765. The names of those known to have spoken on the American side are as follows: Sir William Baker (M.P. for Plympton Erle), Issac Barré (M.P. for Chipping Wycombe), William Beckford (M.P. for London), Hon. Henry Conway (M.P. for Thetford), Rose Fuller (M.P. for Maidstone), Charles Garth (M.P. for Devizes), Richard Jackson (M.P. for Weymouth and Melcombe Regis), Sir William Meredith (M.P. for Liverpool), Thomas Townshend, jun. (M.P. for Whitchurch). Of these, Conway, Meredith, and Townshend held office under Rockingham, while Baker and Fuller were good friends of his Administration. Barré and Beckford were followers of Pitt, and Garth and Jackson unattached American agents. In addition three other friends of the 'Old Whigs', George Dempster (M.P. for Perth Burghs), Sir John Gibbons (M.P. for Wallingford), and Joseph Mawbey (M.P. for Southwark) spoke in the debate, though it is not certain that they favoured the American case. Charles Yorke, of course, who was Attorney-General in the Rockingham Administration, spoke on the Government side in these debates.

[32] *Fitch Papers*, ii. 334: Ingersoll to Fitch, 6 Mar. 1765.
[33] Add.MS. 32965, f. 346: 6 Feb. 1765.
[34] *Papers of Franklin*, ed. L.W. Labaree (New Haven, 1959), xii. 207: Franklin to Thomson, 11 July 1765.
[35] C.O. 5/1368, f. 133: Board of Trade's Representation, 27 Aug. 1765.
[36] See Add.MS. 32969, f. 257: Minutes of 'a meeting of his M[ajesty]'s Serv[an]ts at his R[oyal] H[ighness] the Duke of Cumberlands'. Conway's despatch of 14 Sept. adhered very closely to the directions of the Minute.

the resulting despatch from the Secretary of State's office
was not transmitted until 14 September. The tenor of the
discussion and despatch was firm but far from harsh.
Lieutenant-Governor Fauquier's report that the Resolves
were the work of 'Young, hot, and Giddy Members'[37] permitted Conway to express the hope that they would quickly
be revoked in the next session; his directions were confined
to a general exhortation 'by every prudent Measure in your
Power, at once to maintain the just Rights of the British
Government, and to preserve the Peace and Tranquillity of
the Province committed to your Care'.[38] It would seem that
at this juncture the Ministry was not particularly dismayed
by developments in America which would provide them with
an opportunity simultaneously to discredit Grenville and
demonstrate their own preference for a liberal and popular
policy. That this was so is also suggested by a letter of Joseph
Harrison's. A customs officer at New Haven, Harrison had
come to England to further his career, and had established
contact with Rockingham and Dowdeswell, later becoming
an assistant to Edmund Burke in his secretarial work for
Rockingham.[39] By 11 October he was writing to his colleague
John Temple in Boston:

Wee have lately had strange accounts from Boston of the riots and dis-
orders there and at Rhode Island. Surely the people are distracted and
infatuated. The ministry would certainly have relieved them from those
grievances they have so much complained of had they behaved with toll-
erable decency. But now they must expect no favour. What measures will
be taken is not determined. I shall know when any resolutions are formed;
and shall give you the earliest advice.[40]

Harrison's belief that the Boston riots, in which the property
of royal officials was destroyed, and all possibility of operating
the Stamp Act without military backing nullified, dramatically
affected imperial policy, was undoubtedly correct. 'All
America is in confusion', Conway told Rockingham on
10 October.[41] Almost overnight, a relatively minor colonial

[37] C.O. 5/1331, f. 29: Fauquier to Board of Trade, 5 June 1765.
[38] C.O. 5/1345, f. 84: Conway to Fauquier, 14 Sept. 1765.
[39] On Harrison, see D.H. Watson, 'Barlow Trecothick and other Associates of
Lord Rockingham during the Stamp Act Crisis' (Sheffield Univ. M.A. thesis
1958), pp. 100–28.
[40] *Bowdoin and Temple Papers* (Collections of Massachusetts Hist. Soc., 6th Ser.
(1897)), p. 70.
[41] WWM.R1–502.

problem was transformed into virtual rebellion. The Ministry recognized this by referring a long-term solution to the consideration of Parliament. By way of the formal machinery of the Privy Council, the reports of the American governors and representations of the Board of Trade were henceforth directed to await the attention of the legislature.[42] However an immediate policy was required and this time there was little delay. The critical information from Governor Bernard of Massachusetts was received on 5, 13, and 14 October.[43] The Treasury despatched orders as early as 8 October; the Secretary of State, who had to await the results of a Cabinet meeting on the 13th, dispatched his on the 24th. These instructions were quite explicit. Cooper, as Secretary to the Treasury Board, ordered Bernard to appoint a new stamp distributor (Oliver, the old one, had been compelled by the mob to resign) and to 'inforce a due Obedience to the Laws, and to take care that His Majesty's Revenue suffers no Detriment, or Diminution'.[44] Conway expressed surprise that troops had not already been used and while advising 'lenient and persuasive Methods' where possible, specifically ordered 'such a timely Exertion of Force as the Occasion may require'.[45] Later on there was to be much dispute as to the precise implications of these orders. Once the Ministry had come to a decision to repeal the Stamp Act, it was naturally anxious to insist that it had never wavered in its attachment to this policy. The Opposition's interpretation varied. Charles Lloyd's pamphlet, *The Conduct of the Late Administration Examined*, published in 1767, characterized 'the whole tenor' of Conway's despatches as 'languor and debility'.[46] On the other hand, in February 1766, when Grenville sought to demonstrate the inconsistency of his opponents, he constantly reiterated that the Ministry's policy of October 1765 had been one of en-

---

[42] *Acts of the Privy Council of England: Colonial Series*, ed. J. Munro (London, 1911), iv. 732. The clearest summary of the proceedings of the Treasury, Council, and Secretary of State is at P.R.O., Treasury Papers, Series 1, vol. 447, ff. 135–6.

[43] C.O. 5/755, ff. 261–300; 891, ff. 541–78: Bernard's letters of 15, 22, and 31 Aug. (the last was received first) to Secretary of State and Board of Trade.

[44] T.1/439, ff. 67–8.

[45] WWM.R29: Three different despatches were signed by Conway on 24 October, that to Bernard, a circular to all American governors, and instructions to Gage. All used similar expressions.

[46] C. Lloyd, *The Conduct of the late Administration Examined, Relative to the American Stamp-Act* (2nd edn., London, 1767), p. 74.

forcement. In the debates of 3 and 7 February, after Conway had rashly asserted that 'he would sooner cut off his hand' than employ force, Grenville waxed sarcastic at his expense:

The present administration eager and desirous to carry orders into execution. They will not sleep till orders are sent to the Admiralty and the misery that will follow it was of no consequence, as all the Governors have already orders by Conway's circular letter to carry the laws into execution.[47]

It is difficult not to sympathize with Grenville's interpretation. When Newcastle later re-examined the orders of October 1765, he was compelled to note that they strongly recommended 'The Execution of The Stamp Act', and if necessary the 'Use of Force',[48] while something like an impartial assessment is provided by John Campbell, M.P. for Corfe Castle, and a correspondent of Lord Holland's. Campbell did not attend the repeal debates of 1766 and wrote to Holland on 6 April of that year, 'I have seen some letters (in the printed Papers) from the submissive secretary, to Gov[erno]r Bernard and another, which seem to me quite inconsistent with the repeal of the Stamp Act. Surely both cannot be right.'[49]

In fact it is perfectly clear that, at the time, Conway and his colleagues really did intend the use of force in America. General Gage, the Commander-in-Chief in North America, received explicit orders to supply troops to governors who required them, and Lord Colville, the naval commander, was directed by the Admiralty to provide transport where necessary.[50] Even Sir Roger Newdigate, a Tory with intensely authoritarian views on the American crisis, who noted, on hearing the despatches of 24 October read in the Commons three months later, 'Total Languor and want of Energy in Government', felt compelled to add, 'P.S. orders sent to L[or]d Colville etc. to send forces from Nova Scotia'.[51] As Grenville maintained in the Commons, bloodshed was averted not because the Ministers refused to endorse it but because the machinery of enforcement in America proved incapable

---

[47] 'Ryder Diaries', *Camden Miscellany*, xxiii. 258.
[48] Add.MS. 33001, f. 54: 'Mem[orandum]s upon The American Abstracts', 24 Jan. 1766.
[49] Add.MS. 51406, f. 138: 6 Apr. 1766.
[50] C.O. 5/83, f. 449: Conway to Gage, 24 Oct. 1765; P.R.O., Admiralty Papers, Series 1, vol. 4126, f. 129: Conway to Admiralty Lords, 15 Oct. 1765; *Acts of Privy Council: Colonial Series*, ed. J. Munro, iv. 733.
[51] Newdigate MSS., B2545–17: Notes, 31 Jan. 1766.

of effective action. The critical drawback lay in the fact that the military could only be employed at the specific request of the civil power, in this case the Governors and their Councils. But colonial Councils proved understandably reluctant to call in troops against countrymen who were unanimous in their opposition to the Stamp Act and with whom in many cases they were in complete agreement. At Boston, for example, the Council flatly refused to ask for military aid, and although Bernard had the courage to write privately for troops to Gage, who devised an elaborate procedure for them to act independently if the Council attempted to restrain their use, he preferred to back down in the event.[52] In New Jersey, Governor William Franklin, who strongly advised the use of force, found his hands tied by his Councillors,[53] and at New York, where Gage actually had his headquarters, the same difficulty prevented action, even though the Commander-in-Chief had asked Colden, the Lieutenant-Governor, to make a requisition.[54]

Notwithstanding what has passed, [Gage wrote home] No Requisition has been made of Me for assistance, which I must acknowledge I have been sorry for, as the disturbances which have happened, have been so much beyond riots, and so like the forerunners of open Rebellion, that I have wanted a pretence to draw the troops together from every post they cou'd be taken from, that the Servants of the Crown might be enabled to make a stand in some spot, if matters should be brought to the Extremitys, that may not without reason be apprehended; And I have been the more anxious in this Affair, as from the distance of the Troops, and the Season of the Year it wou'd require a very Considerable time before a respectable force could be assembled, and if the Requisition from the Civil Power is postponed 'till sudden emergency's do happen, it will not be in my power to give the assistance that will be wanted.[55]

By the time the Ministry's orders reached America, it was perfectly clear that the cumbersome procedure required for the employment of the military, the unhelpful deployment of

[52] *The Barrington-Bernard Correspondence and Illustrative Matter, 1760–1770,* ed. E. Channing and A.C. Coolidge (Cambridge, Mass., 1912), pp. 227–38.
[53] C.O. 5/987, ff. 135–8: W. Franklin to Conway, 23 Sept. 1765; D.L. Kemmerer, 'New Material on the Stamp Act in New Jersey', *Proceedings of New Jersey Hist. Soc.,* lvi (1938), 220–5.
[54] *Letters and Papers of Cadwallader Colden* (Collections of New York Hist. Soc., vii (1923)), pp. 57–71.
[55] *The Correspondence of General Thomas Gage with the Secretaries of State, and with the War Office and the Treasury, 1763-1775,* ed. C.E. Carter (New Haven, 1931, 1933), ii. 334: Gage to Barrington, 16 Jan. 1766. See also J.R. Alden, *General Gage in America* (Baton Rouge, 1948), pp. 113–14 et seq.

troops in North America, and the total paralysis of colonial administration in the face of a united opposition to the Stamp Act all made impossible the execution of those orders. As reply after reply to the despatches of Cooper and Conway explained the impossibility of carrying out the instructions from home, it must have been with considerable relief that the Ministers, by then committed to a policy of repeal, found that their initial measures had miscarried.[56]

While there is no positive evidence, there are strong indications that Cumberland was the prime mover of the Ministry's policy of enforcement and repression. The critical Cabinet meeting of 13 October which resulted in Conway's despatch of 24 October was held at Cumberland's house; a policy of enforcement, if necessary with troops, would certainly coincide with his conservative and military cast of mind and there were those who did not hesitate to lay the policy at his door. 'Mr. Jackson', Thomas Hutchinson's son wrote home, 'in Conversation gave it as his Opinion that if the Duke of Cumberland had not died, instead of a repeal of the Act, there wou'd have been a number of Regiments in America before this;'[57] while a correspondent of Jenkinson's postulated a similar outcome, 'if a certain great Duke had lived. Entre nous God has been most kind to this Kingdom, if we were but sensible of it'.[58] Certainly his death came at a fortunate moment for the Americans. It is difficult to believe that the conciliatory policy adopted by Rockingham and his friends at the close of 1765 could have been pursued under Cumberland's regime.

In one important sphere Cumberland is known definitely to have taken a major part. On foreign policy he had his own views and did not hesitate to make them known. He made detailed recommendations to Ministers,[59] and personally advised, for example, the new ambassador to the French Court.[60] Moreover the most important element in the Admin-

---

[56] The replies, almost all of which insisted on the impossibility of enforcing the Stamp Act without large reinforcements, are to be found at C.O. 5/310, ff. 84–5; 390, ff. 70–1; 658, ff. 112–17; 755, ff. 455–8; 934, ff. 54–6; 1098, ff. 36–9; 1280, ff. 37, 123–4, 176–7.

[57] 1 July 1766, quoted in M.G. Kammen, *A Rope of Sand* (New York, 1968), p. 123.

[58] Add.MS. 38205, f. 32: T. Ramsden to Jenkinson, 15 Jan. 1766.

[59] Add.MS. 32969, ff. 197–8, 365: Newcastle's Memoranda of 27 Aug. 1765 and 11 Sept. 1765.

[60] *Walpole's Memoirs*, ii. 161–2.

istration's new foreign policy—the project for an Anglo-Prussian alliance—was submitted to him for his explicit approval before it was finally agreed.[61] Indeed before the onset of the colonial crisis, Cumberland and his colleagues were primarily concerned with external affairs, which gave them more scope for positive measures than did their other commitments. In essence their new policy was simple; designed to counteract the Bourbon-Habsburg combination in southern Europe, it sought to create a balancing system of alliances in the north and to take a tougher, more uncompromising stance towards France and Spain. Though this scheme seemed both coherent and plausible, it implied not a shred of statesmanship on the part of its ministerial advocates. It was based not so much on a clear analysis of international politics and on constructive diplomatic thinking, as on a desire to discredit the Ministries of Bute and Grenville, a slavish obeisance to the theories of Pitt, and an acute anxiety to demonstrate the new Ministers' aspirations to patriotism and popularity; precisely the elements, in fact, which were to characterize the attitudes and measures of the Rockinghams in general, and were ultimately to ensure their return to the political wilderness.

They had after all gone into formal opposition on the issue of the Peace of Paris, and, in the two years which preceded their return to power in 1765, repeatedly sought to take issue with the Bute and Grenville Ministries on their alleged appeasement of the Bourbon powers and alienation of Prussia. Though this tactic had never gained them the least success,[62] mainly because the country gentlemen at Westminster were more interested in financial recovery after the war than in bellicose 'patriot' policies, it was natural that the new Ministers should attempt to vindicate their earlier attitudes. More important, however, was the fact that Pitt had publicly declared his views on foreign policy, and indeed, in the abortive negotiations of May and June 1765, had insisted on the King's agreement to a triple alliance of Britain, Russia, and Prussia, as a *sine qua non* of his taking office.[63]

[61] Albemarle MSS., Conway to Cumberland, 23 July 1765 and Cumberland to Conway, 23 July 1765.
[62] For example, in the division of 4 April 1765, on the 'patriot' issue of the Newfoundland fisheries, the Opposition was severely beaten by 161 votes to 44.
[63] *Jenkinson Papers*, p. 376; *Newcastle's Narrative*, p. 23; *Grafton Autobiography*, pp. 83–4.

This alone ensured that Rockingham and his friends, who had agreed to 'follow Mr. Pitt's Plan', would pursue this policy.[64] Thus when Newcastle heard that Pitt had cast doubts on the Ministry's readiness to 'agree with Him', he assured Rockingham 'The Minute of The Other Night, If carried into Execution, as I hope, It will be, will give Him full Satisfaction upon That Point.'[65] However the new system was also part of a far wider drive for popularity in and out of Parliament. The political capital to be made out of a 'patriot' foreign policy was, or was thought to be, very great. For example, when Conway apparently made some progress in negotiations with the French for the demolition of the Dunkirk fortifications in accordance with treaty obligations, notices to that effect were proudly inserted in the *London Gazette*, much to the amusement of the Opposition press.[66] The extraction of concessions from the Bourbon courts on the various points of dispute was eagerly sought to provide 'an opportunity of opening the Parliament with great *éclat*,'[67] and the political consideration was never absent from the Ministers' minds. Thus Conway wrote to the ambassador in Paris, the Duke of Richmond, urging a settlement of the Anglo-French dispute over the Canada Bills, 'This Thing was mentioned on Tuesday in the House by Mr. Pitt, with great Warmth; and, I assure You, was received in a manner that makes me certain, it would be taken up with very great Warmth; so that, in every Light it seems of the utmost Importance to finish it soon.'[68]

If it is true that foreign policy can never be wholly directed without reference to domestic politics, it is also clear that in the mid-1760s the two had become entangled to a degree which could only damage Britain's international position. At the very time when the general quality of continental statesmanship, as represented by Choiseul, Frederick II, Catherine II, and Kaunitz, was almost unprecedently high, the instability

[64] Add.MS. 32968, ff. 177–8: Newcastle: 'Measures'.
[65] Add.MS. 32968, f. 212: Newcastle to Rockingham, 24 July 1765.
[66] *London Gazette*, 24–7 Aug. 1765. See *Public Advertiser*, 5 and 18 Sept. 1765 for Anti-Sejanus's remarks.
[67] *Letters of Horace Walpole*, ed. P. Toynbee, vi. 362: Walpole to Conway, 29 Nov. 1765.
[68] P.R.O., State Papers, Series 78, vol. 269, f. 19: Conway to Richmond, 17 Jan. 1766.

of politics in England seriously weakened the effectiveness of British diplomacy. Of course this problem was not peculiar to the Rockingham Ministry. Throughout the 1760s British diplomatic strategy, such as it was, was racked at home by political instability, and abroad by foreign awareness of the domestic situation. But it was a difficulty with which the Rockingham Administration, the most insecure of the period, was especially afflicted. As early as November 1765 Richmond was disturbed to have to report concerning the French foreign minister's attitude towards his urgings on the subject of the Canada Bills, that 'he seemed strongly possessed with the Idea, that you wanted this business concluded in order to make a Merit of it in Parliament.'[69] As the winter of 1765-6 revealed the disunity at Court, the strength of Pitt, and the complete failure of Rockingham and his colleagues to achieve political credibility, it became virtually impossible to conduct an effective foreign policy. In February 1766 the interception of an official despatch from Copenhagen to the Danish Minister in London revealed to the Ministry just how low foreign estimation of their prospects had sunk. The despatch expressed approval for a proposed Anglo-Danish alliance, and continued:

Mais si le Roy Approuve ainsi les Propositions et le Plan du Duc de Grafton, n'en est que plus fâché de la Position chancellante, dans laquelle ce Seigneur et Ses Amis se trouvent. Sa Majesté conclue des Paroles échappées au Lord Bute, que leur Credit court Risque d'être renversé par l'Embarras des Affairs, et par le Génie indomptable de Mr. Pitt, soutenu d'une Faveur Populaire sans exemple et Elle prescrit avec Peine, que tout ce qui se traite Aujourd'hui a Londres avec les Ministres actuels, pourra etre nul en peu de semaines ou en peu de Mois. . . .L'Embarras de cette Occasion est grand. Il est impossible de rien faire de bon, tout que le Systeme sera si peu assuré.[70]

Such comments could scarecely have given confidence to Conway and Grafton in their attempts to reorientate British diplomacy.

If contemporaries were aware of the motivations behind the foreign policy adopted by the Rockingham Ministry, they were less clear as to its merits. Doubtless most were agreed as to the basic problem. Whatever the advantages of the Peace of Paris from the British point of view, it was undeniable that it

---

[69] S.P.78/268, f. 112: Richmond to Conway, 22 Nov. 1765.
[70] Grafton MSS., 228: Bernstorff to Bothmar, 1 Feb. 1766.

had humiliated the Bourbon powers without destroying their potential for recovery. That the triple alliance[71] of France, Spain, and Austria was a serious threat to the security of the British Empire was obvious. 'There is the greatest Reason', Newcastle remarked at the end of 1765, 'to apprehend, That, in some Shape or Other, There will soon be a Rupture with France',[72] and indeed many expected war in the near future. However there was less agreement as to the nature of the expedient needed to counteract this threat. Pitt, and therefore the 'Old Whigs', argued strongly for a Prussian alliance, though George III objected that it would involve 'ramming Austria deeper with France and kindling a new War by unnecessary alliances'.[73] Sandwich and his colleagues in the Grenville Ministry had favoured the detachment of Austria from the Bourbon alliance. An additional alliance with Russia was, or was considered, consistent with either of these schemes.

With the advantage of hindsight, it is clear that neither view was very secure. Both made the fundamental assumption that in the event of a new war it would be possible to employ the strategy which had been so successful in the Seven Years War, to fight the French to a standstill in Germany and sweep the board overseas. Yet this strategy had never been an option at the command of the British; it had rested on the French conviction that the Hanoverian possessions of the English crown put the British at a critical disadvantage. Once it had become clear that this was not so, the French strategy, and with it the grounds for the traditional policy of their opponents, dissolved completely. After the disaster of the Seven Years War, neither Choiseul nor Vergennes was prepared to risk involvement in the morass of central Europe.[74] Their conversion to a 'blue-water strategy' required a corresponding transformation of English policy; a switch from 'system-seeking' to 'the maintenance of a two-Power naval

---

[71] Not strictly a triple alliance, but two alliances—the Family Compact of 1761 between Spain and France, and the Second Treaty of Versailles of 1757 between Austria and France. One of the anxieties of British statesmen in the mid-sixties was the possibility of a formal alliance between all three powers.

[72] Add.MS. 32972, f. 229: Newcastle; 'Mem[orandum]s from the Letters I read', 12 Dec. 1765.

[73] *Correspondence of George III*, i. 124—5: 'Heads of My conversation with Mr. Pitt', June 1765.

[74] J.F. Ramsay, *Anglo-French Relations: 1763-70* (Univ. of California Pubs. in Hist., xvii, No. 3 (1939)), p. 161.

standard'.[75] Unfortunately this was not perceived by English
statesmen, partly because the critical reorientation of French
policy was not appreciated in London, partly because
national opinion as reflected at Westminster preferred—then
as ever in peacetime—cheap diplomacy to expensive armaments

However, even granted the validity of the diplomatic
response to the Bourbon threat, there were important bars to
its successful application. Conditions in central and eastern
Europe had changed dramatically since the days when sub-
sidy treaties with Britain or France had been almost axiomatic.
The emergence of Prussia and Russia as great powers had the
curious effect of disentangling the major diplomatic problems
in Europe. For a century before, the extensive nature of
French ambitions and influence had led to the mingling of
issues and problems. In particular German rivalries and overseas conflicts had become inextricably entwined until the
Seven Years War at least temporarily resolved them. After
1763 there was no necessary connection between the Anglo-
French conflict in western Europe and the intricate manoeuvres of the three great eastern powers, Russia, Prussia,
and Austria, whose concern lay primarily with Poland and the
Ottoman Empire. In particular there was no conceivable
community of interest between Britain and these eastern
powers, unless France again demonstrated a capability and
desire to bedevil the European scene with her intervention.
In short, every circumstance combined to nullify the policies
advocated by British statesmen. The system of European
alliances, though few contemporaries in England apparently
appreciated the fact, was moribund.

None the less, with confidence born of optimism rather
than experience, Rockingham and his colleagues set out to
redesign British foreign policy. The main plank of the new
programme was the Prussian alliance. Under Grenville, Anglo-
Prussian relations had steadily deteriorated, and in 1765 it
was necessary to re-establish ambassadorial relations before
proceeding to the question of alliance. Elaborate arrangements
were made to set the new system in motion. In addition to
the direct approaches made through the British chargé in
Berlin, Colonel Faucitt (an officer previously engaged on
German matters) was despatched to obtain the cooperation

[75] *The Fourth Earl of Sandwich: Diplomatic Correspondence: 1763-65*, ed.
F. Spencer (Manchester, 1961), p. 60.

of Prince Ferdinand of Brunswick. In principle, both a 'General System, by which It should be endeavour'd To unite All the Powers of the North together with Prussia; The States General and Great Britain, in order To form a powerful Ballance to The Family Compact, and Alliances of The Houses of Bourbon and Austria',[76] and its particular application in the case of Prussia, were endorsed by the Cabinet 'as a good Foundation, for our Foreign Plan',[77] in the third week of July 1765. There were, of course, doubts within the Ministry. Cumberland, while anxious for 'a real counter-Ballance to the new alliance of the House of *Bourbon*', warned against giving 'just Grounds to your Enemies, for taking fire, before you are prepared'.[78] Northington urged caution,[79] Egmont was and always had been strongly pro-Austrian,[80] and the King, whose wish was ever to 'be in a situation to be courted not to court foreign Powers',[81] was known to have reservations. However, by the end of August, Faucitt's mission was under way. His report that Prince Ferdinand was enthusiastic for the project and that 'the idea of a reconciliation with our Court, had already been suggested to the King of Prussia, by one of his own Ministers; which had moreover met with His ready concurrence, and approbation' provided grounds for optimism.[82] None the less it soon became apparent that the new policy was doomed to imminent failure. By the middle of November, the Ministry was informed that the King of Prussia, 'declines entering into any new Treaty at present', and was left to draw comfort from the fact that a resumption of ambassadorial relations was agreed.[83] Despite the self-congratulation which accompanied this event, nothing could hide the fact that the Ministry's much-heralded new foreign policy was in ruins, though whatever the failings of Rockingham and his friends, this was scarcely their fault. A year later, when Frederick II's

---

[76] Add.MS. 32968, f. 167: Minute of 'a Meeting at His Grace The Duke of Grafton's', 22 July 1765.

[77] Ibid., ff. 185–6: Newcastle to Rockingham, 23 July 1765.

[78] Albemarle MSS., Cumberland to Conway, 23 July 1765.

[79] Northamptonshire Record Office, Northington MSS., Northington to [Conway, after 11 Aug. 1765].

[80] Add.MS. 32971, f. 319: Newcastle, 'Considerations To be laid before My Lord Rockingham only', 9 Nov. 1765.

[81] WWM.R1–2137: King to Rockingham, [7 Jan. 1766]; M. Roberts, *Splendid Isolation, 1763-1780* (Reading, 1970), p. 20.

[82] S.P. 81/117, (not foliated), Faucitt to Grafton, 3 Sept. 1765.

[83] Add.MS. 33078, f. 75: Newcastle to Duchess of Newcastle, 20 Nov. 1765.

champion, Pitt, was in power, the Prussian King proved no more cooperative. Quite clearly, what was at issue was not the perfidy and unreliability of British Ministers, as Frederick insisted, but a firm belief at Berlin that nothing was to be gained by a re-establishment of the British connection.

The collapse of the Prussian project, together with the growing seriousness of the Stamp Act crisis, largely destroyed the Administration's enthusiasm for foreign policy. By early December, Newcastle, the one Minister who had some knowledge and experience of foreign affairs, was complaining: 'I find (forgive my short way) by the Secretaries Correspondences, that there is little regard had to foreign Affairs, and the forming *a System of defensive* Alliances.'[84] Little was salvaged from the wreck of the new foreign policy. The Russian alliance, which had been in the air some time, failed to materialize, because the Ministers in London would not meet the terms demanded by the Russian Court. Panin's great 'Northern System' was in most respects similar to that advocated by Pitt and the Rockingham Ministry, but whereas the British saw it as a shield against the Bourbon powers, the Russians were naturally more interested in its implications for Poland and the Ottoman Empire. British Ministers, under both Grenville and Rockingham, consistently refused to agree to a Turkish clause pledging assistance against the Ottomans, and as long as this was so, there could be no serious possibility of a treaty.[85] Effective alliances with the other northern powers, Sweden and Denmark, were also precluded by disagreement over the terms. The demands of both for subsidies met with firm refusals in London, where it was reiterated that subsidies could only be granted for an 'alliance with such a foreign Power, whose Fleet joined to ours may still maintain the Superiority against all the endeavours of the united force of the House of Bourbon'.[86] In fact all that remained of the scheme for a great northern alliance was a treaty of friendship with Sweden and a commercial treaty with Russia. Neither was properly the achievement of the Rockingham

[84] Add.MS. 32972, f. 193: Newcastle to Rockingham, 10 Dec. 1765.
[85] See M. Roberts, *Splendid Isolation, 1763-1780*, pp. 25–8.
[86] S.P. 95/107, f. 221: Grafton to Goodricke, 6 Dec. 1765; also S.P. 75/119, f. 70: Grafton to Titley, 14 Mar. 1766, and M. Roberts, 'Great Britain, Denmark and Russia, 1763-70', pp. 247, 267, in *Studies in Diplomatic History in Memory of D.B. Horn*, edd. R. Hatton and M.S. Anderson (London, 1970).

Ministry though they were claimed as such. Both had been planned and initiated by the Grenville Administration, and the latter, which was much delayed by the haggling over the terms in general, and the inexperience and insubordination of Macartney (the British representative at St. Petersburg) in particular, was not in fact ratified until after the fall of Rockingham in the summer of 1766.[87] Both treaties were of value, the Swedish in the negative sense that it registered a reverse for the traditional French influence in the Baltic,[88] the Russian more positively, because it ensured the continuance of a trade which was to become increasingly important in the following decade.

The new 'patriot' policy proved no more rewarding in relations with the Bourbon powers than in the plans for a northern 'system'. A whole series of disputes, mostly financial, between London and the Paris-Madrid axis, had grown out of the circumstances of the Peace of Paris in 1763, on which, Rockingham and his friends argued, the Grenville Ministry had displayed undue pusillanimity. One of them, the settlement of the costs of maintenance of prisoners of war, had been concluded by Grenville in 1765. The Rockingham Ministry successfully settled another, the problem of the Canada Bills (debts originally owed by the French Crown to its Canadian subjects, many of which had been taken over by British merchants), after a good deal of haggling over the terms.[89] The demolition of the port of Dunkirk, a subject of contention which went back over half a century, and on which Rockingham laid great stress, was not effected. It is true, as John Almon the printer later asserted, that the Rockingham Ministry was the first to make a very serious or intelligent attempt to obtain the demolition of the jetties at Dunkirk, but the delaying tactics of the French Court ensured that little would be achieved.[90] The same was true

[87] For an account of the negotiation, see W.F. Reddaway, 'Macartney in Russia, 1765-7', *Cambridge Hist. Journal*, iii (1931), 260–94.

[88] The French foreign minister told Richmond that 'We had counteracted their ancient Alliance in Sweden (and if We liked the Swedes he wished us Joy of them).' (S.P. 78/269, f. 68: Richmond to Conway, 23 Jan. 1766.)

[89] S.P. 78/269, f. 260: Conway to Lennox, 1 Apr. 1766. The printed convention is at ff. 251–9.

[90] J. Almon, *Anecdotes of the Life of the Right Hon. William Pitt, Earl of Chatham* (London, 1810), ii. 7–9. After some initial advances, the work of demolition at Dunkirk came to a complete halt. See S.P. 78/267–270 for Colonel Desmaretz's reports of progress on the works, which Richmond ostentatiously visited *en route* to his post in Paris.

of the Manila Ransom, the sum of two million dollars which
the local authorities had promised the English commander
at the taking of Manila in 1763 in order to avert the pillage
of the city, and which the Spanish government refused to
authorize.[91] Despite strong pressure for the settlement of
the demand, pressure so strong that the Spanish considered
war not unlikely, neither cash nor the suggested equivalent
of New Orleans was forthcoming,[92] an outcome which was
parallelled in the case of British complaints made over the
conduct of the French in the Newfoundland fisheries.[93] On
all these issues the British case was very strong, and Rockingham
and his friends were technically justified in charging their predecessors with neglect of British interests. But the weakness
of London throughout these negotiations lay in one obvious
fact, of which foreign ministers were well aware. 'Dunkirk',
Cumberland told Richmond, 'is not worth going to war for',
a comment which was equally applicable to the Canada Bills,
the Manila Ransom, and the Newfoundland fisheries.[94] As a
result, the energy with which the Ministry pursued its objects
was largely counter-productive. In this as in so much else, the
'Old Whig' enthusiasm for the measures which they had
demanded in opposition, which their idol, Pitt, advocated
from the safety of his hearth, and which seemed to promise
popularity for the future, led them to neglect and ignore the
realities of power. On the international scene, as on the
domestic, Rockingham and his associates were innocents
abroad.

If the 'Old Whigs' were innocents, it was not in the sense
they would have appreciated. A century later, when the
polemical arguments and assertions of Burke were taken at
their face value,[95] Rockingham and his associates came to be
regarded as champions of integrity and purity in politics. This

[91] The English arguments were summarized by the commander concerned, in a
pamphlet on which Conway relied heavily for his instructions to Rochford in
Madrid. See *Colonel Draper's Answer to the Spanish Arguments Claiming the
Galeon, and refusing Payment of the Ransom Bills, for preserving Manila from
Pillage and Destruction* (London, 1764).
[92] H.M.C. *Weston Underwood MSS.*, p. 398; Grafton MSS., p. 291: Conway to
Grafton, 8 Apr. 1766; J.F. Ramsay, *Anglo-French Relations: 1763-70*,
pp. 167–8; WWM.R49–16: Rockingham's notes.
[93] S.P. 78/268, f. 7: Hume to Conway, 3 Oct. 1765.
[94] *Walpole's Memoirs*, ii. 161.
[95] See Burke's *Short Account of a Late Short Administration* (London, 1766),
a pamphlet which made extravagant claims on this score; printed in *Burke's
Works*, i. 182–4.

would be surprising if it were true. Pensions and places were part of the armoury of all eighteenth-century politicians, and when in power the Rockinghams were no more averse to their use than their contemporaries.[96] They paid ample attention, if often ineffectually, to political tactics, and indeed there are far more lists and analyses extant for the Parliamentary session of 1765-6 than for others of the period.[97] 'Indeed', Newcastle told Rockingham on 1 August, 'you give more Attention to a New Parliament Than you need to do.'[98] At Shoreham Rockingham steadfastly resisted the pressure exerted by Newcastle to restore an old Pelhamite to a minor office, on the grounds that doing so would alienate an M.P. who might otherwise be won over from Opposition.[99] On the level of electioneering too, the 'Old Whigs' were no more high-minded than their opponents. At Rochester for example, where the Administration had a strong interest in the outcome of a by-election, the Lords of the Admiralty, who naturally wielded considerable influence in the Medway region, spent three days in the town beating up support for their candidate.[100] 'Sure', Newcastle wrote to Rockingham, 'It was very Imprudent in our Friends, To Hold, . . . an Admiralty Board, at Rochester. The same Thing might have done without that *Eclat*; Sir Robert dared not do *That*.'[101]

The successful candidate at Rochester, where the Administration spent over £5,500,[102] was a minor acquisition for the Ministry. Grey Cooper, according to Newcastle, 'a very able Man, but a thorough Nattering Coxcomb, and an absolute Creature of Charles Townshend',[103] was a lawyer who had distinguished himself as counsel at the bar of the Commons in February 1765, and who had written two well-timed pamphlets—*A Pair of Spectacles for Short-Sighted*

---

[96] See for example, Rockingham's cash-account books; WWM.R15-1, 2, 3, 4.
[97] In fairness it should be pointed out that the position of the Ministry, in both Lords and Commons, in 1765-6, was, for a variety of reasons, a good deal more problematical than was normally the case.
[98] Add.MS. 32968, f. 386.
[99] WWM.R1-499, 14-9: Newcastle to Onslow, 9 Oct. 1765, Newcastle to Rockingham, 11 Aug. 1765.
[100] *Chatham Correspondence*, ii. 337-8.
[101] Add.MS. 32972, f. 96: 1 Dec. 1765.
[102] WWM.R15-4: Rockingham's cash-account book. The precise figure given is £5527 10s.
[103] Add.MS. 33078, f. 35: Newcastle to Duchess of Newcastle, 31 Oct. 1765.

Politicians and *The Merits of the New Administration Truly Stated'*—soon after Rockingham and his colleagues took office.[104] Neither was a dazzling performance, though the second was tolerably well reviewed in the press,[105] but he had satisfactorily rebutted the charges of Grenville's hack Charles Lloyd, that the new Ministers were incompetent dupes of Bute and hangers-on of Pitt, and drawn a certain amount of attention to himself.[106] This and his connection with Townshend produced the offer of the office of Joint Secretary to the Treasury from Rockingham, though it was only 'after many arguments and remonstrances on both sides', and the promise of an irrevocable annuity, that he accepted.[107] Evidently he had little confidence in the future prospects of the Ministry which he had defended so stoutly in the press.

However the acquisition of Cooper was among the least of the domestic matters occupying the attention of the Ministers in the late summer and early autumn of 1765. More important were their discussions as to the Parliamentary prospects of the Administration. It was in this connection that the question of a dissolution arise, apparently first suggested by John Roberts as early as July.[108] On the face of it there appeared little necessity to call a general election three years early. The copious lists of the likely attitude of M.P.s to the new Administration which were made out by Rockingham within two or three months of taking office, seemed to provide grounds for confidence.[109] All forecast handsome majorities for the Min-

---

[104] On Cooper, see F.B. Wickwire, *British Subministers and Colonial America, 1763-1783* (Princeton, 1966), pp. 39–40, and R. Rea, *The English Press in Politics, 1760-1774* (Lincoln, Neb., 1963), pp. 122–3, where, however, three pamphlets are mistakenly attributed to him.

[105] See for example *Monthly Review*, xxxiii. 238–9.

[106] The pamphlet which provoked those of Cooper was Lloyd's *An Honest Man's Reasons for Declining to take any Part in the new Administration*. Lloyd also wrote a counterblast to Cooper's efforts, *A Critical Review of the New Administration*.

[107] WWM.R1–493: Cooper to Mellish, [1 Sept. 1765].

[108] Add.MS. 32967, f. 206: Roberts to Newcastle, 1 July 1765, 'Scheme for a New Administration'.

[109] Most of the lists are at Northamptonshire Record Office, Fitzwilliam MSS., 1076. The precise dates are not clear, though one is endorsed 30 June 1765

istry, and there seemed some justification for boasting that 'the Opposition would not at the most reach one hundred in the House of Commons and twenty-five in the House of Lords.'[110] However there was one critical calculation in these estimates which was less than secure. In every list it was assumed that the King's Friends, the men who had held office while the 'Old Whigs' were in opposition and who had remained under the new Ministry, would support Rockingham as faithfully as they had once supported Bute. Newcastle was rightly concerned that this assumption might be faulty.

I admit, [he told Albemarle] That The Administration *may* have a Considerable Majority in Both Houses: But That Majority must be made up of Their Enemies, Creatures of The Two last Administrations, and such as are influenced only by Their Employments, and Their Interest. Such a Majority will last no longer, Than They find, The Administration carries Every Thing clearly, and roundly; The Moment There is The least Check, *They* return to Their Vomit, and vote according to Their Consciences, (If They have any,) or at least consistently with Their Manner of voting during This Reign.[111]

Thus there was a strong case for a dissolution which would provide an opportunity to reorganize and rediscipline the Court interest after the confused and factious politics of the previous four years, so that 'the members', as one of Newcastle's correspondents put it, 'who are entangled with the old minsters, may either be excluded, or brought under new and fresh

and some of the others clearly relate to discussion about a dissolution in September, when Newcastle made reference to the work of listing. The following are the totals in the Ministers' assessments.

For	Against	Doubtful	Reference
317	72	135	Fitzwilliam MSS., 1076/9
275	106	142	Fitzwilliam MSS., 1076/4 and /11
296	129	117	Fitzwilliam MSS., 1076/12 and /2
242	140	158	Fitzwilliam MSS., 1076/10
270	106	160	Add.MS. 33077, f. 178

In addition there are lists of M.P.s and constituencies clearly intended to forecast the likely results of a general election, at 1076/10 and /13. Newcastle's 'R[oug]h Dr[af]t of Observations on [a] List', 17 Sept. 1765 (Add.MS. 32969, ff. 411–18) may refer to these, though it may equally relate to a list made out for Cumberland and destroyed with his papers. See Add.MS. 32969, ff. 390, 393: Albemarle to Newcastle, 15 Sept. 1765 and Newcastle's reply of the same date.

[110] Grenville (Murray) MSS.,: Buckinghamshire to Grenville, 17 Oct. 1765, quoting 'Spanish' Charles Townshend.

[111] Add.MS. 32969, f. 392: 15 Sept. 1765.

engagements'.[112] That the object of a general election was
indeed the reconstruction of a united Court and Treasury
party under the firm and undisputed control of the 'Old
Whigs' is made clear by Newcastle's insistence that if there
were to be a dissolution it must be on the clear condition
that 'The Administration should be at Liberty, To make use
of The Influence of The Crown, in *all Places*, In Support of
Those, who are Their real Friends, and who, by Their principles, and Conduct, have shew'd Themselves so', and in
particular that the Ministry should have complete control
of the Crown's political machinery in Scotland.[113] Once
rumours of an impending general election began to spread,
it was quickly realized that the King's Friends, and not the
Opposition factions, would be the principal victims of the
Ministry's attentions. 'He can't hope', Welbore Ellis wrote of
Lord Bute, 'to have so many friends in a Parl[iamen]t not of
his chusing, as he has in this.'[114]

Not surprisingly there was a good deal of enthusiasm for
the project of a dissolution among the new Ministers, none
of whom showed much apprehension of a 'septennial convention'.[115] 'Lord Rockingham', Newcastle wrote on 30 July
'seems inclined to dissolve The Parliament—To be very well
consider'd',[116] while Newcastle himself was on balance in
favour of a general election, and some of their friends were
no less zealous. 'I wish to God you would dissolve the Parliament', Sir William Meredith wrote to Portland, 'The whole
North crys out for it.'[117] It was Horace Walpole's belief that
Rockingham scotched the notion of dissolving.[118] But Walpole,
though in general a remarkably reliable authority on the mid-

[112] Add.MS. 32970, f. 392: 'Revolution' to Newcastle, n.d. received 30 Sept. 1765.
[113] Add.MS. 32969, ff. 392–3: Newcastle to Albemarle, 15 Sept. 1765.
[114] Add.MS. 51387, ff. 166: Ellis to Holland, 26 Oct. 1765.
[115] See B. Kemp, *King and Commons* (London, 1957), pp. 76–82. At least in the
discussions about a dissolution in 1765 there is little indication of the
existence of a 'septennial convention'. While Cumberland and Newcastle
described a premature dissolution as 'bold' and 'strong' (Add.MS. 32969,
ff. 401, 392), their objections in no sense amounted to recognition of a
convention. Indeed the advocacy by John Roberts, a thoroughly conservative
politician, of a declaration in favour of triennial elections by the Ministry,
does not suggest that septennial Parliaments were held in great reverence
(Add.MS. 32967, f. 206: Roberts to Newcastle, 6 July 1765).
[116] Add.MS. 32968, f. 336: Newcastle, 'Private Memorandums for The Duke of
Cumberland'.
[117] Portland MSS., PwF6711: 24 Aug. 1765.
[118] *Walpole's Memoirs*, ii. 165.

sixties (in part as a result of his connection with Conway), spent the latter part of 1765 in Paris, a fact which considerably reduces the value of his testimony for that period. In reality it was Cumberland who killed the proposal to dissolve Parliament. Though Rockingham and Newcastle went to great lengths to calculate the likely results of a general election, Cumberland was 'rather against' the idea from the beginning and continued to 'think it a hazardous, as well as bold measure, and that much more may be said against than for it', despite the blandishments of his colleagues.[119] Thereafter the scheme was quietly dropped. In this, though there is no positive evidence, Cumberland was probably assisting the views of the King. Since dissolution represented a violent method of solving the problem of the King's Friends, and since his own desire was for a voluntary and mutually acceptable coalition of his Ministers and his friends, George III could hardly approve it. However, in retrospect, the decision not to dissolve is important. A correspondent of Newcastle's had starkly outlined the alternatives. 'A new Par[liamen]t with a declared majority will check all opposition, and such a majority your Grace can hardly now fail of securing . . . if you let it slip, I apprehend your Grace will have a very troublesome and turbulent time of it.'[120] This prediction was to be amply fulfilled in the ensuing Parliamentary session.

The way in which Cumberland's decision over a dissolution was accepted as final by his colleagues is characteristic of the authority which he wielded in the early months of the new Administration. In every sense his was the key role in the summer and autumn of 1765. It was he who formed the Ministry; he who possessed the confidence of the Crown and the respectful obedience of the Ministers, and he who had the last word in ministerial consultations and deliberations. Doubtless the fact that he held no office put him at a slight disadvantage in one respect. Without any departmental brief himself, he relied entirely on his colleagues to refer matters or supply information to him. Consequently much of his work lay in approving or rejecting the solutions and decisions of others. On the other hand he was normally present at Cabinet meetings and frequently gave advice which ran counter to the opinions of the Ministers, or which the

---

[119] Add.MS. 32969, f. 390, 401: Albemarle to Newcastle, 15 and 16 Sept. 1765.
[120] Add.MS. 32970, f. 105: 'Revolution' to Newcastle, n.d. received 30 Sept. 1765.

Ministers accepted without venturing to express any opinion themselves. In the last analysis Cumberland was indeed the 'head and soul of all'.[121] If anyone in the eighteenth century is entitled to be regarded as a Prime Minister, it is he.

This is not to claim for Cumberland a constitutional role identical to that of other eighteenth-century chief ministers. On the contrary, because he was a prince who held no responsible office, yet exercised authority far beyond that of any other royal aspirant to power who had not the Crown, such as Queen Caroline or Prince Albert, his case was very different from that of characteristic eighteenth-century ministers like Walpole, Pelham, North, and the Younger Pitt. All the latter depended for their power on the confidence of the Crown and Commons, linking the two by their control of patronage on the one hand and their hegemony among their colleagues on the other—both exercised through the office of First Lord of the Treasury. Cumberland, however, owed his supremacy wholly to the support of the King and the submission of his friends in office. Neither the Treasury nor any other office was needed to sustain an authority which rather resembled that of a monarch than a minister.

It was because Cumberland had played such an important part in the early months of the Ministry that his death, which occurred on 31 October, 'about 8.0'Clock after being at the drawing room and looking remarkably well',[122] was so serious an event. It was generally expected that there would be political repercussions, and the Opposition was of course especially anxious to read ministerial doom into the Duke's death. 'This stroke causes great uneasiness to these people', Augustus Hervey wrote to Grenville,[123] while one of Bute's friends commented that 'The Duke of C[umberlan]ds death happened at a very critical time and is a severe blow to our young ministers as from him they had their being and on him depended for their existence.'[124] The invective of Anti-Sejanus was predictably harsh.

They have lost their Father, and like so many poor Orphans are left to the wide World, to struggle with every Variety of Distress and Danger . . . They have lost their Leader, whose unconquered Spirit would have

[121] *Grenville Papers*, iii. 83: Mackintosh to Temple, [30 Aug. 1765].
[122] Bedford MSS., lii, f. 173: Marlborough to Bedford, 31 Oct. 1765.
[123] *Grenville Papers*, iii. 106: [2 Nov. 1765].
[124] H.M.C. *Polwarth MSS.*, v. 361: J. Pringle to W. Scott, 8 Nov. 1765.

enabled them to have surmounted some of those Difficulties, under which we shall soon see them totter and sink. They have no Man of Authority amongst them.[125]

There was much more truth in this prognostication than the Ministers would have been happy to concede. The loss of Cumberland's political capacity and experience alone was a stunning blow. When the Ministry had been forming, he had seemed its main strength, and the fundamental weakness of the rest of the Ministry was glaringly exposed by his demise. 'I do not see any way through this Wood', Lord Hardwicke wrote to his brother, 'I think the Ministry will soon feel the *Defects* of their original Arrang*ement*', and reports were rife that 'a total change in the ministry must soon ensue.'[126] But it was not merely incapacity or weakness which appeared to characterize a Ministry deprived of its commander; it was also disunity. 'His authority and weight being withdrawn', Welbore Ellis insisted, 'which controlled and cemented some discordant parts of this Administration they will most probably fall into great disputes and irreconcilable quarrels.'[127] Undoubtedly there was some substance in this view. Even among the Ministers who had come into office in the previous July there were differences caused partly by disagreement over the importance of obtaining Pitt's assistance and partly by personal difficulties between Rockingham, Newcastle, and Grafton. There was also the gap between the 'Old Whig' members of the Ministry on the one hand and the King's Friends in office, in particular Northington and Egmont, on the other. Northington, especially, had already, in the previous August, demonstrated his independence and dislike of his new colleagues in ministerial discussions of the Anglo-Russian commercial treaty.[128] Whether these divisions were necessarily fatal to the continuance of the Ministry, however, is far from certain. Lord Holland, admittedly a thoroughgoing cynic, dismissed the notion with contempt. 'I don't see why the Administration', he replied to Ellis, 'should fall into *great*

---

[125] *Public Advertiser*, 6 Nov. 1765.
[126] Add.MS. 35361, f. 236: Hardwicke to C. Yorke, 7 Dec. 1765; *Walpole Correspondence*, xxii. 375: Mann to Walpole, 14 Dec. 1765.
[127] Add.MS. 51387, ff. 170–1: Ellis to Holland, 3 Nov. 1765.
[128] Grafton MSS., 213, 215, 216, 218 and S.P. 91/76, ff. 211–212: Correspondence between Grafton and Northington, Sept. 1765; J. Barrow, *Some Account of the Public Life, and a Selection from the Unpublished Writings, of the Earl of Macartney* (London, 1807), i. 28–9.

disputes and *irreconcilable* Quarrels, Nor what it signifies if
they do, An Administration with *discordant parts* may go on
as well as one United or perhaps better.'[129] However this
view was untypical. It was almost universally believed that
the loss of the prince who had formed and headed the Ministry would cause severe, if not fatal, difficulties for his
protégés.

One aspect in particular of Cumberland's death especially
alarmed the Ministers. 'We lost', wrote Grafton, 'a support in
the Closet which we all felt.'[130] However, ministerial fears on
this score were soon put to rest. 'His Majesty', Rockingham
wrote on the day after Cumberland's death, 'is much
concerned—but hopes that *we* are not dismayed. His Majesty
pleased me much throughout the whole;'[131] and four days
later, 'Everything here goes on well . . . It seems like Vanity
to puff that we are well in the Closet—and therefore on that
Subject It may be decent to be silent—Events and Circumstances will fully evince that We are so.'[132] There is indeed
no reason to doubt that George III gave the fullest assurances
of support. By 9 November Newcastle was writing 'The King
behaves like an Angel, upon This Occasion. I had a very long
Audience of Him, The Day after, and I was most entirely
satisfied with what passed.'[133] Conway and Grafton were
equally emphatic, the former telling his brother, 'I know
you'll think our affairs quite desperate, after the chasm the
poor Duke has made, Yet we don't at all think so—nor does
his Majesty; but rather flatter ourselves the strength on the
whole is good and promising.'[134] In this there was nothing
strange. If George III 'seemed determined to go on with
those persons whom his Uncle recommended to his service',[135]
it was because the alternatives were as repugnant in November
as they had been in June. Grenville, whom he loathed, and
Pitt, whose arrogant conduct had severely tried his patience,
were in the autumn of 1765 both out of the question. Indeed
not the least absurd aspect of the ancient myth that George

[129] Add.MS. 51387, f. 172: Holland to Ellis, 5 Nov. 1765.
[130] *Grafton Autobiography*, p. 61.
[131] WWM.R156-2: Rockingham to Lady Rockingham, 1 Nov. 1765.
[132] WWM.R156-4: Rockingham to Lady Rockingham, [6] Nov. 1765. See also
R156-3: Rockingham to Lady Rockingham, 2 Nov. 1765.
[133] Add.MS. 32971, f. 333: Newcastle to Lady Bateman, 9 Nov. 1765.
[134] *Companion to the Newspaper* (1835), p. 365: Conway to Hertford, 7 Nov. 1765.
[135] Add.MS. 35428, f. 25: Hardwicke, 'Private Memoirs'.

III was plotting against the Rockingham Administration almost from the moment of its inception is the evident truth that success in such plotting could only expose him to humiliations worse even than those of the previous year. Doubtless the King had no great enthusiasm for his young Ministers, but he had pledged his support and had good, if rather negative, reasons for continuing it. Other ministers—Walpole both with George I and George II, and Pelham with the latter—had had far less promising bases to start from.

However there was more to political survival than the support of the Crown. The want of political credibility which had dogged the ministry from the beginning, and which was ultimately to prove its downfall, was noticeably intensified by the death of Cumberland. However reassuring the lists with which Rockingham and his colleagues sought to 'make up their majorities in both Houses'[136] there was a general feeling that the Ministry was weak. 'Strength must be got Somewhere', Newcastle insisted, and the ministerial need for 'more Assistance of able and experienced Persons' was amply reflected in the flood of offers and overtures which Rockingham authorized in the month after Cumberland's death.[137] Not all these offers were made with much hope of success. Lord Halifax, for example, who had been dismissed as Secretary of State for the southern department only the previous July, and who now received tentative approaches through Lord Talbot and Frederick Montagu, predictably relied on his old colleagues (most unwisely in the event) for a return to office.[138] Newcastle's prophecy that 'Nothing can come of That', proved to be well-founded.[139]

Other refusals were more significant. Hans Stanley, who had lost his seat at the Admiralty Board in August, was offered restitution by Rockingham.[140] He refused, 'after declaring my intention to support the measures I had formerly voted for', and only retained the sinecure governorship of the Isle of Wight from the King himself, 'as his own immediate gift to

[136] *Newcastle's Narrative*, pp. 37–8.
[137] Add.MS. 32971, f. 366: Newcastle, 'Mem[orandum]s for The King', 13 Nov. 1765; Add.MS. 35361, f. 235: Hardwicke to Yorke, 7 Dec. 1765.
[138] *Grenville Papers*, iii. 221–2; Add.MS. 32971, f. 177: Rockingham to Newcastle, 9 Dec. 1765; *Bedford Correspondence*, iii. 362–3.
[139] Add.MS. 32972, f. 60: Newcastle to Rockingham, 26 Nov. 1765.
[140] History of Parliament Trust transcripts, Grenville Letter Book, Grenville to Stanley, 31 Oct. 1765.

me'.[141] Lord North, who was offered 'a considerable employ-ment'[142] through his relations Lord Dartmouth and 'Spanish' Charles Townshend, had left the Treasury Board on the ac-cession of Rockingham. Yet despite Townshend's belief that 'he is free, as he has several times repeated to me in the course of this summer, from the least degree of engagement', North declined to join the Ministry.[143] Most discouraging of all, Charles Townshend, whose services were badly needed in the Commons, refused to become Leader of the House and a member of the Cabinet. Despite Conway's anxiety for the arrangement, and despite the blandishments of Grafton and Cooper, Townshend continued to play the waiting game which he had practised the previous July. 'Charles Townshend', Rockingham told Newcastle, 'continues professing the most Favourable Intentions—but does not seem to chuse to be now called to the Cabinet.'[144] These refusals were, from the ministerial vantage-point, matter for concern. Newcastle fore-cast that they 'will have bad Effects',[145] and Grenville drew comfort from his discovery that 'from all hands the Ministers were everywhere trying to detach individuals, and were looked upon by most people to be in a falling state.'[146] Men such as Stanley, North, and Townshend were precisely those essential to the survival of eighteenth-century administrations. None were committed to any party or faction, though all were ready to seek shelter in factious quarters when necessary. Their sole political objective was office, and if they refused to join with Rockingham and his friends, it was because they saw no prospect of stability in the Ministry. It is not without significance that a year later, when the Chatham Administration was formed, secure in the undoubted confidence of the Crown and with every appearance of public support, all three thank-fully accepted office.[147]

The one acquisition which the Administration succeeded in making in the weeks after Cumberland's death did more

---

[141] Add.MS. 22359, f. 48: Stanley to Buckinghamshire, 26 Oct. 1765; also *Grenville Papers*, iii. 99, 104.
[142] Add.MS. 32972, f. 25: C. Townshend to Newcastle, 23 Nov. 1765.
[143] Add.MS. 32972, f. 25: Townshend to Newcastle, 23 Nov. 1765.
[144] Ibid., f. 93: 1 Dec. 1765.
[145] Ibid., f. 95: Newcastle to Rockingham, 1 Dec. 1765.
[146] *Grenville Papers*, iii. 221–2: Grenville Diary, 9 Dec. 1765.
[147] Stanley accepted a diplomatic mission to Berlin and St. Petersburg; North became Joint Paymaster-General, and Townshend, Chancellor of the Exchequer.

harm than good to its reputation. Lord George Sackville, one of the most controversial of eighteenth-century figures, had been seeking political rehabilitation ever since his disgrace six years before. His aim was simply and solely 'to be in employment, were it but for a week' and the alliance which he had formed with Charles Townshend to this end had already come close to success in July when Townshend had 'found a disposition to treat with you', and Sackville had received overtures from Egmont.[148] According to Shelburne, his appointment as a Vice-Treasurer of Ireland and his restoration to the Privy Council in December 1765 was 'for no other reason than that they [the ministers] were under an apprehension that they should have nobody to speak for them the first day of the Session, on account of the seats of the principal persons of the party being vacated in consequence of their accepting office till they could be re-elected'.[149] In fact it seems to have stemmed from the ministerial anxiety to fill some of the vacant offices in Administration and from Rockingham's discovery that, before Cumberland's death, Sackville had offered to bring 'in a Person—who was attach'd to his R[oyal] H[ighness] and to the Administration', into Parliament.[150] This measure, however admirable as a gesture, was not particularly wise. Sackville, though always grateful to Rockingham for the 'grand point of his being once more producible to great employment',[151] did not turn out to be a regular supporter of the Administration (he voted against the Court in the Anstruther division of 31 January and the repeal of the Stamp Act division of 22 February). Moreover his elevation gave Pitt, who was an old enemy of his, a useful factor to assign 'as one Cause of Disapprobation of The present Ministry';[152] —so much so indeed that Rockingham and his colleagues became acutely embarrassed by an action which Newcastle had from the beginning criticized as 'Hard of Digestion'.[153] 'None of the Ministers own it their act', it was reported, 'and Mr. Pitt is excessively disgusted at that

[148] H.M.C., *Stopford-Sackville MSS.*, i. 103: Sackville to Irwin, 23 Dec. 1765. Ibid., i. 63: Townshend to Sackville, 9 July 1765; also i. 62—6.
[149] Fitzmaurice, *Life of Shelburne*, i. 356: 'Account of Lord George Sackville'. Sackville kissed hands on 20 Dec. 1765.
[150] Add.MS. 32971, f. 94: Rockingham to Newcastle, 1 Dec. 1765.
[151] Fitzmaurice, *Life of Shelburne*, i. 357: 'Account of Lord George Sackville'.
[152] Add.MS. 32972, f. 178: Newcastle to Rockingham, 9 Dec. 1765.
[153] Ibid., f. 186: Newcastle, 'Mem[orandum]s for the King', 10 Dec. 1765.

measure.'[154] The acquisition of a broken and dishonoured soldier merely further discredited the reputation of a Ministry which desperately needed more weight, if not ability, in its councils.

Above all Cumberland's death again raised the problem which had confronted the 'Old Whigs' in July and which the Duke had then partially rather than finally solved. The refusal of minor politicians to join Rockingham was as much a symptom as a cause of the basic difficulty—that the Ministry lacked credibility in the public eye. The general belief that a reconstruction of the Ministry was ultimately inevitable was the most persistent anxiety of the Ministers, and in November, as in July, their remedy was the wrong one. Again it was believed that the publicly declared support of Pitt was the panacea to solve all. It was not so much that Pitt's assistance was considered essential for the transaction of business, as that his prestige was needed to bolster the reputation of the Ministry. 'All That is wanted', wrote Newcastle, 'is Mr. Pitt's avowed Approbation of, and Connection with The present Ministers . . . In short, Any Thing, That might show some Connection between Him, and The Administration.'[155] Again, as in July, much of the pressure for such a measure came from the 'Younger Part of the Ministry'[156] —the 'young friends and 'little Whigs' who in the Minority of 1762-5 had been as much attached to the name of Pitt as Newcastle.

Almost immediately after Cumberland's death, Grafton proposed, apparently with the full support of Rockingham, Conway, and Newcastle, to write to Pitt on the Ministry's behalf,[157] and a Cabinet meeting was held on 7 November, 'particularly on the Intention of a Private Letter to a Great Person'.[158] However, despite the Opposition's belief that a positive approach was made to Pitt,[159] the scheme was dropped, much to the annoyance and mystification of Newcastle, who was strongly in its favour. Thomas Walpole,

[154] *Letters of Sarah Byng Osborne; 1721–1773*, ed. J. McClelland (Stanford Univ., 1930), p. 94: Mrs. Osborne to J. Osborne, 17 Jan. 1766.
[155] Add.MSS. 32971, f. 290: Newcastle to Grafton, 6 Nov. 1765; 32972, ff. 78–9: Newcastle to Featherstonhaugh, 30 Nov. 1765.
[156] Bedford MSS., lii. f. 188: Rigby to Bedford, 10 Nov. 1765.
[157] Add.MS. 32971, f. 249: Newcastle to Rockingham, 4 Nov. 1765.
[158] Ibid., f. 287: Rockingham to Newcastle, 6 Nov. 1765.
[159] *Jenkinson Papers*, p. 391.

a devoted follower of Pitt's, was also puzzled by the Ministry's inactivity:

daring neither [he wrote] to go forwards nor backwards, [they] stand like men staggering in the dark, till the building falls about their ears. They are very sensible of the breach which has lately happened, as well as of the only means to strengthen and support the fabric; and yet I had the misfortune to see, before I left England, that, with the best dispositions, I know not by what fatality, they were not in the right way of procuring that assistance.[160]

Almost certainly George III was behind this change of plan. Despite Newcastle's statement that 'I proposed That Application, *in a proper Manner*, to the K[ing]; He consented to it, and most readily came into it', the King later revealed to Bute that he had exerted pressure on the Ministers to stop the scheme.[161] In any event no more was heard for a few weeks of the notion of an overture to Pitt. Rockingham contented himself with a series of absurd attentions through Lady Rockingham at Bath. 'If a *Real Great Man* comes there', he wrote, 'I would have you consider him and as such and am not afraid of your Conversation with him as I don't believe it will be *Criminal*.'[162] The sequel was a contrived purchase by the Marchioness of some horses owned by Pitt, and the transmission, again through her, of an important Treasury Minute, 'as meer matter of Attention to him in communicating an Affair of some Consequence to the Commerce of the Nation',[163] a farce which was completed by the efforts of the Duchess of Newcastle, who was also in Bath, to carry on the Newcastle-Rockingham rivalry by proxy.[164]

As always, the corollary of the Ministry's predilection for Pitt was its contempt for the King's Friends. Relations between the two components of the Court party—the 'Old Whigs' on the one hand and the King's Friends on the other—which had been marked by an uneasy truce since the formation of the new Ministry, took a critical turn at the death of Cumberland. Throughout August and September the King's Friends, unsure

[160] *Chatham Correspondence*, ii. 334: T. Walpole to Pitt, 21 Nov. 1765.
[161] Add.MS. 32972, ff. 21–2: Newcastle to Offley, 23 Nov. 1765; *Letters from George III to Lord Bute*, pp. 242–3: [10 Jan. 1766.]
[162] WWM.R156–4: Rockingham to Lady Rockingham, [6] Nov. 1765.
[163] WWM.R156–5: Rockingham to Lady Rockingham, 23 Nov. 1765; see also R156–6; R151–1, 2, 3, 4; R168–175, 178; Chatham MSS., liv. ff. 230–5.
[164] See Add.MS. 33078, ff. 21–81, for the letters of Newcastle and his wife from 18 Oct. to 16 Dec. 1765.

of Rockingham's attitude to them in the long-term, had awaited some sign of cooperation. 'L[or]d Darlington's solliciting a small office in the Port of London', Grenville told Whately, '. . . seems to be a mark, and that he and Sir J[ame]s Lowther, with whom I have always understood he is connected, are not indispos'd to the present Administration'.[165] But by October it was becoming clear that little was to be hoped for from the Ministry. 'It is expected', Jenkinson informed Lowther, 'that in the meantime the present Ministers will negotiate some where or other; the world support that it will be with some of those that you and I wish well to; but as for myself I see not the least symptom of it.'[166]

In fact the impression given in the press was that the prejudices of the 'Old Whigs' were stronger than ever. Cooper, for example, the Ministry's most effective publicist, was equivocal on Bute's position in his first pamphlet at the end of August, but in the second a few weeks later, was compelled to state firmly that the Ministers 'since their Entrance into Office, have acted like Men, not only *independent* of him, but *adverse* to him'.[167] Not unnaturally the King's Friends were less than happy about the campaign against them. ' 'tis certain', Augustus Hervey told Grenville, 'his [Bute's] friends in place have been very openly censorious on the present Ministers, and appeared much dissatisfied at being made the sacrifice to their game.'[168] In this worsening situation it was hoped that Cumberland's death would lead to an improvement. It was generally and quite erroneously believed that Cumberland had been personally responsible for the Ministry's hostility to the King's Friends, and that on his demise a new policy would be initiated by Newcastle, whose influence in the Ministry was widely overestimated in this as in much else.[169] However the error of these assumptions was soon revealed. At the end of November, Mackenzie wrote to Baron Mure in Scotland:

Most people thought that the Duke of Cumberland's death would have made the new people wish to strengthen themselves a little, either by making up matters with the King's friends, or by treating with some of the Opposition; however, that event has not as yet produced any thing of that kind. With respect to us, they are so far from making any advances

[165] Grenville (Murray) MSS., 13 Aug. 1765.
[166] *Jenkinson Papers*, pp. 386–7: 26 Sept. 1765.
[167] G. Cooper, *The Merits of the New Administration Truly Stated*, p. 21.
[168] *Grenville Papers*, iii. 87: 3 Oct. 1765.
[169] Ibid.; Bedford MSS., lii. ff. 176–7: Rigby to Bedford, 3 Nov. 1765.

that, by all one can judge from their language and conduct, they seem afraid that it should even be suspected that they have the smallest disposition to unite with us.[170]

The distance separating the attitudes of the 'Old Whigs' and King's Friends was clearly visible at the time when the possibility of a dissolution was being discussed in September 1765. Then the Ministers simply assumed, in their calculations of the Parliamentary balance of power, that those who had been allowed to retain their offices in July would automatically support the Ministry, however loudly the latter declared its contempt for them. Thus Newcastle, enquiring of Lord Edgcumbe as to three Cornish borough-mongers who were known friends of Bute and remained in office under Rockingham, declared that they 'are far from being Friends of Mine; But I suppose, They will go, as They have always done, *with The Court*'.[171] Yet at the very time the Ministers were so unequivocally assuming the Parliamentary support of the King's Friends, Mackenzie was writing to Jenkinson, on the subject of a reported meeting of Parliament for mid-November, '[I sh]ould not have thought our new Ministry would have been in such a hurry for a meeting of Parliament where, without the support of those whom they have not treated with much indulgence, the Kings firmest friends, they must in all probability, make but a very indifferent appearance.'[172] Similarly Sir James Lowther, a week later, was urging a thoroughly independent role for the King's Friends. 'We ought all', he wrote, 'to be in Town a fortnight or 3 weeks before the meeting in order to settle and fix our plan; see who are our friends and who we may depend upon to know what the other sides are doing and upon what ground we stand.'[173]

In the last analysis the significance of Cumberland's death was that it left Rockingham and his colleagues to work out their own political salvation. While Cumberland lived, the more imprudent of the 'Old Whig' prejudices had been under restraint, the King's Friends' rebelliousness held in check, and in general a clear and authoritative lead given to the Ministry. The 'Cumberland Administration' could so easily have been

[170] *Caldwell Papers*, part ii, vol. ii, p. 46: 30 Nov. 1765. See also H.M.C. *Polwarth MSS.*, v. 361.
[171] Add.MS. 32969, f. 242: 31 Aug. 1765.
[172] *Jenkinson Papers*, p. 384: 16 Sept. 1765.
[173] *Jenkinson Papers*, p. 386: Lowther to Jenkinson, 23 Sept. 1765.

the transitional phase during which the 'Old Whigs' returned
to Court and resumed their old place in the Court and
Treasury bloc; had the Duke lived a year or two longer, it is
difficult to believe that this would not have been the case.
But his premature death at the age of forty-four left his young
friends to the consequences of their own inexperience and
incapacity. Bereft of a leader who combined political experience with judgement and good sense, and being themselves
deficient, as Shelburne rather unkindly though accurately put
it, in 'both penetration and fortitude',[174] they were in future
to tread their own course through the dramatic events and
awesome difficulties of the succeeding months. That course
was to defy the dictates of prudence and common sense and
ultimately lead to their downfall. But it was also—perhaps
precisely because it ignored the convictions and conventions
of less naive politicians—to provide a long line of Whig
apologists with ample material for praise and veneration.

[174] Fitzmaurice, *Life of Shelburne*, i. 356: 'Account of Lord George Sackville'.

IV

ROCKINGHAM AND THE IMPERIAL PROBLEM
(NOVEMBER 1765 TO JANUARY 1766)

THE MOST serious problem which the young Ministers faced
at the beginning of November was clearly that of the Stamp
Act, which had indeed been intended for discussion on the
night of Cumberland's death.[1] However, the Ministerial
attitude to the Stamp Act crisis was to take a novel and unexpected turn after the loss of the Duke. In part this was
simply because Rockingham, on whose shoulders Cumberland's
mantle naturally fell, did not hold his master's views on the
American question. Some hint of his attitude even in October
is clear from his remark to a Yorkshire friend that 'the notable
confusion which he [Grenville] has raised in America, tho'
it lays difficulties upon the present administration, yet so far
it serves them, as it shows that he had neither prudence or
foresight.'[2] In November this obvious desire to discredit his
predecessor at the Treasury was augmented by the discovery
of a completely new angle to the Stamp Act crisis. In the
week after Cumberland's death Rockingham received two
letters of critical importance, which convinced him that the
arguments involved in the problem were as much economic
as constitutional. One was from his old friend Sir George
Savile, whose influence on Rockingham was great. Savile
enclosed a letter from a Boston man complaining bitterly
that 'The Government at home has taken the most effectual
Methods to destroy all Trade'.[3] Though this complaint was a
vague one, Savile pointed the moral:

They speak as ignorant men. *Our trade is hurt, what the devil have you
been a doing? For our part, we don't pretend to understand your politics*

[1] According to Conway there was no fixed agenda for the Cabinet meeting on
31 October (see p.73) but a paper in the Northington MSS. is endorsed 'My
Opinion intended to be told at the Meeting summond on Am[erican] B[usine]ss
at Cumberland House, the Ev[enin]g the D[uke] of Cumb[erland] died'.
[2] H.M.C. *Various Collections*, viii. 183: Rockingham to [Viscount Irwin], 25 Oct.
1765.
[3] WWM.R1–482: 'Extract of a Letter from Boston', 16 Aug. 1765. It is a reasonable assumption that this was the enclosure in Savile's letter.

and American matters, but our trade is hurt; pray remedy it, and a plague of you if you wont.[4]

The second letter, received a few days later, on 6 November, was from Barlow Trecothick. Trecothick was a prosperous and prominent figure in the American trade, who had led the London North America Merchants in their opposition to the Stamp and American Mutiny Acts in the previous spring.[5] When and how he first made contact with the 'Old Whigs' is not certain; but his business connections were with the Thomlinson family (old friends of Newcastle), and in September Newcastle had asked him to stand as candidate for the borough of New Shoreham, though significantly Trecothick declined the offer on the grounds that it would spoil his chances of being elected for the City of London at the next general election.[6]

Clearly he was very much a coming man when he wrote to Rockingham. His letter forecast disaster not merely in the colonies but in Britain if speedy action were not taken. Since the Americans were evidently determined not to accept the Stamp Act, he argued, all commercial business requiring stamps would grind to a halt, the British export market in America would collapse, the manufacturing industries would experience a severe slump, and chronic unemployment would ensue—with large numbers of labourers 'soon to be without Employ and of course without Bread!

here I must stop, not daring to pursue any further the dreadful Chain of Consequences . . . My great fear is, that too great Delay and Caution in administering the Remedy, may render the Deseases of this embarrassed Nation incurable; and even a virtuous Administration may therefore be deemed accountable for Effects proceeding from the Error of their Predecessors.[7]

The effect of these two letters on their recipient can scarcely be exaggerated, for they established a line of argument, a causal chain between Grenville's legislation, economic distress

[4] *Rockingham Memoirs*, i. 253. The original, which is not quite accurately reproduced by Albemarle, is at WWM.R1—519: Savile to Rockingham, 1 Nov. 1765.
[5] For details of Trecothick, see T.D. Jervey, 'Barlow Trecothick', *South Carolina Historical and Genealogical Magazine*, xxxii. (1931), 157—69; and D.H. Watson, 'Barlow Trecothick and other Associates of Lord Rockingham', pp. 20 et seq.
[6] Add.MS. 32970, ff. 50, 52, 54—5, 76, 82: Correspondence of Newcastle and Trecothick between 24 and 27 Sept. 1765.
[7] WWM.R24—43a: Trecothick to Rockingham, 7 Nov. 1765.

in America, and a fatal slump in Britain, which was to lead
first Rockingham, then the Administration, and finally
Parliament itself, to a liberal and conciliatory colonial policy.
Rockingham himself was an almost immediate convert to the
cause of relief. While expressing anxiety about the constitutional
issues raised, he arranged a meeting with Trecothick and began
to search for corroborating evidence. By 15 November Richard
Jackson, the Connecticut agent, was aware that the Cumberland
policy was to be reversed.

> I have within the Compass of a week conceived hopes, [he wrote to
> Governor Fitch] that Measures may be taken here, that will perfectly
> conciliate the minds of the Americans, but have reason to believe that
> such Measures are by no means, what were to have been expected a
> Month ago and yet depend upon the Moderation of what we hear from
> New York.[8]

At the end of the month Rockingham's rough notes of a 'Plan
of Business' for the Parliamentary session were already in the
strain which was in fact to be adopted three months later.

> Que. Consideration of N[orth] A[merica] in the Commercial—to be
>   first brought on—
> Que. to avoid the discussion on the Stamp Act—till Good Principles are
>   laid down for Easing and Assisting N[orth] America and being
>   well informed of the high Importance of the Commerce to N[orth]
>   A[merica] respectively to the Mother Country.[9]

On 28 November, the day on which these notes were written,
Grenville was writing to Bedford of reports that the Ministers
were 'resolved (if possible) to repeal the American tax'.[10] In
fact at that time a precise policy was far from formulation.
Trecothick himself had only asked for 'repeal or suspension'
and certainly Rockingham had not yet decided on the former.
What is certain is that already he saw the problem in economic
rather than legalistic terms, and that already he was disposed
to advise a policy of relief for the colonies on the basis of
British commercial interests.

This need not be surprising, for Rockingham was always
ready to listen to the merchants. In part this was doubtless
connected with the general anxiety of the 'Old Whigs' to
attract the support of 'out of doors' and 'popular' elements,

---

[8] *Fitch Papers*, ii. 376: 15 Nov. 1765.
[9] WWM.R49—6: Rockingham's notes, dated 27 Nov., but from the day of the
  week given, in fact [28] Nov.
[10] Bedford MSS., lii, ff. 228—9; the version at *Bedford Correspondence*, iii. 323,
  is not wholly accurate.

among which the merchants were important if not pre-eminent but it was also a very personal interest closely related to Rockingham's Yorkshire heritage. Since his father's death he had played a major part in the politics of his home county, and Yorkshire politics had not a little to do with the commercial and industrial concerns of the West Riding and Humber regions. Throughout the 1750s he had taken great care, with his ally Sir George Savile, to concern himself with the economic problems of the north. Of course this was partly self-interest. Referring to the threat to bullion imports in October 1765, he told Charles Yorke, 'I don't know what will become of Yorkshire Rents—*If Portugal Coin*—was not brought there—in Return for Cloth etc.'[11] None the less his background had inevitably given him, impressionable as he was, a quite genuine and sincere belief in the importance of trade. In notes made in the early months of 1766 for a speech on American business which was never given, he stated proudly: 'Bred in a Manufacturing County—Fond of giving every Encouragement—The Existence of the Country'.[12] Yorkshiremen were certainly aware of his uncharacteristic energy when it came to commercial matters. One of them informed Rockingham in early December that the country gentlemen and manufacturers of Yorkshire intended, though only if he approved their doing so, to petition for a prohibition on grain exports, and added:

they who have so often experienced your Lordships readiness to serve them on all Occasions wherein either their Trade or their Interest were concerned, can think of no Person to whom they can so properly apply as to your Lordship to Present their Petition if you will Please to permit them so to do so.[13]

Rockingham himself placed great emphasis on this aspect of his work. 'It is with no small Satisfaction', he was to inform the Bristol merchants on leaving office, 'that I can look back upon the Measures of the last Session of Parl[iamen]t because I think that at no Time the Commercial Interest of this Country was more the Object of Government.'[14]

Rockingham's Ministerial interest in commercial affairs had been made clear even before Cumberland's death. A

[11] Add.MS. 35911, f. 64: 24 Oct. 1765.
[12] WWM.R49—31: Notes in Rockingham's hand, undated.
[13] WWM.R1—538: Samuel Lister to Rockingham, 7 Dec. 1765.
[14] WWM.R1—670: Rockingham to ?William Reeve, Aug. 1766; unfinished draft.

golden opportunity to display his concern with mercantile interests and simultaneously to discredit Grenville in the public eye arose in relation to the Anglo-Spanish trade in the West Indies, which had long been immensely valuable from the British vantage-point. Once dependent entirely on English 'interlopers', it had gradually become largely, though by no means wholly, reliant on the visits of Spanish ships to ports in the British West Indies. Since it consisted essentially of the exchange of 'Dollars, *Drugs, and dying Woods*'[15] for English manufactured goods, it clearly performed a valuable function in the imperial economy, providing both raw material and a ready market for the manufacturing industries at home, supplying essential bullion directly to England and financing the balance of payments deficit sustained by the American colonies in their commercial relations with the mother country. The legal status of the trade was dubious since the exchange of commodities involved, and perhaps even the import of bullion, ran counter to the Navigation Acts, though the legal objections to a trade so patently beneficial to the British economy had long been traditionally ignored. Unfortunately Grenville's regulations of 1763-4 which sought to reinforce the Navigation Acts, chiefly with a view to terminating the illicit trade between the American colonies and the French West Indies, was also applicable to the Spanish trade to the south. In consequence when a major slump afflicted the trade in 1764, when the market for English manufacturers in Spanish America collapsed dramatically, and the supply of specie and important raw materials dried up, it was scarcely surprising that the aggrieved parties blamed Grenville's measures.[16] Grenville, however, was not unwilling to listen to the complaints, and in 1764 and 1765 orders were despatched in an effort to re-establish the old laxity in dealing with Spanish vessels visiting British ports. There were high hopes of these orders, though they explicitly forbade the importation of 'any Foreign Goods or Merchandize'.[17] 'The Spanish trade', Jared Ingersoll wrote home to Rhode Island, 'you may depend is opened, as much as the Same can be

---

[15] Add.MS. 33030, f. 72: 'Trade', Nov. 1765; an unsigned paper.
[16] See B. Edwards, *The History, Civil and Commercial, of the British West Indies* (London, 1793), i. 238.
[17] Add.MS. 33030, f. 190: evidence of Beeston Long in Commons' Committee on American Papers, 17 Feb. 1766.

without Speaking loud.'[18] None the less it soon became obvious that the new measures were ineffectual. Trade failed to revive and again it was natural for the sufferers to blame the Administration. By the summer of 1765 complaints of continuing depression in the West Indian trade were rife, complaints which were inevitably referred to the new Ministry.[19]

The volume of protest 'with regard to the total ruin which was threatened to the Spanish trade',[20] was impressive, and the Treasury's reaction to it was immediate and favourable. The Ministry went to some lengths to obtain information and evidence, and it was reported in Bristol that 'L[or]d Rockingham and Mr. Dowdeswell have this point much at heart.'[21] However there were considerable legal difficulties involved. Three basic points were at issue—the legality of the bullion trade in terms of the Navigation Acts, its compatibility with treaties then in force between the English and Spanish Courts, and finally, the competence of the Administration to act in such a case without reference to Parliament.[22] On each of these points there was ample room for dispute, and the opinions gathered by the Ministers varied considerably.[23] In particular, Charles Yorke, the Attorney-General, was not encouraging. While he agreed that the statutes of 12 Charles II, and 7 and 8 William III amounted to recognition of the legality of bullion imports, he was emphatic that this did not cover the trade in raw materials and manufactured goods, had severe doubts whether engaging in a trade explicitly forbidden by the Spanish authorities was consistent with treaty obligations, and in general showed great anxiety to avoid all formal consultation and

[18] *A Selection from the Correspondence and Miscellaneous Papers of Jared Ingersoll*, ed. F.B. Dexter (Papers of New Haven Colony Hist. Soc., ix (1918)), p. 323: Ingersoll to G. Malbone, 7 Apr. 1765.

[19] See for instance, 'Mercator' in the *St. James's Chronicle*, 25 July 1765; and for discussion of this problem in general, see A. Christelow, 'Contraband Trade between Jamaica and the Spanish Main, and the Free Port Act of 1766', *Hispanic American Hist. Rev.*, xxii, (1942), 309–43; and F. Armytage, *The Free Port System in the British West Indies* (London, 1953), chapter ii.

[20] *Burke's Works*, i. 412.

[21] T. Townshend, jun. to R. Nugent, 5 Nov. 1765; quoted in W.R. Savadge, 'The West Country and the American Mainland Colonies, 1763-1783, with special reference to the merchants of Bristol' (Oxford Univ. B. Litt. thesis 1951), p. 204.

[22] The last point caused particular concern. (Add.MS. 32971, f. 14: Newcastle to Rockingham, 22 Oct. 1765; WWM.R1—513: Northington to Rockingham, 23 Oct. 1765.)

[23] The various opinions submitted are to be found at Add.MSS. 32971, ff. 16—21, 29—34, 44; 33030, ff. 68—73.

statement on such a delicate matter, a 'Clandestine Trade' which had been 'suffered and winked at rather than allowed'.[24] Naturally Rockingham did his best to pressurize Northington and Yorke, as the Ministry's chief legal authorities, into taking the Treasury view of the problem, which had been summarized in a paper drawn up by Dowdeswell.

The Earnest Requests [he told Yorke] of All the Principal Trading Parts of England and The Demonstration which has been made out to us of the Great National Advantages which would accrue, is really of such Importance in *All Considerations*—that there never was a Time or an Occasion—where *Liberal Construction* could be more justified.[25]

The result, after a favourable opinion from the Crown's law officers,[26] was the Treasury Minute of 13 November, which ordered the despatch of instructions to the customs officers concerned, to admit vessels carrying bullion 'any late Practice to the contrary notwithstanding'.[27]

Unfortunately the new measures were no more effective than their predecessors. The Anglo-Spanish trade did not recover and within a few months the whole problem was to be referred to the legislature. The truth was that the diagnoses of both merchants and Ministry were faulty. The real problem was not, as is now known, the Grenville Ministry's orders, which in the case of the West Indian trade had never in fact been very seriously enforced, but in a combination of circumstances. The renewed efforts of the Spanish government to suppress a trade which it had never legalized, the glut in Caribbean markets after the great boom of 1763-4, and above all the general economic recession which afflicted the western world after the Seven Years War, all played a part in a problem which was far more complex than most contemporaries recognized.[28]

None the less the measure did yield valuable political results for the Administration. It had been aimed as much at the Opposition as at the trading recession. 'As strong an Article of Impeachment, against George Grenville, as can be formed',[29]

---

[24] WWM.R1—515: Yorke to Rockingham, 25 Oct. 1765.
[25] Add.MS. 35911, f. 63: Rockingham to Yorke, 24 Oct. 1765. The original draft of Dowdeswell's 'Proposal' is at WWM.R35—6b, d, e: 9 Oct. 1765.
[26] P.R.O., T.1/455, ff. 182—5: 'Attorney and Solicitor-Gen[era]l['s] Opinion', 11 Nov. 1765.
[27] T.29/37, f. 115.
[28] Add.MS. 38339, f. 225: J. Salvador to Jenkinson, 28 Jan. 1765.
[29] Add.MS. 32971, f. 422: Newcastle to Rockingham, 19 Nov. 1765.

Newcastle called the Treasury Minute of 13 November, while Rockingham himself remarked to a Yorkshire friend, 'I don't imagine Mr. G. Greenville's popularity is very high in your neighbourhood. The difficulties he has thrown upon trade by very inconsiderate regulations must affect any opinion in his favour among the mercantile gentlemen'.[30] Opinion outside the Ministry was equally aware of the significance of the Treasury's activities. Lord Holland forecast to his friend Welbore Ellis, 'That the breach between Mr. Grenvill, and all those, who concern themselves, with Trade, will be [permanent], I will venture to foretell.'[31] That the Opposition was well aware of the Ministry's tactics is clear from its efforts to defeat the campaign in the provinces. At Bristol especially a strong attempt was made to foil the Administration. Grenville personally urged Lord Botetourt to use his influence in Merchants' Hall to oppose a petition to the Treasury since it would 'cast . . . some reflections upon the late ministry and particularly upon your humble servant'.[32] His friend Nugent, who was M.P. for Bristol, was equally industrious. When he heard that a meeting of merchants was to be convened in the first week of November, he wrote to their leader, William Reeve, to

insist [as he informed Grenville] upon the falsehood of the report that the obstructions given to the Spanish trade were by orders from the Ministry, which I apprehend may be the principal object of the meeting, and I relate what you did upon the first complaint made here of the seizure of Spanish effects, and the ordering Spanish vessels to depart from our coasts.[33]

Strenuous, though equally vain, efforts were made at Lancaster and Liverpool, by Grenville's Lancashire friends.[34] Economic distress in the ports which relied a good deal on the Anglo-Spanish trade was considerable and the merchants were quick to blame Grenville for their difficulties. The corollary of the discredit of the old Ministry was the benefit of the new. 'I am just come from Manchester', Sir William Meredith wrote to Burke, 'and am happy to tell you, that Mr. Pitt was never more popular, than L[or]d Rockingham and the present

[30] H.M.C., *Various Collections*, viii. 183: Rockingham to [Viscount Irwin], 25 Oct. 1765.
[31] Add.MS. 51387, f. 178: 11 Nov. 1765.
[32] Grenville Letter Book, 3 Nov. 1765.
[33] Grenville (Murray) MSS., 31 Oct. 1765.
[34] Grenville (Murray) MSS., Nugent to Grenville, 31 Oct. 1765.

administration. T'is the same at Liverpool and all over this country.'[35] Rockingham was immensely proud of the flood of addresses from the provincial merchants, which indeed praised Ministers 'who have given us this early and convincing Proof both of their knowledge of the Commercial Interests of their Country, and their Resolution to support them'.[36] This was merely the beginning of an immensely important phase of cooperation between the Ministry and the merchants, which was to have a monumental impact on imperial policy in the following months, and which was to influence the conduct and theories of Rockingham and his friends in Opposition in the following decades.

Rockingham must soon have been made aware that the recession in the North American trade, of which Savile and Trecothick informed him, and the concurrent commercial crisis in the West Indies were intimately connected. It was significant that when the merchants of Manchester thanked him for the Treasury orders of 13 November, they none the less complained that these applied only in the West Indies and southern colonies, 'whereas the Northern Provinces of America are the great Mart where the Manufactures of this Country are vended'.[37] Though Rockingham very reasonably replied that this was a quite new and separate grievance, it was none the less a significant one. Ever since the autumn of 1764 it had been obvious that something was seriously amiss with the North American economy. In the spring of 1765 London merchants were testifying that returns from the American colonies 'are fallen very short', while colonial merchants like John Hancock of Boston, William Davidson of New York, and William Allen of Philadelphia, all complained bitterly of severe business difficulties.[38]

At first the Sugar Act and Grenville's customs regulations were blamed for this recession, but the Stamp Act put previous legislation into the background. 'I hear the stamp act is like

[35] WWM.Bk1–39: 11 Dec. 1765.
[36] WWM.R56–11: Liverpool Merchants to Rockingham, Nov. 1765. Other letters came from Bristol (R56–1), Lancaster (R56–8), Leicester (R56–7), and Manchester (R56–4).
[37] WWM.R56–4: 27 Nov. 1765; for Rockingham's reply, see R56–6: Rockingham to Strange, Dec. 1765.
[38] *Fitch Papers*, ii. 316–17: Jackson to Fitch, 9 Feb. 1765; A.E. Brown, *John Hancock His Book* (Boston, 1898), pp. 63–4; 'Letters of Dennys de Berdt, 1757-70', ed. A. Matthews, *Pubs. of Colonial Soc. of Massachusetts*, xiii (1910-11), 441; *The Burd Papers*, ed. L.B. Walker (1897-9), i. 67.

to take place,' wrote Hancock, 'it is very cruel, we were before bothered, we shall not be able much longer to support trade, and in the end Great Britain must feel the ill effects of it. I wonder the merchants and friends of America don't make a stir for us.'[39] Gradually, as it became clear that colonial society as a whole was heavily opposed to the Stamp Act, it turned into the principal grievance of the merchants, and ultimately its repeal came to appear synonomous with the return of economic prosperity. By the autumn of 1765 American merchants were warning their British counterparts that unless relief were speedily granted, trade would grind to a complete halt. The logical conclusion of their argument was reached with the non-importation agreements, which were passed in the three great centres of New York, Philadelphia, and Boston, respectively on 31 October, 7 November, and 9 December, and which were to take effect from 1 January.[40] The agreements were carried out with some vigour. Thus Richard Neave and Son of London soon learned from Samuel Mifflin of Philadelphia that all orders for shipment were countermanded,[41] while Barnards and Harrison were similarly informed by Hancock that, unless the Act were repealed, they would lose a customer who refused to be a 'Slave to enrich Placemen'.[42] In the face of such action it is scarcely surprising that the merchants in Britain acted quickly. Whether they agreed with the American attitude—whether even, they accepted the logic of the colonial merchants—was irrelevant. With business bad for the past year, and faced now by the prospect of complete disaster, they had little choice but to obey their clients' demands. Thus Hancock bluntly informed Barnards and Harrison:

You may bid Adieu to Remittances for the past Goods, and Trade in future . . . We are a people worth a saveing and our trade so much to your advantage worth keeping that it merits the notice of those on y[ou]r side who have the Conduct of it but to find nothing urg'd by the merch[an]ts on your side in our favour Really is extraordinary.[43]

[39] A.E. Brown, *John Hancock His Book*, p.69: Hancock to Barnards and Harrison, 22 Mar. 1765.

[40] On these, see A.M. Schlesinger, *The Colonial Merchants and the American Revolution, 1763-83* (New York, 1917), pp. 79–80.

[41] H.M.C. *Dartmouth MSS.*, ii. 23.

[42] A.E. Brown, *John Hancock His Book*, p. 104: Dec. 1765.

[43] A.E. Brown, *John Hancock His Book*, pp. 86–7: 14 Oct. 1765.

English merchants were by no means slow to take the hint.

There was nothing new about an attempt by the mercantile interest to influence imperial policy. Only the previous winter, Trecothick, a 'steady, cool but firm friend to America',[44] as Ingersoll called him, had led the London North America Merchants in an organized effort to modify Grenville's colonial legislation. Though their opposition to the Stamp Act was unsuccessful, they succeeded, in cooperation with the American agents, in having a clause in the American Mutiny Act for the billeting of troops in private houses deleted.[45] 'The Colonys', the Rhode Island agent, Joseph Sherwood, wrote home in May, 'are under great Obligations to the Merchants of London, for their Assistance and Influence in this most Important Attack, had it not been for their Aid, I do believe the Measure would have been carried'.[46] However, influencing a Minister to alter minor legislative provisions was scarcely comparable to the task of completely converting opinion both inside and outside Westminster from an attitude of total hostility to the colonies to one of readiness to repeal the Stamp Act. If the Americans were right in thinking that the most effectual way to get the stamp tax revoked was through the British merchants, success was not to be achieved without considerable skill and labour on the part of the latter.

Their campaign began in the metropolis on 4 December when a new London North America Merchants Committee, which included well-known names like Barclay, Mildred, Hanbury, Neave, and De Berdt, was elected under the chairmanship of Trecothick to work for the repeal of the Stamp Act.[47] Two days later, on the 6th, the Committee agreed on a circular which was to be despatched 'to the outports and to the manufacturing Towns',[48] and which revealed the two essential points in the merchants' campaign; that the object was a concerted movement to petition Parliament and pressurize local M.P.s in favour of repeal, and that there was

[44] *Ingersoll Correspondence and Papers*, ed. F.B. Dexter, p. 332: 'Communication to Connecticutt Gazette', 10 Sept. 1765.
[45] See J.M. Sosin, *Agents and Merchants* (Lincoln, Neb., 1965), pp. 33–6.
[46] *Correspondence of Colonial Governors of Rhode Island*, ed. G.S. Kimball, ii. 363–4: Sherwood to Governor Hopkins, 2 May 1765.
[47] WWM.R1–537: Trecothick to Principal Magistrate of Leeds, enclosing Minute of Proceedings of 4 Dec. 1765, 6 Dec. 1765.
[48] WWM.R1–535: 'General Letter from Com[mitt]ee of North American Merchants', 6 Dec. 1765.

to be no discussion of the constitutional issues, or indeed of
the colonists' resistance to imperial authority at all. 'We mean
to take for our sole Object,' it ran, 'the Interest of these
Kingdoms it being our Opinion, that conclusive Arguments
for granting every Ease or Advantage the North Americans
can with propriety desire, may be fairly deduced from that
Principle only.'[49] According to Trecothick this circular was
sent to some thirty towns throughout the provinces.[50] The
response was enthusiastic. At Bristol, for example, where a
good deal of press coverage was given to American problems
in general and the non-importation agreements in particular,
both the Society of Merchant Venturers and traders outside
the Society, petitioned Parliament and sent three representatives, William Reeves, the Quaker leader of the Bristol merchants, Joseph Farrel, and Thomas Farr, to bear the petitions
to London.[51] At Birmingham, where there was great anxiety
about unemployment, the local manufacturers met on
23 December to elect a committee, and by 4 January had
produced not merely a petition to the legislature, but letters
to all the M.P.s and peers in the district.[52] Altogether some
twenty-five towns, from all the key trading and industrial
areas, petitioned Parliament.[53]

Not every appeal was successful, and when the Mayor of
Norwich replied in distinctly cool vein to the circular,
Trecothick assured him:

[the Committee] desire me to acquaint you that they confine their
object in the intended Application to Parliament to the Honour and
Real Interest of Great Britain, which in their Apprehension are both

[49] Ibid.
[50] Add.MS. 33030, f. 105: Trecothick's evidence in Committee on American
Papers, 11 Feb. 1766.
[51] W.R. Savadge, 'The West Country and the American Mainland Colonies',
pp. 212–13 et seq.
[52] Dartmouth MSS., Garbett to Dartmouth, 21 Dec. 1765; Garbett to Dartmouth,
4 Jan. 1766,
[53] The petitions, with dates of presentation to the House of Commons, were as
follows: from the Lancashire region: Liverpool, Lancaster, Manchester,
(17 Jan.), Macclesfield (20 Jan.); from Yorkshire: Halifax, Leeds (17 Jan.),
Sheffield (27 Feb.); from the Midlands: Leicester town and county (17 Jan.),
Birmingham, Coventry, Wolverhampton, Stourbridge, Dudley (20 Jan.),
Nottingham (28 Jan.), Worcester (24 Feb.); from the West Country and
Cotswolds: Bristol, two petitions, Bradford (17 Jan.), Frome (20 Jan.),
Minehead (21 Jan.), Taunton (22 Jan.), Witney (23 Jan.), Chippenham
(27 Jan.), Melksham (30 Jan.); also London (17 Jan.) and Glasgow (27 Jan.).

inseparably connected with the Welfare of the Trade to North America, they propose to petition Parliament on the Subject of the present Declension and the Prospect of a total Failure of that Trade. And hope for the Concurrence of a City so greatly concerned as yours is in the Event. the present State of the Demand for the Manufactures will doubtless afford Matter whereon to found such Petition from you. And they wish to have it supported by the Countenance of the worthy Members for the City and County.[54]

Yet despite this pressure, despite the fact that there was undoubted and publicized economic distress in Norwich,[55] and despite the existence of sufficient organization and vigour for a petition about grain prices there, the Stamp Act campaign was ignored. Doubtless this was because the chief political interest in the city was that of Grenville's friend, the Earl of Buckinghamshire, who received copies of the correspondence with Trecothick from the Mayor together with congratulations on sentiments 'founded on such principles as can alone Support the Honour and true Interest of Great Brittain'.[56] At Liverpool too the corporation had political interests which differed from those of the merchants. There Trecothick's circular was suppressed, and produced only after Sir William Meredith had informed the local traders of its existence.[57]

However these cases were untypical. For the most part the circular was astonishingly productive. Indeed the response was so widespread that the Opposition was forced to doubt not its extent but its authenticity. Faced by a flood of petitions and evidence from the provincial towns, Grenville and his friends could only argue that a gigantic fraud had been practised; that the manufacturers had 'been deceived by false representations',[58] and that the Ministry, in this deception, 'took the lead, and employed for this purpose every engine in their power',[59] 'encouraging petitions to P[arliamen]t, and instructions to Members from the trading

---

[54] Add.MS. 22358, f. 33: Trecothick to J. Poole, 27 Dec. 1765. For Poole's original reply, see f. 33: 14 Dec. 1765, and for the circular sent, f. 32.
[55] F.J. Hinkhouse, *The Preliminaries of the American Revolution as seen in the English Press: 1763-1775* (New York, 1926), p. 63.
[56] Add.MS. 22358, f. 34: J. Poole to Buckinghamshire, 10 Feb. 1766.
[57] WWM.Bk.1—44: Meredith to Burke, 1 Jan. 1766.
[58] Bedford MSS., liii. f. 18: Bedford's notes.
[59] C. Lloyd, *The Conduct of the Late Administration Examined, Relative to the American Stamp Act* (2nd edn., London, 1767), p. 117.

and manufacturing towns, against the act'.[60] Certainly there was a good deal of suspicion of the merchant classes. One of Charles Jenkinson's Scottish friends refused to believe 'the sad Tales—which the Glasgow Sugarmongers and Tobacconists sour their Punch and light their Pipes with', while from the embassy at the Hague Sir Joseph Yorke opined 'as to the Clamour of the Merchants and Manufacturers that is all an artifice, (I don't mean there is not a Stagnation or Embarrassment) to force Government to give up its Powers'.[61]

How much truth there was in these charges is not easy to determine. Trecothick was certainly anxious to avoid the imputation, which was made to his face in the Commons' Committee on 11 February, that the London merchants had dictated the pattern of the protests.[62] In this respect the activities of the Bristol merchants were somewhat embarrassing. They had obtained a copy of the Liverpool petition 'that we may be as uniform as possible in our application',[63] and had also offered to send Birmingham a copy, though fortunately the manufacturers in that town declined the offer.[64] When Reeve and his colleagues asked Trecothick for instructions as to the petition, he insisted that 'the particular distresses of Commerce in each port and in each manufacturing Town will best be expressed from their own feelings', and that 'such only as either are or soon expect to be aggrieved should complain'.[65] None the less he did go on to outline the London petition, and in drawing up their own, the Bristol merchants proved remarkably slavish in following its pattern. However, despite Grenville's scornful question in the Commons—'Is it difficult for Ministers to get Pet[itio]ns ag[ain]st Taxes. I opposed the Tax upon Beer, could not I first Com[issione]r of Treas[ur]y have got Pet[itio]ns from all the Mughouses in London'[66] —the sheer volume of protest throughout the

[60] Nugent in the Commons, on 14 Jan. 1766, as reported in the *Universal Magazine*, xxxviii. 244.
[61] Add.MS. 38205, f. 12: G. Middleton to Jenkinson, 1 Dec. 1765; Add.MS. 35368, ff. 3–4: Sir J. Yorke to Hardwicke, 14 Jan. 1766.
[62] Add.MS. 33030, ff. 105–6: Trecothick's evidence on 11 Feb., and Newdegate MSS, B2545–20: Newdigate's notes of the evidence, mistakenly dated 10 Feb. 1766.
[63] Quoted in W.E. Minchinton, 'The Stamp Act Crisis: Bristol and Virginia', *Virginia Magazine of Hist. and Biog.*, lxxiii (1965), 153.
[64] W.R. Savadge, 'The West Country and the American Mainland Colonies', p. 216.
[65] Trecothick to Reeve, 2 Jan. 1766, quoted in W.R. Savadge, op. cit., p. 221.
[66] Grey Cooper's report of the debate of 3 Feb. 1766 in the Commons, in 'Debates on the Declaratory Act and the Repeal of the Stamp Act, 1766', edd. C. Hull and H.V. Temperley, *Am. Hist. Rev.* xvii (1911-12), 572.

country belied the notion that it was largely an invention on
the part of the Ministry and the London merchants. As
Trecothick remarked in the Commons, 'In General I believe
the petitions would have come though Letters had not been
sent.'[67]

More serious was the charge that deliberate deception of
another sort was involved. One of the reasons for the great
success of the campaign was the relative importance of the
manufacturing, as against the mercantile, element among the
petitioners. Though Trecothick and his friends provided the
basic organization it was the great outburst of opinion from
manufacturing towns in Yorkshire, Lancashire, and the Black
Country, which with its serious implications for local society,
made a deep impression on opinion inside and outside
Westminster. Their contribution stemmed in the first instance
from the cessation of orders from the merchants who marketed
their wares in North America, and in one case at least it is
certain that a degree of disingenuity was practised. Henry
Cruger, a Bristol merchant of American birth, informed one
of his Rhode Island customers that although he had received
no instructions to cancel orders from him, he had taken upon
himself the responsibility of doing so. 'I cou'd not think of
giving out any of your orders untill I saw which way this
Momentous Affair wou'd turn, and terminate.'[68] However,
this case was doubtless exceptional. There can be little question
that demand had indeed severely decreased, and for the most
part, the pressure on the manufacturers was both spontaneous
and genuine.

The precise relationship between the Ministry and the
merchants' campaign is somewhat obscure, though there is no
doubt that some of the Ministers cooperated closely with the
merchants. Rockingham was in constant touch with Trecothick—
indeed according to the endorsement on the copy of the merchants' circular preserved among the Rockingham Papers, it
was 'concerted between the Marquess of R[ockingham] and
Mr. Trecothick'[69] —and was regularly informed of the progress
of the movement, writing, for example, to Newcastle on

[67] Add.MS. 33030, f. 106: Trecothick's evidence of 11 Feb. 1766.
[68] *Commerce of Rhode Island, 1726-1800* (Collections of Massachusetts Hist. Soc.,
7th ser., ix and x, 1914-15), i. 145: H. Cruger, jun. to A. Lopez, 1 Mar. 1766.
[69] WWM.R1—535. According to D.H. Watson, 'Barlow Trecothick and other
Associates of Lord Rockingham', p. 36, Lady Rockingham was the author of
this endorsement.

2 January, 'Tregothick [sic] and the Merchants and Trading and Manufacturing Towns, etc. go on well'.[70] Similarly Dartmouth at the Board of Trade advised Samuel Garbett, the leader of the Birmingham industrialists, and received regular reports on the headway made in the Midlands.[71] It is interesting that in each of these cases, the wheels of cooperation were oiled by personal interests. Trecothick was incidentally the leader of the Grenada proprietors who were petitioning the Privy Council for an island assembly,[72] while Garbett was corresponding with William Burke as well as his superiors in the Administration about problems involving the iron industry.[73] It is evident from the interest which Rockingham and his more liberal friends took at this time in the concerns of the merchants in general, and their petitioning campaign in particular, that they were as much the directors as the victims of the mercantile and manufacturing lobby which was so rapidly gaining strength.

This was probably equally true of the other interests and groups with which the Ministry was in contact. Inevitably Rockingham and his colleagues were subject to immense pressure from interested parties on the American issue. A mass of material and information from American agents, merchants, manufacturers, speculators, administrators, writers, experts, and mere busybodies, is still to be found among Rockingham's papers at Sheffield.[74] Dartmouth, as well as receiving the usual flood of advice and information, was also much influenced by quite close friends and acquaintances. Dennis De Berdt, a London merchant who plied him with a stream of propaganda on the Stamp Act controversy, had been specifically selected as special agent for Massachusetts because of his known connection with Dartmouth,[75] while Dr. John Fothergill, a noted Quaker with extensive American connections, and a friend of Dartmouth's, was constantly in

---

[70] Add.MS. 32973, f. 13.
[71] Dartmouth MSS., 130, 147: Garbett to Dartmouth, 21 Dec. 1765, 4 Jan. 1766; Fitzwilliam MSS., A.xxvi. 18: [Garbett] to Dartmouth, 9 Feb. 1766.
[72] WWM.R43−8, 9, 10, 11: Trecothick to Rockingham, 30 Nov., 6 Dec. 1765; *Journal of the Commissioners for Trade and Plantations, from January 1764 to December 1767* (London, 1936), pp. 226−7.
[73] *Calendar of Home Office Papers of the Reign of George III*, ed. J. Redington (London, 1878-9), *1760-65*, pp. 605−6, 620, 637−8; *1766-69*, pp. 24−5, 27, 37, 38, 41−2; H.M.C. *Dartmouth MSS.*, iii. 180.
[74] For a detailed analysis of much of this material, see D.H. Watson, 'Barlow Trecothick and Other Associates of Lord Rockingham'.
[75] Dartmouth MSS., T. Cushing and S. Adams to [?], 11 Nov. 1765.

touch with him.[76] However Ministers were as anxious to consult the experts as the latter were to influence them. Quite apart from the better-known Americans like Franklin and Ingersoll, who were constantly being consulted by Rockingham, Conway, and Dartmouth, far less distinguished figures were involved. A West Riding manufacturer like Joseph Milnes could be asked to supply information about the American trade when calling at Wentworth Woodhouse,[77] and a friendship as non-political as that between Dartmouth and George Whitefield could be used to obtain evidence from the other side of the Atlantic.[78] Whatever the amateurism and naivety of the young Ministers, there is no denying their industry or enthusiasm in the autumn of 1765. As in the case of the campaign organized by Trecothick and the London merchants, so in relation to the activities of the innumerable groups and individuals around the Ministry in 1765-6, it is clear that what began as an attempt to pressurize the Ministers soon became a great movement, in cooperation with them, to influence public and Parliamentary opinion.

It is a curious fact that despite the enthusiasm with which Rockingham and some of his colleagues supported the campaign for repeal, they were surprisingly slow to come to any formal decision on imperial policy.[79] On the one hand it was almost universally believed that they were wholly committed, if not to a policy of repeal, at least to one of redressing American grievances. The Opposition of course was anxious to credit the reports that the Ministry were intent on revoking the stamp tax.[80] But colonial agents and advocates were no less convinced of the Ministerial desire to assist the American cause.[81] Indeed so emphatic was the flood of information that

[76] For Fothergill's letters to Dartmouth, see Dartmouth MSS., 75, 81: 7/8 Aug. and 29/31 Aug. 1765, and WWM.R65–5: 6 [Dec. 1765].
[77] WWM.R24–37, 38, 39: Milnes to Rockingham, 21 and 24 Nov. 1765.
[78] H.M.C. *Dartmouth MSS.*, i. 331–2.
[79] Despite the extensive literature devoted to the Stamp Act crisis, little has been written on the evolution of imperial policy from the domestic angle. The most useful works on this problem are D.M. Clark, *The Rise of the British Treasury* (New Haven, 1960), chapter v., and C.R. Ritcheson, *British Politics and the American Revolution* (Norman, 1954), chapter ii. The two principal articles on this subject (W.T. Laprade, 'The Stamp Act in British Politics', *Am. Hist. Rev.* xxxv (1930), 735–57; A.S. Johnson, 'British Politics and the Repeal of the Stamp Act', *South Atlantic Quarterly*, lxii (1963), 169–86) are not very helpful.
[80] *Bedford Correspondence*, iii. 323.
[81] See for example, 'Letters of de Berdt', ed. A. Matthews, pp. 308, 309, 310.

crossed the Atlantic on the subject of Ministerial intentions that Governor Bernard of Massachusetts could assure Conway on 25 January that his Assembly had high hopes of repeal. 'In this they have been a good deal encouraged', he wrote, 'by letters from some Merchants in London; one of which, who claims an intimacy with a Minister of State, says in positive terms, that it is *resolved to take off the Stamp duty*.'[82] Yet despite these reports there is no evidence that a formal decision in favour of repeal had been carried before Parliament met. Not until the end of December was some form of Declaratory Act decided on, and not until the middle of January did the Ministry opt definitely for a policy of repealing the Stamp Act.

This paradox is explained not so much by the vacillation and indecision of the Ministry as by its disunity. On the whole, 'the Younger Part of Administration'[83] were strongly in favour of conciliatory measures. Rockingham had been early converted to the cause of relief, and well before the end of November had apparently told his American relative John Wentworth that

he would give his Interest to repeal 100 Stamp Acts, before he would run the Risque of such Confusions, as would be caused by Enforcing it. That he knew there were already 10000 Workmen discharged from Business, in Consequence of the Advices from America.[84]

Conway was similarly inclined, not least because he had so completely committed himself to opposing the Stamp Act at its inception. 'Our Americans', he wrote to his brother in mid-November, 'are very riotous indeed; it is a serious business, and for me doubly difficult, unless we find lenity the plan.'[85] Grafton was to take a similar view, while Dartmouth, though incensed almost to the point of resignation by Rockingham's initial failure to consult him on imperial policy, had expressed his dislike of the stamp tax in the summer.[86] Winchilsea would follow Rockingham's lead, and Newcastle, if not quite as

[82] P.R.O., C.O. 5/755, f. 494.
[83] Chatham MSS., xxiv, f. 196: Cardross to Pitt, 20 Jan. 1766.
[84] *Diary and Autobiography of John Adams*, ed. L.H. Butterfield (Cambridge, Mass., 1961), i. 287; the diary entry is dated 7 Jan. 1766, but a minimum of six or seven weeks for Wentworth's letter to cross the Atlantic must be allowed. On Wentworth see D.H. Watson, 'Barlow Trecothick and other Associates of Lord Rockingham', pp. 75–99.
[85] *Companion to the Newspaper* (1835), pp. 364–5: 14 Nov. 1765.
[86] H.M.C., *Dartmouth MSS.*, ii. 20.

quick to adopt the popular view on the American question as
he liked later to imagine, soon came to believe that 'The
passing That Bill, was almost the most Unfortunate Measure,
That has ever passed, since my Time.'[87] But between this
group, drawn largely from the old Minority of 1762-5, and
the men who had been in office when the Stamp Act had
been introduced, there was a wide gulf. The King's Friends
in general, and three key figures in the Ministry in particular—
Northington, Charles Yorke, and Charles Townshend—took a
view diametrically the reverse of that of the 'Old Whigs'.

The Lord Chancellor's opinions were well known to be
strongly anti-American. As early as October he had drawn up
a paper declaring,

I am of opinion that the Stamp Act ought to be carried into Execution
in support of the Sovereignty of the British P[arliamen]t over the
Colonies. That for this Purpose immediate Orders should be given to
the Respective Governments to execute this Order and that they should
be furnished with the Assistance of a military Force for this Purpose.[88]

Charles Yorke was no less determined in favour of strong
measures. According to Newcastle, he 'said, My Notions about
The American Affairs, were *Insanity*; I think, He talked more
like a Madman, than I did'.[89] Charles Townshend, as ever,
kept a watchful eye on the political climate. However he had
strongly defended both the principle and expediency of
colonial taxation in the previous session, and for the moment
at least was apparently prepared to do so again. 'Cha[rle]s
T[ownshend]', Newcastle learned in early December, 'will
support The Stamp Act', a prediction borne out at the opening
of Parliament.[90]

The opinions of these three men formed an almost insuperable obstacle to the aims of Rockingham and his closer colleagues. In the Commons, with Grenville in opposition and
Pitt's attitude uncertain, it would have been almost impossible
to proceed in the face of the opposition of a lawyer as
respected as Yorke, and an orator as eloquent as Townshend,

---

[87] Add.MS. 32973, f. 440: Newcastle to Rose Fuller, 14 Feb. 1766; for Newcastle's
equivocation as late as 25 Dec. 1765, see Add.MS. 32972, f. 333: 'Mem[orandum]s
for My Lord Rockingham only'.
[88] Northington MSS.: 'My Opinion intended to be told at the Meeting summond
on Am[erican] B[usine]ss at Cumberland House, the Ev[enin]g the D[uke] of
Cumb[erland] died'.
[89] Add.MS. 32973, f. 275: Newcastle to Rockingham, 25 Jan. 1766.
[90] Add.MS. 32972, f. 231: Newcastle, 'Mem[orandum]s for the King'.

from the Treasury bench itself. Northington's uncompromising stance was equally awkward. His power in the Closet and his standing in the Lords would inevitably endanger the success of a precipitately adopted repeal policy. Indeed the need to gain his assistance, or at least to neutralize his influence, was demonstrated early on. Northington's report to George III of the Cabinet meeting of 11 December exposes the difficulties with which Rockingham and the other Ministers were faced.

The American Papers being read, I asked what was the purpose of the Meeting, whether to give our Opinions on the State of America to be submitted to Y[ou]r Majesty or only to converse together, which had been, I thought improperly and unprecedentedly the Business of former Meetings? I was asked what I considered the Meeting? I said a regular Council for, Advice on that, as Your Maj[es]ty knew of It and approved for I had mentioned the meeting in the Closet. However I found they did not consider It as a Council where we were to give our Opinions the Subject not being ripe; and therefore can't treat any body's Sentiments, as Opinions, but my own that differed from the other Lords. However I found that their Politics seemed to be fixed unanimously to yield to the Insurrections and Clamours and not to support the Stamp-Act, in which I differed and declared my Opinion, as thinking It full Time to have found some fixed Opinion on so national a Subject.[91]

The Ministry's obvious disarray and disunity compelled Rockingham to resort to devious measures. In the following month, it was what Hardwicke described as 'L[or]d Rockingham's proposed Committee', a body even more informal than the 'conciliabulum' which faced the task of thrashing out a policy for America.[92] To Newcastle's bitter complaints about this committee, from which he was excluded, Rockingham replied on 4 January,

there will be a *real* Council tomorrow Evening at the Chancellors—and I hope another on Tuesday . . . Some Benefit has arose from the *Dinners*—which we have had and tho' Your Grace was rather angry and called them *Councils*—yet I am very sure Your Grace will not be displeased when you know the whole.[93]

In fact it is quite clear that Rockingham's committees practically superseded the ordinary Cabinet, which during this period met only for routine discussions of the Anglo-Russian

---

[91] *Correspondence of George III*, i. 428—9: 12 Dec. 1765 (*Additions and Corrections*, p. 68).
[92] Add.MS. 35361, f. 241: Hardwicke to Yorke, 25 Dec. 1765.
[93] Add.MS. 32965, ff. 42—3.

commercial treaty.[94] Their composition varied, and was consistent only in the exclusion of Northington, Winchilsea, and Newcastle, disregarded respectively because of their truculence, inconsequence and interfering ways. Of the other Ministers, Rockingham, Conway, and Dowdeswell were usually present, Grafton, Dartmouth, and Egmont sometimes. Barrington, the Secretary at War, attended one of the later meetings, while Townshend and Yorke, as the two men whose support was considered essential for the success of any policy, were also regular attenders, together with the latter's elder brother, Hardwicke. Others invited to one or other of the meetings were independent M.P.s with friends in the Ministry—such were Sir George Savile and Richard Hussey—and prominent figures in the City and the mercantile community, whether M.P.s, like Sir William Baker and George Aufrere, or not, as in the case of Barlow Trecothick. Edmund Burke, after his spectacular début in the Commons, was also called in to at least one meeting.

On the face of it these gatherings were unwieldy and ineffectual. In fact they performed a valuable function, giving Rockingham the room for manoeuvre essential to convert the opponents of a conciliatory policy and to evolve a workable plan, which the ordinary Cabinet, dominated as it was by Northington and of course religiously reported by him to the King, would not have availed him. It was in his 'committee' that the formula which was to resolve the Stamp Act crisis, and which represented the most sensible colonial policy of any statesman in these years, emerged.

Three policies, discussed *ad nauseam* in the press and later in the legislature, were possible in relation to the Stamp Act—enforcement, modification, and repeal.[95] By December, Rockingham and his younger colleagues, influenced by the

---

[94] The dates of the informal meetings and dinners, as recorded in the papers of Rockingham, Newcastle, Dartmouth, Portland, and George III, are as follows: 8, 13, 16, 27, 31 Dec., 19, 21 Jan. All these were held at Rockingham's house, except the second, which was a 'great Dinner at Dowdeswell's of Americans'; also a meeting at Rockingham's house on 24 Jan. consisted solely of peers and was apparently convened to discuss tactics in the Lords. There were only two meetings of the ordinary Cabinet in the last three weeks of December—on the 19th and 24th—and only two or three in January, whereas the five weeks after Cumberland's death had seen seven.

[95] Strictly speaking there was a fourth alternative—suspension, though it represented not so much a policy as a temporary expedient. While it was not unpopular with pamphleteers and publicists, it does not appear to have been very seriously considered either by the Ministry or the Opposition.

intensity of colonial agitation and by the force of the English
merchants' arguments, had fixed their preference on the last.
Charles Yorke, however, at the important meeting of
27 December, urged the middle course, a bill to 'alter, explain
and amend [the] Stamp Act', which would obviate the juster
grievances of the colonists about the specie shortage in
America, the Vice-Admiralty Courts, and stamp duties on
customs clearances.[96] This compromise, which was attractive
to many moderates, was always the most serious threat to the
cause of repeal. How Rockingham and his friends regarded it
at this stage is not entirely clear. On the one hand Newcastle
later believed that Rockingham had 'amused himself, and
flattered others, with senseless notion of *modification*';[97] on
the other it is evident from Charles Yorke's own account of
the meeting of the 27th, that either Rockingham or one of
his colleagues, perhaps Conway or Dowdeswell, urged the
need for outright repeal, appealing to his legalistic mind with
an array of rather dubious precedents—Walpole's excise
scheme, the Jew Bill and the Occasional Conformity Act.[98]
On the whole it is unlikely that Rockingham's attachment to
a policy of repeal was very gravely shaken by the Attorney-
General's arguments.

In any case the chief problem at this stage was not so much
to choose between modification and repeal, as to discover
how either could be made acceptable to a monarch, legislature,
and indeed public opinion, which regarded the violence of the
colonists' activities with horror and outrage, and which at the
end of 1765 thirsted more for American blood than at any
time before the Boston Tea Party. Even given the immensely
strong economic arguments for granting the Americans relief,
the difficulties of appeasing British opinion into a readiness
to listen to those arguments, seemed almost insuperable.
Conway, though he was convinced that the 'Stamp Act must
be repealed', expressed the general attitude when he told a
colonial acquaintance 'that there was some difficulty about
coming off with Honor, and that America would boast that
she had conquered Britain'.[99] Since this remark, made in

---

[96] Add.MS. 35881, f. 276: Yorke's 'Substance of what I said at [the] M[arquess]
of Rockingham's,' 27 Dec. 1765.
[97] *Newcastle's Narrative*, p. 75.
[98] Add.MS. 35881, f. 276: Yorke's 'Substance of what I said at [the] M[arquess]
of Rockingham's,' 27 Dec. 1765.
[99] *Diary and Autobiography of John Adams*, ed. L.H. Butterfield, i. 287.

November, news of fresh disturbances in New York, which even a pro-American like George Onslow could describe as 'Nothing less than a Rebellion', had added to the problem.[100] There were those who had already foreseen that one way out of the dilemma would be measures to impress on the colonists the mother country's insistence on the reality of Parliamentary sovereignty and the illegality of the agitation against the Stamp Act. As early as 12 December, William Strahan, the printer and friend of Benjamin Franklin, remarked to an American correspondent,

I suppose they will first assert their Right to impose Taxes on the Colonies, and signify at the same time that upon their humble Remonstrances, that any part of the Stamp Act is particularly grievous, they will be heard, and will have such Redress as his Majesty's Subjects Inhabitants of Great Britain would in a similar Case be entitled to.[101]

It was at the two meetings held in the week after Christmas, on 27 and 31 December, that a similar idea was adopted by the Ministry. Yorke's notes of the first meeting show that the more negative, yet in the event critically important, part of the Administration's policy—a King's Speech and resolutions strongly condemning the activities of the colonists, and a statute 'to Assert the Authority of Parl[iamen] t in general words',[102] —was entirely his own work. The scheme he put forward on the 27th is remarkably close to that which the Ministry was to carry through Westminster five or six weeks later.[103]

None the less no formal decision was made. 'Administration', Burke correctly surmised on 31 December, 'has not yet conclusively (I imagine) fixed upon their plan.'[104] The distracted state of affairs at the commencement of the new year is clear from a letter which Rockingham wrote to Newcastle in reply to his complaints of neglect by the younger Ministers. The meeting of 27 December he described,

merely as taking an opportunity of bringing persons together to talk over their Ideas and as preparatory for coming to some fixed Plan. I am sure the Variety of the Opinions of what is right to be done—is no very easy matter to reconcile and I for one shall heartily rejoice when a real concerned Plan can be determined upon . . . Upon the whole that has yet

---

[100] Add.MS. 32972, f. 202: Onslow to Newcastle, [11 Dec. 1765] .
[101] Printed in J.A. Cochrane, *Dr. Johnson's Printer* (London, 1964), p. 186.
[102] WWM.R49—2: Rockingham's notes of this meeting.
[103] Add.MS. 35881, ff. 275—8: Yorke's 'Substance of what I said . . . ', 27 Dec. 1765.
[104] *Burke Correspondence*, i. 229: to O'Hara.

passed—either at the former or at this latter dinner [31 December] —I think one thing seems to be the General opinion—that is—that the Legislative Right of this Country over the Colonies—should be declared— and upon the Plan of Act The 6th of Geo[rge] the 1st relative to Ireland. I think it also seemed the General Opinion—that in the King's Speech and in all the Parliamentary Proceedings—the Intention of giving the Colonies every possible Relief in Trade and Commerce should go hand in hand with declarations of Authority or Censures of the Riots and Tumults.

The main matter in which as yet I can not see exactly where and how the different opinions can be brought to agree—is—what must finally be done upon the Stamp Act. *All* would agree to various Amendments and Curtailings of the Act—*some as yet* not very many to a Suspension and *Very Few* to a Repeal. Your Grace knows that among *even ourselves* there are difference of Opinions—and I am sure Your Grace knows that we must but have one opinion and stick steadily to it when this Matter comes into Parl[iament].[105]

Though Rockingham was anxious about the forthcoming session of Parliament, he had already had some experience as a Minister at Westminster. The brief session before Christmas had been planned as little more than a formality to enable the issuing of writs (forty-one in all) for the re-election of those who had accepted office in July. To this end a short speech merely referring the American disturbances to the consideration of the legislature in the new year, with the 'Address of *Importance*, after The Recess', was scheduled.[106] However it could hardly have been surprising that Grenville and the Bedfords agreed on a 'brisk attack the first day of the session'.[107] Inevitably the approaching opening of Parliament on 17 December was seen as a trial-at-arms, and on both sides 'a general Muster' ensued.[108] Despite the innumerable calcu- lations by which the Ministry had convinced itself of its Parliamentary strength,[109] the event was far from certain. 'It is not easy as yet to judge what the enemies' force will be', Rockingham had informed a Yorkshire friend in the last week of October.[110] As it turned out, he need not have been con- cerned. On the opening day in the Commons, Grenville, after a bitter attack on the Ministry's pusillanimity and vacillation, found so little support for an amendment to the Address that

---

[105] Add.MS. 32973, ff. 11—13: Rockingham to Newcastle, 2 Jan. 1766.
[106] Add.MS. 32972, f. 143: Newcastle to Conway, 5 Dec. 1765.
[107] *Bedford Correspondence*, iii. 322—3: Rigby to Bedford, 23 Nov. 1765.
[108] Add.MS. 32972, f. 21: Newcastle to Offley, 23 Nov. 1765.
[109] See pages 94—5 above.
[110] H.M.C., *Various Collections*, viii. 183: Rockingham to [Irwin], 25 Oct. 1765.

he withdrew it, while the same amendment proposed in the
Lords by his ally the Earl of Suffolk was heavily defeated by
80 votes to 24. Two divisions on 18 and 20 December in the
Lower House were no more encouraging for the Opposition,
beaten respectively by 70 to 35 and 77 to 35, despite the
enforced absence of almost all the Ministry's representatives
at by-elections. Rockingham was naturally jubilant at so
'flattering an Appearance', and Newcastle even considered
'This Administration is thoroughly established, as far, as *King*,
and Parliament can establish Them.'[111]

In retrospect, however, it is doubtful if there was cause for
unalloyed delight. In the first place the session had witnessed
several instances of the kind of 'Inexperience, and Insuffiency'[112]
which did much in the succeeding months to whittle away
the Ministry's public credit. Rockingham had displayed his
total incapacity to speak in the Lords. He was only saved, by
Hardwicke's agreeing to move the Address there, from being
'in any pain about it', and felt compelled to confess to the
King in his report of the debate 'Lord Rockingham is ashamed
to inform his Majesty that he did not attempt to speak upon
this Occasion'.[113] Moreover there had been some notable
mismanagement; an Opposition motion calling for American
papers and materials, accepted by the Ministry in the Lords,
was rejected in the Commons—an unfortunate blunder caused
by the 'Duke of Grafton forgetting to acquaint the Ministers
in that House that he had granted the demand to the Lords'.[114]

However such problems paled by comparison with the
central question of the allegiance of the King's Friends. There
can be no doubt that it was their refusal to join Grenville in
the divisions against the Govenment that was responsible for
the Opposition's weakness. 'All My Lord B[ute's] Party',
wrote Lauchlin Macleane, 'have certainly joined Them, (the
Ministers) so that they muster at least four to one.'[115] In the
Lords, the Minority on 17 December included only one
follower of Bute—the Earl of Abercorn—while Bute himself

[111] *Correspondence of George III*, i. 204: Rockingham to King, 17 Dec. 1765;
   Add.MS. 33078, f. 85: Newcastle to Duchess of Newcastle, 18 Dec. 1765.
[112] Add.MS. 35361, f. 248: Hardwicke to C. Yorke, 13 Jan. 1766.
[113] Add.MS. 32972, ff. 193–4: Newcastle to Rockingham, 10 Dec. 1765;
   Correspondence of George III, i. 203: 17 Dec. 1765.
[114] *Walpole's Memoirs*, ii. 167–8.
[115] Add.MS. 30868, f. 213: Macleane to Wilkes, 20 Dec. 1765.

was present and with almost all his better-known friends
voted with the Ministry.[116] There are no definitive voting
lists for the Commons, but with the Opposition unable to
muster more than 35, it would be surprising to find any but
committed Grenville and Bedford followers in the Minority.
Conway's list of eleven of the latter, which consisted wholly
of Grenville's friends, would hardly have omitted Bute's had
there been any.[117] However the readiness of the King's
Friends to support the Ministry in the December session was
less promising than at the time it appeared. Essentially it
stemmed not from a genuine desire to assist Rockingham and
his colleagues but rather from an anxiety to avoid association
at this stage with what was clearly a formal Opposition. Though
Newcastle's description of the latter—'a most violent *Motley*
Opposition, . . . To the most Innocent Speech, and The most
Innocent Address That ever was made, or proposed. That
can be Nothing but factious Opposition.'[118] —did not come
very well from the Duke, it was none the less accurate.
Jenkinson and his friends were most anxious to warn
Grenville that 'they would not stick by him' in a premature
and gratuitous assault which could only damage their standing.'
In this they were not unaware of the King's attitude. Though
Gilbert Elliot (one of Bute's best-known friends) and Charles
Townshend (currently posing as one), took exception to the
Address and threatened to oppose it on the 17th, both lost
their nerve when it came to the point. 'In walking up the
floor', Elliot recorded, 'Mr. Townshend whispered me he had
changed his mind; that opposing the Address he understood
would offend the King. I answered, 'twas very well, I remained
of the same mind as before.'[120] None the less Elliot had not
the courage to support Grenville, and the incident was a

---

[116] Two lists of the minority are extant—Add.MS. 51387, f. 187 (another copy
51406, f. 123) and Add.MS. 33035, ff. 206, 208, made out respectively by
Holland and Newcastle. At WWM.R53—13, there is a list of the bishops' votes,
sent by the Archbishop of York to Rockingham, 19 Dec. 1765 (WWM.R53—12).
There is no full list of the majority, but virtually all those recorded as being
present on 17 Dec. in the Lords Journals, and not listed in the minority, must
have voted with the Administration.

[117] *Correspondence of George III*, i. 205: Conway to King, [18 Dec. 1765]
(*Additions and Corrections*, p. 42).

[118] Add.MS. 32972, f. 247: Newcastle to Bishop of Worcester, 15 Dec. 1765.

[119] *Jenkinson Papers*, p. 402: Jenkinson to Lowther, 16 Dec. 1765.

[120] G.F.S. Elliot, *The Border Elliots and the Family of Minto* (London, 1897),
p. 397.

significant one. For the moment the King's Friends had rallied
to the Government. Horace Walpole was driven to absurd
expedients to explain this fact. 'Whatever the intentions of
the Crown might be', he wrote, 'it was thought proper that a
majority should first be secured lest the Cabinet should again
be taken by storm.'[121] The truth was simpler. At this stage
the King wholeheartedly supported his Ministry; his attachment to it had yet to be shattered by its overtures to Pitt and
its insistence on repealing the Stamp Act. Of course there was
no cause for complacency. Even in the December session, one
or two of the King's Friends who held no office, notably
Wedderburn, had shown signs of going with the Opposition,[122]
and there was certainly no guarantee of their future conduct.
As early as the end of November Mackenzie had written 'I
hope all our friends will attend before we reassemble after
Christmas holidays, that, whatever line we then take, we may
all act together in a respectable body . . . as prudence shall
direct, according to circumstances, in the most critical and
difficult times.'[123] This was distinctly ominous for the Ministry. Strahan, the printer, had already noted that as far as
American matters were concerned, 'almost all' the twenty or
so speakers in the debate of 17 December, 'seemed to be for
supporting and adhering to the Legislative Authority over the
Colonies, and their undoubted Right to impose taxes upon
them'.[124] If, before the Stamp Act problem had been seriously
posed in Parliament, there was a question mark over the attitude of the King's Friends to the Ministry, their conduct,
once the Ministry had asked both King and Parliament to
approve an unashamedly liberal policy, could hardly be vouched
for.

　　If ever there was a moment for resolution and initiative, it
was in the Parliamentary recess following the December session,

---

[121] *Walpole's Memoirs*, ii. 166.

[122] It emerges from the main accounts of the December debates (*Correspondence
of George III*, i. 205; *Chatham Correspondence*, ii. 351–2; *Walpole's Memoirs*,
ii. 166–8) that most of the King's Friends—notably Townshend, Elliot,
Norton, Wedderburn, Dyson, and Oswald—supported Government, but that
on 18 Dec. Wedderburn apparently spoke for Rigby's motion on the
Opposition's behalf.

[123] *Caldwell Papers*, part ii. vol. ii, pp. 46–7: Mackenzie to Baron Mure, 30 Nov.
1765.

[124] 'Correspondence between William Strahan and David Hall, 1763-77',
Pennsylvania Magazine of Hist. and Biog., x (1886), 91: Strahan to Hall,
11 Jan. 1766.

a breathing-space provided by what Burke called 'a sort of Cessation from the exterior operations of Politicks'.[125] Yet this was not to be. Instead, as Charles Yorke sensed, the Ministers were seeking external help. 'It vexes me,' Yorke told Rockingham on 30 December, 'to see the disjointed state of things for I know not what Reason, and with what expectation of a *Messiah*. Give me leave to say, it is absurd, and to individuals unjust.'[126] The Messiah, of course, was Pitt, who, as Holland predicted with his customary acumen, would 'show his Countenance to the Ministry and then their success wil be imputed to his protection which with a grain of Courage, they might be sure of without it'.[127]

In part the decision to turn to Pitt was indeed an act of weakness, an indication that the Ministers lacked what Charles Yorke's brother Sir Joseph described as a 'proper portion of Courage'.[128] Rockingham, of course, was deficient in the essential qualities of political nerve and determination. He had no liking for the in-fighting of politics, and when the pressure was on, showed signs of weakness. However the responsibility was not altogether his. The fact was that the great majority of those who had come into office in July still considered Pitt's accession essential, and in particular the two Secretaries of State, Grafton and Conway, felt committed to the 'Declarations We set out with, that we would get Mr. Pitt at any Rate'.[129] It was they who, at the beginning of January insisted on a further attempt to obtain his support, and they who kept up the pressure in the following fortnight, even threatening to resign on this issue. The loss of the Secretaries was widely considered equivalent to the collapse of the Ministry. 'If Conway will but stand it', Onslow remarked, 'we may certainly weather this. . . . I know his Consequence, and I know how our People look up to him.'[130]

It was not surprising therefore that Rockingham yielded to the pressure of his colleagues and agreed to an approach to Pitt. Though this was the first formal overture since the formation of the Ministry, there had been no let-up in the attempt to attract his approval in the preceding months. For example,

[125] *Burke Correspondence*, i. 229: Burke to O'Hara, 31 Dec. [1765].
[126] WWM.R1–544.
[127] Add.MS. 51389, f. 45: Holland to Macartney, 20 Dec. 1765.
[128] Add.MS. 35368, f. 4: Sir Joseph Yorke to Hardwicke, 14 Jan. 1766.
[129] Add.MS. 32973, f. 104: Onslow to Newcastle, 11 Jan. 1766.
[130] Ibid., f. 91: Onslow to Newcastle, 10 Jan. 1766.

George Cooke, a former Tory well known to be one of Pitt's followers, had been asked to second the Address at the opening of Parliament on 17 December, avowedly to 'have the sanction of an independent man at their setting out', in fact 'to hold out to the public an appearance of connection'.[131] Equally significant were the renewed offers of office made to Barré and Shelburne together with a declaration by Rockingham that he was 'certain of Mr. Pitt's good wishes, and that they were most ready to be disposed of as he pleased',[132] a gesture that was scorned not merely by the recipients of the overtures but by Pitt himself.[133] None the less the first week of January saw the journey to Bath by 'Tommy' Townshend, a young Lord of the Treasury known to be on good terms with Pitt, and authorized to communicate 'not only that we requested to be favored with Mr. Pitt's advice on the measure then under consideration, but that we desired much to receive him at our head, now, or at any time he should find it suitable with his views for the public'.[134]

The response was not encouraging. Pitt not only declined to give his opinion on the American crisis, but insisted on the dismissal of Newcastle, and at least an offer of the Treasury to Temple, before he would consider taking office. The first condition, which was a gratuitous insult to Newcastle, came as a complete surprise, and the Duke's incredulity at hearing it was understandable.[135] As Sackville remarked, 'the best joke is that the Duke of Newcastle has been so violent for bringing Mr. Pitt into employment that he has disobliged many people by it, and yet Mr. Pitt looks upon him as his greatest enemy.'[136] Pitt had long hated Newcastle, especially since the latter's so-called desertion of him in 1761, and had repeatedly rebuffed his attentions during the years in opposition to Bute and Grenville. However his objection to Newcastle was not simply a matter of malevolence, or even of a desire to occupy that office himself which was held by the Duke; it was also a convenient expedient. Particularly

---

[131] *Chatham Correspondence*, ii. 341: Cooke to Pitt, 5 Dec. 1765; 343: Pitt to Cooke, 7 Dec. 1765.
[132] *Chatham Correspondence*, ii. 356: Shelburne to Pitt, 21 Dec. 1765.
[133] *Chatham Correspondence*, ii. 358–61. [134] *Grafton Autobiography*, p. 62.
[135] Add.MS. 33078, f. 108: Newcastle to Duchess of Newcastle, [7 Jan. 1766], wrongly endorsed 22 July 1766.
[136] H.M.C. *Stopford-Sackville MSS.*, i. 104: Sackville to Irwin, 17 Jan. 1766.

after the death of Cumberland, it became useful to cite
Newcastle's imagined power as the reason for his rejection of
the Ministry's overtures, and to declare that he could 'never
have confidence in a system, where the Duke of Newcastle
has influence'.[137] Newcastle himself, despite his natural
indignation at Pitt's demand, and despite the generally unfavourable reaction—even among those most attached to
Pitt's cause—to such a stipulation, acted with considerable
dignity, begging the King to let him resign and 'remove any
Obstacle to The Settlement of Your Administration'.[138]

The other condition laid down by Pitt was equally unreasonable. He had no political relations with Temple by this
time,[139] and Temple himself had played a prominent part in
the Opposition's attack on the Ministry at Westminster in
December. That the Treasury should be offered to the latter
and then, only after his certain refusal, be returned to
Rockingham, was as outrageous a demand as the dismissal of
Newcastle.[140] It was, as Rockingham himself mildly remarked,
'an unbecoming request, to desire L[or]d Rockingham to
continue in an office dependant on the option of L[or]d
Temple'.[141] The consequence was that he was for the moment
at least, though not without reluctance and irresolution,
brought around to the King's view that 'so loose a conversation
as that of Mr. Pitt and Mr. Townshend is not sufficient to risk
either my dignity or the continuance of any administration,
by a fresh treaty with that gentleman; for if it should miscarry,
all public opinion of this ministry would be destroyed by such
an attempt.'[142] Despite tremendous pressure from Grafton
and Conway, with the former flatly threatening to resign and
George III struggling to sustain Rockingham's will—witness
his urging Egmont to 'see L[or]d Rockingham . . . and *keep
him steady*; for I fear least the Secretarys should stagger him'[143]

[137] *Chatham Correspondence*, ii. 360: Pitt to Shelburne, [Dec. 1765].
[138] *Correspondence of George III*, i. 210–11: 8 Jan. 1766 (*Additions and Corrections*, p. 44).
[139] Despite Temple's claims to the contrary, See *Walpole's Memoirs*, ii. 167, 168.
[140] According to Horace Walpole (*Walpole's Memoirs*, ii. 183), Pitt stipulated that Rockingham was not to be given the Treasury even if Temple declined it, an assertion contradicted by all the other evidence. This error, rare indeed in Walpole, is doubtless a product of his absence from the scene at this time.
[141] WWM.R1–557: Memorandum (a suggested draft for the King of a reply to Pitt).
[142] *Rockingham Memoirs*, i. 266: King to Rockingham, 9 Jan. 1766.
[143] *Correspondence of George III*, i. 220: 11 Jan. 1766.

no further move was made. Grafton's scheme for a letter to be despatched to Pitt promising 'that the King wou'd be glad to hear his sentiments on the occasion, when he arrived', was quashed, and all discussion of the advisability of an official approach to Pitt postponed at least until 'the Person comes to Town'.[144]

Pitt's appearance in London, which was a characteristic piece of theatre, was not long delayed. He had previously made it known that he would, in typically oracular fashion, 'deliver my mind and heart upon *the state* of America',[145] an event all the more dramatic because he had not attended the Commons at all in 1765; and though the speculation and mystification aroused by his tactics were considerable, they were as nothing to the attention focused on the celebrated speech which he duly made in Parliament on 14 January, when the new session began. That speech was also typical of the man, packed with naive and fallacious arguments which were to be cut to pieces by the lawyers in both Houses, yet distinguished by that brand of highly theatrical and oratorical eloquence in which his audience delighted.[146] On the face of it the speech was not calculated to add to his popularity. 'Unconnected and unconcerted',[147] he expressed a mixed sentiment of lofty censure and condescending approval towards the Ministry, 'Condemn'd Every measure of the Late Administration',[148] and in general by his vehement denial of the authority of Parliament in the taxing of the colonies, did much to alienate the country gentlemen in particular and the House as a whole.[149] Yet Pitt's sheer presence and prestige, which it must be remembered, had not yet suffered the blow dealt by his collapse in 1766-7, ensured an awed reception for his views. The remarks of William Rouet, a friend of Bute's, were exaggerated and ironical, but none the less captured the mood of euphoria which, especially in the press, greeted Pitt's pronouncements:

such is his influence, that not a man will be found to arraign his reasoning, nor one lawyer to prove that we have a right to tax our colonys . . . He

[144] *Grafton Autobiography*, p. 63; Add.MS. 35430, f. 29: Rockingham to Yorke, 11 Jan. 1766.
[145] *Chatham Correspondence*, ii. 362: Pitt to Nuthall, 9 Jan. 1766.
[146] For the sources for the debates of 14 Jan. and subsequent dates, on the Stamp Act, see Appendix A.
[147] Some authorities have 'unconsulted'.
[148] *Correspondence of George III*, i. 224.   [149] *Walpole's Memoirs*, ii. 191.

must be king William the Fourth, for he holds in the greatest contempt a law enacted by all the powers of the Legislature.[150]

The burden of the great speech was simple. The Stamp Act had to be repealed, not because it was inconvenient, inexpedient, or even inequitable, but because it was totally unconstitutional—*'That House had no right to lay an internal tax upon America, that country not being represented'*.[151] Since this unhesitating commitment to the colonial cause preceded any public declaration of intent by the Administration, it was considered by many contemporaries, and indeed since by many historians, that the Ministry's policy of repeal was adopted in slavish obedience to the views of the Great Commoner. This notion was not without corroborating evidence. There was for example the complete uncertainty as to the Ministry's intentions right up to the opening of Parliament, not merely among the ill informed public, but even among friends of the Administration like Richard Jackson, who as late as 11 January, was in considerable gloom and doubt about the prospects of repeal.[152] Again there was the tenor of the formal King's Speech with which Parliament was opened. 'I think', a friend of Burke's wrote from Ireland, 'the great Com[mone]r has thrown a fire brand amongst you, which must embarrass a good deal; as tis directly contrary to a plan which appears by the Kings speech to have been concerted.'[153] There was some substance in this. The speech had been almost entirely the work of Charles Yorke, who in the first week of January had exerted considerable pressure on Rockingham, with the result that it 'breathed much more vigour than the Address at the first opening in December. It appeared from this change', or so Gilbert Elliot believed, 'that the Ministers had altered their system and did not intend to repeal the Stamp Act'.[154] The Opposition in the Lords made great play with 'the Appearance—as they conster'd it—of there being an Intention of as Vigorous Measures as they would recommend', and Sandwich 'jocosely threw out that he could not but think a certain late able minister, meaning

[150] *Caldwell Papers*, part ii, vol. ii, pp. 60–1: Rouet to Mure, 16 Jan. 1766.
[151] *Walpole's Memoirs*, ii. 186.   [152] *Fitch Papers*, ii. 383–4.
[153] WWM.Bk. 1–46a: O'Hara to Burke, 25 Jan. 1766.
[154] G.F.S. Elliot, *Border Elliots*, p. 397; for the speech and address, see *Journals of the House of Commons*, xxx (London, 1803), 446–7, and for Yorke's activities, see Add.MSS. 35886, ff. 275–8; 35430, ff. 25–7; WWM.R1–544.

Mr. Grenville, had been consulted, as it so entirely agreed with his sentiments'.[155] Equally significant, it appeared, was the 'servile adulation to Pitt', which was the immediate, indeed precipitate, reaction of the Ministers in the Commons to his speech on 14 January.[156] Both Conway and Dowdeswell paid excessive compliments to Pitt and declared their enthusiasm for his championship of repeal. The former was especially effusive, and even his warm admirer and colleague, Edmund Burke, felt constrained to confess 'Conway went perhaps too far in his compliments to Pitt; and his declared resolution to yield his place to him.'[157] To one onlooker it seemed perfectly plain that

Administration had in a manner agreed to enforce the execution of the Act, finding they cou'd not carry their friends with them in the repeal of it . . . but on Mr. P[it] t's declaring his sentiments the ministers in the House of Commons took courage and declared their sentiments to be quite conform to those of that great and wise man.[158]

However, appearances were deceptive. That no formal decision on repeal had been made by 14 January may be conceded, despite Burke's assertion to the contrary eight years later.[159] What is not true is that Rockingham had in any way opted for a reactionary policy. The speech and address, as Lord Villiers and Thomas Townshend made clear in their proposal of the latter in the Commons,[160] were merely part of the 'Plan of Authority and Relief' which had been evolved in the recess and which Rockingham was determined to pursue, whatever his anxiety at the prospect of declaring it.[161] In any case the view that the Ministry was converted to the cause of repeal by Pitt's speech on 14 January makes the assumption that before it was delivered they had little or no notion of the line he would take. This was certainly not the case. Even in March 1765 he had apparently told Rockingham in a personal interview that he was 'not without his Complaints of the American Tax being not sufficiently objected to *this* year',[162]

[155] *Correspondence of George III*, i. 226: Rockingham to King, 14 Jan. 1766; H.M.C. *Hastings MSS.*, iii. 146: W. Crowle to Huntingdon, 16 Jan. 1766.
[156] Add.MS. 35374, f. 282: J. Yorke to Hardwicke, [18 Jan. 1766].
[157] *Burke Correspondence*, i. 232: Burke to O'Hara, 18 [Jan. 1766].
[158] H.M.C. *Polwarth MSS.*, v. 362: J. Pringle to W. Scott, 16 Jan. 1766.
[159] *Burke's Works*, i. 414.
[160] G.F.S. Elliot, *Border Elliots*, p. 397; *Universal Magazine*, xxxviii. 244.
[161] Add.MS. 32973, f. 13: Rockingham to Newcastle, 2 Jan. 1766.
[162] Add.MS. 32966, f. 69: Onslow to Newcastle, 19 Mar. 1765.

and by December Onslow had been assured by Pitt's friend
and disciple Beckford, that 'the thing Mr. Pitt doubts about,
is nothing material. In the American matter he does *not* doubt
indeed.'[163] By this time Pitt was naturally anxious to conceal
his opinions on the American problem until the opening of
Parliament—he was furious to learn from Cooke that Newcastle
might know enough of them to have a 'hearty resolve to determine the question about the stamp act . . . exactly conformable
to your ideas of it'—but they inevitably leaked out through
his friends. Cooke was informed of them during 'some conversation . . . at Burton Pynsent', while Shelburne, though
characteristically anxious to avoid espousing any specific
policy before Pitt had pronounced,[164] had committed himself to the American cause in the House of Lords on 17
December. 'The concurrence of Shelburne and the retiring of
Lord Camden', Walpole wrote of that occasion, 'spoke sufficiently that they knew or suspected Mr. Pitt would take
part for the repeal'.[165] In short the Ministry could hardly
have been in much doubt that Pitt would opt for repeal when
he finally declared his views in Parliament. What was unexpected in his speech on the 14th, as he must well have known,
was not his advocacy of a repeal of the Stamp Act, but his
total rejection of the legislature's right of taxation,[166] precisely the position in fact which the Ministry consistently
declined to adopt as its own. The wisdom of his other
proposal—repeal—had long been apparent to them.

   This is not to argue that Pitt's pronouncement had no
effect on the evolution of the Administration's policy. However, its function was rather that of a catalyst than an actual
cause. Pitt's speech gave Rockingham the moral courage
openly to avow the policy already formulated in the recess.
In short, it emboldened rather than decided the Ministers.
The final decision emerged from two of Rockingham's informal
gatherings 'at which Meetings, Things are, in a Manner,
determined',[167] on 19 and 21 January. At the first, Conway,

[163] Add.MS. 32972, f. 251: Onslow to Newcastle, 15 Dec. 1765.
[164] *Chatham Correspondence*, ii. 339–40, 344: Cooke to Pitt, 5 and 10 Dec. 1765;
ii. 357: Shelburne to Pitt, 21 Dec. 1765.
[165] *Walpole's Memoirs*, ii. 167.
[166] This even took his followers by surprise. Shelburne, in the Lords had, by his
own account, acknowledged 'the power of parliament to be supreme'
(*Chatham Correspondence*, ii. 355).
[167] Add.MS. 32973, f. 241: Newcastle, 'Continuation of what pass'd, last Night,
with My L[or]d Rockingham', 23 Jan. 1766.

Grafton, Dowdeswell, and Charles Townshend met at
Rockingham's house.

the Ideas we join in [Rockingham informed Yorke] are nearly what I
talked of to you this morning. That is—a *Declaratory Act*—in General
Terms afterwards to proceed to *Considerations of Trade* etc.—and
finally Deter*mination on the Stamp Act*—ie—a *Repeal.* and which its
own Demerits and Inconveniences *felt here* will justify.[168]

Further important meetings were held in the following week—
'a pretty mix'd set of Company' on 21 January,[169] and a
meeting of peers on the 24th.[170] By 25 January Rockingham
could finally report,

Convinced as I am that the Confusion at Home will be much too great
(if the Repeal is not obtained) for us to withstand either as private or
publick men—my opinion being entirely for Repeal—I shall certainly
persist in that measure of tho' many in the House of Commons—may
be against us—and particularly some who have lately called themselves—
under the denomination of L[or]d B[ute's] Friends—yet I am persuaded—
that The House will repeal the Stamp Act—by a Great Majority. *If it
does*—we shall then shew *how* we stand *as Administration.*—If it does
not—I wish no Man so great a Curse—as to desire him to be the Person
to take Administration and be obliged to Enforce the Act.[171]

Thus Rockingham finally committed himself to the execution
of the scheme which he had personally favoured for some
weeks. Admittedly he did so under the pressure of the Parliamentary time-table and secure in Pitt's declaration, yet with
a degree of resolution for which credit has rarely been accorded
him. The process of deliberation was by no means over—the
last fortnight of January saw much wrangling over details—
but henceforth the fate of the Ministry, in the last analysis
because Rockingham himself was determined on it, was tied
inextricably to that of the Stamp Act.

More important than the implications of Pitt's speech for
colonial policy were its political repercussions. The day after
it had been delivered Rockingham formally advised the King,

---

[168] Add.MS. 35430, f. 32: Rockingham to Yorke, 19 Jan. 1766; endorsed
17 Jan. in error.
[169] Add.MS. 32973, f. 224: Lady Rockingham to Newcastle, 21 Jan. 1766. Those
present were Rockingham, Conway, Townshend, Dowdeswell, Dartmouth,
Yorke, Egmont, Barrington. Burke joined them after dinner. Hardwicke and
Hussey were invited but did not attend.
[170] Those present were Rockingham, Dartmouth, Grafton, Marchmont, Egmont,
Winchilsea. Newcastle was invited but did not attend (Add.MS. 32973, f. 263:
Rockingham to Newcastle, 24 Jan. 1766).
[171] Add.MS. 35430, ff. 38—7: Rockingham to C. Yorke, 25 Jan. 1766.

That the events of yesterday in the House of Commons have shown the amazing powers and influence which Mr. Pitt has, whenever he takes part in debate, and That your Majesty's present Administration will be shook to the greatest degree, if no further attempt is made to get Mr. Pitt to take a candid part, is much too apparent to be disguised.[172]

This advice heralded six days of intense and anxious activity.[173] With Rockingham insisting on negotiations with Pitt, George III turned, as he had foreseen he might, to 'my true friends to form an Administration'.[174] Mainly through Egmont he attempted the construction of a Ministry independent of the factions, to be headed by Northington, with Egmont and Charles Townshend as Secretaries, and including Northumberlan Hardwicke, Lord Townshend, Conway, and Charles Yorke.[175] This system did not materialize, partly because Northington would 'be made uneasy by an Offer of the Treasury in Lieu of the Seals',[176] partly because it was patently not credible— even Townshend, who was plainly intended to be the guiding light in the new Administration, advised the King to call on the services of Pitt.[177] In consequence he had no option but to agree to the demands of Grafton, who had already seen Pitt privately, and start a formal negotiation. On the 18th Rockingham and Grafton visited Pitt with two simple questions from the King—firstly as to Pitt's disposition to take office, secondly (and wisely in view of the farce of the previous summer) as to whether a refusal of office by Temple would lead him to decline taking part.[178] On the first point Pitt insisted on the old terms—'He was ready To form an Administration with Lord Rockingham, The Duke of Grafton and Gen[era]l Conway', but 'This Administration must be dissolved', there would have to be a *transposition* of offices', and Newcastle would have to go, for 'that Duke was of so irksome, and meddling a nature that He would marr, and

---

[172] *Rockingham Memoirs*, i. 271.
[173] The sources for the history of these negotiations are as follows; *Rockingham Memoirs*, i. 270–1; *Correspondence of George III*, i. 215, 233–5, 237–40, 244–5, 350; *Chatham Correspondence*, ii. 317–18, 371–3; *Grafton Autobiography*, pp. 63–8; WWM.R1–557; Add.MS. 32973, ff. 148, 156, 158–9, 162, 186, 188, 194–6, 237–40.
[174] *Letters from George III to Lord Bute*, p. 245: [10 Jan. 1766].
[175] Add.MS. 47012 (Egmont Papers), f. 173: a list of the proposed Ministry; see also *Correspondence of George III*, i. 350 (*Additions and Corrections*, p. 57).
[176] *Correspondence of George III*, i. 234: Egmont to King, 16 Jan. 1766.
[177] *Grafton Autobiography*, p. 65.   [178] Ibid., p. 67.

cramp all Councils'.[179] On the other point, his reply was equally irritating and considerably more obscure:

as to the second Question, He calld it a cruel One; that he could not come into Office unless L[or]d Temple was desir'd also to come, that they were not on a foot for him to propose it to L[or]d Temple, for that they had not met except at Court since He came from Somerset Shire that He was therefore if He was to negociate it, certain L[or]d Temple would decline, that for that reason the Ministers must find out the proper Channel; that if L[or]d Temple accepted but demanded that some of his *new Associates* should come in with him; that he (Mr. Pitt) would decline taking a part; and that he must be excus'd declaring any thing of his own conduct if L[or]d Temple would not accept.[180]

It was scarcely surprising that George III replied on the 21st, through Rockingham this time (Grafton would not accompany him),

His Majesty is sorry Mr. Pitt found himself, from the situation of the times, unable to answer his Majestys first question more directly. His Majesty does not see any method, by which he can sound Lord Temple, in his Majesty's uncertainty whether, and how Mr. Pitt woud come in.[181]

Despite the failure of both negotiations of January 1766, the first at Bath in the first week of the new year, the second in London in the third week, they were not without significance. Though Rockingham and his friends did not realize it, they represented something of a watershed for the Ministry, if only because of the change they registered in the King's attitude. Since Cumberland's death his attitude had been one of loyal and at times enthusiastic support. Particularly during the brief session of Parliament before Christmas he had constantly encouraged and assisted his Ministers, assuring them, 'A steady perseverance, unattended by heat, will overturn all oppositions, even in Parliament.'[182] His sentiments were explained at length in a letter to Bute on 10 January.

I will now open my ideas with regard to this Ministry undoubtedly their still imbibing those strange ideas in government, that they addopted

[179] Add.MS. 32973, f. 194: 'Lord Rockingham's Account of what passed with Mr. Pitt', 20 Jan. 1766; *Grafton Autobiography*, p. 67; *Correspondence of George III*, i. 238: Memorandum by the King, [22 Jan. 1766] (*Additions and Corrections*, pp. 48–9).
[180] *Correspondence of George III*, i. 238: Memorandum by the King, [2 Jan. 1766] (*Additions and Corrections*, pp. 48–9).
[181] WWM.R1–546: the draft of the message, [20 Jan. 1766].
[182] *Rockingham Memoirs*, i. 296: King to Rockingham, *c*. 23 Dec. 1765, wrongly dated 2 Feb. 1766. See also i. 276, 277 (two letters placed under Jan. 1766; in fact dated respectively 18 and 17 Dec. 1765).

whilst in opposition, cannot make me anxious for their continuance; but when I receiv'd them into my service I promis'd them ample support, this I am as a man of honour oblig'd and will punctually act up to, for they have not rose in any one term that they made at first accepting; but should they find themselves unable to go on then they quite me not I them; I feel the more the necessity of this conduct because every set that have retired have ever said I drove them to it, and laid the principle blame on you; nay Mr. Pitt in the last negotiation frequently hinted at that . . . [The letter concluded] on the whole I mean to support these men if they can go on if not I am free to do what I should think best.[183]

From George III's point of view the Ministry's insistence, first on sending Townshend to Bath, and a fortnight later on opening direct negotiations with Pitt, amounted to an infraction of his tacit contract with them. It was they who were breaking trust by attempting to admit Pitt on terms which amounted to 'a total change of Aministration'.[184] Thus did the King defend his action to Grafton, in initiating a negotiation for an Administration of the King's Friends:

however misinterpreted his own conduct might be, he acted most honorably by those whom he had called to his service; that whilst they saw a possibility of going on, he had [supported] , and would support them to the utmost of his power; but as he saw it likely to be broken, he was determined to acquaint him with his design.[185]

Above all the King insisted that if there was to be a change of Administration, it must be negotiated by himself. As Walpole reported, 'When it was first proposed to call in Mr. Pitt, the King was said to reply: "Go on as long as you can; but if there is to be a change, I will choose my next Ministers myself." '[186] In retrospect it is plain that for the King the January negotiations were something of a turning point. Fundamentally he had lost faith in his young Ministers; an attitude of genuine, if rather forced support, had given way to one of growing doubt, indifference, and irritation. Behind the remark reported by Albemarle on 20 January—'the King was in Prodigious Spirits yesterday, and told me that a little Firmness would do, and re-establish those ministers he *wished* to be served by'[187] —a remark which doubtless reflected George III's relief at the breakdown of the negotiations with Pitt, was a posture more faithfully represented by a statement

[183] *Letters from George III to Lord Bute*, pp. 242, 245.
[184] *Correspondence of George III*, i. 213: King to Northington, 8 Jan. 1766.
[185] *Grafton Autobiography*, p. 65.   [186] *Walpole's Memoirs*, ii. 222.
[187] Add.MS. 32973, f. 206: Albemarle to Newcastle, [20 Jan. 1766].

made to Egmont nine days earlier; 'all I desire is that they will act firmly till the arduous business of the American Colonys is over, then I can stand upon my own feet.'[188]

While the January negotiations compelled George III to look around for an alternative Ministry, they also showed him his limitations. If anything was clear after that episode, it was that the King's Friends, the men with whom his own preference lay, could not help him materially. When, in the middle of the month, he had attempted the formation of a new Ministry, a number of the King's Friends had met to 'discourse in confidence with each other on the present state of affairs'.[189] In their discussions, recorded by Charles Jenkinson, they naturally remarked on

Those who have always hitherto acted upon the sole principle of attachment to the Crown. This is probably the most numerous body and would on trial be found sufficient to carry on the publick business themselves if there was any person to accept of a Ministerial office at the head of them, and this is all they want. This defect however makes it necessary that they should be joined if possible to some one of the other parties.[190]

Yet there was little prospect of a suitable alliance for the King's Friends outside the Ministry. The most obvious candidate, Pitt, who combined immense public popularity with highly regarded abilities, had for the moment at least put himself out of consideration by his antics in the summer of 1765 and again in the January negotiations. It is difficult not to agree with Hardwicke's comment: 'I never thought the Negotiation w[i]th Mr. P[itt] w[oul]d do; the Man is absolutely Impracticable, Invidious, and Mischievious. I am sorry to say so, but I doubt It is Truth.'[191] Fortunately this had at least demonstrated to the supporters of Pitt in the Administration that their idol was totally unpractical, and had thus taken considerable pressure off Rockingham. 'I am glad,' Rockingham himself remarked, 'that this affair has gone as far as it has. Because It will *prevent* the Difference *amongst us*—which was the thing I most dreaded.'[192] With this problem out of the way, the essential need was for a firm policy of uniting with

---

[188] *Correspondence of George III*, i. 220.
[189] *Jenkinson Papers*, p. 404: 'Observations on the probable dissolution of Lord Rockingham's [first] Administration', [16-18 Jan. 1766?].
[190] Ibid., pp. 405–6.
[191] Add.MS. 35361, f. 255: Hardwicke to C. Yorke, 19 Jan. 1766.
[192] Add.MS. 32973, f. 181: Rockingham to Newcastle, 18 Jan. 1766.

the King's Friends and mastering the Closet. More than ever, in January 1766, the future of the Ministry depended on the relations between the Ministers and the King's Friends.

Despite his awareness of the hostility with which the 'Old Whigs' regarded the King's Friends, George III, in default of an alternative, was not wholly without hope. Grenville had ruined his credit for ever in this respect, and Pitt did not appear to be a much better prospect. According to the belief crudely expressed by Walpole, 'He [the King] did not despair of gaining Mr. Pitt alone and unconnected, who, the King and the Favourite flattered themselves, would be more complaisant than either of the factions.'[193] This was quite untrue. George III had no faith in Pitt's readiness to conciliate his friends, and indeed, in his letter of 10 January, told Bute that Northington had remarked that 'I might see Pitt did not mean to take them by the hand.'[194] In consequence, dissatisfied and disillusioned with his Ministers though he was, the King could still entertain hopes of Rockingham and his colleagues. Thus he informed Bute of Northington's expectation that 'those of the Ministers that remain will try to approach my Dear Friend and his friends; I find he and Egmont never cease to tell them they are mad if they don't attempt it.'[195] Clearly the failure of the King's Friends to form their own Administration, and the almost simultaneous breakdown of the attempt to negotiate Pitt's accession, put the ball very much in the Ministry's court at the end of January. Whether Rockingham would seize the chance, indeed the reprieve, offered him, and rebuild a stable Court party, united within itself and secure in the King's confidence, remained to be seen.

[193] *Walpole's Memoirs*, ii. 184.
[194] *Letters from George III to Lord Bute*, p. 244.   [195] Ibid.

V

PARLIAMENT AND THE IMPERIAL PROBLEM
(JANUARY TO MARCH 1766)

ROCKINGHAM'S thoughts in the last week or two of January
were less preoccupied with the subject of the King's Friends
than with that of his colonial policy and its likely reception
in Parliament. He had some reason to be concerned; the
Stamp Act crisis undoubtedly presented one of the most
serious issues in decades and Burke was not alone in considering that 'since this monarchy, a more material point
never came under the consideration of Parliament'.[1] But it
was not only the momentous importance of the issue which
so concerned Rockingham; it was also the question of its
likely fate at Westminster. It was generally agreed that Parliament would not relish the prospect of yielding to the colonists' demands. 'There will be great opposition to the repeal of
this odious act', John Wentworth had declared in November.

Many members of Parliament, who were closely attached to Mr. Grenville
and voted for it, will adhere to the rectitude of the measure. I have con-
versed with some of them upon the subject and find them very warm
against us, alleging the necessity of enforcing it, as the colonists have so
violently refused submission to it, and not only avowed independence
but also broke loose from all law and government.[2]

The almost universal belief was that an important and legit-
imate principle was involved, and that the intemperance with
which the colonies had rejected it necessitated its reassertion.
There had never been any doubt about the former. At the
time when the Stamp Act was passed it had been made quite
clear that the legality of taxing the colonies was simply not
at issue in England. 'Both within doors and without', one
American had noted, 'all I have heard speak on the subject at
once give it against the Provinces, and allow the Power and
Right.'[3] This overwhelming consensus in favour not merely

---

[1] *Burke Correspondence*, i. 229: Burke to O'Hara, 31 Dec. [1765].
[2] L.S. Mayo, *John Wentworth, Governor of New Hampshire, 1767-75* (Cambridge,
Mass., 1921), p. 19: Wentworth to D. Rindge, 29 Nov. 1765.
[3] *Bowdoin and Temple Papers*, p. 46: J. Nelson to J. Temple, [Feb. 1765].

of the Stamp Act but of the principle of imperial taxation had only been strengthened by the violence with which the Americans resisted it. As the London North America merchants later pointed out to their transatlantic colleagues, 'the difficulties of the Repeal would have been much less; if they had not by their violence in Word and Action, awakened the Honour of Parliament'.[4] The opinion of Edward Sedgwick, a minor official of great experience if little originality, may stand for all;

The only thing I am clear in, [he informed his friend Weston] and that I have been from the beginning, is, that the Right of the British Legislature to tax the Colonies is clear and incontestable, and that it must not, cannot be given up, without annihilating the British Constitution in British America.[5]

Such a sentiment, which was characteristic of the attitude of Englishmen to the Stamp Act crisis, was a simple fact of Parliamentary life with which the Ministry had to come to terms. It did not necessarily require the enforcement of the Stamp Act, especially if it could be shown that the tax was as fatal to British commerce as to American liberties, but it did demand some sort of concession. What was needed, Lord Digby correctly diagnosed, was 'to find means to appease the Tumults in America without giving up the authority of the Legislature here'.[6]

It was Rockingham's design, first evolved in the Christmas recess, to supply this need and exploit the existence of the many who were 'for supporting the authority and powers of a British Parliament, yet seem to think a violent exertion of either, in the present crisis, ought to be avoided'.[7] The essence of his scheme, which was later to be elaborated into a theory of empire by Burke, was to take the colonial view of what should be done and the imperial view of what should be said, to repeal the offending tax and yet defend the principle on which it was founded, on the basis that this was the only solution which would satisfy both the legislature and the colonies. Conway explained the thinking behind the Ministry's strategy to Dennys De Berdt.

[4] 'London Merchants on the Stamp Act Repeal', *Massachusetts Hist. Soc. Proceedings*, lv (1923), 216.
[5] H.M.C. *Weston Underwood MSS.*, p. 399: 24 Dec. 1765.
[6] Add.MS. 51341, f. 78: Digby to Ilchester, 18 Jan. 1766.
[7] *Caldwell Papers*, Part ii, vol. ii, p. 65: Rouet to Mure, 31 Jan. 1766.

Mr. Conway told me there was 3 Parties in the House, one was severe method the other for a Repeal but for previous resolves to assert the right and Power of Parliament, the Third which Includes the ministry for a Repeal without any previous resolutions at all but in Order to secure the Repeal they were obliged to agree to the resolves in order to secure a majority for a Repeal which by that means He apprehended they should be secure in the great Question, in which light He hoped the Americans would take their resolutions.[8]

The 'resolves' which Conway alluded to, were worded, like the Speech and Address of 14 January, in surprisingly strong terms. 'To be sure', Newcastle later remarked; they 'might as well be followed by an Act To enforce The Stamp Act, as by a Bill to repeal it, But They say, (and They should know) That *That* was necessary, To bring some into The Repeal'.[9] The five resolutions intended by the Ministry for adoption by both Houses of Parliament, roundly condemned the activities of the colonists 'in manifest violation of the laws and legislative authority of this Kingdom',[10] charged the colonial assemblies with fomenting resistance, and recommended that the authors of the riots should be punished and their victims compensated. Most important, however, was the resolution, consciously modelled on the Dependency of Ireland Act of 1719, and likewise intended to be put on the statute book, which declared that the King in Parliament 'had, hath and of a right ought to have, full power and authority to make laws and statutes of sufficient force and validity to bind the colonies and people of America *in all cases whatsoever*'.[11]

These resolutions, which had first been mooted in December, were largely the work of Charles Yorke,[12] and his brother Hardwicke even boasted later that 'It was principally owing to my Brother that the Dignity and Authority of the Legislature were kept up by the Bill for asserting the Dependancy of the Colonies.'[13] From Rockingham's vantage-point, Yorke was representative of conservative opinion in Parliament; concession to his demands, as well as ensuring his own support,

[8] 'Letters of de Berdt', ed. A. Matthews, p. 312: De Berdt to S. White, 15 Feb. 1766.
[9] Add.MS. 32973, f. 344: Newcastle to Secker, 2 Feb. 1766.
[10] *Rockingham Memoirs*, i. 285.
[11] Ibid., i. 287. The wording of the Declaratory resolution differed from that of the Act of 1719 only in the addition of the words 'in all cases whatsoever'. See *Statutes at Large*, v. (London, 1786), 6 Geo. I, c. 5.
[12] Add.MS. 35881, f. 275: Yorke, 'Substance of what I said . . .,' 27 Dec. 1765.
[13] Add.MS. 35428, f. 26: Hardwicke's 'Private Memoirs'.

provided some means of gauging the minimum conditions
which had to be satisfied at Westminster before the repeal
could be secured. In general therefore, his views were accom-
modated as far as possible. In some cases, Rockingham
attempted to restrain the Attorney-General's enthusiasm for
a strong phrase, and in particular he declined to accept the
suggestion that the Declaratory resolution should end with
the words, 'as well in cases of Taxation, as in all other cases
whatsoever', which he feared would gratuitously offend
Pitt.[14] But for the most part Yorke's demands were approved.
'The Resolutions in general', Rockingham informed him on
25 January, 'exceed in Spirit what the Generality of our
Friends wish—but in Expectation that coming into them—will
pave the way for the *Actual Repeal of the* Stamp Act I think
they will be agreed to.'[15] There is no doubt that many in the
Administration, especially those who regarded themselves as
followers of Pitt, disagreed with the strategy by which
Rockingham hoped to obtain repeal. Newcastle, strongly
influenced by this element, warned Rockingham, 'I hope,
They [the Commons] will come *Soon* to The Repeal, Or,
believe me, My Dear Lord, you will see great Confusion
amongst your own Friends.'[16] As early as the beginning of
January, when Rockingham had first suggested a 'Plan of
Authority and Relief' the Duke had declared that 'for one, I
shall incline rather to be Deficient, in That, which is only a
Declaration in Words, than in The Other, on which depend
The most Material Interests of This Country'.[17] Newcastle's
view was arguably more logical than Rockingham's, but it is
difficult to accept that it provided a practicable solution to
the problem. Oddly enough, it was his old friend Archbishop
Secker who put the argument against his position most
cogently.

Will it not be better [he asked] to comply with the general Opinion as
far as one well can, and try to stand upon that Ground, rather than run
the Risque of being instantly overturned by keeping on a situation,
which however good it may otherwise be, is not suited to that of
Affairs? If the approaching parliamentary storm can be weathered by
such precautions, gentle methods may be gradually interposed with
safety in future proceedings, to prevent Inconveniences from strong
Declarations now. Permit me to add, that if by conciliating Applications

---

[14] *Rockingham Memoirs*, i. 287; WWM.R49–8: Rockingham's notes.
[15] Add.MS. 35430, ff. 37–8.   [16] Add.MS. 32973, f. 305: 28 Jan. 1766.
[17] Add.MS. 32973, f. 25: Newcastle to Rockingham, 3 Jan. 1766.

and Advances, though such as one would not on less Occasions chuse,
any neutrals could be gained over, though it were but in part, the
Acquisition might be extremely seasonable and important.[18]

Later on of course, when the question of British sovereignty
in terms of taxation again became the central point of conflict between the mother country and the colonies, this issue
acquired additional significance. Burke and his friends then
maintained, with every justification, that the Declaratory Act
had been a political necessity,[19] though they did not attempt
to deny their conviction of its validity. Others took a different
view. Grafton, writing nearly forty years after the Stamp Act
crisis, declared:

I shall never change my opinion in thinking that, under Mr. Pitt's accession, the nation would have been brought to a conviction, at least,
of the expediency of giving up all right of *taxation* over the colonies.
He would have made the attempt at least; and if he should have succeeded, what scenes of woe might there not have been avoided?[20]

In the light of such a contention, the historical problem of
the Declaratory Act—the question of whether Rockingham's
strategy was necessary and justified—is all the more crucial.

In fact it was not long before the approach devised by
Rockingham and Yorke was put to the test. On 27 January
the House of Commons was presented with petitions for the
repeal of the Stamp Act from the Congress of colonial
committees which had met in New York three months previously. As early as December Charles Yorke had warned
Rockingham that if petitions were to be accepted from the
Americans, they would have to come from the colonial agents,
and represent 'Reasons for *repealing* or *altering* the Stamp
Act etc., without disputing or touching the Legislative power'.[21]
Yet the petitions which George Cooke delivered on 27 January
were overt challenges to imperial authority in matters of
taxation—'from an illegal congress, calling the right of Parliament in question', as Hardwicke described them.[22] Several
weeks before, Conway had 'hoped the Americans would
Petition; He longed to receive some Petitions', but he had

[18] Ibid., f. 332: Secker to Newcastle, 1 Feb. 1766.
[19] These claims are conveniently marshalled in W.E.H. Lecky, *A History of
England in the Eighteenth Century* (London, 1878–90), iii. 342.
[20] *Grafton Autobiography*, p. 68.
[21] Add.MS. 35881, ff. 277–8: Yorke, 'Substance of what I said . . . ', 27 Dec. 1765.
[22] *Rockingham Memoirs*, i. 290: Hardwicke to Yorke, 28 Jan. 1766.

expected, like Yorke, that they would be based on arguments of expediency, not on provocative statements of constitutional right.[23] The Ministry's reaction when the petitions arrived was consistent with the strategy enshrined in the resolutions already drawn up. 'I saw plainly', Charles Garth wrote to his superiors in Maryland, 'the wish of our Friends not to hazard any Question that might endanger the Loss of a single Voice upon the Point in Prospect.'[24]

Conway tried to stop the presentation of the Congress petitions, though in vain.[25] Pitt predictably supported the petitioners and there were those in the Ministry (notably George Onslow) who took his part. However Conway and Dowdeswell argued against receiving the petitions, and their judgement was vindicated by the clear sense of the House.

> Mr. Pitt [Conway reported to the King] had said some imprudent things which I thought indispos'd the House much to the Petition; particularly that he thought *the Original Compact with the Americans was Broke, by the Stamp Act*—on which words he was strongly attack'd by the Late Attorney-Gen[eral] who rais'd a strong cry against him upon them and intimated he shou'd have been call'd to the Bar for them.[26]

Pitt was indeed severely mauled by Sir Fletcher Norton, a coarse lawyer with a talent for violent and at times devastating vituperation; he himself realized that for once he had badly blundered in his treatment of the Commons. 'He soon perceived that he had gone too far', David Hume was to write later, 'and like an able man, he has ever since lowered his tone, and talked with great submission and deference to the House, so that he has entirely recovered the good will of his audience.'[27] There could have been no clearer vindication of Rockingham's strategy of evading conflict on the constitutional issue than Pitt's almost unprecedented humiliation in a House which he was accustomed to dominate. Not surprisingly the petitions were quietly dropped 'without either being accepted or Rejected'.[28]

This lesson was driven home barely a week later when the Commons, after reading the various state papers on the Stamp

[23] *Diary and Autobiography of John Adams*, ed. L.H. Butterfield, i. 287.
[24] 'Stamp Act Papers', *Maryland Hist. Mag.* vi (1911), 289: Garth to Tilghman, etc., 5 Mar. 1766.
[25] *Correspondence of George III*, i. 246.
[26] Ibid., Conway to King, 28 Jan. 1766 (*Additions and Corrections*, p. 49).
[27] *Letters of David Hume*, ed. J.Y.T. Greig, ii. 18–19: Hume to Hertford, 27 Feb. 1766.
[28] 'Letters of de Berdt', ed. A. Matthews, p. 312: De Berdt to S. White, 15 Feb. 1766

Act crisis, and orally examining four victims of the riots on
31 January,[29] came to consider the first of the resolutions
proposed by the Ministry—that which was later to become
the Declaratory Act. The resolution was overwhelmingly
approved, despite an attempt by Pitt and Barré to exclude the
words 'in all cases whatsoever' and by implication renounce
the authority of Parliament in matters of colonial taxation.
Apart from Burke's eloquent exposition of 'a real distinction
between the ideal and the practical right of the constitution',[30]
the level of debate was not very high. Most of the relevant
points had been made in the press and, as John Yorke remarked,
Pitt's 'Arguments seldom require great abilities to answer'.[31]
But it was nevertheless an important debate, for it demonstrated
once for all that Pitt's 'opinion and his manner of declaring it',
as the young Philip Francis noted, 'were universally condemned
by every Englishman above the rank of a Blacksmith'.[32] The
view of a country gentleman, rare because country gentlemen
did not often commit their sentiments to paper, but significant
because it was the authentic voice of the backbencher, may be
taken for all. 'Mr. Pit's opinion', wrote Sir Edward Turner,
'even Mr. Pit's opinion, that Great Britain hath no right to
tax the Colonies, cannot convince me or many others of
inferior, common, and unrefined understandings. If that Right
be given up (but I think it impossible) good by [i.e. goodbye]
America.'[33] In fact Pitt did not even bother to put his motion
to a division. According to Charles Garth, when the Declaratory
resolution was passed, 'from the Sound there were not more
than ten dissenting Voices'.[34] When Grafton proposed the
same resolution in the House of Lords, the event was even
more decisive. After a debate considerably more distinguished
than that in the Lower House, in which the argument put
forward by Pitt's old friend Camden was comprehensively
demolished by his still older enemy Mansfield, the Ministry's

---

[29] See B.R. Smith, 'The Committee of the Whole House to Consider the American
Papers, (January and February, 1766)' (Sheffield Univ. M.A. Thesis 1957),
pp. 38–83.

[30] 'Ryder Diaries', *Camden Miscellany*, xxiii. 273.

[31] Add.MS. 35374, f. 278: J. Yorke to Hardwicke, 4 Feb. 1766.

[32] *The Francis Letters*, ed. B. Francis and E. Keary (London, 1901), i. 72:
Francis to Allen, 4 Feb. 1766.

[33] *An Eighteenth Century Correspondence*, ed. L. Dickens and M. Stanton
(London, 1910), p. 431: Turner to S. Miller, 18 Jan. 1766.

[34] 'Stamp Act Papers', *Maryland Hist. Mag.* vi. 300: Garth to Ilghman, etc.
5 Mar. 1766.

resolution was carried by the overwhelming majority of 125 to 5. After the debates in both Houses on 3 February, as after that in the Commons on 27 January, Rockingham could reasonably feel that his strategy had been completely vindicated against the doubts of Newcastle on the one hand and the opposition of Pitt on the other.

In the midst of these Parliamentary successes the Administration was rocked by a new if not unheralded menace—the revolt of the King's Friends. The possibility of such a development had long been recognized. Thus Conway had told his brother at the end of December, 'A certain party keep aloof, and the world says are certainly forming a *bande à part*: I mean Lord B[ute] 's friends—the two Townshends particularly and if they have a mind, the American affairs will give them an opportunity to be troublesome.'[35] The failure of the projected Northington-Townshend Ministry, the Administration's continued refusal to conciliate Bute's friends, and the growing commitment of Rockingham and his friends to a policy of repeal, all assisted the evolution of a rebellious movement which was commonly described as a 'flying party', a *'Flying Squadron'*, or a 'camp-volant'.[36]

The gravity of the revolt was registered in three Parliamentary divisions at the end of January and beginning of February On 31 January when a disputed Scottish election came up for consideration, the Ministry was all but defeated. The petition which Alexander Wedderburn presented against the sitting member, Sir John Anstruther, was deferred at the Administration's instigation, but by only 148 votes to 137, 'too small a majority', in Chesterfield's words, 'to carry anything'.[3] Worse was to come. In the House of Lords, on 4 and 6 February, the Government was actually defeated by majorities of respectively 60 to 63 and 59 to 55, which, as Bamber Gascoyne rather mildly recorded, 'occasion'd Ministerial stock to be under par'.[38] In each division the apparent issue was

[35] *Companion to the Newspaper* (1835), p. 366: Conway to Hertford, 27 Dec. 1766.

[36] *Letters from George III to Lord Bute*, p. 245: [10 Jan. 1766]; History of Parliament Trust transcripts, Bute MSS., extract from *London Evening Post*, sent by Lord Townshend to Bute, 28 Jan. 1766; *Caldwell Papers*, Part ii, vol. ii, p. 57: Rouet to Mure, 10 Jan. 1766.

[37] *Letters of Chesterfield*, ed. B. Dobrée, vi. 2712: Chesterfield to P. Stanhope, 11 Feb. 1766.

[38] Strutt MSS., Gascoyne to Strutt, 6 Feb. 1766.

trivial; in the first case the Opposition altered a resolution 'recommending' the colonial assemblies to compensate the victims of the Stamp Act riots to one 'requiring' them to do so, while in the second, a resolution congratulating those officers who had attempted to execute the law was modified to include a specific reference to the Stamp Act. But the underlying significance of these defeats was considerable. They plainly served notice on the Administration that the Lords would have little sympathy for a conciliatory policy towards the colonies.

There could be no ignoring these divisions, which quite clearly represented a concerted defection by 'those who call themselves Lord Bute's friends'.[39] In the Commons, Bute's better-known connections, whether in office, like Oswald, Dyson, and Elliot, or out, like Wedderburn and Norton, were prominent in the Opposition's ranks,[40] while the Lords saw the 'first appearance . . . of Lord Bute or his friends taking any open part in opposition to the administration'.[41] On 4 February, Despenser led the attack in debate, while Bute himself, his more important followers—notably Talbot, Lichfield, Harcourt, Denbigh, and Townshend—and a solid block of Scottish peers, all voted with the Bedford-Temple group. Even the King's brother, the Duke of York, and the Lord Chancellor, Northington, did so.[42] At one stroke, the great majorities which the Ministry had won in the December session of Parliament were wiped out by the calculated desertion of men who, at least since the beginning of the reign, had consistently supported Government, and many of whom indeed held office.

This, of course, was the commencement of what Burke was later to describe as 'an opposition of a new and singular character; an opposition of placemen and pensioners',[43] and

[39] *Chatham Correspondence*, ii. 380: G. Onslow to Pitt, [31 Jan. 1766], misdated 14 Feb. 1766.
[40] Conway listed seventeen 'particularly remark'd' as voting against Administration on 31 January. (*Correspondence of George III*, i. 249–50 (*Additions and Corrections*, p. 50).)
[41] *Newcastle's Narrative*, p. 47.
[42] A division list is extant for 4 Feb., though the minority consists only of 59 names and one of these (Roxburgh) is queried. (Add.MS. 33035, ff. 274, 278–9). There is no list for 6 Feb., but according to Holland (Add.MS. 51406, f. 131: to J. Campbell, 7 Feb. 1766) three of Bute's friends, Talbot, Harcourt, and Lichfield, (probably at the King's instigation) voted with the Ministry.
[43] *Burke's Works*, i. 183–4.

the almost unprecedented spectacle of an Administration utterly divided; an 'undecipherable state of affairs', Chesterfield called it, 'which, in fifty years' experience, I have never seen anything like'.[44] Its significance is not illuminated by the mountains of propaganda in which it has figured so long and so prominently. At the time it was widely regarded as a manoeuvre by Bute to destroy the Ministry which had treated him so shabbily, and later it came to be seen as a strategem of George III's to rid himself of an odiously liberal and constitutionalist Government. Yet in January George III himself had warned Bute that there was a distinction between political and conscientious motivations in the conduct of the King's Friends.

I owne [he wrote] I should think I had great reason to complain if those of my friends that are still in office try'd to overturn those that I employ; for then they would be acting towards me the very part I have met with from all, that is making disturbance that they may profit by it; ... as to my friends differing from Ministers where they think their honour and conscience requires it, that I not only think right, but am of opinion it is their duty to act so; nay I think that it is also incumbent on my Dear Friend to act entirely so also.[45]

How the opposition of the King's Friends should be classified is far from obvious. On the American issue it is possible to give them the benefit of the doubt. Later on they were to vote *en bloc* against the repeal of the Stamp Act in all four divisions in the Commons, and also the only one in the Lords. Throughout the period of the American Revolution, placemen, bureaucrats, and office-holders in general tended to have anti-American views, and most of the King's Friends had been in office when the Stamp Act was so overwhelmingly passed. Bute himself felt especially committed to the defence of a tax which had been first mooted during his Administration, while some of his friends, like Jenkinson and Norton, had helped to organize its introduction. However the Anstruther election is clearly in a different category. It is true that it was a matter in which some of Bute's followers happened to be personally involved,[46] and as George III pointed out, it was

[44] *Letters of Chesterfield*, ed. B. Dobrée, vi. 2712: Chesterfield to P. Stanhope, 11 Feb. 1766.

[45] *Letters from George III to Lord Bute*, p. 242: [10 Jan. 1766].

[46] Wedderburn, Oswald, and Bute himself all had an interest in the Anstruther election. See *Memorials of the Public Life and Character of the Right Hon. James Oswald of Dunnikier*, p. 418. The dispute was finally settled when Rockingham promised a seat elsewhere to the Bute candidate (Add.MS. 32974, f. 187: Gilmour to Newcastle, 17 Mar. 1766).

scarcely an issue of confidence. 'By what L[or]d Rockingham drop'd to me', he told Conway, 'that both Sir John Anstruther and Mr. Alexander, were good Men, I did not know Administration meant as such to be active on this occasion.'[47] On the other hand Horace Walpole thought that, 'according to Parliamentary divination, it had all the aspect of an overthrow',[48] and if this was a little strong, Conway's summary of the considerations involved was eminently fair.

Had there been no previous Appearance of any Sort of design or Separation from Your M[ajesty]'s Service [he told the King] less notice wou'd have been taken of this; but the buzz there has been for some time of such a plan, made it matter of great observation. —I must observe to Your M[ajesty] that Personal friendships and local connexions may have naturally also had a share in this, as generally happen's in Election matters, tho' I cannot think it was the whole and it was too trifling a question for conscientious distinctions.[49]

Even the King seems to have been disturbed by the incident. 'The late silly division', Bute told his friend Samuel Martin on 2 February, 'has had bad effects I too much apprehended, and has certainly brought the Person in question nearer these Governors again.'[50] Of course this revolt was not the well-drilled exercise in treachery which Burke liked later to paint it. George III was distressed and alarmed by the development; Bute, though quite clearly anxious to defend the Stamp Act, and perhaps tempted by the prospect of intrigue, was not the conscious director of a party in the way that Bedford was and Newcastle had been. None the less the King's Friends were obviously bent on compelling the Ministry to come to terms with them; some of them, especially Norton, Lowther, Jenkinson, Stanley, and Ellis, were eager to regain office, many felt (as yet unaware how deep was the King's enmity for Grenville) that Grenville and Bedford were both more able and congenial as Ministers than the 'Old Whigs', and all were certainly disgusted with the attitude of Rockingham and his colleagues to Bute and themselves.

If the object of the King's Friends was the actual destruction of the Ministry, they came very close to success. There were constant reports and rumours of such an event, with

[47] WWM.R1–567: [1 Feb. 1766]; the version printed in *Rockingham Memoirs*, i. 295, is not accurate.
[48] *Walpole's Memoirs*, ii. 196.
[49] *Correspondence of George III*, i. 249: 1 Feb. 1766.
[50] Add.MS. 41354 (Martin Papers), f. 97.

Hardwicke assuring his brother Charles on 3 February, 'The *talk* is of a new Administration'.[51] Rockingham's own reaction to the Anstruther division was first to demand the dismissal of some of those who had voted against the Ministry, and secondly to consider resignation. In fact neither of these courses was effected. Newcastle was not surprised to learn that George III would dismiss nobody 'for voting with My Lord Bute in a Scotch Election',[52] while on the other side Dartmouth strongly advised Rockingham against resignation. 'The Case', he urged, 'is not yet desperate, and while there is the least shadow of hope of doing good, I would on no account give up the game to those who will, undoubtedly, do mischief.'[53] This advice was apparently taken by Rockingham, who assured the King of his 'resolution, of standing firmly by the fate of the American question'.[54] However his determination was shaken not a little by the defeats which the Administration suffered on the colonial issue in the Lords. Though Grafton pressed strongly for a concerted resignation, a meeting of the 'Old Whig' leaders, including Portland, Albemarle, Bessborough, and Lord John Cavendish, as well as the principal Ministers, again decided to await the fate of repeal and 'stake their credit on this point'.[55] If they failed, as Newcastle pointed out, 'they had done their part and, in either case, then and not till then, would be the proper time for them to consider what part they should take either for resigning or strengthening their administration'.[56]

While the Ministry was deciding on a course of action, it was receiving a buffeting in the House of Commons, where the resolutions which it had drawn up to accompany the Declaratory clause were severely mangled on 5 February. One resolution was withdrawn, another replaced by one of Grenville and Pitt's making, and two completely new resolutions devised by Grenville added. These alterations were of no practical importance, though the last provided for a necessary legal technicality—a statute indemnifying those who had

[51] *Rockingham Memoirs*, i. 297.
[52] Add.MS. 32973, f. 340: Newcastle to Rockingham, 2 Feb. 1766.
[53] WWM.R1–574: [2 Feb. 1766]; the incomplete version printed in *Rockingham Memoirs*, i. 303, is mistakenly dated 12 Feb. 1766.
[54] *Rockingham Memoirs*, i. 297.
[55] H.M.C. *Polwarth MSS.*, v. 363: J. Pringle to W. Scott, 4 Feb. 1766.
[56] *Newcastle's Narrative*, p. 48.

failed to use stamps in the colonies—but they did not reflect well on the credit of the Administration which, as Bamber Gascoyne remarked, 'look'd very small'.[57] No one factor can account for the Ministry's pusillanimity in the Commons. In part it was sheer inefficiency. Already the new session had seen one mishap, when a motion made by the Opposition for the printing of the American papers was initially rejected in the Lords, accepted by the Ministry in the Commons, and then hastily revoked when it was discovered that 'this was getting into a scrape, and the worse scrape, as the Lives of some in America would be endangerd by such a publication.'[58] This lack of 'concert' and crass mismanagement was aggravated by the absurd way in which the Ministers in the Commons paid court to Pitt. The latter had now recovered his credit in the House, having 'profess'd his *submission* to the opinion of the House upon the Right to tax, because they had resolv'd it', and assisted by the subservience of Conway and Dowdeswell, 'took the directions of the proceedings upon him as if he had been in office'.[59] Finally, design may have played some part in the Ministry's readiness to alter its carefully planned schedule. The alterations were after all essentially matters of detail, and the basis of the Administration's strategy was to avoid conflict on the constitutional issues. It would have served no purpose to challenge Grenville on questions which had little to do with repeal. 'No division—Expected every minute but Min[istr]y seemed to fight off—', Newdigate noted in his diary on 5 February.[60] It is conceivable that common sense as much as cowardice dictated the apparently humiliating course which the Ministry pursued in the Commons on that day.

By Friday 7 February, when the various resolutions had been dealt with in both Houses, Grenville, 'animated with his former success',[61] might have been forgiven for feeling some complacency. The Ministry exhibited every symptom of

---

[57] Strutt MSS., Gascoyne to Strutt, 6 Feb. 1766.

[58] *Burke Correspondence*, i. 252: Burke to O'Hara, 18 [Jan. 1766]. This incident bore a remarkable similarity to the blunder in the December session. See p. 133 above.

[59] Add.MS. 35374, f. 285: J. Yorke to Hardwicke, 6 Feb. 1766; H.M.C., *Stopford-Sackville MSS.*, i. 107: Sackville to Irwin, 10 Feb. 1766.

[60] Newdigate MSS., A.7.

[61] *Cust Records*, ed. Lady E., L., and Sir J. Cust, iii. 96: Revd. R. Palmer to Revd. Dr. R. Cust, 8 Feb. 1766.

decline; it was clearly disunited and demoralized, its majority in Parliament and such solidarity as it had ever possessed had been shattered by the concerted desertion of a large section of the Court's followers, and its chosen American policy seemed about to expire conclusively and ingloriously. From the Opposition's viewpoint the moment had obviously arrived for the frontal attack with which to complete the Ministry's destruction, and Grenville and his friends had some excuse for thinking that it would be more in the nature of a *coup de grâce* than a serious contest. The occasion for the onslaught was to be a motion for a formal address to the Crown requesting the enforcement of all laws and statutes, and of course by implication the Stamp Act. Such a policy would not be inconsistent with the American resolutions passed so far, for the essence of the Administration's scheme, even before it had been altered by Parliament, had been to ensure that there was no compromise on matters of authority; and it was calculated that the Opposition could muster well over two hundred votes, almost certainly sufficient for a majority.[62] The Ministry had already been defeated in the Lords and come near to disaster in the Commons, as a result of the junction of the Opposition and the King's Friends. It was a not unreasonable assumption that the same alliance on the repeal issue would complete the process.

However the result was a great surprise. When, after a long debate, Charles Yorke moved to adjourn the Committee, a motion amounting to the rejection of Grenville's address, the event was an overwhelming victory for the Administration.

to my great astonishment [wrote Lord George Sackville] the ayes on the right were 274, noes on the left 134, majority 140. The most sanguine on our side did not expect to carry it by above seventy, because upon that division all the Bute following declared itself, ... and what was more extraordinary Mr. Grenville produced my Lord Granby, and prevailed upon him to speak in opposition, and yet with all this the minority made only 134. This event has staggered all the politicians. The stocks, which fell three or four per cent. on Wednesday, Thursday, and Fryday rose as quickly on Saturday, and the conversation is that the ministry may now stand their ground.[63]

Rockingham rejoiced at 'so compleat a day', while Newcastle was delighted with 'the greatest Day, and the most useful to

---

[62] *Walpole's Memoirs*, ii. 204; according to Walpole, Sandwich estimated the Opposition's strength at 130 and Bute's friends put their own at 80 or 90.
[63] H.M.C. *Stopford-Sackville MSS.*, i. 107: Sackville to Irwin, 10 Feb. 1766.

the publick, That I ever saw in Parliament'.[64] Evidentlv the division of 7 February in the Commons was for the Ministry as welcome as it was unexpected.

The sequel to this great victory, like so much else in this confused and distracted period, was utterly unpredictable. The Strange affair is probably the most celebrated episode in the history of the First Rockingham Administration. Fortunately there is ample evidence to reconstruct it and assess its significance. On 7 February Rockingham had had an interview with the King. After it he had told many inside and outside the Ministry that the King had authorized him to declare his support for the policy of repeal, a declaration which was accepted as authentic, until Lord Strange intervened. Strange was a strong opponent of repeal, a friend of Grenville's rather than Bute's, but none the less essentially a placeman and courtier. As Chancellor of the Duchy of Lancaster he had access to the Closet, and on Monday 10 February he was permitted by the King to state publicly that he was 'for a modification of the Act, but not for the repeal of it'.[65] Indeed Strange promptly 'came down to the Ho[use] of Commons and went about to the Members assuring them the King disapproved of the Repeal'.[66] Rockingham's reaction to news of this was one of surprise and anger. After a stormy interview with the King, in which he declared 'that He stood accus'd of having falsely stated my opinion',[67] the final outcome was a confrontation between George III, Rockingham, and Strange in the Closet to 'reconcile this seeming contradiction'.[68] In the end the honour of all three was satisfied by George III's explaining that both reports were correct so far as they went. Being against enforcement he was indeed in favour of repeal, but his own preference against either was for modification, a middle course. Rockingham produced a paper declaring 'That L[or]d Rockingham was on Friday allow'd by his Majesty to say that his Majesty was for the Repeal', to which George III agreed after adding the qualification 'the conversation having only

---

[64] *Correspondence of George III*, i. 268: Rockingham to King, 7 Feb. 1766; *Newcastle's Narrative*, p. 51; WWM.R1−579: Newcastle to Rockingham, [7 Feb. 1766].

[65] Dartmouth MSS., Dartmouth's Notebook, 12 Feb. 1766.

[66] WWM.R161−5: Lady Charlotte Wentworth's account.

[67] *Correspondence of George III*, i. 269: King's Memorandum [after 12 Feb. 1766] (*Additions and Corrections*, pp. 50−51.)

[68] Dartmouth MSS., Dartmouth's Notebook, 12 Feb. 1766.

been concerning that or enforcing'.[69] For the moment the
episode was forgotten, though later on it was to acquire great
significance. Even at the time it was described in some quarter
as 'an equivocation' and 'great Duplicity' on the King's part,[70]
but Whig historiography was to turn it into a calculated act of
hostility towards his own Ministers, a deliberate order to the
King's Friends to vote against the Administration, and even a
treacherous conspiracy to destroy the Government and set up
a new, constitutionally irresponsible Administration of Bute
and his friends, in its place.

    The substance of these allegations can be dismissed without
much difficulty. The notion that George III was plotting to
replace the Rockingham Ministry with an alliance of Grenville
and Bute is patently absurd. It is true that the air was full of
rumours of such a design, and that the Opposition entertained
high hopes of it. A whole crop of negotiations flourished in the
first fortnight of February, not because either Bute or George
was seriously interested in them, but because some of their
less scrupulous underlings were intent on giving the impression
that they were. The King's brother, the Duke of York, and his
follower Charles Cadogan, various friends of Bute, notably
Colonel Graeme and William Hamilton, and Lords Eglinton,
Denbigh, Harcourt, and Marchmont, as well as one or two of
Grenville's supporters, in particular Lord Hyde, were intriguing
to this end.[71] In every case the claims made were quite
fictitious, though Grenville, Temple, and Bedford were all
anxious to believe them. George III was approached through
Harcourt and the Duke of York but coldly rebuffed their
overtures, while the clandestine negotiation which Temple
imagined he was conducting with the Queen proved to be
illusory. The only concrete result of this welter of intrigue
was an extraordinary meeting at Eglinton House between
Bute and the Opposition leaders. Grenville and Bedford, 'as
meek as lambs', apologized for their conduct towards Bute in
1764 and 1765.[72] With some dignity Bute accepted the

[69] WWM.R161-3; inaccurately printed in Rockingham Memoirs, i. 301.
[70] Walpole Correspondence, xxii. 401: Walpole to Mann, 1 Mar. 1766; Commerce
    of Rhode Island, i. 141: H. Cruger, jun. to H. Cruger, sen. 14 Feb. 1766.
[71] For these intrigues, see Grenville Papers, iii. 353-7, 360-1, 367-73;
    Correspondence of George III, i. 271-3; Bedford Correspondence, iii. 326-9;
    J. Almon, Anecdotes of the Life of Pitt, ii. 1-6; Add.MS. 42084 (Grenville
    Papers), ff. 7-8: Grenville to Hyde, 28 Jan. 1766; Grenville (Murray) MSS.,
    Hyde to Grenville, 10 and 16 Feb. 1766, Suffolk to Grenville, 31 Jan. 1766.
[72] Bute MSS., Eglinton to J. Home, 12 Feb. 1766.

apology but refused a political alliance, insisting that he was interested in a coalition solely for the purpose of defending the Stamp Act, and the unfortunate Eglinton, the intermediary, was savaged by both sides for forming 'a language for each side from a desire of bringing them together'.[73] The net result of these negotiations, despite the efforts of historians to construe them as evidence of George III's treachery,[74] was the well-deserved ridicule which the Opposition met with for its attempts to curry favour with the object of its professed contempt and hatred. At no point in these intrigues is there a shred of evidence that the King, whose loathing for Grenville was one of the few fixed points in a fluid and unstable political scene, even considered for a moment the possibility of appealing to him for assistance.

Nor can it be said that George III set out to wreck his Ministers' American policy, though it is true that he did not agree with it.

From the first conversations on the best mode of restoring order and obedience in the American Colonys; [he afterwards wrote] I thought the modifying the Stamp Act, the wisest and most efficacious manner of proceeding; 1st, because any part remaining sufficiently ascertain'd the Right of the Mother Country to tax its Colonys and next that it would shew a desire to redress any just grievances.[75]

He had never been one of those who demanded immediate enforcement of the Stamp Act, from the beginning recommending great circumspection in what he considered to be 'undoubtedly the most serious matter that ever came before Parliament'.[76] Though by January he was convinced that modification was 'more consistent with the honour of this Country, and all the Americans would with any degree of Justice hope for',[77] he was determined that his own opinion

---

[73] Add.MS. 41355, f. 208: 'Relation of a *meeting* and *conversation* 12 Feb. 1766'. A slightly different version is in the Bute MSS.

[74] It is remarkable that the stories in the *Grenville Papers*, etc., have been swallowed even by twentieth-century historians. Thus A.S. Johnson, ('British Politics and the Repeal of the Stamp Act', *South Atlantic Quarterly*, lxii. 182–3) for example, accepts that the King was seriously negotiating with Grenville and Temple, though there is no reliable evidence to suggest that this was in fact the case.

[75] *Correspondence of George III*, i. 269: Memorandum [after 12 Feb. 1766] (*Additions and Corrections*, pp. 50–1).

[76] B.M. Egerton MS. 982, f. 12: George III to Conway, 6 Dec. 1765.

[77] *Correspondence of George III*, i. 268–9: Memorandum by King, [11 Feb. 1766] (*Additions and Corrections*, p. 51).

should not be allowed to influence Parliament's verdict, and
equally that no Member of Parliament should be punished for
voting either with or against his Ministers. Repeated attempts
by the Opposition to enlist his cooperation failed totally.
Thus the Duke of York was told 'I do not think it Constitutional for the Crown personaly to interfere in Measures
which it has thought proper to refer to the advice of Parliament',[78] while Harcourt, as was noted in Grenville's Diary,
learned that

he was strenuously for supporting and asserting the right of Great
Britain to impose the tax, was against the repeal of the Bill, but thought
it could perhaps be modified . . . Lord Harcourt suggested at a distance
that His Majesty might make these his sentiments known, which might
prevent the repeal of the Act . . . The King seemed averse to that, said
he would never influence people in their parliamentary opinions, and
that he had promised to support his Ministers.[79]

In so far as George III departed from this position at all, it
was not to encourage the opposition of the King's Friends,
but to assist the Ministry. Though he consistently refused to
dismiss members for voting against Government, he was
personally prepared to countenance the possibility of a repeal
and even to urge supporters of the Court to do the same. Thus
he reported on 21 January to Rockingham, 'Talbot is as right
as I can desire, in the Stamp Act—strong for our declaring our
right, but willing to repeal.'[80] Again in an interview with
Newcastle on 5 February, when questioned as to his own
views on the Stamp Act, he assured the Duke, 'I am; I was
always against enforcing it, I have thought some middle way
might be taken, but I am now convinced that nothing but the
repeal will do',[81] and when Newcastle urged him to tell his
servants this, he replied 'he had done so. "But what can I say
when they tell me they can't in conscience vote for the
Repeal?" '[82]

In all this, George III's concept of his duty was perfectly
proper, and indeed verged on the platitudinous. The doctrine
that the Crown is required by the constitution to support its

[78] Ibid. i. 273: 18 Feb. 1766.   [79] Grenville Papers, iii. 353: 31 Jan. 1766.
[80] Rockingham Memoirs, i. 271–2: King to Rockingham, [21 Jan. 1766].
[81] Dartmouth MSS., Dartmouth's Notebook, 12 Feb. 1766. It may seem perverse
to employ Dartmouth's rather than Newcastle's account (see below) but the
former was written soon after the event, whereas Newcastle did not record it
until 27 February.
[82] Newcastle's Narrative, p. 50.

servants in all their measures had no place in the eighteenth century. All that can be argued against George III is that in permitting Lord Strange to declare his opinion publicly he departed from the standards he had set himself.[83] Yet he did so only in the conviction that that opinion had already been misused by his Ministers. Strange exploited this belief to the maximum, assuring him that 'it was currently reported that in all cases I was for the Repeal'.[84] Where the truth lies in this matter is not easily ascertained. George III's own view of the Stamp Act problem—he disliked enforcement, would accept repeal, but personally favoured modification—was quite coherent, but capable of varied interpretations. Doubtless Rockingham stressed the King's readiness to endorse repeal, and Strange his preference for modification. The former may possibly have been somewhat disingenuous, and certainly used as evidence of George III's support for repeal a letter which by no means sustained his claim.[85] On the other hand, Strange was unquestionably mischievous. Having failed with his friends in the Commons to carry the policy of enforcement on 7 February, he did his utmost to wreck the Administration's programme by playing on the King's desire for modification. In any event it was not George III who was guilty of misconduct. For him this period was one of intense anxiety and stress—on 2 February, for example, he was reported as being 'in a good deal of agitation, and burst out into an expression before the physicians, saying he was willing to do anything for the good of his people, if they would but agree among themselves.'[86] This was not the picture of a King coolly plotting the destruction of his Ministers and their policies, but of a conventional and conscientious monarch all but overwhelmed by the difficulties which beset him. It is difficult in such circumstances to convict him of anything worse than an 'unintentional indiscretion'.[87]

---

[83] It may also be pointed out that in 1763 and 1764 George III had flung himself without reservation into the defence of General Warrants, even insisting on the dismissal of Conway and other army officers for their voting in Parliament. On the other hand, this is a double-edged argument; Rockingham and his friends were in 1766 demanding a degree of intervention from the Crown which they had strongly condemned two years earlier.

[84] *Correspondence of George III*, i. 269: King's Memorandum, [after 12 Feb. 1766] (*Additions and Corrections*, pp. 50–1).

[85] Ibid. i. 270.   [86] *Grenville Papers*, iii. 357: Grenville Diary, 2 Feb. 1766.

[87] I.R. Christie, *Crisis of Empire* (London, 1966), p. 64.

Strictly speaking the historical importance of the Strange affair is slight, for it had remarkably little effect on the outcome of the Stamp Act crisis. It is of course true that great play was made with the King's name. 'Both sides give out that the King's opinion goes with them', Sackville wrote on 11 February,[88] and indeed there were considerable hopes of this manoeuvre. According to David Hume, Rockingham's publication of George III's views on 7 February 'was understood to be a general declaration in favour of his Ministers, and brought them an accession of force'.[89] Similarly, after Strange's attempt to reverse this impression, James West assured Newcastle that 'The Report of a Great Person having this day told Lord Strange, his Opinion was against the repeal, does Infinite damage in the City and in the House'.[90] However the ultimate result of the confrontation between Rockingham and Strange, and George III's efforts to square them, seems to have been to neutralize the King's opinion as a factor in the decision of Parliament. 'Many who would wish to know the King's secret wishes, and act accordingly', William Rouet remarked, 'are quite puzzled what to believe', while Hume wrote of 'men uncertain which was the surest way of paying court to his Majesty. Some wags have remarked that the Bench of Bishops itself was obliged to vote according to conscience, for want of better direction'.[91] On the whole it seems likely that George III's earnest desire that Parliament's conduct should not be affected by his views was gratified, if in rather unexpected fashion. The Ministers themselves were certainly not too dismayed by the Strange episode, Newcastle remarking that 'the Explanations come out Tolerably well; ... Thus it now stands; His Majesty seemingly in good Humour with us all.'[92]

This is not to argue of course that there was no opposition among supporters of the Court to the Administration's American policy after the Strange affair. On the contrary the revolt of the King's Friends which had developed in the first week of February, first in the Anstruther division, then in the

---

[88] H.M.C. *Stopford-Sackville MSS.*, i. 108: Sackville to Irwin, 10, 11 Feb. 1766.
[89] *Letters of David Hume*, ed. J.Y.T. Greig, ii. 20: Hume to Hertford, 27 Feb. 1766
[90] Add.MS. 32973, f. 411: [11 Feb. 1766].
[91] *Caldwell Papers*, Part ii, vol. ii, p. 73: W. Rouet to Mure, 18 Feb. 1766; *Letters of David Hume*, ed. J.Y.T. Greig, ii. 18: Hume to Hertford, 27 Feb. 1766.
[92] Add.MS. 32974, ff. 5–6: Newcastle to Archbishop of Canterbury, 15 Feb. 1766.

Lords' Committee, and finally on Grenville's motion to enforce the Stamp Act on 7 February, continued as the struggle for repeal evolved. There were three major divisions in the Commons on the repeal issue, on 22 and 24 February and 4 March, and one in the Lords, on 11 March, and in all of these there was a pronounced desertion from the ranks of those who normally voted with the Court.[93] Its precise extent is a matter for debate. Hardwicke stated flatly that '*half the Court at* least voted in opposition to administration',[94] a verdict with which most 'Old Whigs' agreed. Yet Grafton, writing long after the event, remarked that, although 'the Repeal of the Stamp Act went heavily down with those, who passed under the denomination of *king's friends*; . . . most of them voted for the Repeal', and recent historians have not been wanting to endorse this view.[95] On the evidence of the voting lists it is indisputable that a large number of placemen did consistently oppose repeal. Newcastle drew up a list of 52 in the Commons and 19 in the Lords,[96] though this is a rough starting point rather than a definitive total, since, as always in such problems, there are awkward difficulties of classification. However, allowing for these difficulties, it is clear that roughly a third of the Court's placemen voted against repeal. This was scarcely enough to justify Horace Walpole's view that George III's informing the King's Friends that 'they *were at liberty to vote against him and keep their places,* . . . was, in effect, ordering his servants to oppose his Ministers',[97] but it was a considerable number by any standards. While the Court and Treasury men were not expected in the eighteenth century to be lobby-fodder, such a concerted defection was most unusual. Even given the fact that the Stamp Act presented a clearer issue of principle than perhaps any problem since the Hanoverian Accession, and even given the confusion of politics in general in the 1760s, it quite clearly represented a major rebellion by placemen.

On the whole the 'Government side of the Administration, largely staffed by 'Old Whigs', was predictably loyal to

[93] For the voting lists on the Stamp Act issue, see Appendix B.
[94] Add.MS. 35428, f. 26: Hardwicke's 'Private Memoirs'.
[95] *Grafton Autobiography*, pp. 68–9; C.R. Ritcheson, *British Politics and the American Revolution*, p. 61.
[96] The list is printed in D.A. Winstanley, *Personal and Party Government* (Cambridge, 1910), appendix iii.
[97] *Walpole's Memoirs*, ii. 183.

Rockingham. Lord Barrington, the Secretary at War, two or three members of the Board of Trade retained from Grenville's regime, and the Ordnance Board under Granby's leadership, all opposed repeal, but for the most part the opposition came from other quarters. Especially noticeable were the military men with regiments, of whom a dozen opposed the Administration, and above all the Household officers, men who held sinecures on a fairly long tenure. Both masters of hounds, the Treasurer of the Chamber, the Comptroller of the Household, the Chamberlain of the Exchequer, and Chancellor of the Duchy of Lancaster, the Captain of the Band of Gentlemen Pensioners, no less than six Lords of the Bedchamber and two Grooms, as well as the entire Queen's Household, all voted either in the Lords or Commons, in opposition to the King's Ministers. In short the revolt was essentially of those described by Lauchlin Macleane as the 'Butean Part of the Administration',[98] the men who had in the early sixties acquired so many of the Court's offices, and who had survived the fall of Grenville to remain under Rockingham. Many were Scots, most well-known friends of Bute, and almost all career placemen and minor politicians.

It is quite unnecessary to resort to the influence of the Crown to explain this defection. It was after all a continuation of the revolt which had been building up in the previous months and which stemmed from the deep division between the two component parts of the Administration. As the repeal issue evolved, it was clearly augmented by other factors. One was obviously conscience. The voting of Lord Barrington and Lord George Sackville, for example, was probably not political. Neither had voted for Grenville's motion to enforce the Stamp Act on 7 February, yet both felt compelled to oppose outright repeal. Some of Bute's close friends also felt quite genuinely on this issue. 'People will not be brought to give up the sovereignty of this Kingdom, either to please Mr. Pitt or follow the desire of Ministers', declared Gilbert Elliot,[99] and indeed there is no need to question the sincerity of men like Dyson and Oswald, however inflexible and conservative their thinking. Still more crucial was Bute's own attitude. His views on this question were simple to the point of bigotry. He was wholly convinced both of the legality and expediency of the

[98] Add.MS. 30869, f. 16: Macleane to Wilkes, 22 Jan. 1766.
[99] G.F.S. Elliot, *Border Elliots*, pp. 398–9: to Sir Gilbert Elliot, 27 Jan. 1766.

Stamp Act, which had first been seriously mooted during his Ministry, and he insisted that the only alternative to its enforcement was to 'sit tamely by and see our country, this great Empire crumble into pieces'.[100] Nor did he hesitate to declare these views, first to his friends, and then publicly in the House of Lords on 6 February. He must have known that his conduct would have an influence on events. It is no coincidence that the section of the Administration which voted against repeal was precisely that associated with Bute's name, and many of those were Scots. Given his own attitude and conduct, the discontents of the King's Friends, and the important issues of conscience raised by the Stamp Act crisis, it is most unlikely that even an unequivocal and vigorous declaration by George III would have altered their voting.

Less surprising than the courtiers' championship of the Stamp Act was the fact that repeal was carried despite it. 'What made this more Extraordinary', Holland remarked of the key division of 22 February, 'is, that all Lord Butes Friends, almost every Scotch Man, and many Country Gentlemen, were in the Minority.'[101] The triumph of repeal had not of course been inevitable after the defeat of Grenville's address on 7 February. It was not the case that the rejection of enforcement automatically entailed repeal, despite Conway's belief on 13 February that 'our disposition for it is too strong in the House of Commons for *anything now to conquer*'.[102] Modification, as the King's Friends, and Lord Strange in particular, appreciated, was still a possibility. None the less the confidence of the Ministry proved to be justified. After a further fortnight of debate and discussion, the crucial division on a resolution in Committee to repeal the Stamp Act, in the early hours of Saturday 22 February, was carried by 275 votes to 167. This was reaffirmed by a majority of 107 when the resolution was reported to the House on 24 February, and again after a bill to this end was brought in by one of 124 votes on the third reading on 4 March. These majorities were indeed remarkable given the

---

[100] Bute MSS., 'Heads I intended to have used on the Debate on the Resolutions, 1766, but did not'.
[101] Add.MS. 51406, f. 132: Holland to J. Campbell, 25 Feb. 1766.
[102] *Companion to the Newspaper* (1835) p. 366: Conway to Hertford, 13 Feb. 1766.

opposition of 'Lord Bute's friends, Mr. Grenville's party and the rank Tories'.[103] The attitude of the last, when first registered in the division of 7 February on Grenville's motion to enforce the Stamp Act, had seemed particularly ominous. It was to be expected that the formal Grenville-Bedford Opposition would vote against repeal, and it had equally to be recognized that Bute's connections would do so. But the opposition of the Tories was disturbing. Some forty of them voted against repeal on 22 February, a remarkably solid performance, given the fact that most of the 113 Tories identified by Namier in the 1761 Parliament,[104] had either died or dispersed among the political parties by 1766. During the 1760s the old Tory party was rapidly disintegrating—many joined the followings of Bute, Grenville, Bedford, Rockingham or Pitt, and the remainder were gradually absorbed into the ranks of the independent country gentlemen, from whom by the 1770s they were quite indistinguishable. But those who still liked, rather anachronistically, to call themselves Tories, men like Sir Roger Newdigate, M.P. for Oxford University, or knights of the shire like Sir James Dashwood, Sir Armine Wodehouse, and Sir John Hynde Cotton, were not prepared to compromise on the colonial issue, whatever the pressures. 'Country party' men under the first two Hanoverians, they were none the less unashamedly authoritarian in their imperial attitudes, and it was one of the more bizarre consequences of the repeal of the Stamp Act that it provoked the final, and appropriately futile, convulsion of eighteenth-century Toryism as a distinct force.

Fortunately the Tories were not typical of Independents in general, for it is perfectly clear, despite the absence of voting lists for the majority in the repeal divisions, that a very large number of Independents cast a solid vote of support for the Administration's American policy. Nothing else could account for a majority of over 100 in a very full House with heavy Court defections. In the most general terms the Commons comprised about 350 M.P.s with some degree of political motivation, either as career placemen or 'politicians' currently in government and opposition, and some 200

---

[103] 'Ryder Diaries', *Camden Miscellany*, xxiii. 318: from a letter of Sir William Meredith, read in the Commons on 4 Mar. 1766.

[104] Sir L. Namier, *England in the Age of the American Revolution* (2nd ed., London, 1961), Appendix A.

Independents. Of the former, about 130 voted against repeal. Even if the remainder (220) all supported the Ministry—in fact many must have been absent—it would have required a considerable degree of Independent assistance to bring the Administration's total to 275. It is that factor that resolves the apparent contradiction between the division of 31 January when the Ministry had come near to defeat, and those on repeal in which it was overwhelmingly successful. The Anstruther election was the last kind of issue to attract the interest of Independents, so that voting was confined largely to the 'politicians'. The repeal divisions on the other hand were of altogether more importance, and the weight which the Independents threw into the balance turned it heavily in favour of the Administration. The significance of this unexpected flood of support from the politically uncommitted was not lost on the Ministers. '*Our* majority', George Onslow wrote to Newcastle, 'consists *now* of Men not to be wrought upon',[105] while Rockingham boasted to the King within hours of the critical division, 'it is a Confirmation that the Opinion he had humbly submitted to his Majesty was well founded in point of Publick Opinion.'[106] If nothing else this is eloquent testimony to the relative impartiality of the eighteenth-century Commons, and demonstrates the absurdity of the charge of corruptibility. Those who might be considered most open to the 'influence of the Crown', the placemen, proved exceptionally unreliable in this instance, while those who were immune to the power of corruption rescued the Administration from disaster. This indeed is the central problem in the passing of the repeal of the Stamp Act; what persuaded so many Independents, who had no interest in political or personal profit, 'so grossly', as one of their opponents put it, to 'Change their late opinion'?[107]

It is most unlikely that the answer to this question lies in the great set-piece debates in the Commons. For the most part the arguments expressed there were exceedingly stereotyped and repetitive. They had already been rehearsed in countless pamphlets and papers, and were not noticeably improved by their airing at Westminster. 'Every point now turns immediately into something American',[108] wrote John Yorke after

105 Add.MS. 32974, f. 71: Onslow to Newcastle, 23 Feb. 1766.
106 *Correspondence of George III*, i. 275.
107 Add.MS. 42084, f. 21: A. Hervey to Grenville, 3 Mar. 1766.
108 Add.MS. 35374, f. 286: J. Yorke to Hardwicke, 14 Feb. 1766.

a debate on army estimates had been used to discuss the
Stamp Act, and it was scarcely surprising that many began to
find the arguments tedious. 'Mr. Burke', the young William
Baker remarked after the debate of 24 February, 'was the
only man who could keep up the attention of the House on
a subject already threadbare', while Burke himself recorded
of the debate on the third reading of the repeal bill, that
'The house was teezed to Death and heard nobody willingly.'[109]
The debating strategy of both Administration and Opposition
was simple enough. The essence of the Ministry's approach
throughout had been to concede everything demanded in
terms of constitutional rights, in order to clear the way for a
repeal based on expediency. The King's Speech and Address
of 14 January, the rejection of the Stamp Act Congress's
petitions on 27 January, the elaborate series of resolutions
condemning the colonists' activities, and above all the
resolution which was to become the Declaratory Act, all
were intended to pave the way for what Newcastle called
'the immediate Repeal of The Stamp Act; not as an Illegal
Act; But, as the most Imprudent, and pernicious One, That
ever was made'.[110]

Against this the Opposition was concerned to treat the
repeal of the Stamp Act as a purely constitutional question—
to describe it as a 'glaring absurdity'[111] to declare a right
while repealing its only legislative application, to point out
that 'the disgrace of departing from the inforcing the laws by
constraint, and by open rebellion of the Colonists, can't be
wiped off by the power of any words whatsoever',[112] to
insist that the Americans were seeking not the redress of
specific grievances but ultimate independence, and to prophesy
that repeal would merely encourage them to make new
demands. The sole object urged by the Opposition was the
submission of the Americans—'the Palladium', Bedford
called it, 'which if suffered to be removed, puts a final period

[109] 'William Baker's Account of the Debate on the Repeal of the Stamp Act',
    ed. D.H. Watson, *William and Mary Quarterly*, 3rd Ser., xxvi (1969), 262;
    Burke Correspondence, i. 241: Burke to O'Hara, 1, 4 Mar. 1766.
[110] Add.MS. 32973, f. 342: Newcastle to Secker, 2 Feb. 1766.
[111] Bedford MSS., liii. f. 18: a paper of about Feb. 1766 in Bedford's hand. The
    Opposition held meetings to marshal its arguments at Halifax's house on
    24 Jan., and at the Star and Garter on the 29th (Bedford MSS., liii. ff. 14–15,
    22–3).
[112] Bedford MSS., liii. f. 14: Bedford, 'Thoughts on the Proper Manner',
    24 Jan. 1766.

to the British Empire in America'[113] —and the sole solution suggested was the enforcement of the Stamp Act, 'with this Argument, that since you snarle and begin to shew your Teeth, they ought to be knocked out before you are able to bite'.[114] This was the essence of the arguments employed in the debates on the imperial problem, the framework on which the 79 speakers in those debates, all but a handful of them committed party politicians, hung their remarks.[115] It was obviously important to state the different viewpoints clearly, but it can hardly be maintained that they were decisive as such. It was evidence, not argument, that was responsible for what Bamber Gascoyne described as 'such an alteration in men's minds'.[116] The Administration had hit on a formula acceptable to the House, provided it could demonstrate that the Stamp Act was as damaging from the purely British point of view as it was for the colonies. In consequence the decisive battle was fought not in the drama of debate but during the examination of evidence and witnesses to the effects of the Act. It was this battle, notable for what Charles Garth described as 'the very great Attention and minute Enquiry which has been had and given upon this Occasion in the House of Commons',[117] which it was the Administration's concern to win.

To a great extent the Ministry's task had been eased in advance by the change wrought in the climate of opinion in which the legislature found itself considering a course of action. If it is true that the initial reaction in England to news of the disturbances in America had been one of intense hostility, it is also the case that by February 1766 public opinion appeared to be overwhelmingly in favour of repeal. The immense flood of propaganda poured out with the active connivance of the Ministry had had an undoubted impact.

---

[113] Bedford MSS., liii. f. 14: Bedford, 'Thoughts on the Proper Manner', 24 Jan. 1766.
[114] *Commerce of Rhode Island*, i. 141: H. Cruger, jun. to H. Cruger, sen. 14 Feb. 1766.
[115] The breakdown of the 79 speakers is as follows: 9 Grenvilles, 8 Bedfords, 7 Pittites, 10 Independents (including 3 Tories), 16 King's Friends, 29 Administration.
[116] Strutt MSS., Gascoyne to Strutt, 8 Feb. 1766.
[117] 'Stamp Act Papers', *Maryland Hist. Mag.*, vi. 304: Garth to Tilghman, etc. 5 Mar. 1766.

Pamphlets, newspapers, petitions, even cartoons,[118] had been employed by the merchants on the one hand and the Ministry on the other, to influence opinion. Pitt's declaration in support of repeal and the Administration's readiness to satisfy all scruples on the score of rights had assisted this development. 'The Vox Populi', wrote Henry Cruger on 14 February, 'now begins to gain ground, and I think since the Legality of Taxation is allowed, the Act will be repeal'd upon the Grounds of *Expediency*', while Richard Champion, another Bristol merchant, thought that 'Out of Doors the whole Kingdom seem to be united upon the same Sentiment'.[119] This extraordinary turnabout was bound to have its effect at Westminster. Indeed, according to Hume, the pressure was so great that some of the King's Friends, 'voted against the repeal but from party and in full hopes and confidence of being out-voted. Some have confessed it to me'.[120]

However the main emphasis must be on the efforts made to pressurize M.P.s and peers directly. For Ministers who had a reputation (which they posthumously retain) for being ineffectual, Rockingham and his friends showed unexpected efficiency in organizing this campaign. From the beginning they had worked in harness with the merchants' petitioning movement; in the critical period of January-February 1766, Ministers, merchants, American agents and experts, all joined in the attempt to ensure the maximum impact for their case in Parliament. For example, Samuel Garbett, the Birmingham industrialist, circularized Staffordshire and Warwickshire peers and M.P.s with long and detailed accounts of the plight of the local economy as a result of the Stamp Act crisis.[121] Henry Cruger was also very busy. 'I was three Weeks in London', he later wrote to his father, 'and every Day with some one Member of Parliament, talking as it were for my

[118] See D. Adair, 'The Stamp Act in Contemporary English Cartoons', *William and Mary Quarterly*, 3rd Ser., x (1953), 538—42; M.D. George, 'America in English Satirical Prints', *William and Mary Quarterly*, 3rd Ser., x (1953), 517—18.

[119] *Rhode Island Commerce*, i. 142: Cruger to H. Cruger, sen., 14 Feb. 1766; *The American Correspondence of a Bristol Merchant, 1766-1776*, ed. G.H. Guttridge (Univ. of California Pubs. in Hist., xxii. 1934), p.11: Champion to C. Lloyd, 15 Feb. 1766.

[120] *Letters of David Hume*, ed. J.Y.T. Greig, ii. 20—1: Hume to Hertford, 27 Feb. 1766.

[121] Fitzwilliam MSS., A. xxvi. 18: Copies of letters to Barré, Newdigate, J. Mordaunt, Denbigh, Shelburne, Sir C. Mordaunt, and Dartmouth, 5-13 Feb. 1766.

own Life. it is surprising how ignorant some of them are of *Trade* and *America*.'[122] Similarly, William Strahan's account of Benjamin Franklin's activities commented that

the assiduity of our friend Dr. Franklin is really astonishing. He is forever with one Member of Parliament or other (most of whom by the bye seem to have been deplorably ignorant with regard to the Nature and Consequence of the Colonies) . . . This is the most necessary and essential Service he could possibly perform on this Occasion; and so effectually hath he done this, and I will venture to say, he hath thrown so much Light upon the Subject, that if the Legislature doth not now give you ample redress, it is not for want of the fullest and most distinct Information in respect of the real Merits of the Case.[123]

Of course the main effort took place in the Commons' Committee of the Whole House on the American Papers. Twenty-two witnesses gave evidence in favour of repeal. On 31 January, four victims of the American riots had testified to the violence of the disturbances in the colonies, and the remainder were heard, once the constitutional questions had been resolved, on the consequences of the Stamp Act: three London merchants prominent in the American trade on 11 February, three Americans with some knowledge of commerce as well as six manufacturers from the English provinces on the following day, and on 13 February, three merchants from the outports, two manufacturers, a goldsmith, and quite unclassifiably, the celebrated Franklin.

The Ministers obviously chose these witnesses with great care, though occasionally they met with difficulties. For example, Garbett, who had throughout played a major part in the campaign in the Midlands, told Dartmouth that he 'should with great reluctance attend the House of Commons upon the Plan your Lordship mentions or be Instrumental in Occasioning any of my Neighbours to Attend'.[124] However there was no shortage of witnesses. Fifty-three were ordered to attend the Commons' Committee, though of course some were summoned by the Opposition, and in any case less than half were actually examined at the Bar. The basis of this selection was obviously to demonstrate the unanimity not

[122] *Commerce of Rhode Island*, i. 139: 14 Feb. 1766.
[123] 'Correspondence between Strahan and Hall', *Pennsylvania Mag.*, x. 92: 11 Jan. 1766; see also, E. Wolf, 'Benjamin Franklin's Stamp Act Cartoon', *Proceedings of Am. Philosophical Soc.*, xcix (1955), 388–96.
[124] Fitzwilliam MSS., A.xxvi. 18: [Garbett] to Dartmouth, 9 Feb. 1766. Garbett seems the most likely author of this letter, which exists only in the form of a copy in the hand of Joseph Harrison.

merely of the Americans but, far more important, of the British merchants and manufacturers in their opposition to the Stamp Act. Already the Commons had been subjected to a carefully marshalled onslaught of twenty-seven petitions from the trading and manufacturing towns,[125] and now the impression of an economy under siege was to be driven home by viva voce evidence from all quarters. Various friends of the Ministry in the Commons were apparently allotted specific tasks to ensure that when the witnesses were questioned in Committee the maximum effect would be achieved. For example, Sir George Savile was active in coordinating the evidence of the West Riding textile manufacturers with whom he was well acquainted, and the copious lists of prearranged questions which he drew up with them still survive.[126] Burke directed the activities of the merchants of Lancaster and Glasgow and manufacturers of Birmingham,[127] while Sir William Meredith dealt among others with the Liverpool representatives.[128] Richard Jackson methodically rehearsed with William Kelly, a New York merchant, the questions he was to ask him in the House,[129] and Barlow Trecothick, whose role was probably more important than that of any other witness, was equally well-prepared. The questions he was asked were based on his own paper 'Proofs and Observations on Allegations in the London Merchants' Petition';[130] and when he was examined in the Commons, West reported to Newcastle that he 'stated every thing as he did to your Grace this morning'.[131] Naturally the Opposition did all in its power to reduce the impact and credibility of the witnesses— apparently the procedure was for alternate questions from each side, with Conway and Grenville taking the lead; but as little as possible was left to chance, and the result was impressive

[125] See D.H. Watson, 'Barlow Trecothick and Other Associates of Lord Rockingham', pp. 40–2, for the organized presentation of the petitions.
[126] WWM.R42–5 to R42–12. Savile's friend David Hartley also helped to organize the Yorkshire campaign (Berkshire Record Office, Hartley MSS., 0.19: Hartley to ?, 7 Feb. 1766).
[127] *Burke Correspondence*, i. 235; Fitzwilliam MSS., A.xxv. 79: Burke, notes: 'Names to the Birmingham Petition'.
[128] WWM.R42–2, 3, 4: 'Minutes of Evidence from Sir William Meredith'; Bk. 1–44: Meredith to Burke, 1 Jan. 1766.
[129] WWM.R96–11, 12: 'Papers relating to the Questions that Mr. *Jackson* asked Mr. *Kelly*'; a number of draft questions with answers.
[130] WWM.R57–2. The petition itself is at WWM.R57–1.
[131] Add.MS. 32973, f. 411: West to Newcastle, [11 Feb. 1766]: Franklin was similarly prepared; see *Papers of Franklin*, ed. L.W. Labaree, xiii. 129.

Thanks to the preservation of the written record of the viva voce evidence,[132] it is possible to be certain of the principal considerations which interested the Committee of the Whole House in its examination of witnesses. There can be little question that the emphasis was on the damage done to the British economy by the Stamp Act and its repercussions. Recently some weight has been attributed to the military and diplomatic factors—the expense and difficulty of reducing the Americans to submission by force, and the threat of Bourbon intervention in any Anglo-American conflict, a view which apparently rests primarily on some remarks made by Conway in his speeches of 7 and 21 February.[133] But Conway's allusions to the problems of imperial strategy must be seen in the context of long perorations largely concerned with the economic aspects. Indeed, in his great speech of 21 February, they were apparently so insignificant that some of those who reported the debate and speech made no note of them.[134] Beyond this there is in any case little to suggest that the military and diplomatic considerations had any influence. One or two questions were asked of the American witnesses as to the military potential of the colonists, though very little attention or emphasis was bestowed upon the subject. It would be surprising if the contrary were the case. A few years after Bourbon power had been shattered by English arms, and over a decade before it was demonstrated how formidable American antagonists could be, Englishmen were not likely to be impressed by such an argument, and tended to agree with Pitt's assertion that if necessary, 'the force of this country can crush America to atoms'.[135] That it was a minor

---

[132] The official record, which bears witness to the inability of the clerks to keep pace with the speakers, is to be found at Add.MS. 33030, ff. 78–203 and WWM.R27. Other sources for the evidence are 'Ryder Diaries', *Camden Miscellany*, xxiii. 291–302; *Commerce of Rhode Island*, i. 139–40; Add.MS. 32973, f. 411: West to Newcastle, [11 Feb. 1766]; Newdigate MSS., B2545–15, 16, 17, 18, 19, 20, 21, 22: Newdigate's notes. A useful analysis of the evidence is in B.R. Smith, 'The Committee of the Whole House to Consider the American Papers'.

[133] L.H. Gibson, 'The Great Debate in the Committee of the Whole House of Commons on the Stamp Act 1766, as reported by Nathaniel Ryder', *Pennsylvania Magazine of Hist. and Biog.*, lxxxvi (1962), 40–1; also L.H. Gipson, *The British Empire before the American Revolution* (Caldwell and New York, 1937–), x. 408–9.

[134] Add.MS. 32974, f. 45: West to Newcastle, 21 Feb. 1766; *Cust Records*, edd. Lady E., L., and Sir J. Cust, iii. 96.

[135] Pitt's speech of 14 Jan. as reported in *Universal Magazine*, xxxviii 248.

consideration which needed stating may be conceded. That it
was the critical one is suggested neither by the evidence of
the debates, nor the observations of contemporaries.

The primary concern of the Administration was to demonstrate, in Newcastle's words, 'That the Interest, and The very
being of This Country, as a Trading Nation, depends upon
The immediate Repeal of The Stamp Act'.[136] Of course much
of the evidence was concerned necessarily with the situation
in America, though the Ministry vainly attempted to limit
the scope of the enquiry to safer topics.[137] The inability of
the colonists to pay the sums required by the Stamp Tax, the
total unacceptability of modifying as opposed to repealing
the Stamp Act, and the certainty of a grateful submission to
British authority on the part of the Americans once repeal
had been obtained—these points were driven home time and
time again by the American witnesses despite strenuous
efforts by the Opposition to demolish them. Franklin was
particularly useful in this respect. His knowledge of American
conditions and his skill in evading the attempts of the Opposition's questioners to trap him into expressing constitutionally
subversive doctrines made a considerable impact. Rockingham
himself apparently attributed great weight to Franklin's
testimony.

To this very Examination, [Strahan wrote to his partner in Philadelphia]
more than to anything else, you are indebted to the *speedy* and *total*
Repeal of this odious Law. The Marquis of Rockingham told a Friend
of mine a few Days after, That he never knew Truth make so great a
Progress in so very short a Time. From that very Day, the *Repeal* was
generally and absolutely determined, all that passed afterwards being
only mere Form.[138]

This was probably something of an exaggeration, and indeed
it is possible that the publication of Franklin's evidence and
the predominance of the constitutional issue in the later
stages of the American Revolution have bestowed on his

[136] Add.MS. 32973, f. 342: Newcastle to Archbishop of Canterbury, 2 Feb. 1766.

[137] Meredith's motion to this effect on 11 February was negatived (Add.MS.
32973, f. 411: West to Newcastle, [11 Feb. 1766]).

[138] 'Letters between William Strahan and David Hall', *Pennsylvania Mag.*, x. 220–1
10 May 1766.

role rather more significance than it strictly merited.[139]
The essential task was to prove that, quite apart from other
considerations, purely British interests were at stake, and this
was achieved not by Franklin, but by Trecothick and his
friends.

Most of the witnesses were British merchants and manufacturers, who had first to paint a dire picture of home industry
and commerce, and secondly to establish that it was Grenville's
American legislation, and in particular the Stamp Act, that
was to blame. Six merchants, Trecothick, Hanbury, and
Mildred from London, Glassford from Glasgow, Reeve from
Bristol, and Halliday from Liverpool, all testified to the
drastic decline of the American trade in 1765, the refusal of
their colonial colleagues to place orders until the Stamp Act
had been repealed, the huge British debts tied up in the
colonies at the mercy of the insurgents,[140] and in general the
prospect of a total collapse of Anglo-American commerce
unless the colonists' grievances were redressed. Equally
significant were the testimonies of the manufacturers, no less
than eight of them, representing the key industrial centres of
Manchester, Leeds, Bradford, Nottingham, and Leicester, as
well as London. Again their reports of a major slump and
chronic unemployment in the manufacturing trades were
carefully linked to the cessation of orders from America, so
that the clear impression was gained of an almost catastrophic
economic crisis directly caused by the colonial disturbances.
What must finally have decided the issue was Grenville's total
failure to reverse this impression when he called his own
witnesses on 17 and 18 February. The only authority he was
able to summon on the colonial trade was Richard Oswald,
who, it transpired, had abandoned his American business

---

[139] For the examination, which was later printed, see *Papers of Franklin*, ed.
L.W. Labaree, xiii. 124–62. Though the most quoted point made by Franklin
is the celebrated distinction between internal and external taxes, the most
influential was probably his insistence that modification of the Stamp Act,
the only alternative by this stage to repeal, would be totally repugnant to the
colonists. For the impression made by his testimony on this matter, see
Caldwell Papers, part ii, vol. ii, pp. 72–5, and for the problem of Franklin's
role in general, B.R. Smith, 'The Committee of the Whole House to Consider
the American Papers', p. 275.

[140] Much was and is made of the importance of these debts (see, e.g., E.G. Evans,
'Planter Indebtedness and the Coming of the Revolution in Virginia', *William
and Mary Quarterly*, 3rd ser., xix (1962), 511–33). It must be stressed
however that their influence lay less in affecting the Commons than in moving
the merchants to press for a repeal campaign in the first place.

some twelve years previously in favour of government con-
tracting in Germany. In the course of the interrogation, his
complete ignorance of current American affairs was exposed
and his testimony utterly demolished by the Administration's
questioners. He was dismissed with the withering question:
'When you was a Contractor in Germany and wanted Flour
in a distant Country did you enquire of the Price of it from
a Person who had not been in that Country for twelve years.'[1]
For the rest Grenville seems to have been concerned partly to
exculpate himself from the charge that his customs reforms
had been responsible for wrecking the Spanish bullion trade
in the West Indies,[142] and partly to play for time. His patent
inability to produce any expert evidence on his side greatly
enhanced the impact of the testimonies procured by the
Administration.

That the commercial consideration was the decisive one
in the ultimate triumph of the campaign for repeal can scarcely
be doubted. According to Horace Walpole 'it was the clamour
of trade, of the merchants, and of the manufacturing towns,
that had borne down all opposition',[143] and his verdict must
be confirmed by the historian. But it must not be assumed
that the Commons were motivated in their decision simply
by a concern for the merchants in particular, or the economic
plight of the country in general. One of the topics raised in
the Committee had a significance which went beyond the
purely economic. This was the unemployment which was
said to be a product of the Stamp Act crisis, a matter on
which many witnesses were most emphatic. For example,
Robert Hamilton, a Manchester fustian manufacturer,
claimed to have laid off some 2400 workmen; William Reeve,
the leader of the Bristol merchants, spoke of heavy unemployment among the West Country nailmakers, and Benjamin
Farrer of the West Riding testified to the dismissal of thirty
per cent of the labour force of his district.[144] A Cheapside
shoemaker connected with Trecothick, one John Hose, was
trapped by an Opposition questioner into the unfortunate
admission that he thought boots and shoes bore a Stamp duty.[145]

[141] Add.MS. 33030, f. 200.
[142] *Chatham Correspondence*, ii. 387; Grenville called seven witnesses on 17 and
   18 February. The evidence for the 18th is not in the official record, but some
   of it was noted by Newdigate (Newdigate MSS., B. 2545—15).
[143] *Walpole Memoirs*, ii. 211—12.
[144] Add.MS. 33030, ff. 154, 151, 145.   [145] Ibid., f. 180.

But this transparent ignorance merely added point to the patent honesty and therefore effect of his testimony—that he had turned off all but 45 of his 300 workmen and that he had done so because Trecothick's American orders had suddenly dried up. The corollary of this anxiety about unemployment was concern about the American industrial potential, and the determination of the colonists to manufacture for themselves the goods, which they declined to order from Britain, seemed scarcely less important than the non-importation agreements themselves. The possibility of industrial expansion in the colonies was repeatedly raised during the Committee's examination of witnesses with some knowledge of America,[146] though this fear was in reality a superfluous one. The labour shortage and bias in favour of agricultural and commercial enterprise in the colonies militated strongly against serious industrial development during the foreseeable future, and Thomas Whately's belief that 'all Attempts to establish Manufactures in *America*, to an Extent that may be alarming to *Great Britain* must prove abortive in the End', was quite justified.[147] None the less much was made of this danger, and the claims of Franklin and his friends that the Americans were indeed capable of dispensing with British manufactures were most influential,[148] endorsing the view that what was at issue was not merely a temporary depression, but a long-term threat to English industry.

The Commons' evident anxiety about unemployment reflected their concern with the social as well as economic consequences of the Stamp Act crisis in England. An industrial slump was potentially as dangerous to law and order as to commercial prosperity. As Grafton later pointed out in the Lords, at the very least there was the prospect of an appalling burden on the poor rates, at most the danger of severe disturbances,[149] even, according to De Berdt, the possibility

---

[146] Ibid., ff. 99, 100, 111, 119, 131, 144, 150, 168, and 170.

[147] T. Whately, *The Regulations lately made concerning the Colonies, and the Taxes Imposed upon Them, considered* (London, 1765), p. 67.

[148] For Franklin's testimony on this point, see *Papers of Franklin*, ed. L.W. Labaree, xiii. 143, 160–1, and for its incompatibility with other remarks made by him, see V.S. Clark, *History of Manufactures in the United States* (New York, 1929), i. 218.

[149] 'Debates on the Declaratory Act', *Am. Hist. Rev.* xvii. 581; see also J. Fothergill, *Considerations Relative to the North American Colonies* (London, 1765), p. 14.

that the unemployed might 'fall on the Lands of the Nobility and Gentry'.[150] This consideration had been heavily emphasize to the Ministry by the merchants and agents in the previous autumn and great use was made of it in the Commons. According to Henry Cruger, it was the most influential factor there. Referring to the evidence of a Leeds manufacturer that he had turned off half his employees, he remarked:

this fact will have great weight when added to many more evidences of the like kind. The Country Members are somewhat alarmed at so many People losing Employ, if anything repeals the Act, it must be this. the present Ministry see and have declared the *Expediency* of repealing on *this ground*. if the late Ministers come in again, and enforce the Act, they will have 20,000 unemployed Poor in a suppliant manner petitioning a Repeal of the S[tamp] Act.[151]

How seriously these prophecies should be taken is uncertain. It is difficult to believe that the fears expressed were never a little extravagant and fanciful. On the other hand many were quite obviously very alarmed.

Every member of the Community [Garbett assured Dartmouth] from his Majesty to the Peasant must soon feel the Effects in numberless Instances—here I must Stop—as Dangers arise which I must not point out—for I would most unwillingly be thought Seditious—but I will venture to say that Gentlemen are not aware of the numerous ill consequences that will be produced by Violence by Indecision or by suspence in their determination respecting America.[152]

Another Birmingham man, John Twiggs, was equally apprehensive, writing to William Reeve in December that 'We are very fearful the Country will rise before [that] Time [the meeting of Parliament] comes; but sho[ul]d not the Act be repeal'd 'tis impossible to prevent it, dreadful and alarming indeed is our Situation.'[153]

Whatever the truth of that matter it was an effective ploy. That it was a critical consideration is confirmed by the attitude of the Opposition, which treated the grievances of the merchant as the deceptions of 'Interested Men',[154] but which did not

[150] 'Letters of de Berdt', ed. A. Matthews, p. 429: De Berdt to Halifax, n.d.
[151] *Commerce of Rhode Island*, i. 140: H. Cruger, jun. to H. Cruger, sen., 14 Feb. 1766.
[152] Fitzwilliam MSS., A.xxvi. 18: Garbett to Dartmouth, 9 Feb. 1766.
[153] J. Twiggs to W. Reeve, 26 Dec. 1765; quoted in W.R. Savadge, 'The West Country and the American Mainland Colonies', p. 217.
[154] A remark apparently made by Lord Coventry in the Lords; Add.MS. 33001, f. 155: Newcastle's Notes 'from the Book', 11 Mar. 1766.

PARLIAMENT AND THE IMPERIAL PROBLEM   185

attempt to deny the 'distress of our manufactures at home'.[155]
Bedford considered that 'they ought in such an emergency to
be employed by Government',[156] and the very concern to
find a solution to the problem amounted to a tacit recognition
of its importance. Its impact was heightened by what De Berdt
called 'a recent instance thereof'—the Spitalfields riots of
May 1765.[157] These riots have been obscured in historical
perspective by the Gordon Riots, but heavy concentrations
of troops had to be employed before they subsided, and they
made a deep impression at the time. Fundamentally the riots
had been the product of a slump in the silk industry in the
year or two after the Seven Years War, and there was some
excuse for expecting a repetition of such disturbances in 1766.
It was scarcely surprising that Newcastle, alarmed by the rapid
growth of unemployment, could write, 'I dread The Consequence of what may happen even in This Capital',[158] or that
the Commons recognized the domestic implications of the
Stamp Act crisis. It was not only the prospect of a decline
from commercial greatness that ensured the success of the
repeal agitation; it was also the threat of popular disturbances
and the spectre of severe social dislocation.

Fundamentally the Commons approved the policy of
repeal because it accepted the existence of a causal link
between Grenville's American legislation and the commercial
and industrial crisis in Britain. Whether the historian should
be equally trusting is more than doubtful. In this connection
a paper probably drawn up by Charles Jenkinson at the close
of 1766, merits extensive quotation.

It was represented to Administration, and afterwards given in Evidence
in Parliament, in March 1766, by those who solicited the Repeal of the
Stamp Act, that a very considerable Part of the Orders for Goods, which
had been transmitted from America in the Year 1765, had been afterwards suspended; but that, in Case the Stamp Act was repealed, those
Orders were to be executed in the present Year 1766, in Addition to
the Orders for the Supply of that Year; that in Consequence, the Exports
to the Colonies had, in the Year 1765 been greatly diminished, and the
Trade of Great-Britain thither entirely at a Stand. Whereas, should the
Stamp-Act be repealed, Trade would again flourish, and the Exports to

[155] 'Ryder Diaries', *Camden Miscellany*, xxiii. 305: Jenkinson's speech on
     21 Feb. 1766.
[156] Bedford MSS., liii. f. 18: a paper of about Feb. 1766 in Bedford's hand.
[157] 'Letters of de Berdt', ed. A. Matthews, p. 432: De Berdt to Dartmouth,
     [July 1765].
[158] Add.MS. 32974, f. 5: Newcastle to Archbishop of Canterbury, 15 Feb. 1766.

the Colonies, in the present Year 1766, would be at least double the Value of the Exports in the past Year. The Stamp-Act was repealed, and every other American Proposition adopted; and from the Custom-House Entries, it now appears, that the Exports to the North American Colonies in the Year 1766, instead of being double the Value, as was promised, actually *fell short* of the Exports in 1765, no less than 176, 884£ so greatly was the Administration and Parliament abused by those they confided in, and so dangerous it is to allow interested Traders to direct the Measures of Government.[159]

Though Jenkinson was admittedly an opponent of repeal, his comments were substantially correct. Lavish promises of great improvement had been made in order to ensure the passage of repeal and these promises were indeed belied by events. Exports from the American colonies, far from reviving after repeal, continued to decline. For example the value of goods exported to New York, which had fallen some £130,000 from their 1764 figure of half a million, fell a further £50,000 in 1766.[160] Shipments to Pennsylvania, which stood at £435,000 in 1764, fell by a sixth in 1765 and a further ninth in 1766. These figures were typical of the general pattern. Apart from Georgia, a tiny plantation which for no clear reason did not conform, exports to the colonies suffered a general decline. It was not surprising that by the end of 1766 the New York merchants were again complaining of their commercial troubles, and, in their mystification at the origin of these troubles, were blaming both Rockingham and Grenville, or that John Hancock, the most celebrated of the Boston merchants, was writing 'Our trade is very dull, money very scarce and but an indifferent prospect of carrying on Business to any advantage.'[161] Not until two years later, long after the remedies applied by the Rockingham Administration had been carried out, were there any signs of improvement.

The failure of the colonial economy to respond to the measures of 1766 must largely be explained by reference to

[159] Add.MS. 38339, f. 303: 'Exports to North America in 1765 and 66'. There is another copy of this document at P.R.O., Granville MSS., 3/1/16.
[160] The statistics are taken from Sir C. Whitworth, *State of the Trade of Great Britain in its Imports and Exports* (London, 1776), which was based on the Inspector-General of Customs' ledgers. While the general value of this work is limited, it is adequate for the purpose of year-by-year comparisons of exports in this period.
[161] A.E. Brown, *John Hancock His Book*, p. 134: Hancock to Barnards and Harrison, 15 Oct. 1766.

the fact that the depression in American markets was by no means local. Trecothick pointed out in the Commons that '[The] Trade of Gr[eat] Britain to every Q[uarte]r of the World is upon the decline',[162] and certainly all the key markets for British manufactures suffered heavily in the mid-sixties. Export values to Germany, which had reached a record £2·3 million in 1764, sank steadily to £1·2 by 1770. Those to Holland, over £2 million in 1764, fell by a quarter in 1765 and 1766, while the Portuguese trade, which could normally absorb up to a million a year, accounted for less than half that figure in the middle sixties. The Spanish trade displayed a similar trend and even exports handled by the East India Company were reduced by over a third between 1764 and 1766. Only Ireland and Russia of the important markets sustained their level of demand in what Ashton has described as a 'reaction—common to all overseas markets—from the post-war boom'.[163] Indeed the recession was not limited to commerce. A major financial crash originating at Amsterdam in 1763, a succession of bad harvests and exceptionally high food prices, together with the stresses and strains consequent upon a return to peacetime conditions, all aggravated the basic problem of the depression which followed the inflated prosperity of 1763 and 1764.

The precise connection of the Stamp Act crisis with this depression is not easily assessed. However it is clear that there were two major fallacies in the argument which the House of Commons heard and endorsed in 1766. One lay in the undue significance attributed to colonial trade. It is true that great emphasis was placed on the American market in the overall picture of British trade by some merchants and manufacturers, and that historians have also stressed its strategic importance; 'the principal dynamic element in English export trade,' it has been called.[164] None the less it is possible to overestimate its significance. In the great year of 1764, British exports to America amounted to some £2·8 million. Yet Germany and Holland each took over £2 million in that year, while Ireland, Spain, Portugal, and the

[162] Newdigate MSS., B.2545–20: Newdigate's notes of 11 (wrongly dated 10) Feb. 1766.
[163] T.S. Ashton, *Economic Fluctuations in England, 1700–1800* (Oxford, 1959), p. 154.
[164] R. Davies, 'English Foreign Trade, 1700-1774', *Econ. Hist. Rev.* 2nd Ser., xv (1962-3), 290.

East Indies all commanded well over a million each. It was natural for merchants who derived their livelihood from the American trade to stress the national importance of their business; but it must be remembered that the continental colonies accounted for only an eighth of all exports, a very large, but by no means a dominating proportion.

The second misapprehension was scarcely less serious. The basic assumption on which both Administration and the House of Commons acted, namely that the severe decline in colonial commerce was directly attributable to the legislation of the Grenville Ministry, was far from sound. There was and is no reliable evidence that the Sugar Act and Stamp Act were responsible for the slump in the colonial economy. In particular the impression was deliberately given that the heart of the problem lay in the non-importation agreements which so dismayed British merchants. Yet these agreements were not made until November 1765 (the earliest, that of New York, was reached on 31 October), and were not to come into operation until 1 January 1766, long after the symptoms of a commercial malaise had begun to appear in Britain and America in the autumn of 1764.[165] Doubtless the Sugar and Stamp Acts and accompanying measures had an adverse effect on the colonial economy both in the restrictions they imposed on trade and in the demands they made on specie. But the fundamental cause of the economic problem lay elsewhere. Wartime conditions, especially the artificial stimulus injected by the presence of large military concentrations across the Atlantic, and the temporary British possession of the great Spanish and French islands in the West Indies, had raised commercial activity to quite unprecedented heights. The consequent glut in continental and Caribbean markets and the drastic shrinkage produced by the coming of peace led inevitably to a severe recession. One Opposition M.P. properly enquired of Trecothick 'whether [the] encrease in 1764 did not occasion the market being glutted and decrease the y[ea]r 1765'.[166] Both the American and Spanish trades were victims

---

[165] The standard authorities (T.S. Ashton, *Economic Fluctuations in England, 1700-1800*, p. 154 and similarly W.E. Minchinton, *The Growth of English Overseas Trade in the 17th and 18th Centuries* (London, 1969), p. 17) recognize the existence of a deep-seated depression after the Seven Years War, yet persist in attributing a key role to the agreements, though the timing does not correspond.

[166] Newdigate MSS., B.2545—20: Newdigate's Notes of 11 (wrongly dated 10) February 1766.

first and foremost of this development. In consequence it is
scarcely surprising that the nullification of Grenville's colonial
measures by the Rockingham Administration and Parliament
in 1766 failed to produce any significant improvement. What
was at issue was not a regional decline in American trade but
a widespread depression—aggravated by, but fundamentally
independent of, political discontents and government
measures—which had afflicted Britain, its empire and indeed
the whole western world. The Americans, the merchants and
manufacturers in Britain, Rockingham and his colleagues,
and in the last resort, the House of Commons, all came to an
essentially erroneous conclusion—that the critical factor in
the crisis at home and in the colonies was the Stamp Act and
Grenville's other imperial policies.

Had Grenville been able to prove to the House of Commons
that the premises on which the Administration based its case
for repeal were false, had he been able to show that repeal
would not improve the economic situation, it is unlikely that
Rockingham's policy would have found the favour it did.
However the fact that the economic basis of the Ministry's
policy was faulty rather adds to its significance. It is no
coincidence that the British Parliament came nearer than ever
after to a genuinely conciliatory attitude at a time of severe
economic unrest. Ten years later the situation was very
different. Apart from the financial crash of 1772-3, the early
1770s were a prosperous period for English trade and industry.
The political inactivity of the merchants in 1774-5 as opposed
to 1765-6 is well known.[167] But in 1765 the commercial
scene was almost universally black. In 1775 it was surprisingly
bright—even the American trade on the eve of the War of
Independence prospered,[168] while employment was full and
industrial growth rapid. Not until the American War was well
under way and Bourbon intervention inevitable did the
severe economic recession of the late 1770s develop. It would
be unwise to underrate the differences between the Administrations of North and Rockingham or to attribute changes
in imperial policy to crude economic factors. Yet the fact

[167] B. Donoughue, *British Politics and the American Revolution* (London, 1964),
pp. 152–6.
[168] Little attention has been bestowed on this problem from the British angle in
any detail, but for one useful if limited investigation see M.L. Robertson,
'Scottish Commerce and the American War of Independence', *Econ. Hist. Rev.*
2nd Ser. ix (1956-7), 123–31.

remains that in 1766, in the midst of an alarming if largely fortuitous depression, both Government and Parliament opted for a conciliatory policy, while in 1774-5, when commercial prospects were so good that not even those 'interested men', the merchants, were inclined to protest, there was over-whelming support for a rigidly authoritarian policy.

From a purely domestic point of view the economic basis of repeal was equally significant. The agitation for repeal is usually treated as an affair of the merchants. Certainly it was so in America; but in Great Britain, while the role of Trecothick and his friends in supervising the campaign was of the first importance, a critical part was also played by the manufacturers, so that the Opposition could even talk of 'The Manufacturing Interest against The Interest of The Nation'.[169] Nearly twenty years before the period of industrial take-off and the political activities of Wedgwood and his fellow manufacturers, Parliament was displaying intense interest in the economic problems and social reper-cussions of British industry and its development. Their preoccupation, not merely with trade and navigation, but with manufactured exports and industrial employment is a pointer to the rapidly changing balance of power in the community. The prominence of the disparate financial and mercantile interests—North America, East India, and West India—in the early years of George III's reign must not be allowed to obscure the role of the manufacturing interest, as yet unorganized and incoherent, but none the less a growing power in the land. Not the least remarkable feature of the Stamp Act crisis is its powerful testimony to the burgeoning importance of the new cities and new men of the industrial north and midlands, as against the traditional influence of the mercantile élites of the metropolis and outports.

Once the Commons had accepted that the economic arguments in favour of repeal were overwhelming, the passage of repeal was not long delayed. After the American resolutions of the Committee of the Whole House were reported on 24 February, the major proposals—for the repeal of the Stamp Act and the declaration of 'the dependency of the American colonies'—were embodied in two bills introduced on the 26th. Further efforts by the Opposition to forestall repeal and an

---

[169] Add.MS. 33001, f. 155: Newcastle: Notes 'from the Book', 11 Mar. 1766; a remark apparently made by Lord Coventry in the Lords on that day.

attempt by Pitt to amend the Declaratory Act did not prevent
the bills passing on 4 March. By this time the Lower House
was heartily tired of colonial problems; Sir Matthew
Fetherstonhaugh told Newcastle on 4 March that 'the Temper
of the House is such that it will not admit long or much
Debating.'[170] However the reception to be expected in the
Upper House for these measures was a matter for much
speculation, Sir William Baker's son noting, for example, that
'People seem divided in their Sentiments about the reception
the Bill will meet with in the Lords.'[171] The Ministers themselves were certainly anxious as to the outcome, and took far
greater pains to calculate the likely voting pattern than they
had in the Commons.[172] Though it had originally been
intended to subject the Lords to the same shower of information and evidence as the Commons, this approach was
soon abandoned. Apart from a few petitions from the more
important of the trading towns, and an order, soon revoked,
for the attendance of four witnesses to the disturbances in
America, no serious attempt to present the detailed case put
forward in the Lower House was essayed.[173] This was
probably a wise decision. The Lords had already, in the
divisions of 4 and 6 February, demonstrated their intense
hostility to the attitudes and activities of the colonists, and
there was no great phalanx of Independents to be persuaded
one way or the other of the merits of the case. It was not to
be expected that the peers' minds would be changed by the
kind of evidence presented in the Lower House. Other arguments were plainly required.

Fortunately they were forthcoming. The essential fact was
that the Stamp Act, and therefore the bill repealing it, were
supply bills. The great danger in the Lords was the possibility
of an attempt to implement the policy favoured by the King
and many of the King's Friends—the policy of modification.
Yet despite Chesterfield's fear of 'any of *Lord Strange's*

[170] Add.MS. 33069, f. 397.
[171] 'William Baker's Account of the Debate on the Repeal of the Stamp Act',
William and Mary Quarterly, 3rd Ser. xxvi. 265.
[172] Newcastle made out no less than eight lists in his attempts to anticipate the
voting; see Add.MS. 33001, ff. 96–7, 99–100, 102–3, 104–5, 113–15,
128–30, 148–50, 151–3.
[173] *Journals of the House of Lords*, xxxi. 292, 296–7, and 250, 252, 253.
According to Newcastle (Add.MS. 32973, f. 415: to Wight, 11 Feb. 1766),
there were difficulties about the precedents for the examination of merchants
in the Lords.

modifications',[174] such a ploy was generally conceded to be unwarranted in the case of a supply bill.

as you know [William Rouet wrote to a friend] they cannot make any amendment to such bills, the question must be confined to repeal, or enforce the Act as it now stands, and I don't find that even the Father of the bill would have given his vote for the last alternative; so that the Lords may probably be unanimous, though after a good deal of speechifying.[175]

Though this was not of course a matter of statutory obligation, the Commons had resolved in 1678 that 'all Aids and Supplies, and Aids to his Majesty in Parliament, are the sole Gift of the Commons: . . . which ought not to be changed, or altered by the House of Lords',[176] and ever since the serious disputes between Lords and Commons in the last decades of the seventeenth century, this had been accepted as a convention not to be violated.

This was not the only difficulty for the opponents of repeal. If modifying the Stamp Act was out of the question, there were grave doubts as to the propriety of rejecting its repeal completely.

It is impossible [James West assured Newcastle] for the Lords in prudence to reject the repeal of a Tax, which would thereby, be *really and substantially* imposed on the Subject by the Lords only, an Imposition that no Subject either in Great Britain or America has ever submitted to, in the most just, necessary and equal Tax, much less, in a disputed, inexpedient, and oppressive one, would occasion fresh disturbances in the Colonies, and almost certainly, a breach between the two Houses.[177]

In this case no constitutional convention could be convincingly pleaded. The Lords had recently divided, though not without adverse comment, on a supply bill—the Cider Excise of 1763— and much later, in the celebrated instances of 1860 and 1909, were actually to throw out financial legislation.[178] None the less such a course in 1766 could only cause a major controversy, and create, in Newcastle's words, a 'Division of The Two Houses of Parliament, The Worst of all Divisions'.[179]

[174] *Letters of Chesterfield*, ed. B. Dobrée, vi. 2714: Chesterfield to Newcastle, 25 Feb. 1766.
[175] *Caldwell Papers*, Part ii, vol. ii, p. 76: Rouet to Mure, 1 Mar. 1766.
[176] *The Law and Working of the Constitution: Documents 1660-1914*, edd. W.C. Costin and J.S. Watson (London, 1961), i. 154.
[177] Add.MS. 32974, f. 153: 7 Mar. 1766.
[178] This problem was of course finally settled by the Parliament Act of 1911.
[179] Add.MS. 33001, ff. 163–4: Newcastle, 'Farther Considerations upon The Stamp Act', 16 Mar. 1766.

The Opposition naturally had arguments to advance against this. The repeal, Sandwich urged, had 'forced its way thro' another Ho[use] by means of that Democratic Interest w[hi]ch this Ho[use] was constituted to restrain—In this Assembly Men have a Seat by Birth not Election so that no Influence by Electors can be used'.[180] Again, the official protest drawn up by Lyttelton once the Lords had passed the repeal bill, invoked the ancient cause of Lords against Commons. To 'give our Consent to it here, without a full Conviction that it is right, merely because it has passed the other House', it insisted, would be to 'annihilate this Branch of the Legislature, and vote ourselves useless'.[181] However these arguments were unavailing against the Lords' apprehensions of 'the danger that would attend the continuing this tax after the Commons had repealed it by so great a majority',[182] and the Ministers had some reason for confidence, Burke for instance believing that 'their Courage will never carry them to those Lengths, which their Strength might enable them to go.'[183]

Even so it was, as Richmond predicted, 'a very near thing'.[184] There was only one division in the Lords—on the motion to commit the repeal bill on 11 March, and the Ministry's majority, excluding proxies, was 73 votes to 61.[185] The critical factor in this victory was a change of attitude by some of those who had voted against the Administration's American resolutions in the first week of February. 'I flatter myself', Archbishop Secker remarked, 'that the House of Commons may have enlightend several members of our House.'[186] Involved were some eight or nine peers who, by their conversion to the cause of repeal, turned a majority

---

[180] Add.MS. 35912, f. 83: Sandwich's speech in Hardwicke's account of the debate of 11 Mar. 1766. The version printed at *Am. Hist. Rev.* xvii. 580 is not entirely accurate.

[181] *Lords Journals*, xxxi. 312: 17 Mar. 1766.

[182] H.M.C. *Stopford-Sackville MSS.*, i. 108: Sackville to Irwin, 11 Mar. 1766.

[183] *Burke Correspondence*, i. 239: Burke to O'Hara, 1, 4 Mar. 1766.

[184] *Life and Letters of Lady Sarah Lennox, 1745-1826*, edd. Countess of Ilchester and Lord Stavordale (London, 1901), i. 191: Lady Sarah Bunbury to Lady Susan O'Brien, 8 Mar. 1766.

[185] With proxies the figures were 105 to 71, but proxies could not be called in Committee and it was essential for the Ministry to obtain a majority independent of them.

[186] Add.MS. 32973, f. 399: Secker to Newcastle, 10 Feb. 1766.

against the Administration into one in its favour.[187] They were led by Northington who, though he had throughout been one of the most committed and outspoken opponents of repeal, changed sides once the Commons had reached their decision. In the debate of 11 March he spoke 'very strongly', as Rockingham reported to the King, 'for the Houses not disagreeing'.[188] His speech was concerned not at all with the merits of repeal, but solely with the importance of averting a major constitutional crisis. Expressed by the Lord Chancellor, such an argument was probably of critical importance. Had the Repeal of the Stamp Act not been a supply bill, overwhelmingly endorsed by the Commons, it is most unlikely that it would have emerged from the Upper House without considerable modification.

The Declaratory Act and the Repeal Act received the royal assent on 18 March, barely a year after the Stamp Act had passed onto the statute book. The preamble to the Repeal stated emphatically that 'the Continuance of the said Act would be attended with many Inconveniencies, and may be productive of Consequences greatly detrimental to the Commercial Interests of these Kingdoms'.[189] But if the Rockingham Administration's American policy was concerned primarily with the interests of the British economy, it also involved the assumption that it would bring the crisis in the colonies to a peaceful conclusion. Of course not everyone accepted this assumption, which was open to two lines of attack. On the one hand it was argued by the Opposition that the repeal was an unjustified concession, that the real aim of the colonists was independence and that the ultimate result of a policy of appeasement would be to advance that event. On the other hand it was claimed by some of Pitt's friends that insufficient concessions had been made, that the Declaratory Act was an intolerable insult to the Americans and that it could only create further strife. A definitive

[187] The Duke of Argyll, the Earls of Hardwicke and Northington, Lord Willoughby de Broke, and the Bishop of Llandaff voted for repeal on 11 March, while the Earls of Morton and Lords Cadogan and Boston either did the same or abstained (precisely which is not clear). The Earl of Exeter supported repeal by proxy. All these had voted in opposition on 4 February; the remainder of the Majority on that date also voted against repeal on 11 March. This information is drawn from lists compiled by Newcastle—Add.MS. 33035, ff. 276–7 for the division of 4 Feb. and ff. 385–7 for that of 11 March.
[188] *Correspondence of George III*, i. 281: 12 Mar. 1766.
[189] *Statutes at Large*, vii. 6 Geo. III. c. xi.

answer to this problem is out of the question, simply because the Rockingham policy was scarcely given a chance. Less than two years after the repeal of the Stamp Act, the Townshend Duties were introduced and henceforth the logic of events led inexorably to the Boston Tea Party and Lexington. Those two years hardly constitute an adequate period for a definite judgement on the efficacy of the measures of 1766. Only the most tentative of assessments can be attempted.

The Administration was naturally concerned about the reception of its measures in America. It had been emphasized again and again during the examination of witnesses in the House of Commons, that the Opposition's prophecies would be proved wrong and that 'If the Stamp Act was repealed this House wo[ul]d soon have speciments of that [the colonists'] Gratitude.'[190] So anxious were Rockingham and his colleagues to ensure that the colonies would not ruin their own and the Ministry's credit by an unfavourable reaction to the policy embodied in the Declaratory Act, that yet another campaign was organized. A whole series of letters was sent across the Atlantic, urging the need to avert 'improper Triumph' on the news of repeal, and 'impress the minds of all people with a dutiful sense and spirit of gratitude, submission, peace and good will'.[191] As in November 1765 it was Sir George Savile who had much to do, in his unostentatious way, with the initiation of this campaign. On his recommendation, an official letter was despatched by the London Committee of North America Merchants to their colonial counterparts, pleading for an attitude of moderation and gratitude on the grounds that

It has been a constant Argument against the Repeal, that in case it should take place, the Parliamentary Vote of Right will be waste paper, and that the Colonies will understand very well, that what is pretended to be adopted, on mere Commercial Principles of Expedience, is really yielded thro' fear; and amounts to a tacit but effectual Surrender of its right or at least a tacit Compact that it will never use it.[192]

---

[190] Add.MS. 33030, f. 102: Trecothick's evidence, 11 Feb. 1766.

[191] *American Correspondence of a Bristol Merchant*, ed. G.H. Guttridge, p. 14: R. Champion to C. Lloyd, 23 Feb. 1766; *Grenville Papers*, iii. 238: Moffat to Styles, 18 Mar. 1766.

[192] 'London Merchants on the Stamp Act Repeal', *Massachusetts Hist. Soc. Proceedings*, lv. 216: 28 Feb. 1766. For Savile's draft, see *Rockingham Memoirs*, i. 303–6.

The results were encouraging. Though the New York merchants replied to the letter with some truculence, declaring 'you can hardly expect, at least of a sudden, such a Surprising Revolution, so repugnant to the Force of Custom, and all the Motives of Interest', they promised to pacify 'your Fears, that our Conduct will fulfil the Predictions of the Opposition'. The replies from most other quarters were similarly reassuring, and in general, while there was great jubilation in the colonies, it was mostly of a seemly and gratifying nature, with even the pamphleteers emphasizing the benevolence and generosity of the mother country.[195] On this point at least the Ministers need not have worried unduly.

This is not to argue that there were no further troubles in America once the Rockingham Ministry's policy had been implemented. Israel Mauduit, the intensely loyalist propagandist, indeed set out to prove the contrary, declaring 'it is often said that immediately after the repeal of the Stamp Act the people of Massachusetts were all satisfied and the next year was a year of peace', and then going on to show that a 'quarrelsom and spitefull disposition against Government was shewn during the Ministry even of their friends, and in the honey months of their deliverance from the Stamp Act'.[196] There were admittedly serious difficulties in Massachusetts where the Assembly quarrelled violently with the Governor over compensating victims of the Stamp Act riots, while in New York and New Jersey there were great disputes over the provisions of the American Mutiny Act. Even in Virginia, the acting Governor could report that 'everything is contested, a Spirit of Discontent and Cavil runs through the Colony: so opposite is the general Tenor of their Conduct to that Moderation, which the late Indulgencies, received from their Mother Country, ought to inspire them with.'[197] Yet these problems were essentially a result of the growing strife between

---

[193] WWM.R55–1: 6 May 1766.
[194] A.E. Brown, *John Hancock His Book*, p. 125; *John Norton and Sons, Merchants of London and Virginia*, ed. F.N. Mason (2nd edn., Newton Abbot, 1968), p. 14; WWM.R55–5: S. Cary to Rockingham, 21 May 1766; P.R.O., C.O. 5/390, f. 92: Montagu to Board of Trade, 29 June 1766.
[195] See for example, J. Mayhew, *The Snare Broken* (Boston, 1766); N. Appleton, *A Thanksgiving Sermon on the Total Repeal of the Stamp-Act* (Boston, 1766); C. Chauncy, *A Discourse on 'the Good News from a far Country'* (Boston, 1766).
[196] *Jenkinson Papers*, pp. 440, 442: 'Annus Pacificus'.
[197] C.O. 5/1345, f. 138: Fauquier to Board of Trade, 4 Sept. 1766.

colonial assemblies and royal government which had been developing steadily for some years. They did not necessarily imply a conflict of imperial proportions, and indeed neither the issue of compensation and punishment in relation to the Stamp Act riots nor that of the American Mutiny Act succeeded in raising a united opposition to the mother country. Not until the Townshend Duties was there any sign of the concert and combination which had been such a menacing feature of the Stamp Act crisis.

In particular there is little evidence that the Declaratory Act was especially offensive to the Americans. It is true that it was 'the most explicit declaration and justification ever drawn up in support of Parliament's unbounded right to legislate for the Colonies'.[198] Yet Franklin had assured the Commons:

I think the resolutions of right will give them very little concern, if they are never attempted to be carried into practice. The Colonies will probably consider themselves in the same situation, in that respect, with Ireland; they know you claim the same right with regard to Ireland, but you never exercise it. And they may believe you never will exercise it in the Colonies, any more than in Ireland, unless on some very extraordinary occasion.[199]

On the whole this prediction was vindicated by events. There were reports that 'the Americans are less pleased with the repeal, than displeased by the declaration of right',[200] but for the most part the Declaratory Act met with little opposition, partly it seems,[201] because the colonies did not interpret it in the way Parliament had intended it—as a sweeping assertion of sovereignty in all fields—partly for the reasons foreseen by Franklin. The essential fact was that it was no more than a declaration. Only when Charles Townshend wilfully turned it into something more positive did it become a major grievance in America; had Rockingham and his friends stayed in office it would probably have been allowed to remain as a mere form of words without practical implications.[202] If it was true, as

[198] C.R. Ritcheson, *British Politics and the American Revolution*, p. 67.
[199] *Papers of Franklin*, ed. L.W. Labaree, xiii. 141.
[200] *Jenkinson Papers*, p. 413: Bradshaw to Jenkinson, 24 June 1766.
[201] E.S. and H.M. Morgan, *The Stamp Act Crisis*, p. 358.
[202] There can be no certainty about this however. Rockingham and his friends were not in the least averse to laying duties on the colonies (see below, p. 208); on the other hand it is extremely unlikely that they would have adopted the deliberately provacative scheme designed by Townshend.

Savile insisted, 'that the Act would certainly not have been repealed if men's minds had not been in some measure satisfied with the Declaration of Right',[203] it did not necessarily follow that the declaration required implementation in the form of new revenue duties.

It is difficult to withhold all credit from Rockingham and his colleagues for their solution to the Stamp Act crisis. That solution was indeed shaped by expediency rather than principle, despite Burke's later success in weaving it into a sophisticated theory of empire, but given the incompatibility of prevailing views on either side of the Atlantic, this was its great merit. The policy enshrined in the Repeal and Declaratory Acts was acceptable to moderates—in whose hands the future of the empire lay, in both Britain and the colonies—and provided a sensible basis on which to rebuild Anglo-American relations. The Ministry did not however receive much credit for its achievement. Especially in America, Pitt's unreserved advocacy of the colonial cause, though it had limited impact on the policy actually adopted in England, put the Administration's efforts in the shade. Thus from New York it was reported that 'It appears as if that Province had decreed a Statue of Brass in Honour of His Majesty's grace and favour to the colonies on this occasion—and another to Mr. Pitt as the Great Instrument in effecting the repeal—It is strange if not incredible that America acknowledges so little to the present Ministry on this occasion.'[204] In some measure Rockingham and his colleagues, by their constant courting and adulation of Pitt, had provoked such a verdict. Yet it was none the less unjust, for the sensible and statesmanlike policy adopted in 1766 was largely their own work. It was not of course without defects, and historians, if not contemporaries, have pointed out that it was essentially negative.[205] While it undoubtedly terminated the Stamp Act crisis, it provided no answer to the many problems of empire raised after the Seven Years War. In March 1766, with the Repeal and Declaratory Acts safely on the statute book, it remained to be seen whether Rockingham and his friends could come to grips with these problems more successfully than Grenville.

[203] *Rockingham Memoirs*, i. 305: Savile; 'Considerations on the Repeal', [22 Feb. 1766].
[204] WWM.R55—4: 'Memorandums, relating to the manner of Sir H[enr]y *Moore's* introducing the *Repeal* of the *Stamp* Act to the Gen[era]l Assembly etc. 1766'
[205] See for example, D.M. Clark, *The Rise of the British Treasury*, p. 154.

VI

THE ADMINISTRATION IN DECLINE
(MARCH TO MAY 1766)

LONG before the royal assent was given to the Declaratory
Act and Repeal of the Stamp Act on 18 March, the House of
Commons had been disabused of the notion that it had, for a
while at least, finished with the problems of the American
colonies. On 21 February after completing its resolutions in
connection with the Stamp Act crisis, the Committee of the
Whole House had agreed that it should continue to sit on
other matters relating to the colonies. It had probably been
the intention of the mercantile interests throughout to press
for major changes in the regulation of imperial commerce.[1]
Though it was the Stamp Act which by alienating so many
sections of opinion in America had provided the occasion
for effective action, the colonial merchants had always
objected primarily to Grenville's commercial legislation, and
this was equally true of their British counterparts. During the
examination of witnesses in Committee, discussion of the
effects of the stamp tax constantly gave way to digressions on
the trading situation in general, and if the case of Bristol is a
fair example, the Stamp Act problem was positively a distraction from the strictly commercial issues. Throughout 1764
and 1765 William Reeve and his colleagues had pressed, with
their M.P., Robert Nugent, for measures to modify Grenville's
legislation, and while they threw themselves into the campaign
for repeal with great enthusiasm, their deeper and more consistent interests were elsewhere;[2] one of their number, Henry
Cruger, declared frankly at the beginning of March 1766,
'I have been in London with all the great Men in the Kingdom.
The Stamp and Sugar Acts were my two objects.'[3] Indeed
what was surprising about the movement for major changes

---

[1] For the problem of the relations between the mercantile interests and the 'Old
Whigs', see L.S. Sutherland, 'Edmund Burke and the First Rockingham Ministry',
E.H.R. xlvii. 46—72, to which the following account is heavily indebted.
[2] See W.R. Savadge, 'The West Country and the American Mainland Colonies',
pp.193—4 et seq.
[3] *Commerce of Rhode Island*, i. 146: Cruger to A. Lopez, 1 Mar. 1766.

in the regulation of trade was not the fact that it was taken up with such vigour by the merchants, but that it was so completely successful. In the dying months of the Rockingham Ministry, the direction of colonial policy passed largely into the hands of the mercantile pressure groups; at no time in the eighteenth century were Administration and Parliament more at the command of the commercial interests than in the spring of 1766.

That fairly drastic measures were needed was generally conceded. The state of a vast territorial and trading empire, enlarged and consolidated by the Seven Years War, yet afflicted in the years after the war by severe economic difficulties, and racked by the host of measures devised mostly for revenue purposes by Grenville, was clearly not to be neglected. Unfortunately it was easier to agree that action was needed than to agree on the nature of such action. A multiplicity of sectional demands, many in direct conflict with each other, compounded the difficulties of Rockingham and his fellow Ministers. The sheer weight and variety of these pressures were formidable, but individually they were over-shadowed by one issue which lay at the very heart of the Empire's problems. The fundamental question of foreign trade with British colonies raised deep questions of imperial policy, utterly divided the mercantile interests in England, and bade fair to become an issue scarcely less grave than that posed by the Stamp Act.

Trading between the British colonies and foreign settlements whether Spanish, French, Dutch, or Danish, conflicted with one of the most deeply-rooted and sacred principles of the mercantilist theory embodied in the Trade and Navigation Acts. It was essential to that theory that the benefits of colonial possessions should be directed to the mother country, and it was to this end that the many restrictions on trade in the Americas, most of them enforced by prohibitive or punitive duties, had been legislated.[4] Yet by the 1760s it was becoming self-evident that it would be to the great advantage, not merely of individual colonies but of the empire in general, to modify these restrictions. It was almost universally agreed that the trade between Jamaica and Spanish America, which

---

[4] There is of course a considerable literature on this subject, but the most thorough up-to-date account is in O.M. Dickerson, *The Navigation Acts and the American Revolution* (Philadelphia, 1951).

brought in valuable bullion and raw materials, and provided
a ready market for British manufactures, was highly beneficial
to the imperial economy, though the lawyers were adamant
that certain branches of it at least were definitely prohibited
by the Navigation Acts.[5] But far more pressing was the
problem presented further north. On any impartial assessment
the illicit trade between the New England colonies and the
French West Indian Islands, which disposed of surplus
American produce in return for cheap molasses and sugar
(essential elements in the fishery and slave trade), was very
much in the Empire's interest.

Had it been simply a matter of partially repealing or
modifying earlier legislation, there would have been few
problems. Unfortunately the American demand for a freer
trade in the Caribbean was directly at variance with the
hitherto dominant view of West India planters, that it would
shatter their overpriced market for British-grown sugars. 'You
may remember', Sackville reminded his friend Irwin, 'there
are frequently distinct interests between the Islands and
North America.'[6] For long the West India interest had
succeeded in imposing on British Governments its argument
that it was more important to preserve its monopolies and
privileges than to recognize the need to provide the continental colonies with foreign markets and materials, though
the British islands were themselves by no means able to
satisfy that need. Their influence had achieved its greatest
triumphs with the terms of the Peace of Paris in 1763 and
the Sugar Act in 1764,[7] and it was not to be expected that
they would meekly submit to the growing demands in 1765-
6 which ranged from the request for a reduction of Grenville's
duty on molasses to sweeping proposals for free ports in the
West Indies.[8] By the spring of 1766, when the Administration
and Parliament came to consider the problems of imperial

[5] For the legal arguments, see F. Armytage, *The Free Port System in the British West Indies*, pp. 31-3.
[6] H.M.C. *Stopford-Sackville MSS.*, i. 111: 25 Apr. 1766.
[7] See F.W. Pitman, *The Development of the British West Indies: 1700-1763* (New Haven, 1917), chapter xiv. But for a modification of the traditional view of the Sugar Act, see J.M. Sosin, *Agents and Merchants* (Lincoln, Neb., 1965), pp. 46-7. R. Pares deals with American trade in the West Indies in *Yankees and Creoles* (London, 1956), and L.M. Penson with the West India interest in England in *The Colonial Agents of the British West Indies* (London, 1924).
[8] For proposals in favour of free ports sent to the Ministry in 1765, see Add.MS. 33030, ff. 318-23; WWM.R27-2, R37-5, R96-1, R96-2.

commerce, a major conflict between the North America and West India interests was evidently boiling up. 'Their Eyes', Henry Cruger wrote rather optimistically of the Commons in February 1766,

> are at last open'd and they seem convinc'd what vast Benefit will accrue to this Kingdom by giving you almost an unlimitted trade, so farr as doth not interfere with British Manufactures. The West Indians are collecting all their Force to oppose us; but I have reason to say they will at length be defeated.[9]

Cruger's confidence was doubtless a result of the evident sympathy of the Ministry for the views of Trecothick and his friends. Rockingham made no secret of his approval of the North American cause: 'We suffer ourselves to be monopolised by the W[est] I[ndies]', he declared.[10] Rarely had the West India interest found itself so totally out of favour with the Government as in 1766.

At first there seemed a chance that the threatened struggle would be averted. On 12 March Rockingham informed the King that he had received a deputation from the two sides,

> who came to inform him—that several of the Matters which might have occasioned dispute—were nearly agreed between them and L[or]d Rockingham has now full Reason to assure his Majesty that there is the Greatest Prospect of an Advantageous System of Commerce being Established for the Mutual and General Interest of this Country—N[orth] America and the West India Islands.[11]

It is not difficult to understand why the West Indian Committee was prepared to cooperate at this stage. The formal agreement which was drawn up with their antagonists 'at the King's Head Tavern on 10 March',[12] did admittedly surrender an important point. The duty on foreign molasses imported into North America, which had stood at 3d. per gallon since 1764 and 6d. before that, was to be reduced to 1d., the sum levied on British molasses. But if this was a concession, it had in the current climate of opinion become a virtually unavoidable one, and was in any case accompanied by specific

[9] *Commerce of Rhode Island*, i. 143: H. Cruger, jun. to H. Cruger, sen., 14 Feb. 1766.
[10] WWM.R49—31: Rockingham's rough notes for a speech never made.
[11] *Correspondence of George III*, i. 282: 12 Mar. 1766.
[12] The agreement is printed without explanation in L.M. Penson, *The Colonial Agents of the British West Indies*, pp. 284—5; see also WWM.R38—1: 'Proposal for Regulating the Plantation Trade', 14 Mar. 1766; R38—7: 'Argument for Reduction of the Duty on Molasses'.

assurances to protect the West Indian monopoly of sugar and other tropical products at home. In addition to this there was a hope, formally enshrined in a recommendation by the joint committees to the Ministry on 3 April,[13] of statutory measures to permit the trade between Spanish America and the British islands, which had suffered such difficulties in the previous three years. In short, an indefensible and largely unenforceable privilege had been abandoned in return for cast-iron guarantees on more important points, and the prospect of a useful regulation on another. The way, it seemed, was clear for a phase of amicable cooperation between the mercantile interests, a useful programme of commercial reform in Parliament, and a great improvement in the economic climate.

This happy state of affairs did not endure long. In the course of the month of April the unity of the commercial interests was at last shattered by the emergence of a clear demand on the part of the North American element for free ports in the Ceded Isles. Bristol led the way with a petition for a free port in Dominica to the Commons on 7 April, and the Londoners followed suit on the 21st.[14] The immediate reaction of the West Indians was one of predictably intense hostility. Led by William Beckford and supported by Pitt, who refused to be moved by a visit from Burke and a deputation of North America merchants on 11 April,[15] they wrecked all possibility of amicable progress.

Mr. Pitt [it was reported back to Bristol on the 12th] said he intended to be in the house on Monday, that many Doubts and Difficulties appear to the proposal. on the whole he seemed strongly prejudiced against us and Beckford is working hard in Opposition, and the Ministry will not care to Divide the house against Mr. Pitts opinion—thus it stands very unfavourable now w[hi]ch is all you can know at present.[16]

Characteristically the Ministry panicked once Pitt had committed himself to opposing the free ports scheme.

When the Freeport came to be debated in a full Cabinet [Burke informed O'Hara] the old Stagers frittered it down to an address to the King for the opinion of the boards on the matter etc.—so we came

---

[13] WWM.R60: 'Further proposal of the *West India Merchants*'.
[14] *Commons Journals*, xxx. 704, 750.
[15] The merchants who went with Burke were Trecothick, Barclay, Hanbury, and Rawlinson. (Add.MS. 32974, f. 389: 'Memorandums . . .', 16 Apr. 1766).
[16] Rawlinson to Reeve, 12 Apr. 1766, quoted in W.R. Savadge, 'The West Country and the American Mainland Colonies', p. 277.

hopping into the house with half a measure; the most odious thing, I am sure to my Temper and opinion that can be conceived. However, even this miserable remnant is better than nothing.[17]

Yet this was by no means the last volte-face in an extraordinary tale of vacillation and indecision. In the first week of May, when all hope of the free ports had long abandoned, the two sides came together and agreed on a workable plan. The agreement of 8 May provided for the opening of ports not merely in Jamaica for the Spanish trade, but also, given Parliamentary time, to legalize in Dominica the commercial relations of the continental colonies and the foreign islands.[18] In the change of attitude by the West India Committee which permitted this settlement, the decisive factor was doubtless the withdrawal of Pitt's support. Though he assured his follower Nuthall on 11 May of his hope that 'this unsolid idea of a free port is quite rejected and exploded',[19] he had in fact ceased to oppose it in the Commons, a change of front made plain on 30 April when rather than endorse Beckford's proposal to reject the scheme outright, he had advocated the hearing of expert evidence as to its merits.[20] Whatever the reason for his desertion—presumably he was afraid of losing popularity with the increasingly influential North America interests— it decisively weakened Beckford's campaign. Fortunately there were men of more moderation among the West Indians, for George Onslow remarked on the 'Agreement of the West India Committee which Rose and Stephen Fuller have had infinite Merit in procuring'.[21] The Fuller brothers were well-known among the merchants and planters; though Stephen was the Jamaican agent, it was his brother Rose who was the more prominent in 1766—he had taken the chair of the Commons' American Committee of the Whole House, though his tenure was interrupted by illness—and was energetic in pressing for reform of trading regulations. The agreement

[17] *Burke Correspondence*, i. 251: 23, 24 [April 1766].
[18] The agreement of 8 May is printed by L.S. Sutherland in 'Edmund Burke and the First Rockingham Ministry', *E.H.R.* xlvii. 71; printed with this document is a selection of explanatory observations made in a paper entitled 'Notes on Agreement' in Add.MS. 33030, ff. 247–50. These notes were part of a letter sent by Rose Fuller to Newcastle, 10 May 1766, (Add.MS. 32975, ff. 147, 149–51) from which they were apparently separated during foliation.
[19] *Chatham Correspondence*, ii. 421.
[20] Add.MS. 32975, f. 58: West to Newcastle, 30 Apr. 1766; Add.MS. 35607, ff. 255–6: Harris to Hardwicke, 30 Apr. 1766.
[21] Add.MS. 32975, f. 114: Onslow to Newcastle, 8 May 1766.

was chiefly his work, and indeed he stands second only to Barlow Trecothick among the merchants who by their activities in 1766 helped to develop imperial policy in new directions. Fortunately it was less a surrender than an armistice that he was compelled to negotiate. In return for conceding the establishment of a free port in Dominica, the West Indians obtained an impressive array of concessions, free ports of their own with which to tap the Spanish market, the withdrawal of restrictions on the rum trade on the one hand and on cotton imports on the other, and above all two crucial clauses to safeguard the planters against the worst effects of competition from French sugars, one reducing duties on British-grown sugars imported into North America, the other specifying that for taxation purposes all sugars imported to Britain, via Dominica and the continental colonies, should be treated as foreign. Hedged about with these regulations the Dominica free port was scarcely the massive blow at West India monopolies that had been feared.

Once the 'happy Union between the West Indian and North American Merchants'[22] had resulted in a detailed programme of commercial reforms, the House of Commons troubled itself little about them, and the Lords even less. Most members of both Houses were heartily sick of American problems, and were either uninterested in the new measures or anxious to see them finished with. 'In a question of such importance as that now before the House', Thomas Nuthall reported on 8 May, 'concerning the American duties, free port, etc., only seventy members could be found to attend their duty.'[23] Moreover the Opposition was considerably weakened by the defection of prominent figures like Strange and Nugent, both compelled to support commercial measures clearly to the advantage of their constituencies,[24] and Grenville was led to complain bitterly of his isolation.[25] It is true that a great deal of trouble was taken to examine expert evidence on the subject of imperial trade. But there was a marked difference between

[22] 'London Merchants on the Stamp Act Repeal', *Massachusetts Hist. Soc. Proceedings*, lv. 221: 13 June 1766.
[23] *Chatham Correspondence*, ii. 418: Nuthall to Pitt.
[24] Nugent's constituency was Bristol, Strange's Lancashire. See Add.MS. 35607, f. 256: Harris to Hardwicke, 30 April 1766, and *Chatham Correspondence*, ii. 418; also J. Tucker, *A Review of Lord Vis. Clare's Conduct as Representative of Bristol* (Gloucester, 1775), p. 10.
[25] Add.MS. 42084, f. 33: Grenville to Whately, 25 May 1766.

the testimonies given in Committee in February and those of the spring. In the former case the witnesses called had a crucial role to play, giving much-needed information on a matter of undoubted national importance. In the latter though many witnesses were summoned, their significance was necessarily limited.[26] Despite Grenville's fuming over the 'overbearing and delegation of administration to a Club of North America Merchants at the Kings arms Tavern',[27] it was generally recognized that once the merchant interests had come to terms, there was little need for the intervention of either Parliament or Administration. On 6 June the two bills embodying the recommendations of the joint committees one establishing the free ports in Jamaica and Dominica, the other providing for the necessary regulation of customs duties safely received the royal assent after an uneventful passage through both Houses.

These bills were obviously important; one of Rockingham's admirers considered that they 'will make this Sessions the noblest era for extending commerce this Nation ever knew',[28] and if the judgement of the London North America Merchants was more sober, it was scarcely less flattering.

We consider [them] as the basis of an extensive System of Trade between Great Britain and her Colonies framed on liberal principles of reciprocal Advantage, relieving the Colonies from injudicious restrictions and severe Duties, enlarging old, and opening to them, new Channels of Commerce, and by securing to Great Britain an increasing consumption of her Manufactures, and of consequence an extension of her Navigation and Revenue.[29]

None the less the actual results of this legislation were disappointing. Neither the Jamaica nor Dominica free ports were an unqualified success.[30] There was no great expansion of

[26] Twenty-nine were ordered to attend, but only the following are definitely known to have been examined: William Kelly, Brook Watson, John Wentworth, ? Hale (27 Mar.), Captain Collet, Richard Maitland (7 May), ? Brindley (8 May).
[27] Add.MS. 32975, f. 58: West to Newcastle, 30 Apr. 1766; quoted in L.S. Sutherland, 'Edmund Burke and the First Rockingham Ministry, *E.H.R.* xlvii. 66.
[28] WWM.R58–7: R. Hamilton to Rockingham, 16 May 1766.
[29] 'London Merchants on the Stamp Act Repeal', *Massachusetts Hist. Soc. Proceedings*, lv. 220: 13 June 1766.
[30] For a detailed assessment of the results of opening free ports, see F. Armytage, *The Free Port System in the British West Indies*, pp. 42–51, and for Jamaica in particular, A.C. Christelow, 'The Contraband Trade between Jamaica and the Spanish Main, and the Free Port Act of 1766', *Hispanic Am. Hist. Rev.* xxii. 339–42.

the Spanish market for British manufactures and no sudden influx of American bullion into the West Indies. Neither was there a great advance towards the economic 'capture' of the French Sugar Islands from Dominica. Indeed in the years after 1766 there was constant wrangling as to the value of the free ports to the empire and still more anxiety over the difficulty of enforcing the regulations designed to maintain an open and closed system side by side.

None the less the statutes of 1766 were not without historical significance. They were of course essentially elaborate and calculated refinements of the system enshrined in the Trade and Navigation Acts, fairly described in the King's Speech at the close of the 1766 session 'as a Plan of due Subordination to the Commercial Interests of the Mother Country'.[31] Yet they also evinced a new readiness to question assumptions made during the earlier history of the empire. In the last analysis they represented the first significant attempt to launch an experiment in free trade and a portentous, if small, breach in the old imperial system. John Yorke's comment—'I see they are oversetting every American idea that ever was establish'd'—was not wholly without justification,[32] nor did Grenville's efforts to pose as the defender of the Navigation Acts against the heretical onslaughts of the North American interest entirely lack conviction and credibility.[33]

The Rockingham Administration's commercial legislation was also significant in another respect. In terms of revenue the duties enacted in 1766 proved surprisingly valuable.[34] The molasses duty of 1d., which was scarcely onerous enough to justify evasion, was yet sufficiently remunerative to produce £20,000 per annum by 1772, and in all, the exactions made under the Sugar Act as extensively modified in 1766 yielded over £300,000 in the decade before the War of American Independence, about ninety per cent of all revenue raised from the American colonies during that period. Ironically the taxes laid by Rockingham and his colleagues, entirely to satisfy the pressures of their merchant friends for

[31] *Commons Journals*, xxx. 845: 6 June 1766.
[32] Add.MS. 35374, f. 291: Yorke to Hardwicke, 19 May 1766.
[33] *Walpole's Memoirs*, ii. 224.
[34] The figures which follow are from tables in O.M. Dickerson, *The Navigation Acts and the American Revolution*, pp. 185, 201.

commercial reform and carried through Westminster less than
three months after the repeal of the Stamp Act, were far
more productive than any of those avowedly intended as
financial measures by Grenville in 1764 and Townshend in
1767. It must of course be remembered that Rockingham had
never renounced the possibility of taxing the colonies through
their trade. Indeed the free ports scheme had been recommend·
to him as a potentially lucrative source of revenue, provided
it began with 'small duties, such as the people are willing to
pay',[35] while Rose Fuller strongly emphasised the value of
the molasses duty as a measure which would serve to impress
British authority on the colonies, as well as making a sizeable
contribution to the Treasury.[36] On the other hand, if it is
true that the molasses duty was nakedly a revenue levy,[37] it
is also the case that unlike the Sugar Act of 1764 and the
Townshend Duties of 1767, it was unaccompanied by a
specific declaration of intent to that effect. On neither side
of the Atlantic did contemporaries immediately take note
of its constitutional implications, which were largely incidental
   In fact the whole question of colonial taxation, the most
urgent and volatile problem of imperial policy in the seventeen·
sixties, was somewhat neglected by the Rockingham Ministry.
The twin measures of the Declaratory Act and the Repeal Act
were doubtless commendable, and given a chance, might well
have helped to avert the final breakdown between the mother
country and the colonies. Similarly the Free Ports and Duties
Acts represented an important development in the direction
and organization of imperial commerce. But the remaining
legislation of the 1766 session concerned with America was
of little consequence. The Indemnity Act was no more than
a technicality (as was a new American Mutiny Act), intended
to renew Grenville's measure of 1765. Though the latter met
with objections in some colonial quarters, and indeed in the
fractious provinces of New York and Massachusetts was to
lead to considerable strife, it was not intrinsically important
in terms of imperial policy. The eternal problem of defence

[35] Dartmouth MSS., R. Hale to Dowdeswell, 8 Nov. 1765.
[36] Add.MS. 32975, f. 150: R. Fuller to Newcastle, 10 May 1766. See also
   WWM.R38—7: 'Argument for Reduction of the Duty on Molasses'.
[37] The new duty on foreign molasses, being placed at 1d., was thus precisely that
   which was now to be levied on British molasses. With the differentiation
   destroyed in this way, it was no longer possible to claim that the duty was a
   preferential regulation.

and taxation, which Grenville's policies had been intended comprehensively to solve and which Rockingham's measures had re-exposed, was not touched in 1766. Under Walpole and the Pelhams of course, the costs to the mother country of civil and military administration in the colonies had been such as could be borne without too much difficulty. But after 1763 this was no longer the case. Simultaneously the British empire in America was greatly extended, north into Canada and west into the interior, and the peacetime burden on the domestic budget hugely increased.[38] The dual problem of designing a scheme to regulate and develop these vast new territories and of finding adequate resources to finance it, each in the face of colonial hostility and resentment of imperial interference, was one to tax the abilities of the most adept and statesmanlike minister.

There is no sign that Rockingham recognized the nature of these difficulties or attempted to resolve them. It is true that Dartmouth at the Board of Trade and Barrington at the War Office were aware of the problem, though to some extent their hands were tied. The Proclamation of 1763 and the Board of Trade's tentative Indian Plan of 1764 were intended firstly to guard the western frontier fairly strictly against settlement, at least for the immediate future, and secondly to regulate the Indian trade through a system of thorough and efficient supervision. The 'Old Whigs' showed no apparent determination to alter these plans. Though Dartmouth gained a reputation for sympathy towards the American land speculators, he did nothing to implement any of the several schemes for colonies beyond the Appalachians. Under his direction illegal settlements on the Ohio were prohibited,[39] and when Major Mant, for example, presented his own scheme for 'a settlem[en]t and Gov[ernmen]t at Detroit', Dartmouth 'acquainted the Major that it cannot at present be consider'd on acc[oun]t of the Indian Plan'.[40] Barrington took a little more initiative from his angle of the problem. A paper which he drew up in May 1766 envisaged a major reduction in the excessively expensive military establishments in the new

[38] The most authoritative and recent study of the problem of the western territories in imperial policy is J.M. Sosin, *Whitehall and the Wilderness* (Lincoln, Neb., 1961).
[39] *Journal of Commissioners for Trade* (1764-7), pp. 211–12.
[40] Dartmouth MSS., Dartmouth's Minutes, 21 Nov. 1765.

territories.[41] Gage, the Commander-in-Chief, was in fact already moving troops eastwards, not merely for the sake of economies, but also to ensure that in the event of renewed riots in the thirteen colonies the authorities would never again be as helpless as in 1765;[42] but Barrington's scheme would have entailed a critical change of policy, revoking the military dispositions in the west made by the Bute Administration, and concentrating troops in important centres on the eastern seaboard. However, if the significance of Barrington's plan cannot be denied, it is far from clear that it embodied the 'Old Whig' programme in the way that has sometimes been assumed;[43] there is in fact not a shred of evidence that it represented a conscious and considered realignment of imperial policy by Rockingham and his colleagues.

If one half of the colonial problem lay in the regulation of the American interior, the other was concerned with finding the money to pay for it, or indeed for the administration and defence of the continental colonies in general. Again there is no indication that Rockingham had conceived a project to supply the revenue which the Stamp Act had been intended in part to provide. There was of course Benjamin Franklin's elaborate plan for a Treasury loan office in America, which would both equip the colonies with a paper currency and produce a revenue from the interest payable on such an issue.[44] This was a matter of some importance, for one of the colonies, most prominent grievances was the mother country's prohibition of the issue of paper currencies, since 1751 in the case of the northern provinces, since 1764 in that of the southern.[45] Though British merchants were intensely hostile to any scheme likely to devalue the debts owing to them in the colonies,[46] it does seem that Rockingham made promises

---

[41] P.R.O., C.O. 5/84, ff. 114−27: 10 May 1766.

[42] *Correspondence of Gage*, ed. C.E. Carter, ii. 349.

[43] See for example, C.W. Alvord, *The Mississippi Valley in British Politics*, i. 245−8, and C.R. Ritcheson, *British Politics and the American Revolution*, p. 64: 'Although the Rockingham Ministry fell before the report could be considered, it may be accepted as a statement of their view of the west', an assertion for which no evidence is presented.

[44] See *Papers of Franklin*, ed. L.W. Labaree, xii. 47−60.

[45] Pennsylvania's petition against the act of 1764 was presented to the Commons on 20 March 1766; (*Commons Journals*, xxx. 676). See also J.P. Greene and R.M. Jellico, 'The Currency Act in Imperial-Colonial Relations, 1764-76', *William and Mary Quarterly*, 3rd series, xviii. (1965), 484−518.

[46] For an early instance of mercantile alarm at this proposal, see Add.MS. 42084, f. 22: A. Hervey to Grenville, 30 March 1766.

on this point. Franklin himself believed so,[47] and according
to Charles Garth, the Ministers

have given us to understand that this Subject shall during the Prorogation
be taken into Consideration in order that some general and beneficial
Plan for the whole Continent of America may be proposed in the next
Sessions to the Attention of the Legislature.[48]

Whether Rockingham and his colleagues really did believe that
Franklin's plan could form the basis of such a system, and
what in fact they intended to do for the long-term future of
the colonies in the next session must remain a matter for
speculation.

However, if the Administration did not produce a definitive
answer to the problems of empire in the sixties, it is not easy
to join with those who condemn the 'Old Whigs' for providing
'no permanent settlement for the fundamental differences
that divided the English-speaking world'.[49] As it was, the
amount of American legislation pushed through in the 1766
session was unprecedentedly large.

I hope, [wrote Charles Garth] we shall have given Satisfaction by the
Acts of this Sessions, a more fatiguing one, I imagine, was scarce ever
known; from the multiplicity of business of the first Importance in
itself as well as to the Peace and Happiness of the Kingdom and its
Dominions, and from the strong Contests from Difference of Opinions,
the Session has been protracted much longer than could be expected,
and for great part thereof we almost, as it is said, turned Night into
Day, the Day, it should seem, not being sufficiently long for the Transaction of the Business in Agitation.[50]

In the course of a few months a massive programme, much of
it to the advantage of the North American colonies, was
implemented. 'Every Grievance of which you Complained',
Joseph Sherwood pointed out to Governor Ward of Rhode
Island, 'is now Absolutely and totally removed, a joyfull and
a happy Event for the late Disconsolate Inhabitants of
America.'[51] The Americans themselves were delighted with

[47] Franklin even made the highly questionable claim that the Ministry only
agreed to repeal the Stamp Act because they relied on his scheme to provide
an equivalent yield. (V.W. Crane, 'Benjamin Franklin and the Stamp Act',
Pubs. of Colonial Soc. of Massachusetts, xxxii (1933-7), 59.)
[48] *South Carolina Hist. and Genealogical Mag.*, xxviii (1927), 232: Garth to
Committee of Correspondence, 6 June 1766.
[49] D.M. Clark, *The Rise of the British Treasury*, p. 154.
[50] *South Carolina Hist. and Genealogical Mag.*, xxviii (1927), 233: 6 June 1766.
[51] *Correspondence of Colonial Governors of Rhode Island*, ed. G.S. Kimball,
ii. 384: 15 May 1766.

the progress made, and if Rockingham and his friends were to be ejected from office before they had time to put forward a more positive and comprehensive scheme for the future of Anglo-American relations, criticism on this point is a little churlish.

As the session of 1766 wore on, it became increasingly clear that Rockingham was steadily dismembering the legislation of the Bute and Grenville Administrations. 'Rigby writes us word', Burke heard from Ireland, 'that the present Ministers are solely employed in undoing what their predecessors had done', and Burke's reply conceded 'We are, it is true, demolishing the whole Grenvillian Fabrick. Rigby is right. But we must clear the Ground.'[52] Ever since its inception the Rockingham Administration had been committed to an essentially destructive programme, and Grenville had had some reason to predict in the autumn of 1765 'that it is intended to attack during the ensuing Session of Parliament almost every Public measure which I promoted during the two former sessions'.[53] Yet the earnestness with which the Ministry pursued this task surprised contemporaries. Later on it was to be one of Burke's proudest boasts that 'then for the first time were men seen attached in office to every principle they had maintained in opposition',[54] and even his enemies had to concede the consistency of the 'Old Whigs'.

when an opposition gets into office, [William Knox wrote in 1789] and the King trusts them with the exercise of his power, the farce is at an end, and, after a few aukward apologies, and a few ineffectual votes with old connections, by way of consistency, the business of Government is expected to be taken up, and carried on in the usual way. Such, however, way not the conduct of the old Whigs, when they came into office in 1765.[55]

Fundamentally the determination of Rockingham and his friends to carry out in power the measures they had advocated in opposition was related to their general concern with popularity. It was not quite as revolutionary as is sometimes

---

[52] R.J.S. Hoffman, *Edmund Burke, New York Agent*, p. 344: O'Hara to Burke, 15 April 1766; *Burke Correspondence*, i. 252: Burke to O'Hara, 23, 24 [Apr. 1766].
[53] Grenville Letter-Book, Grenville to Fife, 22 Nov. 1765.
[54] *Burke's Works*, i. 330.
[55] W. Knox, *Extra Official State Papers* (London, 1789), pp. 2–3.

claimed; in part the sheer number of contentious issues raised immediately after the Seven Years War gave them an opportunity which few of their predecessors had possessed previously. Moreover some of their repealing measures, notably those relating to Grenville's colonial policy, they had stumbled on rather than planned in advance. None the less the essential fact remains. There were a whole series of 'engagements which', as one independent member of the Commons remarked, 'I look upon the present administration to have absolutely bound themselves to the performance of',[56] and most of them Rockingham and his friends were extraordinarily anxious to put into practice.

Already they had attempted, if somewhat ineffectually, to reverse the foreign policy of their predecessors, and in the sphere of colonial measures had actually done so. But their principal commitment in opposition had been on domestic and constitutional topics. Pre-eminent among these was the Cider Excise. In retrospect it is not easy to sympathize with the opposition to the cider tax. All alcoholic beverages produced at home had been subject to duties for a long time. But in 1760 and 1761 those on beer had been considerably increased with great advantage to the revenue. Bute's cider tax of 1763 had merely been intended to extend this augmentation to ciders and perries. The professed objection, of course, was not to the financial burden but to the excise regulations accompanying it, which, including as they did, extensive rights of search and trial without benefit of jury, could be relied on to provoke popular hostility. But the ale and beer trade was no less subject to the excise, and doubtless the vigour and success of the opposition to the cider tax had less to do with the merits of the case than the fact that the Beer Excise had been levied by Pitt and Newcastle in wartime, whereas that on cider was laid by Bute in peacetime.[57] 'The repealing of the Cyder Tax', Lord Digby remarked in July 1765, 'will probably occasion a greater and more reasonable

---

[56] *Parliamentary History of England* (London, 1813), xvi, 227: Nicolson Calvert's speech on the budget, 18 Apr. 1766.

[57] There were other factors of course; some of the most interesting related to the economic and political characteristics of the West Country as a whole in in the eighteenth century. Unfortunately the campaign against the cider tax from 1763 to 1766 has not been studied in the necessary detail. The only account of any value is in L.H. Gipson, *The British Empire before the American Revolution*, x. 184–94.

clamour about the last additional Tax upon Beer.'[58]

However the cider issue was one on which the Ministry felt no doubts. It was primarily the concern of Dowdeswell, who had led the opposition to the tax in 1763 and 1764, and had irrevocably committed himself to its repeal. It was also just the kind of issue—'patriot', 'country', and 'popular'— which Rockingham was particularly glad to take up. When a new duty on Minorca wines was under consideration, it was agreed that an excise levy should not be employed—'some other tax would be a better and more acceptable exchange, and more becoming that Administration which is to establish it'[59]—so intent were the Ministers on this point. Moreover the scheme suggested by Dowdeswell was a prudent one. The tax of 1763, though somewhat modified in 1764, had been poorly drafted and inefficiently executed; Dowdeswell sought to eliminate the more irksome aspects of the excise collection by transferring the burden of the tax from the maker to the dealer, from the peasant grower to the retail businessman, a solution which provided the relief desired, though it did not yield an increase in the actual sums collected. There was an impressive array of petitions to support the Ministry's intention,[61] and the new-found anxiety of Grenville and his friends to outdo the 'Old Whigs' in their patronage of popular causes, heavily reduced the extent of opposition;[62] in consequence Dowdeswell's resolutions for the repeal of the old cider tax and the introduction of a new one, were passed in Committee on 14 February without a division. Even in the Lords, where Bute's following was strong and there were some doubts of success, the prediction made by one of Newcastle's friends of 'a safe and pretty easy passage' was fulfilled.[63] With this, however, Dowdeswell had shot his bolt. The pledge of a reduction in the land tax was abandoned, (to be carried from

[58] *Letters to Lord Holland*, ed. Ilchester, p. 239: 18 July 1765 (quoting Ilchester).
[59] WWM.R1–545: Note on 'Duty on wines in Minorca . . .'
[60] Dowdeswell's papers on this subject are at Add.MS. 33041, ff. 161, 181–8: 'Some Considerations' etc.
[61] Petitions were directed from the following places: counties of Hereford, Worcester, Gloucester, Devon, Somerset, Cornwall, Monmouth; boroughs of Exeter, Hereford, Tewkesbury, Leominster, Ashburton, Honiton (26 Feb. 1766), and Weobley (5 March 1766).
[62] The opposition even produced their own bill to limit the summary jurisdiction of the excise commissioners in general. It was rejected by 95 to 48 votes on 5 May 1766. See *Commons Journals*, xxx. 796–7.
[63] Add.MS. 33069, f. 423: Page to Newcastle, 30 Mar. 1766.

the safety of the Opposition benches in 1767), a new and not notably popular window tax introduced, and the expectation of economies in the armed forces disappointed; —a significant comment was the laconic entry in the diary of Sir Roger Newdigate for 24 January 1766, 'Mr. Dowdeswell proposed 16000 seamen!'[64] Dowdeswell, essentially a country Tory of the old school, had entered office with high hopes, but like other Chancellors of the Exchequer before and after him, he did not find it easy to fulfil all the hopes he had entertained in opposition.

If there was any issue on which the 'Old Whigs' were more completely committed than the Cider Excise, it was that of general warrants, the most celebrated of the questions which had emerged during the Bute and Grenville Administrations.[65] Strictly speaking however, there was little for them to do. By 1766 the two issues raised by Wilkes's battle with the executive had both been settled by the Courts. Pratt's judgements in Wilkes v. Wood (1763) and Entick v. Carrington (1765) in the Court of Common Pleas had totally demolished the legality of general warrants issued by the Secretaries of State for the seizure of papers in libel cases, while the King's Bench in the case of Leach v. Money (1765) had made it no less clear that general warrants for simple arrest were quite untenable in law. The Rockingham Administration had aided this process by withdrawing all opposition on the part of the Crown's law officers, both in the cases for damages, and in the allied case involving the printer Almon.[66] However the feeling of the 'Old Whigs' that something more should be done was gratified by the events of 22 April in the Commons, when Savile and Meredith, the leaders of the Opposition's campaign against general warrants in 1763-4, obtained resolutions flatly declaring the illegality of both types of warrant.[67] The resolutions, of course, had no practical importance. As Norton pointed out in the Commons and Mansfield in the Lords, a resolution of one branch of the legislature was quite

---

[64] Newdigate MSS., A.7: 16,000 was the number moved by Grenville in 1765, and bitterly attacked by Dowdeswell at that time.

[65] The only attempt to deal with the Rockingham Ministry's measures relating to general warrants in any detail is in R. Rea, *The English Press in Politics: 1760-1774*, pp. 119–21.

[66] *Rockingham Memoirs*, i. 246–8; J. Almon, *Memoirs of a Late Eminent Bookseller* (London, 1790), p. 31.

[67] *Commons Journals*, xxx. 753–4; the only division was 173 to 71. See Add.MS. 32975, f. 11: West to Newcastle, 23 Apr. 1766.

worthless as far as the law was concerned;[68] while the House of Commons was perfectly entitled to regulate its own rules of privilege, its judgements on matters of law in general were valueless.

That the Ministers were in any case anxious to avoid more than a symbolic and conscience-saving gesture is clear from their opposition to the efforts of Pitt and Grenville, in the most unholy of alliances, to condemn all general warrants of any description,[69] and to do so by statute. This manoeuvre, intended by the Ministry's opponents to 'try', as Bamber Gascoyne put it, 'how far these patriots are in earnest and to overturn the grace of their resolutions',[70] succeeded in embarrassing the Ministers. In the end, however, little came of it. Pitt's motion resolving the illegality of a 'General Warrant for seizing and apprehending any Person or Persons', and declaring its execution on a Member of Parliament to be a breach of privilege, was accepted on 25 April.[71] But his attempt to put it on the statute book was rejected.[72] Similarly a bill of Grenville's devising 'to prevent the Inconveniences and Dangers to the Subject from searching for and seizing Papers',[73] though actually read three times and passed in a rather truncated form by the Commons, was consigned to oblivion in the Upper House, doubtless because the Ministry in general, and its Attorney-General in particular, thought it wise to leave its destruction to the peers rather than appear openly in opposition to it in the Lower House.[74]

The problem raised for the Ministry by general warrants were as nothing to the difficulties it faced in relation to their most celebrated victim.[75] John Wilkes, who, outlawed and in

[68] *Select Statutes, Cases and Documents*, ed. C.G. Robertson (8th edn., London, 1947), p. 455; Robertson also prints extracts concerning the cases mentioned above.

[69] The Administration's resolutions had only related to those involved in libel cases, that is of the type attacked by Wilkes.

[70] Strutt MSS., Gascoyne to Strutt, 28 Apr. 1766.

[71] *Commons Journals*, xxx. 771; see also *Rockingham Memoirs*, i. 325–9; Add.MSS. 32975, ff. 25, 27; 33001, f. 198.

[72] *Commons Journals*, xxx. 780; Add.MS. 32975, ff. 49–52: Onslow to Newcastle, 29 Apr. 1766.

[73] *Commons Journals*, xxx. 822.

[74] *Lords Journals*, xxxi. 410. For the Commons debates on the bill, see Add.MS. 35607, ff. 260–1: Harris to Hardwicke, 10 May 1766; Add.MS. 32975, f. 128: West to Newcastle, [9 May 1766] ; Strutt MSS., Gascoyne to Strutt, 20 May 1766

[75] None of the many biographies of Wilkes are wholly satisfactory for the events of 1765-6, but among the more useful are H. Bleackley, *Life of John Wilkes* (London, 1917), R. Postgate, *That Devil Wilkes* (London, 1956), O.A. Sherrard, *A Life of John Wilkes* (London, 1930).

exile had returned to Paris in the summer of 1765 after a tour
of Italy, was more than especially desperate for money and
had high hopes of the change of Administration. Though the
'Old Whigs' had had reservations about Wilkes personally they
had always supported his cause against Bute and Grenville,
and as he himself remarked, 'If I do not return under this
Ministry, what can I expect on any change, except indeed of
one with Lord Temple at the head?'[76] His demands were
characteristically outrageous, comprising a full pardon to end
his legal problems, and a lucrative office, preferably the
Constantinople embassy or the Governorship of Jamaica,
(with his friend Lauchlin Macleane as Lieutenant-Governor),
but failing these a large pension on the Irish establishment.[77]
These demands were made as of right, and were accompanied
by a frankly threatening posture. 'If the Ministry do not find
employment for me', he declared, 'I am dispos'd to find
employment for them. . . . One sett of Ministers I occupied
a year and a half. If the power of the other shou'd last as
long, the chace might not be shorter and little chance of
their being in at the death.'[78]

For Rockingham and his colleagues Wilkes presented a
most awkward problem. Though they had early communicated
their readiness to assist him through George Onslow,[79] there
were considerable difficulties. All those who acted as inter-
mediaries between the Ministry and Wilkes tried to impress
on him the implacability of the King's aversion to him.
William Fitzherbert pointed out that 'The difficulty wh[ic]h
arises is from our having two Pardons to Get, one public—
another private nor can we have one without the other', while
Burke informed his brother, 'Lord R[ockingham] is extremely
averse from asking any thing for him from the K[ing].'[80] It
was obviously unlikely that George III would ever bestow
favours on a charlatan who had publicly abused and vilified

[76] W.P. Treloar, *Wilkes and the City* (London, 1917), p. 45: Wilkes to [Fitzherbert],
    4 Dec. 1765.
[77] *The Correspondence of the Late John Wilkes with his Friends*, ed. J. Almon
    (London, 1805), ii. 204, 210; W.P. Treloar, *Wilkes and the City*, p. 44;
    J. Almon, *Anecdotes of the Life of Pitt*, ii. 10.
[78] Add.MS. 30868, f. 207: Wilkes to Cotes, 4 Dec. 1765 (inaccurately printed in
    Correspondence of Wilkes, ed. Almon, ii. 218,) and W.P. Treloar, *Wilkes and
    the City*, p. 45: Wilkes to [Fitzherbert], 4 Dec. 1765.
[79] *Correspondence of Wilkes*, ed. Almon, v. 240–1.
[80] Add.MS. 30869, f. 2: Fitzherbert to Wilkes, 3 Jan. 1766; *Burke Correspondence*,
    i. 231: Burke to R. Burke, sen., *ante* 14 Jan. 1766.

his name, and who had done so much to disrupt the early
years of his reign. No comment could have been more just
than that of Humphrey Cotes on the Ministry's situation.
'I really think they want the Power of doing you the Essential
Service they wish', he told Wilkes.[81]

The attempted solution of this problem was an extraordinary one. Rockingham and his friends offered Wilkes a
pension of £1,000 per annum, with the possibility of a
further £500, 'to be paid out of the income of their respective
places', until more permanent measures could be taken.[82] The
spectacle of a Ministry paying a blackguard like Wilkes to
stay abroad aroused not a little amusement and derision. At
first Wilkes haughtily declined the offer as 'precarious,
eleemosinary, and clandestine',[83] but then changed his mind,
without notice drawing two bills for £500 on Fitzherbert
from Thomas Foley the banker, a manoeuvre which caused
considerable surprise and confusion. How much he in fact
received over the following year is not certain; estimates
ranged from a minimum of £630 to well over £1,000.[84] What
is clear is that the statement he later made during his violent
quarrel with Horne Tooke—'I never did receive from them
either *pension, gratuity*, or *reward*'[85] —was a blatant lie.

The pension was by no means the end of the story of the
Rockingham Ministry's relations with Wilkes. The latter had
long been threatening to return to England regardless of his
outlawry and finally did so in May 1766. Yet a whole series
of meetings with Rose Fuller, George Onslow, and Sir William
Baker, as well as Fitzherbert and Burke, failed to produce the
desired outcome.[86] To the immense relief of the Ministers,
he returned to Paris with more money from Fitzherbert and
an assurance that something would be done for him. Burke's
tactics must have had a better effect than Fitzherbert's earlier
efforts to pacify him, for Wilkes professed high hopes from
Paris, assuring Burke of his desire 'of becoming your fellow

[81] Add.MS. 30868, f. 199: 18 Oct. 1765.
[82] W.P. Treloar, *Wilkes and the City*, p. 47: Wilkes to Onslow, 12 Dec. 1765.
[83] Ibid., p. 46: Wilkes to Fitzherbert, 8 Dec. 1765, and p. 47: Wilkes to Onslow, 12 Dec. 1765.
[84] The lower and more questionable figure was Cotes's; J. Almon, *Anecdotes of the Life of Pitt*, ii. 15.
[85] *The Controversial Letters of John Wilkes, Esq., the Rev. John Horne, and their Principal Adherents; with a Supplement, containing material Anonymous Pieces* (London, 1771), p. 199.
[86] J. Almon, *Anecdotes of the Life of Pitt*, ii. 10–16.

labourer', and promising to do any 'good word or work of which I may be thought capable, and I live in the impatient hope of returning soon, and perhaps aiding to keep the boars out of the garden'.[87] But before any further developments could occur, the Administration was to fall. On the whole the 'Old Whigs' had little to regret about their difficulties with Wilkes, however comical their attempts to buy him off. Every other Ministry in the first decade of George III's reign managed to fall foul of him, but Rockingham, if more by luck than judgement, did well to escape serious trouble.

At the time of Wilkes's visit to England in May 1766, his demands were among the least of the Ministry's problems. By then it was rapidly becoming clear that the Rockingham Administration was tottering to its fall. Throughout the early months of 1766 there had been many who considered this was the case, and by the spring the air was full of rumours of a ministerial revolution, with the Ministers themselves admitting that they were 'in a most embarrassed situation'.[88] This was curious for, on the face of it, Rockingham and his friends seemed to be in a strong position. They had weathered a constitutional and political crisis of exceptional magnitude, surviving the total disruption of the forces of government, and producing sensible and efficacious measures for the colonies. In addition they were engaged in carrying a host of bills through Westminster, performing promises made in opposition, and overhauling the commercial regulations of the empire. Nor was the Ministry obviously weak in Parliament. Since the defeats in the Lords in February there had been no major reverse there for the Government, and in the Commons the Administration's majority remained a workable one. Given the contentious nature of the plethora of measures pushed through in the 1766 session, it was not surprising that the Opposition forced a large number of divisions. Yet the Ministry's majority never fell below 37 even in the smallest of Houses, and in general it was far higher. The general warrants resolutions, the cider repeal, the window tax, the American bills, all were passed without difficulty, and there was no indication

[87] *Burke Correspondence*, i. 257: 12 June 1766; for Burke's cautious reply, see i. 259: 4 July 1766.
[88] *Companion to the Newspaper* (1835), p. 368: Conway to Hertford, 29 April 1766.

that the Government stood in imminent danger of defeat and destruction.[89] Contemporaries were emphatic that 'Opposition is dwindled to nothing', and 'There is now little opposition here left',[90] and Burke had every reason to assure his friend O'Hara, 'I see nothing in the union, the ability, or the spirit, of opposition, which is able to move them'.[91] Yet he was also conscious of the paradox involved in the Ministry's position. 'We are in an odd way', he remarked, '. . . in the Road of being the strongest ministry ever known in England are our Superiors now; In the probability of being none at all.'[92]

The 'oddity' of this situation was rooted in a general and acute lack of confidence in the Administration's capacity to survive, which despite their record of sound measures and popular standing, dogged Rockingham and his colleagues throughout their tenure of office. In the spring of 1766 this sentiment had grown visibly stronger as the apparent incompetence and disunity of the Administration became more obvious. Much of this impression was owing to grave mismanagement in the Commons, which despite the majorities won by the Ministry, detracted seriously from its reputation.

[89] The following is a list of the significant divisions in the Commons from March.

Date	Admin.	Opp.	Majority	Issue
10 March	127	48	79	Excise
18 March	145	48	97	Cider tax
25 March	105	57	48	Malt tax
18 April	162	112	50	Budget
21 April	179	114	65	Lottery
21 April	169	85	84	Window tax
22 April	173	71	102	General warrants
28 April	92	52	40	Window tax
29 April	130	78	52	Window tax
29 April	130	75	55	Window tax
5 May	95	48	47	Excise bill
6 May	68	28	40	American trade
9 May	87	49 or 50	37 or 38	General warrants
12 May	104	51	53	Window tax
3 June	118	35	83	Princes' money
3 June	109	31	78	Princes' money

Of course not every issue was one of Government against Opposition. In two divisions on general warrants (9 May, 75:40 = 35; 14 May, 55:16 = 39) the Ministry's forces were divided because no clear Government direction was given. In the Lords the only significant division was 57:16 in the Ministry's favour on the window tax on 28 May.

[90] Add.MS. 30839, f. 25: Macleane to Wilkes, 4 Mar. 1766; G.F.S. Elliot, *Border Elliots*, p.399: G. Elliot to Sir G. Elliot, 1 Apr. 1766.

[91] *Burke Correspondence*, i. 248: Burke to O'Hara, 8 Apr. [1766].

[92] Ibid. i. 241: Burke to O'Hara, 1, 4 Mar. 1766.

Typical was one account of a debate on 15 April, when the
two Treasury Lords present, George Onslow and Thomas
Townshend, proposed an alteration of the malt tax.

> Strange management, that a material point was to be the business of
> the day, but no Chancellor of the Exchequer there, or anyone of the
> Ministry to support it . . . Pitt said he was entirely against these measures,
> and totally disliked the whole, so much that they knocked under and
> said it was not a measure of government but a measure entirely of their
> own, which brought a laugh on them and on the Ministry, too, to find
> no head there, and the business to be carried on at the caprice of any-
> one who chose to start up and propose their own schemes. George
> Grenville was there, but said not a word: left it to battle it among them-
> selves, and all the sensible people laughing in their sleeves at such a
> material affair under such management.[93]

At the bottom of such problems lay divided leadership. At
the best of times, eighteenth-century conditions did not favour
an Administration in which the chief Minister was a peer and
the Minister for the Commons a subordinate. In addition to
this, Conway was not the most effective of managers, honest
and conscientious though he was; as it happened, he was
gravely ill for a long period in March and April and quite
incapable of attending to his duties. His stand-in, Dowdeswell,
could hardly compare with Grenville and Pitt. Moreover it
was generally agreed that the Ministry as a whole was 'inef-
ficient and feeble', 'weak, timid and unequal to their important
Station'[94] and above all utterly divided. Even a friend and
member of the Administration like John Yorke could describe
it as 'a Vessel with[ou]t officers, and a crew undisciplin'd . . .
What a Medley of Characters and Connections! They seem to
be composed of the fragments and remains of all the political
systems and coalitions which have made any figure in this
country, since we were born.'[95]

This chronic lack of public confidence in the Administration
was greatly intensified by the resignation of Grafton, who had
long been threatening to retire from office, and on 28 April
apprised the King of his intention to do so as soon as the
Ministry could find a successor. Though rumours were circu-
lating that he was piqued about a patronage disappointment,[96]

[93] *Osborn Letters*, ed. J. McClelland, pp. 99–100: Mrs. Osborn to J. Osborn,
15 Apr. 1766.
[94] 'Correspondence between Strahan and Hall', *Pennsylvania Mag.*, x. 98, 97:
7 Apr. 1766.
[95] Add.MS. 35374, ff. 291, 293: J. Yorke to Hardwicke, 19 May, 4 June 1766.
[96] *Cust Records*, edd. Lady E, L. and Sir J. Cust, iii. 262.

the avowed reason for his action was the fact that Pitt had not been taken into the Administration. 'The footing I stood on with Mr. Pitt', he later declared, 'and my connexion with him left me but little room for much consideration.'[97] By this stage it was clear that there could be no amicable junction between his idol and the existing Ministry, though further efforts had been made since the failure of the negotiations at Bath and in London in January 1766. Rockingham had launched a final attempt to obtain Pitt's assistance at the end of February. 'The time', he then informed Thomas Nuthall, 'is critical. Might I wish to know whether Mr. Pitt sees the possibility of coming and putting himself at the head of the present Administration? I can only say with very sufficient grounds that Mr. Pitt has only to signify his idea.'[98] Yet again, despite this open invitation through Nuthall and equally strong hints through Shelburne,[99] Pitt remained aloof, declaring *He had said His say*' and was 'under an impossibility of conferring upon the matter of *administration* without *his Majesty's commands*'.[100]

For Grafton, who was not moved by Rockingham's very reasonable contention that the failure of the various negotiations was to be laid solely at Pitt's door, this was sufficient; he had come in, he insisted, 'in July last supposing it to be the unanimous opinion of the Administration to serve till Mr. Pitt should be inclined to come forth, then that they were to continue or retire as he would think fit'.[101] Probably there were additional motives for Grafton's decision. He had no great liking for business, and was naturally irritated at Rockingham's persistent inability either to conduct state affairs efficiently or to share the burden of speaking for the Ministry in Parliament. It was on him, as Hardwicke remarked, that 'the labouring oar had lain in the House of Lords'.[102] In any event his resignation was a severe blow to his colleagues, though fortunately it did not lead to a spate of imitations. Conway, anxious though he was to be out of office, and being equally committed to a junction with Pitt,

[97] *Grafton Autobiography*, p. 73.
[98] *Rockingham Memoirs*, i. 312: [27 Feb. 1766].
[99] Fitzmaurice, *Life of Shelburne*, i. 377–81.
[100] Add.MS. 33078, f. 90: Newcastle to Duchess of Newcastle, 9 Feb. 1766 and *Chatham Correspondence*, ii. 401: Pitt to Nuthall, 28 Feb. 1766.
[101] *Letters from George III to Lord Bute*, p. 246: [3 May 1766].
[102] *Rockingham Memoirs*, i. 333.

in 'such a dilemma as I can satisfy myself in neither way',[103] ultimately contented himself with exchanging his own department for Grafton's and thus ridding himself of American responsibilities. The only outright resignation in fact was that of Viscount Howe, the Treasurer of the Navy, who declined to remain in a Ministry which did not include Pitt, though he had found no difficulty in occupying a seat at the Admiralty Board under Bute and Grenville while Pitt was in opposition.[104] 'These Hows', Bamber Gascoyne remarked, 'have always sail'd well in politicks and know the political compass well.'[105] Evidently Howe was convinced that the Rockingham Ministry was a fast-sinking ship.

The unfortunate impression created by Grafton's resignation was only enhanced by Rockingham's attempt to find his successor. Grafton's office was the object of a series of refusals unprecedented since the days of the Pelhams, with all the most likely candidates, Charles Townshend, Egmont, Hardwicke, and Charles Yorke, declining to accept the post of Secretary for the Northern Department.[106] Such a concerted reaction could not but reflect adversely on the Administration's prospects. 'Lord Egmont's Refusal is certainly a *bad Symptom*', one of Hardwicke's friends commented, while Charles Yorke's declining was described by his younger brother as 'a sign that he has no opinion that the system is maintainable'.[107] Hardwicke, though he accepted a place in the Cabinet without portfolio, refused Grafton's office because 'I was very diffident of the strength and stability of that administration'.[108] Townshend was no less emphatic; though he was offered a peerage with the Secretaryship, he assured the Ministers, 'that he meant to keep his place, and that they durst not take it from him if they could, and could not if they durst, which he

---

[103] *Grafton Autobiography*, p.73: Conway to Grafton, 23 April 1766.
[104] According to Sackville (H.M.C. *Stopford-Sackville MSS.*, i. 112: Sackville to Irwin, 10 June 1766), Howe resented the arrangement by which he paid £1,200 per annum from his salary to William Finch, who was removed by Rockingham from the office of Vice-Chamberlain of the Household. See also *Grenville Papers*, iii. 243.
[105] Strutt MSS., Gascoyne to Strutt, 29 May 1766.
[106] In desperation Newcastle also listed Rochford, Albemarle, Hyde, Bristol, Richmond, Portland, Scarborough, Bessborough, and 'For the summer only' Holdernesse, and Grantham, as possible candidates (Add.MS. 33001, ff. 208, 210: Newcastle, 'Secretaries of State'.)
[107] Add.MS. 35425, f. 78: H.V. Jones to Hardwicke, [19 May 1766]; Add.MS. 35374, f. 291: J. Yorke to Hardwicke, 19 May 1766.
[108] Add.MS. 35428, f. 28: Hardwicke, 'Private Memoirs'.

hoped was sufficiently explicit'.[109] Nor were these the only refusals. Lord Townshend turned down the French and Spanish embassies with no less determination than his brother, and North, yet again offered office by Rockingham, declined, though only after some hesitation.[110] His refusal was, as Jenkinson remarked, 'a strong proof of his Lordships idea of their instability'.[111]

From the Administration's viewpoint these developments were of the utmost gravity. What Grafton described as 'the general backwardness to embark with the Ministry'[112] was both a symptom and a cause of the Government's obvious weakness. When career placeme.1 would not accept offices pressed upon them by a supplicant Ministry, and ' 'tis a much greater disgrace to be in than out',[113] the situation was indeed serious. All were agreed that drastic action was required if the Old Whigs were to stay in power. Grafton believed that the Ministry 'could not hold long without some material accession of strength', and the Yorkes were no less convinced that 'with[out] additional strength the Ministry cannot last'.[114]

The obvious quarter in which to seek assistance was that which had held the key to the long-term prospects of the Administration from its beginning. A junction with the King's Friends would have been judicious in July 1765, in November 1765, or in January 1766, and it would have been all the more so in the spring of 1766. Those not imbued with the prejudices of the 'Old Whigs' had no doubts on this score. Thus Lord Holland, above all a political realist, asked Richmond

Will they be hurt or strengthened by the accession of L[or]d Northumberland and of A., B., C., for I name no names, and amongst them by all means Norton, if room can be found for him? I see the appearance of great strength and great stability to this Administration; and no one inconvenience from it, if L[or]d Northumberland . . . were to be Groom of the Stole. Would the Ministry be put in any danger by it?[115]

[109] Grenville Papers, iii. 236: Whately to Grenville, 23 May 1766.
[110] Grenville Papers, iii. 236; Rockingham Memoirs, i. 345.
[111] Jenkinson Papers, p. 410: Jenkinson to Sir R. Jenkinson, 25 May 1766.
[112] Grafton Autobiography, p. 89.
[113] Osborn Letters, ed. J. McClelland, p. 104: Mrs. Osborn to J. Osborn, 30 May 1766.
[114] Grafton Autobiography, p. 88; Letters from George III to Lord Bute, p. 250: [3 May 1766].
[115] Ilchester, Life of Holland, ii. 309.

Moreover by the spring of 1766 circumstances were more propitious to such an alliance than at any time since the death of Cumberland. There were several offices vacant with which to placate Bute's unemployed friends, and the 'Old Whigs', it could be argued, had had sufficient time to get over the prejudices they had acquired during the Bute and Grenville Ministries. The great issues of policy and conscience raised in the winter had for a while at least been laid to rest, and the King's Friends themselves, disappointed in their attempt of January and February to unseat the Government and wreck its American policy, would now have been content to come to an agreement with Rockingham and his friends. 'The terror of passing next summer out of employment', one of their connections remarked, 'seems universal'.[116] It was true, of course, that they maintained an air of detachment and independence; Conway complained at the end of April that 'Lord Bute's people have still been shy, and none of them have given any support; which if it does not alter, it is ridiculous to continue; it must immediately be resolved.'[117] Yet the fact was that once the Stamp Act issue was out of the way, Bute's friends showed some readiness to assist the Government. Gilbert Elliot assured his father, who held that it was the job of the courtier unreservedly to support Administration, 'In other matters [than the repeal of the Stamp Act] I have supported Government, and in some instances with effect',[118] while on the many issues raised between March and May, he and his colleagues ostentatiously avoided combining with Grenville. The cider bill, which after all repealed a measure of Bute's Ministry, they 'opposed very faintly'[119] and when there was an important division in the Lords on the window tax on 28 May, all of Bute's friends joined the Administration to defeat the Opposition almost as heavily as in the divisions of the December session of 1765.[120] Moreover Bute himself had dropped a most significant hint. In his speech on the

[116] *Chatham Correspondence*, ii. 381: W.G. Hamilton to Calcraft [? Mar. 1766] misdated 13 Feb. 1766.
[117] *Companion to the Newspaper* (1835), p. 368: Conway to Hertford, 29 April 1766.
[118] G.F.S. Elliot, *Border Elliots*, p. 399: Mar. 1766.
[119] *Chatham Correspondence*, ii. 384: W.G. Hamilton to Calcraft, [10 Mar. 1766] misdated 17 Feb. 1766.
[120] Only Eglinton among the Opposition votes could conceivably be regarded as one of Bute's connections. See *Correspondence of George III*, i. 343–4, for Rockingham's list of some of those voting.

third reading of the Repeal of the Stamp Act on 17 March, he had maintained his hostility to the Ministry's American policy, yet declared that he would never again take office, remarking that 'all faction and party ought as much as possible to be discouraged; and that the present Ministry ought to enlarge their bottom from different sides.'[121] Sackville was particularly struck by this speech.

He has by that [he commented] so authentically excluded himself from ever holding any ministerial office, and has so strongly deny'd his influence, that I should think it will be ridiculous hereafter for any administration to pretend an alarm or to have any jealousy of his returning to power, so that I must conclude there will be some degree of complaisance and attention to those who belong to him.[122]

The expectations thus aroused appeared to have some substance in the spring of 1766. As early as February Mackenzie, Bute's brother and confidant, had made overtures to the Ministry through Egmont, though nothing came of this communication. Ominously Rockingham took not the least interest in it.

I believe [wrote Newcastle] The Principal Point, viz. Mr. Mackenzie's Conversation with Lord Egmont, is, at present, quite out of The Question. My Lord Rockingham, who now acts as The Sole Minister, never took the least Notice to me of it; . . . I . . . asked His Lordship, Whether He had ever mentioned to The King, My L[or]d Egmont's Report of Mr. Mackenzie's Conversation; He said, No, He look'd upon it, *as a very Idle Thing*, and, *had thought no more about it*.[123]

However this question was reopened by Grafton's resignation, which exposed the fundamental insecurity and weakness of the Ministry more glaringly than ever. Discussion of a junction between the 'Old Whigs' and the King's Friends came up at a Cabinet meeting held on 1 May, which was preceded by a preparatory conversation between Egmont, Rockingham, and Conway. Rockingham revealed that, with the utmost reluctance, he and his colleagues would be prepared to offer Mackenzie a Vice-Treasurership of Ireland in return for the guaranteed cooperation of the King's Friends.

I asked them [Egmont reported to the King] whether they imagined this would be sufficient to ensure them the hearty Concurrence of Lord Butes Friends both in the House of Lords and Commons—They

[121] *Caldwell Papers*, Part ii, vol. ii, p. 82: W. Rouet to Mure, 18 Mar. 1766.
[122] H.M.C. *Stopford-Sackville MSS.*, i. 109–10: Sackville to Irwin, 27 Mar. 1766.
[123] Add.MS. 32974, f. 107: Newcastle to Secker, 28 Feb. 1766.

answered, by saying they could not turn out any of their own Friends to make Room for Lord Northumberland. Lord Rockingham spoke peevishly again of Norton and Dyson, and both joined in saying that if they were to go farther now than taking in Mr. Mackenzie their own Friends would All Leave them, and that adding more of Lord Butes Friends in great Offices would be Construed by all the world, as if they were acting their Parts only under his Patronage, which was what they neither could nor would submit to do. . . . To this I replyd only that they knew my Opinion from the Time they came into Office, to have been uniformly the same—viz—That they had not Strength Sufficient of their own to Carry on Y[ou]r Majestys Affairs, and that they must acquire what they wanted, by a cordial Union with the Friends of Lord Bute, or of the Duke of Bedford (if they could be had) or if they neither could or would do either of these, They must make their Retreat.[124]

The meeting in the evening was little more than a repetition of this conversation, and turned out to be the end of any serious attempt to obtain a coalition between the 'Old Whigs' and the King's Friends. A month later another rather half-hearted offer was made of an employment for Mackenzie,[125] but by then it was too late. In retrospect the consistent refusal of the Rockingham Ministry to contemplate the possibility of an overt alliance with Bute's friends seems the critical factor in its fall. It alienated George III whose not unnatural desire it was to see those conciliated, whom he regarded as having stood by him in the first years of his reign, and it perpetuated that division in the Administration which was the greatest obstruction to the continuance of Rockingham and his friends in power. As Richmond, who was 'for offering handsomely to take in several of Lord Bute's friends',[126] pointed out, cooperation with the Bute party would be doubly useful, on the one hand by placating the King, on the other by convincing the political world of the existence of a secure foundation for the future of the Administration.

Even if it was said that we had actually joyn'd Lord Bute and were in connection with him, such a Report would do us good instead of harm. It would then be believed we had realy the King's heart and that would give us the assistance of those who look for the best of the lay and wish to be always with the Court . . . the assistance of such people could not indeed be depended upon, but . . . while we had it, it was of use and . . . when the world thought us strong many people would engage so firmly as not to be able afterwards to go back.[127]

124 *Correspondence of George III*, i. 298: Egmont to King, 1 May 1766.
125 *Caldwell Papers*, Part ii, vol. ii, pp. 85—6.
126 *Rockingham Memoirs*, i. 350: Richmond's Journal, 17 June 1766.
127 'The Duke of Richmond's Memorandum, 1-7 July 1766', ed. A.G. Olson, *E.H.R.* lxxv (1960), 478.

Certainly contemporaries were puzzled by the failure of the 'Old Whigs' to recognize political realities. 'If the present Ministry', asked Holland, 'either cannot or will not go on without help, and yet will not accept of help, what can be said of them?'[128] The King's Friends themselves remained bewildered and resentful, threatening the revival of overt opposition to the Ministry. There were reports that 'Lord Bute wearied with the Indignities, and Malice with w[hi]ch he has been pursued had in a Manner left those who were attached to him formerly to their own discretion, and that they were ripe to make any Junction out of despair', and indeed Mackenzie and Wedderburn were constantly flirting with the Grenville and Bedford groups.[129]

The author of this conduct towards the King's Friends was undoubtedly Rockingham himself. Conway was not averse to an agreement with the Butes—the King told Egmont 'he declares against all measures that may encrease heat and wishes rather to conciliate which is coming nearly on Your ground'[130]—and Richmond, Grafton's eventual successor as Secretary of State, was strongly in favour of a coalition. Egmont and Northington, of course, were both friends of the Bute connection. It was Rockingham and Newcastle who refused throughout to countenance the idea of an alliance with Bute, rejecting it with extraordinary vehemence. Thus Richmond described their reaction at a Cabinet meeting in June to his suggestion of a new overture to Mackenzie: 'L[or]d Rockingham bounced off his seat and the D[uke] of Newcastle put on his Hat to go away, both exclaiming Good God, would you have us joyn My Lord Bute! no, lett us keep our fingers clean.'[131] On both sides the position was much the same in May 1766 as in July 1765. On the one hand Rockingham was insistent that Bute's party was fortunate not to have been systematically driven from office, and 'would go no further in satisfying Lord Bute's friends, except the keeping them in their places if they acted with and in support of the administration'.[132] On the other hand Egmont was 'of opinion that L[or]d B[ute's] Friends will never come in cordially, without

---

[128] Ilchester, *Life of Holland*, ii. 308.

[129] *Correspondence of George III*, i. 306: Northumberland as quoted by Egmont to King, 4 May 1766.

[130] Ibid. i. 296—7: King to Egmont, 1 May 1766.

[131] 'The Duke of Richmond's Memorandum, 1-7 July 1766', *E.H.R.* lxxv. 477.

[132] *Newcastle's Narrative*, p. 61.

some further encouragement than keeping them in Their Employments', and George III himself argued that 'whilst they were barely tolerated it could not be expected they would with ardour step forward unasked to support the Ministers'.[133] The fundamental issue was the astonishing consistency with which the 'Old Whigs' maintained their aversion to the King's Friends. In part it was sheer prejudice, born of the bitterness created by the violent antagonisms of George III's first years of rule, in part a deep conviction that their party would dissolve if they departed at all from their long-held views. 'This it was said by Lord Rockingham and the D[uke] of Newcastle', Richmond recorded, 'would lose us our Party.'[134] Such fears were probably illusory. When, a few months later, Pitt, by then in office himself, went out of his way to conciliate Bute's Friends, there was no concerted mass of resignations. Those of the 'Old Whigs' who left office in November 1766 did so for quite unconnected reasons, and as it happened most of the 'young friends' whose loss Rockingham feared earlier did not resign at all. Possibly Pitt could get away with much that his less exalted rivals dared not attempt. None the less it is difficult not to believe that Rockingham and his friends greatly overestimated the attachment of their followers to their own prejudices.

This was not the only miscalculation made by the Ministers. The arguments with which they convinced themselves that their rejection of a Bute alliance need not be fatal to their political prospects, were equally fallacious. In part they relied on a coalition with Bedford and his clique as an alternative to the King's Friends. Rockingham seemed particularly intent on this course, hoping, so he declared, to 'buy the Bedfords, that he always reckon'd about £8000 a year would be sufficient to buy most parties'.[135] Whether this was in fact attempted is not certain—according to Horace Walpole, who is usually reliable in such cases, overtures were made and rejected;[136] but it was in any case not the most practicable of ideas. Rigby and his friends had no great liking for men whom they regarded as incompetent dupes of the old Pelham-Cavendish connection,

[133] Add.MS. 33001, f. 213: Newcastle, 'Short Notes of what passed at My L[or]d Chanc[ello]r's', 1 May 1766; *Letters from George III to Lord Bute*, p. 247: [3 May 1766].

[134] 'The Duke of Richmond's Memorandum, 1-7 July 1766', *E.H.R.* lxxv. 478.

[135] 'The Duke of Richmond's Memorandum, 1-7 July 1766', *E.H.R.* lxxv. 478.

[136] *Walpole's Memoirs*, ii. 222–3.

and felt no more confidence in the permanence of the
Rockingham Ministry than anyone else. However the 'Old
Whigs' drew comfort from what appeared to be a more
favourable consideration than the attitude of the Bedfords.
Above all else they relied on the assurance that there was no
obvious alternative Ministry to their own. 'We risked nothing
by being quiet for that it was impossible for any thing else to
be formed that could hurt us.'[137] The Rockingham Administration had been established because no one else whom the
King could tolerate would consent to take office, it had
survived the severe crisis of the winter for the same reason,
and its leaders did not see why this should not continue to
give them the security which their own strength could scarcely
provide.

As it happened this was not an entirely warranted assumption. It was true that the Opposition leaders were as repugnant
as ever to George III and also that the King's Friends were
incapable of forming an Administration without assistance.
But in one quarter, that of Pitt, there was a critical change of
front in March and April. In the first place Pitt's conduct in
Parliament took an unexpected turn. It was noted that he
made great play in public with the possibility of an alliance
with his brothers-in-law in Opposition. There were 'several
conferences with L[or]d Temple and G[eorge] Grenville',[138]
and an ostentatious display of friendliness towards Grenville
in the Commons in the debates about general warrants. But
far more significant was the new and aggressive stance, which
despite his assurances of friendship to his more devoted
supporters in the Government, he began to display towards
the 'Old Whigs'. Hitherto his public attitude towards the
Ministry had been one of lofty and condescending approval;
it could scarcely have been otherwise, given the way he had
been 'flattered, caressed and even cringed to by the Ministry'.[13]
However with the host of measures pushed through Westminste
from March onwards a new posture was to be adopted. Conway
who maintained a rather pathetic faith in Pitt's good intentions
was shocked to learn of the events taking place during his illnes
'the account I have seems to me quite incredible in respect to

[137] 'The Duke of Richmond's Memorandum, 1-7 July 1766', *E.H.R.* lxxv. 478.
[138] *Grafton Autobiography*, p. 87: Conway to Grafton, 20 April 1766.
[139] 'Correspondence between Strahan and Hall', *Pennsylvania Magazine*, x. 222:
10 May 1766.

the unprovoked violence with which Mr. Pitt is said to have
arraign'd the Administration on the slightest occasion, evidently sought for, and with as much passion, as if the highest
provokation had been offerr'd him.'[140] On the Ministry's
militia proposals, which included economies and reductions,
Pitt made a vehement attack, declaring he 'would go to the
furthest part of England to oppose and overturn that Administration that should attempt to destroy the militia'.[141] 'A
greater basting I never heard', Bamber Gascoyne wrote of
the occasion.[142] A similar onslaught was launched on the
free ports scheme, when he made a speech 'paradoxical,
declamatory, and impertinent'.[143] Horace Walpole, newly
arrived from France, was astonished to discover that 'Mr. Pitt
has kicked and cuffed to right and left, and all is disorder.
I don't guess what the sediment will be.'[144]

This conduct was plainly political in motive. The militia
on which Pitt chose first to display his rancour, was admittedly a favourite topic of his; since the Militia Act of 1757, he
had fancied himself its champion. Yet Walpole at least thought
that 'This was all grimace: he did not care a jot about the
militia.'[145] Nor did his remarks on the free ports evidence
serious thought or principle. 'On this point,' wrote Burke,
who had been sent to reason with him, 'I found so great a
man utterly unprovided with any better arms than a few
rusty prejudices . . . But the truth is, he determined to be out
of humour; and this was the first object he had to display it
upon; for he had in a better Temper approved of all the
previous regulations.'[146]

This typified the general verdict on Pitt's behaviour. 'The
Meaning of this Conduct', David Hume opined, 'is commonly
understood to be, that he wants to be Minister with full
Power of modelling the Administration as he pleases.'[147] In
some sense Pitt was returning to the tactics of his younger
days; what was under way was an all-out attack on every
aspect of the Administration's activities in a determined if
rather petulant attempt to demonstrate his displeasure that it

[140] *Grafton Autobiography*, p. 86: Conway to Grafton, 16 April [1766].
[141] *Jenkinson Papers*, p. 409: Robinson to Lowther, 22 April 1766.
[142] Strutt MSS., Gascoyne to Strutt, 22 April 1766.
[143] H.M.C. *Round MSS.* p. 299.
[144] *Walpole Correspondence*, xxii. 416: Walpole to Mann, 20 April 1766.
[145] *Walpole's Memoirs*, ii. 224.
[146] *Burke Correspondence*, i. 251–2: Burke to O'Hara, 23, 24 [April 1766].
[147] *Letters of David Hume*, ed. J.Y.T. Greig, ii. 43: Hume to Hertford, 8 May 1766.

had not capitulated to his demands of the winter and to force it to its knees as quickly as possible.

It is difficult not to sympathise with the horrified bewilderment of Rockingham and his friends at Pitt's extraordinary conduct. For long they had gone out of their way to court and conciliate Pitt, to obtain his approval of their measures on the one hand and to secure his accession, not as a colleague but as a leader on the other. Their consideration, even adulation, he had repaid with the utmost contempt, and yet had the temerity to complain that he

thought Himself greatly slighted by The Administration; That after all The Messages, and Messengers, That had been sent to Him (Mr. Pitt), That, besides the sending Mr. Tho[ma]s Townshend to Bath, He had had Other Overtures, made to Him at Bath, repeated to Him at His Arrival in Town, and continued to This Time; And That yet Nothing had come of it.[148]

Though biographers have chosen to describe his attitude as one of reason and moderation,[149] and that of Rockingham as insulting and arrogant, contemporaries did not share this view. 'Mr. Pitt', remarked William Strahan, 'is generally condemned by sober dispassionate Men for hovering over the Operations of the Ministry, and tho' invited and caressed by them, declining to take part with them.'[150]

In one sense of course the 'Old Whigs' had only themselves to thank for their difficulties. A fundamental miscalculation ran through the entire history of their relations with Pitt; the fact was that he was not the man to be won over in the way they imagined. His characteristic egotism and envy, nurtured in the early, bitter decades of his career, had not been diminished by the power he enjoyed and status he achieved as an almost unprecedentedly successful war minister. By 1766 his terms for returning to office amounted to a total monopoly of power and the public humiliation of the 'Old Whig' leaders, 'such terms', as Burke remarked, 'as no man with a drop of blood in his Veins would hearken to'.[151] By the spring of 176(

[148] Add.MS. 32974, f. 420: 'An Account of Mr. Thomas Walpole's Conversation with Mr. Pitt; and afterwards with The Duke of Newcastle', 18 Apr. 1766.

[149] See for example, O.A. Sherrard, *Lord Chatham and America* (London, 1955), p. 206: Rockingham's 'approaches, in short, were unwilling, half-hearted and unofficial. Bearing in mind their character, Pitt received them with greater encouragement than they deserved'.

[150] 'Correspondence between Strahan and Hall', *Pennsylvania Magazine*, x. 223: 10 May 1766.

[151] *Burke Correspondence*, i. 250: Burke to O'Hara, [21 April 1766].

Rockingham was aware of his error, assuring the King that he would 'not join in pressing me to send for Mr. Pitt and consult him how I should carry on my Government but that he would give his opinion against it, as he look'd on it, after I had in so candid manner called him Mr. Pitt forth in January as very much beneath me, to make any fresh attempt'.[152] But if the Ministers had learned their lesson as far as Pitt was concerned, by this time it was too late. In their servility and deference to Pitt, they had lowered their reputation in the public mind and gravely damaged their own cause. As Burke pointed out, 'by looking for a support exterior to themselves, and leaning on it, they have weakened themselves, rendered themselves triffling [sic], and at length have had drawn away from them that prop upon which they leaned.'[153] The general lack of confidence in the Ministry had not a little to do with its obsequiousness to the 'Great Commoner', the way, according to one rather brutal but not wholly unjust description, 'The mongrel curs of the present times shrink and creep, and fall down at his footstool, watch his nod, and would show implicit obedience to his will'.[154]

Pitt's change of tack, though it helped to diminish the public standing of the Ministry and confirmed the revival of his interest in his political prospects after Cumberland's death, was not itself decisive. In some ways more significant was a deliberate and explicit declaration of his attitude towards the King's Friends, made in a speech on the third reading of the repeal of the Stamp Act on 4 March 1766.

What was the most particular, [Lord George Sackville recorded] he praised my Lord Bute and said though he did not wish to see him minister yet it was shameful to proscribe his relations and his friends, and said that he had said as much to his sovereign, and that he would avow that advice and meet the enraged citizens and support it to their faces, and that the displacing the noble Lord's brother was an insult up on the King, provided the office did not lead to ministerial influence. After much dissertation upon this subject he cleared himself next of his having objected to the Torys and flattered them under the name of the country gentlemen who had so zealously supported the measures of the war, and expressed the highest opinion of them and the truest regard for them, intimating that whatever they were called they would always act upon true revolution [principles], to which Kynaston nodded, some

[152] *Letters from George III to Lord Bute*, p. 246: [3 May 1766].
[153] *Burke Correspondence*, i. 250: Burke to O'Hara, [21 April 1766].
[154] *Osborn Letters*, ed. J. McClelland, p. 102: Mrs. Osborn to J. Osborn, 29 April 1766.

say it was approbation, others declare he was asleep. Upon the whole, that day's behaviour convinced every body that Mr. Pitt wished to be in office, and that he was resolved to declare to every denomination of men in that House that he had not the smallest objection to act with either of them.[155]

Pitt had never joined in the 'Old Whig' loathing for Bute with very much conviction, and ever since the latter's retirement in 1763 he had recognised that neither Bute nor his friends provided a real threat to his own ambitions. This had been made clear for example in the negotiations of June 1765, but the declaration of the following March was none the less important, amounting as it did to a specific assurance to George III and the King's Friends that he would have nothing to do with the vendetta against Bute, and that from him they need fear no imitation of the Rockingham attitude. Nor did it go without notice in the quarters it was aimed at. George III was well aware of Pitt's public commitment,[156] and it was scarcely surprising that there were constant rumours of a firm alliance between Bute's band and Pitt, and reports, as Albemarle noted, that 'Lord Bute, finding the present administration firm in their aversion to him and his friends, has sent to Mr. Pitt, and that he is to come in upon his own terms'.[157]

The varied developments of the spring of 1766 created the necessary conditions for the downfall of the Rockingham Ministry. Grafton's resignation greatly accentuated the lack of confidence in and out of Government in its capacity to survive. The continued refusal of the 'Old Whigs' to form a junction with the King's Friends and reconstruct a stable Court and Treasury party seemed to threaten an indefinite period of the division and discord which had characterized the session of 1765-6. At the same time Pitt's critical realignment in relation to the Ministry and his declaration in favour of Bute's friends created an obvious alternative to Rockingham as Minister. In short by May 1766, the Administration was weak and demoralized, seemed perversely intent on averting the one course which could improve its prospects, and on top of this, faced a powerful and esteemed rival whose return to office was commonly thought to be inevitable.

[155] H.M.C. *Stopford-Sackville MSS.*, i. 109: Sackville to Irwin, 11 Mar. 1766.
[156] *Letters from George III to Lord Bute*, p. 253: [12 July 1766].
[157] Add.MS. 32975, f. 414: Albemarle to Newcastle, 15 June 1766.

However, if the prerequisites of a political change were present, they had yet to be acted on. As always in the eighteenth century, this was in the last resort the prerogative of the King. Of course the relations between the Crown and its servants were far from being cut and dried at this time. In theory the right of the monarch to appoint and direct his Ministers was absolute. In practice it was limited by the circumstances prevalent at any particular moment. It was not always possible, for example, for the King to have the Minister of his choice. A Carteret might lack the requisite power-base, or a Bute might want sufficient political nerve. But the negative power of the Crown in such matters was less limited; a Minister actually repugnant to the King was unlikely to remain long in power. This was especially so in the case of George III. His grandfather had shown a capacity to accept even those for whom he had no liking, as with the Pelhams in the 1740s and Pitt during the Seven Years War. But George III was a good deal more obstinate and single-minded. Grenville in 1765 and the Fox-North Coalition in 1783 were driven from office solely because they were detested in the Closet, and even the Younger Pitt was compelled to retire in 1801 because his views no longer commanded the royal favour. Not a little of the historical controversy aroused by eighteenth-century politics is a product of the contrast between the personalities of George II and George III, and the differing political attitudes and conduct which they generated. Rockingham and his friends, of course, had to deal with the rather more determined of the two; in the last analysis, their fate as they approached the anniversary of their accession to office was in the hands neither of Pitt nor Bute, the candidates favoured in the public mind, but in those of the King.

VII

THE FALL OF ROCKINGHAM
(MAY TO JULY 1766)

As IT happened George III was far from reluctant to take advantage of the developments which were bearing the Rockingham Ministry to its demise. He had never been particularly well-disposed towards the 'Old Whigs'—his declared enemies during the previous four or five years—but his relief at escaping from the clutches of the hated Grenville and the softening influence of the Duke of Cumberland had led him to treat them with some favour in 1765. However, since Cumberland's death, a number of considerations had combined to produce a growing distaste for the Ministers at Court. Though he clashed awkwardly and embarrassingly with Rockingham over the repeal of the Stamp Act, this was scarcely his prime grievance. Much more important was his conviction that his Ministers were simply not up to the job of effective government. 'The King', Newcastle later remarked, 'was weary of an Administration *of Boys*.'[1] George III himself told Bute of his feelings:

tho' I have kept my complaints to myself, I have suffered greatly from the conduct of my Ministers, and my own contempt of their tallents; but as I thought myself in honour engag'd to support them, I was of opinion that nothing but the most undoubted proofs of their weakness even to most of themselves could enable me without giving some handle of blame to dismiss them.[2]

This accent on the weakness of the Administration was a strong card. The marked indifference of so many politicians to tempting offers of office 'shew'd how very prevalent the opinion must be, of their want of strength', and even a member of the Cabinet was compelled to confess, 'As this Ministry is *constituted*, no Business of any Nicety or Consequence can go on.'[3]

[1] Add.MS. 32976, f. 325: Newcastle to C. Yorke, 29 July 1766.
[2] *Letters from George III to Lord Bute*, p. 250: [12 July 1766].
[3] *Letters from George III to Lord Bute*, p. 252: [12 July 1766]; Add.MS. 35362, f. 6: Hardwicke to C. Yorke, 28 June 1766.

None the less this was not the only reason for George III's unhappiness with his Ministry. Above all it was the distaste of Rockingham and his friends for Bute that ruined their standing in the Closet. By 1766 George III was losing the illusions of his adolescence; no longer did he see politics in terms of a crusade for purity and integrity. Gone were his early dreams of a new system in politics and a halcyon future of noble partnership with Bute; all that remained was a feverish anxiety to find a stable, and permanent Government on the one hand, and to obtain places in it for those who had been loyal to him on the other, 'to see,' as he told Bute, 'as many of those gentlemen who were contrary to my inclinations remov'd reinstated particularly Mr. Mackenzie, in short to see you my Dear Friend once quit of the unmerited usage you have so long suffer'd and openly appearing as my private friend'.[4] It had been demonstrated in January 1766 that these men were incapable of forming a Ministry themselves, and in consequence he had to be content with the hope of a firm and amicable alliance between the 'Old Whigs' on the one hand, and the 'King's Friends' on the other. He doubtless agreed with Egmont that, as Bute was informed, 'if they would cordially wish to be reconciled to you, take in some of your friends, that your attachment to me would make you forget all that has pass'd and that the Administration might be formed on a solid basis'.[5] Unfortunately this was the one point on which Rockingham would make no concessions, and indeed nothing did more to alienate the King. Holland's opinion was not very far from the truth; 'when this Ministry came in, immediately on The King's being forc'd to break his Word to Mr. Mackenzie, and in a Year did nothing to restore his Majesty to His Honour, can they wonder He wish'd to change?'[6]

In any event by May 1766 George III was thoroughly dis-satisfied and disillusioned with his Ministers. Any faith he may have retained in their ability to survive was shattered by the resignation of Grafton and the final decision of Rockingham and his colleagues on 1 May to decline a junction with Bute's Friends. 'On the D[uke] of Grafton's retiring,' the King later wrote, 'I immediately turn'd my thoughts how an effective Ministry could be formed, and secondly, how I

---

[4] *Letters from George III to Lord Bute*, p. 253: [12 July 1766].
[5] *Letters from George III to Lord Bute*, p. 247: [3 May 1766].
[6] Add.MS. 51421, ff. 147–8: Holland to Ilchester, 28 July 1766.

could in the best method dissolve the present Administration.'[7]
However the moment was clearly unpropitious.

I believe You will agree with Me [he told Northington on 28 April, a
few days after the news of Grafton's resignation] that at present I
cannot steer myself with any probability of amendment through the
present labyrinth I am right in permitting them to go on if they can;
for if they should not succeed I am then in no worse situation than at
present; I gain time by this mode of conduct and that is a great deal,
for the Chapter of accidents may be favorable to Me.[8]

This was ominous enough, but a few days later, after
Rockingham's formal rejection of Egmont's scheme for an
alliance with the Butes, all optimism had vanished. As he
told Bute, he had agreed that the Ministers were to go on, but
solely because it 'gain'd me time, and pav'd the way that I
could politely get rid of them if they did not propose that I
approv'd of'.[9] Short of a dramatic change of front and a
sensational change of fortune, the fate of the Rockingham
Ministry was settled by the first week of May 1766. Though
it was to drift on for a further three months, this was merely
'to hobble out the session',[10] and give the King time and
space for manoeuvre, essential to avoid 'falling into the error
of the last year, the being without any administration and
thus negotiating'.[11]

The ensuing two or three months were indeed a curious
period during which George III sought a means of escape
from his Ministry, and his Ministers wrestled to secure their
future, quite unaware that their efforts were foredoomed to
futility. It is important to bear this in mind because there
were developments in that period which were by some thought
to be responsible for the downfall of the Administration. First
among these was the appointment of the Duke of Richmond
as Secretary of State in succession to Grafton. Richmond,
though far from being one of the 'Old Whigs' to oppose the
Bute regime, had long been angling for a senior place in the
Rockingham Ministry. He had made strenuous efforts to
obtain high office in July 1765 and accepted the French
embassy only with reluctance and in the assurance that he
would be allowed to return to England for the ensuing

[7] *Letters from George III to Lord Bute*, p. 250: [12 July 1766].
[8] *Correspondence of George III*, i. 295.
[9] *Letters from George III to Lord Bute*, p. 247: [3 May 1766].
[10] Ibid.   [11] Ibid., p. 250: [12 July 1766].

Parliamentary session.[12] Grafton's resignation, and the refusal of the obvious candidates to replace him, came at a fortunate moment for Richmond, and Chesterfield's remark that he 'begged them [the Seals] and has them *faute de mieux*', was not far from the truth.[13] There was no apparent alternative; Conway (related to Richmond by marriage) was strongly in favour of the appointment, and Rockingham was amenable. However this choice aroused not a little derision. Richmond was as inexperienced as his colleagues, and moreover, like Grafton, was the descendant of a royal bastard. Buckinghamshire made great play with

the Whig administration thinking it necessary always to have a Secretary of State of the Line of Charles the Second (for what other motive could determine them to have appointed his Grace to succeed the Duke of Grafton,) the Duke of St. Albans is next Heir to the Seals, and we may yet live to see them in the hands of the Duke of Cleveland.[14]

A more serious objection to Richmond was the fact that he was detested by the King, and not merely on the grounds that 'that Duke had neither the abilities, temper nor experience requeesite [sic] '.[15] In 1760 Richmond had resigned from the Bedchamber, rashly and precipitately, over an imagined insult to his brother's military pretensions, an impetuous act of anger for which he was never really forgiven in the Closet.[16] George III agreed to his appointment only after Rockingham had threatened to resign over this issue. Horace Walpole, who convinced himself that he was (through Conway) the architect of Richmond's elevation, also thought that this was a critical factor in alienating the King from his Ministers. 'In truth, I believe the Seals which I had obtained for his Grace were a mighty ingredient towards the fall of that Administration.'[17] In fact, though the appointment did nothing to ingratiate the 'Old Whig' leaders with George III, the crucial decision had already been taken. As the King himself later informed Bute, his sole object was 'to gain time that I might with some degree of certainty discover whether Mr. Pitt really was desirous of

---

[12] Add.MS. 51424, f. 259: Richmond to Holland, 7 Aug. 1765. Richmond returned on 21 Feb. 1766 (*Correspondence of George III*, i. 266–7, 274).

[13] *Letters of Chesterfield*, ed. B. Dobrée, vi. 2742: Chesterfield to P. Stanhope, 13 June 1766.

[14] Add.MS. 22358, f. 36: Buckinghamshire to Grenville, 11 June 1766.

[15] *Letters from George III to Lord Bute*, p. 251: [12 July 1766].

[16] See A.G. Olson, *The Radical Duke* (Oxford, 1961), p. 4.

[17] *Walpole's Memoirs*, ii. 239–40.

coming into office'.[18]

This was also true of the second matter which arose to plague relations between the Crown and its Ministers at this time—the dispute over a financial provision to be made for the King's three brothers. The latter, and in particular the Duke of York, a notable political mischief-maker in the mid-sixties, had for some time been demanding an increase in their allowances,[19] but in 1765 had achieved little against the combination of Grenville's economies and the King's irritation at his brother's intrigues. Grenville had then pointed out that 'if in the meantime any accident happened to the Duke of Cumberland, it might meet with less difficulty' and the Duke's death did indeed lead directly to an agreement by which Rockingham promised to divide his allowance among his nephews. However the affair was characteristically allowed to drift, and by the time it came up for final consideration in May, it had encountered grave difficulties. The settlement of Cumberland's money on the three princes required Parliamentary authorization by way of the Commons' Committee of Supply, and by this stage of the session the Committee had been closed. Finance was a sensitive topic with the country gentlemen, and as Lord George Sackville remarked, 'had the ministers done it at this season of the year it would have raised a great clamour against them, and might be reasonably called a surprize, as the majority of the members were out of town in full confidence that all the money demands had been fulfilled.'[21]

This was just the kind of consideration guaranteed to drive the 'Old Whigs' into a state of panic. Conway, who had been ill when the scheme was first proposed, was especially anxious and Rockingham was all too easily influenced by his arguments. Unfortunately it was a matter for a Court as well as a Country interest. George III was always intensely concerned by issues directly involving the royal family, such as the Regency Bill

[18] *Letters from George III to Lord Bute*, pp. 250–1: [12 July 1766]. Richmond's appointment took place on 23 May, nine days after Grafton's formal resignation.
[19] York had voted against the Ministry's American policy in the Lords, had consistently intrigued in and out of Court to secure the return of Bedford to power, and in general did his utmost to assist the Opposition. His two brothers presented less difficulty; the Duke of Gloucester had no liking for political intrigue, and Prince Henry was too young to become involved in such matters.
[20] *Grenville Papers*, iii. 142: Grenville Diary, 1 May 1765.
[21] H.M.C. *Stopford-Sackville MSS.*, i. 112: Sackville to Irwin, 10 June 1766.

of 1765, the Royal Marriages Act of 1772, and the Prince of Wales's allowance in 1783. He was thus particularly angered by this problem, alleging that the Ministers refused to carry out their pledge, 'unless they can be sure of continuing, how mean, how very rankorous is this'.[22] This was a most embarrassing dilemma—'a sad *Scrape*', Newcastle called it.[23] Charles Yorke strongly advised the need to avoid losing credit in the Closet:

I think, that the *ministry* are doing *simply* at Court, in not indulging the King, with the establishment of his brothers, etc. (founded on the dropping of [the] D[uke] of C[umberland] 's revenue) before the Parliament breaks up . . . Nobody can or will oppose it, and their Enemies will make a handle of neglecting it.[24]

The Yorkes of course were essentially politicians and courtiers. Rockingham and Conway, whether to their credit or not, were more concerned with what they conceived to be their popularity and public prestige. The method of escape they devised was not very fortunate. After much difficulty the King's brothers were brought to concede that for the moment they would be satisfied with a formal declaration of intent by Parliament for the next session, the occasion being a royal message to both Houses asking for a grant for the marriage of Princess Caroline to the King of Denmark; this and provision for the princes were promised in an Address to the Crown. In the Commons, Dyson and Augustus Hervey moved resolutions obstructing the Administration's tactics, though both were heavily defeated,[25] and Newcastle rejoiced at 'This Happy End put to This Most Embarrassing Affair'.[26] In fact he was unduly optimistic, for the episode as a whole was bound to leave an unfortunate impression in and out of the Closet. Perhaps, as Rockingham assured Hardwicke, 'their Conduct ab[ou]t the Princes Establishm[en]t was a *Bevue* owing to Hurry and Perplexity'.[27] None the less it inevitably appeared

---

[22] *Letters from George III to Lord Bute*, p. 249: [3 May 1766].

[23] Add.MS. 33078, f. 98: Newcastle to Duchess of Newcastle, 1 June 1766.

[24] Add.MS. 35361, f. 284: Yorke to Hardwicke, [29 May 1766].

[25] For accounts of this day (3 June 1766), see *Correspondence of George III*, i. 353; *Walpole's Memoirs*, ii. 234–5; *Bedford Correspondence*, iii. 336–9; *Caldwell Papers*, Part ii, vol. ii, p. 95; H.M.C., *Stopford-Sackville MSS.*, i. 111–2; Add.MS. 32975, f. 339: Onslow to Newcaslte, 3 June 1766; WWM.R49–29: Rockingham's notes.

[26] Add.MS. 32975, f. 323: Newcastle to Rockingham, 1 June 1766.

[27] Add.MS. 35368, f. 87: 'Heads of My Answer', Hardwicke to Sir J. Yorke, 24 July 1766.

as a gratuitous offence to the King, who vented his irritation
by bestowing a number of minor offices on the princes and
their dependents, without consulting the Ministers.[28] So
marked was his anger that when the Ministry ultimately fell,
Hardwicke was convinced that 'the non compliance with
this Court Point was the ruin of Lord Rockingham's
administration'.[29] However this was certainly not the case.
George III may have been infuriated by the affair but it
played no part in his decision, already taken, to rid himself
of his Ministers. On the contrary he saw it in a light which
would have surprised them not a little had they been aware
of it.

I thought the moment was come [he told Bute] that I should be able
with honour to get rid of my administration, nay I had already sent for
the Chancellor that he might have sounded Lord Cambden with regard
to Mr. Pitt when my brothers made the proposal that compromised the
affair, this disappointed me but did not remove my resolution of
encouraging the Chancellor to continue to get lights from the Chief
Justice, whilst I rely'd on Providence to point out the minute when I
could best dismiss my Ministry.[30]

However George III need not have worried about the need
for an issue on which to part with his Ministers. Indeed
Rockingham himself seemed perversely intent on forcing a
confrontation. In the first week of June the King was
presented with a series of demands which clearly evinced the
determination of the Ministry to continue only on the most
uncompromising terms. These amounted to the bestowal of
several peerages among the back-bench friends of the 'Old
Whigs',[31] and the dismissal of two errant placemen for voting
against Government in recent divisions. The latter were
Jeremiah Dyson, who had long irritated the Ministers by his
consistent opposition in the Commons and at the Board of
Trade, and Lord Eglinton, a Scottish peer and Lord of the
Bedchamber who had intrigued with Grenville and Bedford
throughout the previous winter. Dyson, a highly independent

[28] *Newcastle's Narrative*, pp. 70–1.
[29] Add.MS. 35428, f. 31: Hardwicke, 'Private Memoirs'.
[30] *Letters from George III to Lord Bute*, p. 252: [12 July 1766].
[31] The candidates were Gage, Downe, Fetherstonhaugh, Bridgeman, Warren,
Foley, and G. Pitt, though it was agreed to insist on the immediate elevation
of three only (Gage, Downe, Pitt). See *Correspondence of George III*, i. 355;
Add.MSS. 33001, f. 264: Newcastle, 'Proposed to be made Peers', 2 June 1766;
32975, f. 329: 'Mem[orandum]s for the King', 2 June 1766; ff. 343–4:
Fetherstonhaugh to Newcastle, 5 June 1766.

King's Friend of a legalistic cast of mind, was unrepentant when Rockingham taxed him with his conduct, and the latter felt justified in demanding his dismissal.[32]

Clearly the aim of these demands was to restore some credibility to the Administration. The parlous state of its standing in the public eye had only recently received new emphasis from the interception of a despatch sent by the Russian ambassador in London to his Court, which read 'It is generally thought that the present administration cannot last long, as they have not the confidence of the King, their master.'[33] The creation of peers and the dismissal of two rebels would, as Rigby remarked, 'make an example' and demonstrate the King's faith in his Ministers.[34] Indeed the choice of Dyson and Eglinton was largely fortuitous—earlier Lichfield and Talbot had been thought of, on the general grounds of 'The Necessity of making some Removals, If This Administration is to be supported'.[35] The pill was to be sugared with one or two offers of office to more eligible members of the Bute party; Mackenzie to be given a vacant Vice-Treasurership of Ireland, Northumberland to have the French embassy, and Welbore Ellis the Spanish. But even this concession, which was principally Richmond's design, was considered too generous by Rockingham and Newcastle. As a result of their objections—Conway was characteristically ambivalent, alternately agreeing with Richmond and with Rockingham—Northumberland was excluded from the list.[36] As it happened this did not affect the issue, for the terms which accompanied these concessions were so strong, and the spirit in which they were given so grudging, that George III was unlikely to be brought to agree with his Ministers. The limited offer to Mackenzie had already been turned down once, and it was not made more palatable by the simultaneous demand for dismissals and peerages. This was the maximum extent to which Rockingham was prepared to compromise— later on he frankly informed the King that 'at the Close of the Session we had offered the Vice-Treasurership for him [Mackenzie], because It was thought if his Majesty would

---

[32] Sir L. Namier and J. Brooke, *History of Parliament, House of Commons: 1754-90*, ii. 372; *Correspondence of George III*, i. 354.
[33] *Newcastle's Narrative*, p. 72.
[34] *Bedford Correspondence*, iii. 338: Rigby to Bedford, 4 June 1766.
[35] Add.MS. 32975, f. 435: Newcastle, 'Mem[orandum]s for the King', 18 June 1766.
[36] 'Duke of Richmond's Memorandum, 1-7 July 1766', *E.H.R.* lxxv. 481–2.

have indulged in some Removals—we should not suffer in the
Publick opinion—by giving that office to Mr. Mackenzy.'[37] In
any event this was quite unacceptable to George III. The
peerages were refused,[38] the complaint about Eglinton's
conduct was shrugged off,[39] and the King 'said particularly
as to Mr. Dyson's behaviour in the question about the provision for the princes, that as that affair related to the king
himself, he would not turn him out for that'.[40] In fact the
only concession he made was a distinctly disingenuous
promise to dismiss Dyson if his habits of insubordination
were not mended in the ensuing Parliamentary session, a
fairly safe pledge given his determination to have a new
Government by that time.

These varied developments in May and June, the appointment of Richmond, the furore over the financial provision to
be made for the King's brothers, and the ultimatum presented
by Rockingham thereafter, none of them decisively affected
the issue of the Administration's future; on the other hand
they did nothing to reawaken the King's faith in the 'Old
Whigs' and much to reinforce the decision he had already
reached. In retrospect the Ministers' role in them must appear
perverse, even suicidal, since they were either ignoring or
defying the realities of politics, in much the same manner as
they constantly rejected a junction with the King's Friends.
There can be no doubt that the responsibility was Rockingham.
It was he who had throughout reacted violently against all
suggestion of a Bute alliance, he who had held out for the
choice of Richmond as Secretary of State, he who had involved
the Ministry in the embarrassment of the princes' provision,
and he who was intent on compelling George III to dismiss
some of the King's Friends. His reasons for acting in this way
are not easily elucidated, since the whole question of his
political motives and attitudes is involved. It is true of course
that there is one obvious explanation of his conduct. Some
of his contemporaries diagnosed simply a high degree of
incompetence, naivety and over-confidence on his part, and
it is certainly possible that Rockingham consistently miscal-
culated in the formulation and direction of his political
strategy. Richmond for example had a particularly low

[37] Add.MS. 32976, f. 20: Rockingham to Newcastle, 6 July 1766.
[38] *Rockingham Memoirs*, i. 347.
[39] *Walpole's Memoirs*, ii. 236.   [40] *Newcastle's Narrative*, p. 73.

opinion of his perspicacity:

The true state of the case is that Lord Rockingham's disposition is always to deferr, and by too fine spun schemes to bring about what he wishes. He loses many opportunities by being always too late and while he is talking and schemeing perhaps to prevent a thing, it is done. He depends also too much in my opinion upon the difficulties there is to settle another administration for difficult as it may be it certainly may be done. And another great fault he has, is thinking that because he acts honestly and fairly as he certainly does, it will produce a like return. I believe he also flatters himself he is in favour with the King and altho' there has been lately some things happen'd which have to a degree opened his eyes, yett I believe he still think[s] the King likes him and the present Administration.[41]

Certainly Rockingham seemed strangely unaware of the dangers which threatened him. Thus when Grafton, shortly before his resignation, drew attention to the chronic weakness of the Government, Rockingham assured him, 'that he saw no reason why the present Administration, (if they receiv'd assurances from the King that people in office were to hold their posts at the good will of the ministers), should not carry on very well and with honor to themselves the King's business.'[42] Moreover there was the extraordinary complacency with which he reacted to the constantly reiterated warnings of those around him that his days in office were numbered. Richmond again was driven to fury by this behaviour.

By waiting and giving time [he told his colleagues] the King will have time to settle something else. If he is now unprepared, it is just time to push and acquire the power we want and which is so necessary for every administration. But if we do nothing we shall at last be turned out and what is worst of all, with the reputation of Simpletons, who could not keep the game when they had it.[43]

None the less it is dangerous to take too simplistic a view of Rockingham's political character, for it included a number of unusual and intriguing strands. For example, one of the most influential factors in the development of his career was a curious, yet marked, indifference to the allurements of office. It was true, initially at least, that he enjoyed the deference and prestige brought him by his tenure of the most importance office in the land. But the more normal motivations of politicians and placemen—the desire for profit or power,

[41] 'Duke of Richmond's Memorandum, 1-7 July 1766', E.H.R. lxxv. 479.
[42] Grafton Autobiography, p. 71: Grafton to Conway, 22 April 1766.
[43] 'Duke of Richmond's Memorandum, 1-7 July 1766', E.H.R. lxxv. 478.

the ambition to direct men and measures, whether in the lofty operation of political strategy or the everyday conduct of government business—these were foreign to Rockingham, who was fundamentally an indolent, ineffectual, and only spasmodically interested politician. Basically, of course, his abilities were not sufficient for his job. 'I have seen the Burden too weighty for his Shoulders both in Council and Parliament', Hardwicke declared without malice or prejudice,[44] and Rockingham himself must have been at least partially aware of his insufficiencies. In any event his relative indifference to office emerges in several ways. There were, for example his constant threats to resign, over the revolt of the King's Friends in February 1766, over the appointment of Richmond in May, and over the conduct of Dyson in June. So noticeable was this tendency that George III strongly suspected Rockingham of hoping for a suitable excuse with which to leave office. 'They want', he told Bute, 'to lay their not going on at your door and that of your friends.'[45] In addition there was the remarkable equanimity and inactivity which comprised Rockingham's reaction to the news early in July that a new Administration was to be formed. The King noted with some surprise that 'He behav'd very handsomely said He agreed with Me in it, and that whether He made part or no of it He should wish it success.'[46] Hardwicke was particularly appalled by 'the disgraceful manner in which Lord Rockingham and his Administration laid down their arms, without expostulating freely with the King upon his manner of dismissing them when he had no fault of error in conduct to lay to his charge'.[47] Hardwicke of course, in the career of his brother Charles Yorke, had a considerable vested interest in the future of the Ministry; but from Rockingham's personal viewpoint there was nothing very disastrous about departure in the summer of 1766. He had no great ambition to stay in an office, which whatever its gratifications, was altogether too busy and irksome an occupation. Moreover he could look back on a year of personal success and public applause. A few months previously, when he had contemplated resigning at the height of the repeal crisis, he had been adjured by

[44] Add.MS. 35362, ff. 10–11: Hardwicke to Yorke, 10 July 1766; not included in the version printed at *Rockingham Memoirs*, i. 364–5.
[45] *Letters from George III to Lord Bute*, p. 247: [3 May 1766].
[46] *Correspondence of George III*, i. 367: King to Northington, 6 July 1766.
[47] Add.MS. 35428, f. 34: Hardwicke's 'Private Memoirs'.

Dartmouth to continue until the issue of the Stamp Act was settled. 'Your successors may then be left to enjoy the sweets of an honourable coalition, and hug themselves in the possession of employment, which nothing but concern for the public good could make it worth your while to hold.'[48] Such a pleasing combination of private convenience and public benefit may well have been in Rockingham's mind in the spring and summer. There is at least one exceptionally good authority for this view. Where the newcomer Richmond could only account for Rockingham's apathy and inactivity in terms of overconfidence and incapacity, Newcastle suggested a more convincing diagnosis.

My Lord Rockingham, [he told his old friend John White in June] I believe, wishes to go out, and flatters himself that he shall go out with more éclat than any man ever did; that he has done great service to the King, and to the publick; that he had shew'd the King that he could carry the repeal of the Stamp Act, with His Majesty, and my Lord Bute against him; that he could carry the Free Port with Mr. Pitt against him; and had carried all the regulations, that were proper, relating to the American trade.[49]

This is not to argue that Rockingham was determined to leave office in all circumstances, though there were undoubtedly moments when he gave his colleagues that impression. Nor indeed was he wholly without political objects and ambitions, though they were of a rather unusual kind. Where more conventional political leaders like Grenville or Pitt kept their sights on power, place, and profit for themselves, Rockingham's aspirations could be summed up in one word—party. In that concept was enshrined all his experience and thought. This requires some emphasis, given the boundless criticism and derision levelled by twentieth-century historiography at those in the eighteenth century who professed their belief in the Whig party. It was Rockingham's firm conviction (and one which with much else he transmitted to Burke), that he and his friends made up a distinct party, that that party was the direct and only true representative of the Whig tradition, and that his highest personal achievement would be to lead and maintain it as a unit, preferably in government but if necessary in opposition. Moreover this basic conviction was accompanied by a notion which goes

---

[48] *Rockingham Memoirs*, i. 303: [2 Feb. 1766] misdated 12 Feb. 1766.
[49] *Newcastle's Narrative*, p. 75.

far towards explaining his conduct in 1766. This was the
belief that the permanent enemies of the Whig party were
Bute and the King's Friends, some of them Tories of George
II's reign, some of them merely deserters from the old Pelham
regime, but all of them dedicated to the destruction of
Whiggism and the elevation of a new and sinister influence
behind the throne. To claim firstly that Rockingham and his
friends were not Whigs in any meaningful sense, and secondly
that the King's Friends were neither a malignant nor unnatural
element in the politics of the day (no matter how just these
claims might be) does not alter the fundamental fact that
these were seriously held convictions.

Certainly Rockingham's curious role in the events of 1766
cannot be elucidated without reference to these beliefs. They
explain for example his repeated refusal to treat with Bute's
friends, whose accession was considered fatal to the standing
of the Administration and the party. They also explain
Rockingham's readiness to step down from the Treasury for
anyone on whom it was felt that the 'Old Whigs' could rely.
Grafton for instance 'would be the only real security to the
party', whereas if Temple (the brother of Grenville) were
appointed, 'my Lord Rockingham thinks all hopes of saving
the party, by this administration, were at an end'.[50] Above
all it was hoped that Pitt, despite his earlier unhelpfulness,
could be brought forward. 'By this means', Newcastle
reported, 'Lord Rockingham thinks *he* shall keep *the Whig
party* together, and I suppose be himself at the head of it.'[51]
The same factor also casts light on Rockingham's utterly
uncompromising stance towards the King. His demands were
made not so much on the basis that they were bound to
meet with success, as in the assurance that, if they were
rejected, the 'party' could either be protected by a new Pitt
Ministry, or make an orderly retreat into opposition. It was
in this spirit that Rockingham approached the crisis of his
Administration, dictating terms as though he held all the
cards, and declining to make even the most expedient of
concessions. 'We shall either have done with being Administration—or we shall be so—better and more firm and strong
than we have been', he assured Newcastle,[52] while the latter
informed his wife, 'He thinks He shall either get out, or have

[50] *Newcastle's Narrative*, p. 85.   [51] Ibid., p. 56.
[52] Add.MS. 32976, f. 19: 6 July 1766.

His Charles Yorke etc. His Chanc[ellor]. Oblige the King to turn out Dyson, L[or]d Eglinton etc. and made a Solid Administration of True Friends.'[53] To many, Rockingham's obsession with an unrealistic and anachronistic concept of party was incomprehensible. 'Do not think of your party; you have none but what depends upon the Court,' Holland implored Richmond.[54] This was doubtless good advice. The obstinacy of Rockingham and his friends in consulting the popularity and principles of their party rather than cultivating the Closet and Court was fatal to their political future.

By July 1766 Rockingham and his friends had, from George III's point of view, piled error upon error; in addition to their persistent refusal to come to terms with the King's Friends, and their repeated and unnecessary irritations of the King in the spring, they could lay no claim to public support and credibility. If ever there was a Government which totally lacked the confidence of the political world, it was Rockingham's in the summer of 1766. Junius's later remark that 'Lord Rockingham's feeble administration' had 'dissolve[d] in its own weakness',[55] was by no means an exaggeration, and it was typical of the Ministry that at a critical stage it should provide George III with yet more evidence of its disunity and disarray. The Ministers chose this moment to divide bitterly over a minor piece of patronage, the military Governorship of Hull, which fell vacant in June. Rockingham sought to fill it with a reliable supporter as useful to his own Yorkshire interests as to those of the Government, but Richmond and Conway strongly backed the action of their relative the Duke of Argyll who pressed his own claims almost to the point of resigning his other posts.[56] There could have been no clearer indication of the Ministry's inability to unite even in the face of the utmost danger.

None the less it was not lightly that the King turned to Pitt. The latter, 'black-hearted Pitt' of Leicester House days, had never been a great favourite of his and had not increased his credit in the Closet by thrice refusing to propose an

[53] Add.MS. 33078, f. 102: [7 July 1766].
[54] Add.MS. 51424, f. 269: 4 May 1766.
[55] *The Letters of Junius*, ed. C.W. Everitt (London, 1927), p. 105: Junius to Bedford, 19 Sept. 1769.
[56] Argyll was eventually brought to back down. See *Newcastle's Narrative*, pp. 73-4; 'Duke of Richmond's Memorandum, 1-7 July 1766', *E.H.R.* lxxv. 479-80.

Administration when asked to do so in 1763 and 1765. Indeed by 1766 George III was understandably wary of an approach to Pitt, 'declaring so often, that he thought such a *step* would be personally disgraceful to himself, and that he had twice before acted below his dignity, in seeing Mr. Pitt without knowing what he would propose'.[57] Moreover, it was clear to all that acceptance of Pitt's terms would amount to the total submission demanded by a dictator. As Hardwicke remarked, if the King sent for Pitt, it would be 'to put his affairs for the *present* entirely in his hands—as he must be sensible that the Great Commoner always expects implicit acquiescence in his hands. He will save everybody all the trouble of *thinking*.'[58] This indeed turned out to be very much the case. Newcastle, for example, was irritated at the end of July to find 'That His Majesty will not do any Thing, without The previous Concert of His New Minister, His Majesty had not That Delicacy, with Regard to His present Ministers, during the Whole Time, That They served so well'.[59] However once he had recognized the need to call in Pitt, George III was quite prepared to act with determination. Secrecy was essential. His humiliation in 1765 had been the product of dismissing his Ministry before making any attempt to settle preliminaries for a new one in advance, and he was determined not to repeat his mistake. Later on there was to be considerable debate as to the extent to which the change of Ministry had been carefully premeditated, Newcastle, for example, hearing that 'My Lord Camden has had the Management of this Affair, with my Lord Chancellor'.[60] In fact it is quite clear from George III's own testimony that Camden was approached by Northington as early as May. 'Cambden', the King assured Bute, 'said he [Pitt] was ready to come if called upon, that he meant to try and form an Administration of the best of all party's and an exclusion to no descriptions; this I owne gave me great comfort.'[61]

Even after thus assuring himself at least of Pitt's interest in office, George III avoided acting precipitately. He went to

[57] *Rockingham Memoirs*, i. 367: Hardwicke to Rockingham, 10 July 1766.
[58] Ibid. i. 363: Hardwicke to Rockingham, 11 July 1766.
[59] Add.MS. 32976, f. 256: Newcastle to Rockingham, 26 July 1766.
[60] A. Gilbert, 'The Political Correspondence of Charles Lennox, Third Duke of Richmond, 1765-1784', (Oxford Univ. D. Phil. thesis 1956), i. 155: Newcastle to Richmond, 11 July 1766.
[61] *Letters from George III to Lord Bute*, p. 251: [12 July 1766].

elaborate lengths to ensure that he did not give the impression
that he was ridding himself of his Ministers for any other
reason than their own incapacity, 'particularly after the very
scandalous falsitys the last set that I parted with propagated,
when the real cause of my conduct was their insolence and
at the same time their not advancing any public business'.[62]
In consequence he sought some other means than the direct
dismissal of 1765. 'The plan of the Court', William Hamilton
informed Temple, 'is evidently and avowedly, not to remove
these Ministers from their employments, if it can be avoided;
but to reduce them to the necessity of relinquishing them.'[63]
To this end it was important to have an assistant. The obvious
candidate was Egmont, an old friend of Leicester House and
Bute, and a close confidant of the King throughout 1765 and
the early months of 1766; unfortunately he 'could not', as
George III told Bute, 'be instrumental in what I intended'.[64]
Egmont was one of Pitt's most bitter personal enemies, and
moreover, was an unwavering champion of an Austrian
alliance as opposed to a Prussian one in Europe. It was not
surprising that he had been such a strong advocate of an
alliance between the King's Friends and the 'Old Whigs'.
Upon it his own political future rested; when Pitt did in fact
take office, Egmont resigned almost at once.

Fortunately in the Lord Chancellor there was another
obvious choice as 'the grand negotiator for settling an administration'.[65] Since the inauguration of the Rockingham
Ministry Northington had been very much an agent of the
King, and never made the mistake of allowing himself to
become associated with a particular party or faction—'I can't
have Confidence with Parties', he assured the King in March
1766.[66] He had no liking whatsoever for the 'Old Whigs', and
was very much in favour of George III's plans in the spring,
though he properly pointed out, 'if You intend them to go
on with their present Business they must have, for they want,
all Support'.[67] Moreover he had his own reasons for wishing
to see the Rockingham Ministry at an end. Lord Holland's
comment on his ultimate revolt—'Nor do I think He *picked*

[62] *Letters from George III to Lord Bute*, p. 250.
[63] *Grenville Papers*, iii. 257: 1 July 1766.
[64] *Letters from George III to Lord Bute*, p. 252: [12 July 1766].
[65] *Newcastle's Narrative*, p. 82.
[66] *Correspondence of George III*, i. 285: [18 Mar. 1766].
[67] Ibid. i. 356: Northington to King, 5 June [1766].

a Quarrel; (but I judge at a distance). I believe they gave him
a real Cause, and for the sake of Ch[arles] Yorke'—was not
wholly mistaken.[68] At the beginning of May Rockingham,
loyal to Charles Yorke, who had after all been led to expect
the Lord Chancellorship in 1765, suggested a scheme by
which Northington would replace Winchilsea as Lord President
and give up his own office to Yorke. Winchilsea was agreeable,
and the highest law office in the land was Yorke's ardent, even
overpowering, ambition. However the scheme fell through
because Northington flew into a rage at the proposal and
threatened to withdraw from Cabinet meetings.[69] Rockingham
reacted to this with some spirit, declaring that in that case
'Then He must make his *Bow* to morrow'.[70] At that stage of
course, the King was not prepared for such an eventuality,
and after soothing assurances on all sides the affair was
apparently forgotten. But henceforth Northington was
perfectly aware that sooner or later Rockingham would
insist on his replacement by Yorke. This was to some extent
balanced by the knowledge that Pitt's accession would equally
mean his supersession by Camden; doubtless he opted for the
lesser of the two evils, especially when it was plainly favoured
by his royal master. In this he made a wise choice; his ultimate
reward was not merely the office of Lord President, but also
a massive pension of £4,000 per annum, the gift of the appoint
ment to a place in the Hanaper Office for two lives, and a
Tellership of the Exchequer for his son, by any standards
handsome compensation for his exertions in the King's
service. As Hardwicke commented, he 'gained immensely by
the Jobb'.[71]

    In addition to needing a collaborator, George III felt the
need of a suitable issue on which to part with his Ministers.
Fortunately one was forthcoming to supply the place of the
princes' provision. In late June 'a matter came before us,'
Hardwicke confided to his memoirs, 'which was of great
importance, and the rock upon which we split, or rather
served as the match with which the Chancellor was permitted
to fire the mine laid for the demolition of our weak Ministerial
fabric.'[72]

---

[68] Add.MS. 51421, f. 145: Holland to Ilchester, 20 July 1766.
[69] *Newcastle's Narrative*, p. 59.
[70] *Correspondence of George III*, i. 351: Northington to King, [1 May 1766]
(*Additions and Corrections*, p. 57).
[71] Add.MS. 35428, f. 11: Hardwicke, 'A Memorial of Family Occurrences'.
[72] *Rockingham Memoirs*, i. 350: Hardwicke's Memorial.

Quebec, which for some time had been raising difficult problems for the British Government, was an ideal subject over which Northington could create trouble. Fundamentally the task of administering a large and alien province was not a very tractable one. But since the close of the Seven Years War a number of factors had combined to add to its difficulty and create 'a welter of chaos and discontent'.[73] One was the absurd inadequacy of the measures taken after the conquest of Quebec, and its formal cession by the French Court in 1763, for the future regulation of the region. The Proclamation of 1763, which was intended to lay down the broad pattern of government for all the newly-conquered territories, was impossibly obscure and ambiguous in its provisions for Canada. Murray, the first British Governor, did his rather clumsy best to implement its provisions in a tolerably favourable fashion for the French inhabitants. Unfortunately his main achievement in the process was the complete alienation of the handful of new English settlers in Quebec, whose sole concern was the speedy exploitation of the area to their own profit and power. By 1765 the situation in the new province was one of considerable confusion. Ordinances for the creation of courts and assemblies had been promulgated, which irritated the French in so far as they were in accord with the apparent intentions of the Proclamation of 1763 to discriminate against their own customs and traditions, and the English to the extent that they were softened by the Governor's efforts to prove liberal in their application. Indeed relations between the British settlers and the Quebec Administration eventually broke down altogether, their conflict culminating in the celebrated case of Thomas Walker, J.P., whose ear fell victim to what was regarded as a carefully planned assault by military friends of the Governor.[74]

The reaction of the Rockingham Ministry to these problems was predictably one of concession and surrender. The unfortunate Murray, who at worst had been guilty of tactlessness,

[73] W.S. Wallace, 'The Beginnings of British Rule in Canada', *Can. Hist. Rev.* vi (1925), 221. For other useful studies of this problem, see A.L. Burt, 'Governor Murray and the British Government', *Proceedings and Transactions of Royal Soc. of Canada*, 3rd Ser., xxii (1928), 49–56; R. Coupland, *The Quebec Act* (Oxford, 1925), chapters i–ii. The most recent general summary is in H. Neatby, *Quebec: The Revolutionary Age, 1760-91* (London, 1966), chapters iv–v.

[74] See A.L. Burt, 'The Mystery of Walker's Ear', *Can. Hist. Rev.* iii (1922), 233–55.

was recalled on 1 April 1766 to explain his conduct, and new officers were sent out. Ultimately Murray was acquitted by the Privy Council of all charges against him, and indeed the policy pursued by his successor Carleton proved to be not markedly different from his own. Though it was suspected that Murray was recalled by Rockingham because of his association with Bute,[75] it is more likely that as usual the 'Old Whigs' were giving way before the pressure applied by the mercantile interests. To a great extent the mercantile connections of the Canadian settlers were an extension of the North American interest, and were on good terms with the Ministry. Brook Watson, for example, the leading Canadian merchant, was a member of the London North American Merchants Committee, and worked in close cooperation with the Ministers in the matter of the Anglo-French negotiations over the Canada Bills. It was scarcely surprising, as a result, that it was the merchants' and settlers' side of the case which claimed the attention of Rockingham and his friends.

Perhaps a little more remarkable is the action they took, albeit furtively, to solve the religious problem in Canada. Toleration had been granted as part of the settlement in the Peace of Paris and confirmed in the Proclamation of 1763, but the precise status of the clergy had remained unclarified. There were, for example, obvious objections to recognizing a Roman Catholic Bishop (the last had died in 1760), whose allegiance would be to the Vatican if not to Versailles. However, after some consideration the 'Old Whig' Ministers agreed to the acknowledgement of the more moderate candidate, Briand, as Superintendent of Clergy (and tacitly Bishop) in Quebec, permitting his consecration in France. This business was transacted in the most clandestine manner, and some embarrassment occurred when the Board of Trade found itself compelled to restrain the enthusiasm of customs officials intent on burning Briand's books.[76] Yet this was a thoroughly judicious and statesmanlike provision; and one which reflected creditably upon its authors.[77]

However, the recall of Murray and the recognition of Briand were matters of slight importance compared with the

[75] A.L. Burt, 'Governor Murray and the British Government', *Proceedings and Transactions of Royal Soc. of Canada*, 3rd Ser., xxii. 56; R.H. Mahon, *Life of General the Hon. James Murray* (London, 1921), p. 342.

[76] P.R.O., T.1/453, f. 264: J. Fremantle to C. Lowndes, 7 May 1766.

[77] See W. Kingsford, *The History of Canada* (London, 1888-98), v. 174–5.

central problem of the Quebec constitution. As early as
6 August 1765 Dartmouth and his fellow-Ministers had met
'to come to a determination' on this difficult question.[78]
Though the Board of Trade spent a good deal of time drawing
up schemes, the critical decisions were made by Charles
Yorke, who as Attorney-General was required to give a formal
legal opinion on the situation of justice in Canada. His advice
was unhesitatingly on the liberal side; his plan provided for
the revocation of the judicial ordinance of 1764 and
recommended a compromise on the matter of law—the
institution of English law in criminal cases, and the retention
of the old French code in civil.[79] Moreover, the cause of
French conciliation and integration was to be advanced by
the admission of the native settlers both to the practice of
law and to service on juries. In essentials this scheme bore
a close resemblance to that later embodied in the Quebec
Act of 1774. It is ironic that that Act, coinciding as it did
with the Intolerable Acts, contributed not a little to the onset
of the American War of Independence; had Yorke's plan been
pushed through in 1766, events might well have taken a rather
different turn. As it was the scheme was wrecked by the dis-
integration of the Rockingham Ministry, and then effectively
buried during several years of almost total inactivity on the
Quebec problem. For this Northington must bear the
responsibility.[80]

Northington had long held strong views on this matter.
Already in 1765 he had opposed Grenville's proposals for
the establishment of a recognized and fully tolerated Roman
Catholic Church in Quebec, declaring to Sandwich that he
could not 'think this plan . . . either approvable or practicable'.[81] When the Rockingham Ministry came to consider
connected matters in the spring of 1766, he was no less
obstreperous. Carleton for example, who left to take over
from Murray on 19 June, departed, as Richmond told
Newcastle,

---

[78] Dartmouth MSS., Dartmouth's Notebook.
[79] For the plan in its final form, that is the draft drawn up by Yorke and
Pownall of additional instructions to be despatched to Carleton and dated
24 June 1766, see R.A. Humphreys and S.M. Scott, 'Lord Northington and
the Laws of Canada', *Can. Hist. Rev.* xiv (1933), 54—62.
[80] Ibid. 42—54.   [81] Sandwich MSS., Northington to Sandwich, 9 June 1765.

without his instructions owing to some difficulties the Chancellor found or rather put in our way, which have delay'd him till now, and would have stopped him a week longer if he had stay'd for them. It was thought the lesser evil to send him away without them than to delay the Packet any longer.[82]

Nor was this the end of his obstructiveness. At a Cabinet meeting called on 27 June to settle the problem finally, he refused to cooperate in authorizing the instructions for Carleton designed by Yorke. 'Old *Tom*', Hardwicke informed his brother the day after, 'was so Cross and Negative last Night that no Business c[oul]d be done w[i]th Regard to the Affairs of Quebec. He w[oul]d neither Lead, nor be driven, and in short w[oul]d give no Opinion at all, any further than that he thought all was wrong.'[83] In fact Northington did not entirely lack a credible defence for his attitude. One of his basic objections, so he declared, was not to Yorke's scheme as such, as to the fact that it was to be carried out by Carleton with no other sanction than an Order of the King-in-Council. According to his argument—and it was one to which Francis Maseres, Quebec's new Attorney-General, subscribed—only Parliament could provide for the organization of a new legal system in the province.[84] Of course Northington was concerned with a good deal more than the legal merits of the dispute, as his blatant obstruction at the meeting on the 27th demonstrated. His final complaint that he was kept insufficiently informed by his colleagues led on to an emphatic declaration that 'it was ridiculous to expect him to give his opinion upon matters he was not prepared upon, and, therefore, he declared he would attend Councils no more'.[85]

Naturally enough there was some dispute as to whether Northington was acting under orders in this affair, Rockingham for example wondering 'whether this Transaction of the Chancellor's is on a *Plan* or a mere Effect of Passion'.[86] In fact it is clear that Northington's conduct had the King's previous

[82] A. Gilbert, 'Political Correspondence of Richmond', i. 143: 19 June 1766.

[83] Add.MS. 35362, f. 6: 28 June 1766; see also *Rockingham Memoirs*, i. 351–5; *Newcastle's Narrative*, pp. 26–7.

[84] F. Maseres, 'Considerations on the Expediency and Procuring an Act of Parliament for the Settlement of the Province of Quebec', printed privately in 1766 and reprinted in F. Maseres, *Occasional Essays on various subjects, chiefly political and historical* (London, 1809), pp. 327–64.

[85] *Rockingham Memoirs*, i. 355: Richmond's Journal, 27 June 1766.

[86] Add.MS. 32976, f. 21: Rockingham to Newcastle, 6 July 1766.

concurrence and his encouragement, now that Camden had given the necessary assurance that Pitt would not be wanting in resolution if summoned yet again to form a Ministry.

[The Chancellor, George III informed Bute on 12 July] came to consult with me whether he might not decline attending Cabinet meetings and if they ask'd his reason, declare that the little confidence shew'd him was the cause of it, added to his opinion that he could not with honor continue in the station he held unless a stronger Administration was formed; I very much approved of this and said it would bring things to an issue very honourably for myself.[87]

Unfortunately for the plotters, this plan misfired. Doubtless they relied on Rockingham's threatening to resign as he had at the beginning of May when Northington had declared that he would withdraw from the Cabinet. But on this occasion Rockingham's reaction was quite different. 'To my great astonishment' George III reported to Bute, 'the Ministers took no notice of the Chancellors secession.'[88] Indeed Rockingham and his colleagues were not especially alarmed by the loss of a colleague who, since the inception of the Ministry, had been a constant thorn in their flesh, and whose office would very conveniently be filled by Charles Yorke. After Northington's withdrawal two further meetings were held on the subject of Quebec, with Charles Yorke himself present to push ahead his plan.[89]

This rather embarrassing development drove the King and his confidant to new disingenuities. On Sunday 6 July Northington had an audience with his royal master,

saying [as Richmond retailed to Newcastle] he cannot attend Councils, and that to keep the seals and not attend would be indecent, he therefore will resign. He did not confine his reasons to the want of communication he complains of, but said he thought the system weak; that it was intended to gain Strength by the disposal of vacant offices, but that nothing was done, and he could not go on so.[90]

In fact this declaration was no more spontaneous than Northington's retirement from the Cabinet. According to the King's account to Bute,

I . . . on Fryday told him if he really was of opinion that the sooner the Administration ended the better; he must come to me on the Sunday

---

[87] *Letters from George III to Lord Bute*, pp. 251–2.   [88] Ibid., p. 252.
[89] Add.MSS. 35428, ff. 32–3; Hardwicke's 'Private Memoirs'; 35870, ff. 316–17: Hardwicke: 'Heads of My Brothers Speech', 4 July 1766.
[90] A.G. Olson, *The Radical Duke*, p. 115: 6 July 1766.

and declare what he had purposed to have said to them; he accordingly
did so; I upon that told Lord Rockingham that as individuals I wished
my Ministers well but that I agreed with the Chancellor that no one
man of weight having sought for the Vice Treasurership of Ireland,
the Treasurership of the Navy, or the embassy to Spain . . . I owed it
to my Country to make once more an effort whether a solid administration could not be fram'd.[91]

A message was immediately sent to Pitt, and by Wednesday
9 July an effusive reply assured Northington and the King
that he would come to London at once. On the same day
Rockingham and his colleagues were informed in the Closet
that they were to be superseded.

To all intents and purposes this was the end of the
Rockingham Administration. 'Yesterday', Horace Walpole
wrote to Lady Suffolk on 10 July, 'the administration's year
was completed and yesterday the administration ended.'[92]
All that remained was to await the outcome of the King's
discussions with Pitt and subsequent negotiations for the
detailed arrangements of the new Government. On the 23rd
Rockingham was informed by George III that his Ministry
was definitely at an end;[93] and seven days later the formal
changes were made. There had of course been a good deal of
speculation as to the extent of the changes. Rockingham
regarded 'the sending for Mr. P[itt] as one and the same thing
with the dismission of all the present set'.[94] Yet not long after
this, Horace Walpole could assert with some emphasis that
'There will be very few alterations, and no leaven. The present
administration will be retained, or pacified.'[95] This turned
out to be substantially correct. The ministerial changes
associated with the conclusion of the Rockingham Ministry
were certainly not comparable to those which had accompanie
its formation. There were few resignations or dismissals. The
principal leaders naturally had to go, partly to satisfy Pitt's
terms of January, partly to demonstrate to the public, as one
of Wilkes's friends remarked, 'that Mr. Pitt appoints, and that
the Pelham Interest is no more'.[96] Rockingham's departure
was inevitable, though according to Barrington, he was offered

[91] *Letters from George III to Lord Bute*, pp. 252–3: [12 July 1766].
[92] *Walpole Correspondence*, xxxi. 121.
[93] Fitzwilliam MSS., Box 25: Rockingham to ?, 23 July 1766, misdated 24th.
[94] WWM.R1–647: Savile to Rockingham, 13 July 1766.
[95] *Walpole Correspondence*, xxii. 441: Walpole to Mann, 23 July 1766.
[96] Add.MS. 30869, f. 58: H. Lawrence to Wilkes, 16 July 1766.

'any Court office';[97] doubtless acceptance of such an offer
was out of the question after the dignity of the Treasury. The
dismissal of Richmond, Winchilsea, and Newcastle was equally
predictable, Newcastle declining to take a pension. In addition
Charles Yorke resigned after the promotion of his rival Camden
to the Lord Chancellorship. He had some reason to be irked,
for in 1765 he had undoubtedly been promised that office.
Yet in 1766 the only offer made him, 'in a dry way',[98] was
that of Chief Justice of the Common Pleas; had it been
accompanied by a peerage such as Camden had received a
year previously, he would unquestionably have accepted it,[99]
but no such offer was forthcoming. Yorke was one of the
great losers by the violent instability of politics in the 1760s.
'Your Grace', he remarked to Newcastle when he retailed the
story of his latest misfortune, 'will excuse this Short History
of a man Sacrificed to the Times',[100] and nothing could have
been more apt. Yorke was the type of the legal placemen,
brought up to be a sound Court and Treasury man, but
plunged by the accident of his illustrious father's political
connections into the factious strife of George III's early years.
Though he was a natural King's Friend if ever there was one,
Yorke's career, and eventually his life, fell victim to the rise
of party.

Apart from the resignation of Egmont, and the dismissal of
two minor office-holders—Lord George Sackville, long marked
down by Pitt, and the Earl of Breadalbane whose post of
Scottish Privy Seal was needed for its old occupant Mackenzie—
this should have been the extent of the changes required by
Pitt's elevation. There were however one or two others.
Dartmouth had long been agitating for the creation of a new
office of Secretary of State for the Colonies, a demand to
which Rockingham had agreed in principle, and he preferred
to resign rather than 'endure the cutting off his American
pretensions by the New People, when He contended for that
point with his old friends'.[101] Dowdeswell was another
casualty—partly the victim of Grafton's insistence on Charles

---

[97] Add.MS. 6834, f. 72: Barrington to Mitchell, 31 July 1766. There were also
reports that it was intended to offer Rockingham the Lord Lieutenancy of
Ireland. (*Grenville Papers*, iii. 287).
[98] Add.MS. 35428, f. 11: Hardwicke, 'A Memorial of Family Occurrences'.
[99] Ibid., WWM.R1—664, 668: Yorke to Rockingham, 28, 30 July 1766.
[100] Add.MS. 32976, f. 324: 29 July 1766.
[101] *Burke Correspondence*, i. 262: Burke to O'Hara, 29 July [1766].

Townshend being offered the Exchequer, partly of Pitt's characteristic fury at hearing of a certain rumour.

Permit Me, Sir, [he wrote to the King] most humbly to add that if Lord Rockingham's being *Quiet*, as Mr. C. Townshend informs Your Majesty depends on no other Motive than Mr. Dowdeswell continuing Chancellour of the Exchequer I most humbly advise that a Resolution be finally taken that Mr. Dowdeswell be immediately acquainted by Your Majesty's Command, that He is not to remain in that Office.[102]

Dowdeswell was offered the compensation of the Board of Trade or the Paymaster-Generalship, but by this time had a notion of his own importance which prevented him accepting either. 'It might be a misfortune,' he assured the King, 'sometimes to have been raised too high; men could not, after being much exalted, stoop to certain offices which they might have at first accepted.'[103] Dowdeswell was followed out of office by one other member of the Treasury Board. Lord John Cavendish resigned simply on the grounds that 'I have allways thought Mr. Pitts style too high for my temper'.[104]

That there were no great sweeping changes of the kind witnessed a year previously is not altogether surprising. In the first place both Pitt and the King had every reason to retain most of those already in office. 'The D[uke] of N[ewcastle] and his friend the Marquess must give way;' Camden wrote to Grafton on 13 July, 'but I do not believe Mr. P[itt] will wish to remove the Rest in office, unless perhaps they in a pique should scorn to hold on under his appointment, which I do not expect.'[105] Quite apart from any other considerations, Pitt's personal band of followers was far too small to provide the basis of the new Administration. He had little choice but to leave most of the 'Old Whigs', particularly those in minor offices, undisturbed.

Equally important was the fact that the latters' leaders also favoured their remaining. Again it was the obsession of Rockingham and Newcastle with their party that directed their conduct. Both were insistent that 'The Remaining of our Friends in Employment, is The Surest Way to support

[102] *Correspondence of George III*, i. 381: 25 July 1766.
[103] *Sir Henry Cavendish's Debates*, ed. J. Wrighte, i. 580: Dowdeswell to Mrs. Dowdeswell, 30 July 1766.
[104] Add.MS. 32976, f. 269: Cavendish to Newcastle, 26 July 1766.
[105] Grafton MSS., 2.

the Party, and The Cause.'[106] Thus Newcastle enjoined
Portland, 'Pray don't think of quitting; That will ruin all',
while Rockingham was furious at the precipitate resignation
of Lord John Cavendish, 'I was much surprised as I did think
that our Friends would have waited and been more
Temperate.'[107] This attitude was the result of a curious conviction on the part of the 'Old Whig' leaders that it was
possible to maintain unity and discipline, to say nothing of
their own primacy, in a party under Pitt's wing, or rather
that it was possible to enrol Pitt in the party's service by
surrounding him with their friends. It was essential to this
scheme however that the key posts in the Administration
should be in the hands of especially reliable supporters.
Unfortunately it appeared at first that Rockingham's
immediate successor at the Treasury would be Temple, since
Pitt insisted on offering him the post. At this stage Rockingham
was unusually pessimistic; 'this is not at all pleasing to our
Friends in general and probably will be decisive', he told
Yorke on 17th July.[108] However Temple had no intention of
accepting office on his brother-in-law's terms, which he
rightly judged would make him a 'Capital Cypher'.[109] News
of his refusal completely transformed Rockingham's opinion.
Eight hours after his letter to Yorke he informed Newcastle:
'I am much pleased because I now think that the Corps will
be kept together, which indeed I fear'd was doubtful some
Hours ago.'[110] Henceforth the 'Old Whigs' remained secure
in the belief that Pitt was in their power by virtue of his
dependence on Grafton on the one hand and on Conway on
the other. These were the party's 'two friends in the first
departments of Government able and willing to protect
them',[111] though one was a devoted follower of Pitt, and the
other an irresolute sympathizer torn between two loyalties.
Yet Rockingham and his friends acted on the principle that
they were their docile agents in the Cabinet. 'We think ourselves perfectly safe in your Hands, and The Duke of
Grafton's,'[112] Newcastle confided to Conway at the end of

[106] Add.MS. 32976, f. 223: Newcastle to Ashburnham, 24 July 1766.
[107] Add.MS. 32976, f. 221: 24 July 1766; f. 253: Rockingham to Newcastle, 26 July 1766.
[108] Add.MS. 35430, f. 56.
[109] Add.MS. 42084, f. 104: Grenville to Powis, 20 July 1766.
[110] Add.MS. 32976, f. 162.
[111] Add.MS. 32976, f. 269: Cavendish to Newcastle, 26 July 1766.
[112] Ibid., f. 315: 29 July 1766.

July. If this was absurd it was still more so to believe that Pitt
would be vulnerable to such a strategy. After Temple's refusal
of office, Newcastle could seriously write, 'Mr. Pitt must now
make use of us; He has no where else to go; and Both Sides
ought to be *reasonable*' and 'Now is the Time for Conway To
fix Him when His Wrath must be strong against Lord Temple'.
Time was to reveal the total impracticability of the 'Old Whig'
scheme, but for the moment they retained their belief in its
validity. It was customary for Ministers to declare on leaving
office that they had no intention of opposing their successors
without excellent cause, and Newcastle characteristically
announced on this occasion that 'an Idea of a Formal Opposition would be most Impolitick, and Unjustifiable'.[114] But
he and Rockingham must have been among the very few
eighteenth-century Ministers who really did intend to support
the Administration which had supplanted them.

This was all the more surprising when it is remembered that
by this time Rockingham had little reason for faith in Pitt's
friendship or good intentions. Tactically it would have made
sense to conduct an orderly retreat into opposition with such
forces as he could muster. Even if the scheme which he
actually intended to pursue had endured for long, its most
logical result was not the capture of Pitt by the party, but
the capture of the party by Pitt. Moreover, Rockingham's
personal relations with Pitt were now very bad. During July
he grew increasingly angry at Pitt's complete failure to communicate at all with him about the negotiations for a new
Administration. 'There seems to be much anger among many',
he wrote to Newcastle, projecting his own discontent onto
his friends, 'at the Total Silence of Mr. Pitt, and that neither
directly nor indirectly thro' either Conway or the d[uke] of
Grafton any mark of Attention or Civility of even desiring or
wishing for their concurrence has as yet been made.'[115] Just
before Rockingham finally stepped down from office, this
resentment was to lead to an incident which caused something
of a sensation among the gossip-writers.

The episode was on the face of it a trivial one. Conway,
intensely worried by his friends' complaints of neglect at the

[113] Ibid., f. 175: Newcastle to Onslow, 18 July 1766; f. 173: Newcastle to
Rockingham, 18 July 1766.
[114] Ibid., f. 115: Newcastle to Rockingham, 12 July 1766.
[115] Add.MS. 32976, f. 253: 26 July 1766.

hands of Pitt, had with the utmost difficulty managed to persuade his new chief to pay a courtesy call on Rockingham. With Newcastle such a gesture would have worked wonders. However, 'Lord Rockingham came home while Mr. Pitt's chair was at the door, upon which it was carried into the hall, but his Lordship went up stairs and sent word by his servant to Mr. Pitt that he was extremely busy, and could not possibly see him.'[116] This was the snub direct; as Onslow remarked, 'It is as personal as possible'.[117] That Rockingham's motive was the pique aroused by earlier neglect is evident from a letter which he wrote to Conway the day before the attempted visit, a letter which makes it equally apparent that the insult was entirely premeditated.

That after his [Pitt's] total want of attention or civility to many considerable friends of ours, and of positive assurances of his good intentions towards our friends, in general that after all this he should propose an interview, I really think that I should be wanting to myself, and to others, to have any personal communication with Mr. Pitt.[118]

This doubtless rather childish affair was not without its significance. 'Pitt says, I hear,' Lloyd reported to Grenville, 'that he is resolved never to be angry again, but that if this had happened twenty years ago, Lord Rockingham should have heard of it, for he would have taken no such usage from the first Duke in the land.'[119] This was not the most convincing of declarations, ringing as it was with the authentic tone of Pitt's resentment of the Whig aristocracy, and it is difficult not to agree with Walpole's comment that Rockingham 'forced Mr. Conway to draw in Mr. Pitt to receive an affront; and from that day the wound was incurable'.[120] It was certainly not an auspicious beginning to what had been pictured as an amicable partnership between Pitt in office and Rockingham on the back-benches, designed to preserve the cause of true Whiggism for the future. What the future held for Rockingham in particular, and his beloved 'Whig' party in general, was far from certain when he formally surrendered his office on 30 July, just fifty-five weeks after he had assumed it.

[116] Grenville Papers, iii. 287: W.G. Hamilton to Temple, 30 July 1766.
[117] Add.MS. 32976, f. 309: Onslow to Newcastle, 28 July 1766.
[118] Rockingham Memoirs, ii. 6: 26 July 1766.
[119] Grenville Papers, iii. 283: 29 July 1766.   [120] Walpole's Memoirs, ii. 253.

VIII

THE EMERGENCE OF THE ROCKINGHAM PARTY
(JULY TO DECEMBER 1766)

ROCKINGHAM left office to encounter a public reception which verged on the euphoric. Rather surprisingly he met with a tremendous demonstration of support and enthusiasm for his 'most popular administration',[1] and a host of congratulatory addresses were presented to him and his colleagues. The London North America and West India Merchants, for example, expressed their appreciation of a 'Period, short indeed, but, truly memorable for the Noblest exertions of a Patriot Ministry in favor of the Civil and Commercial Interests of these kingdoms', while the Liverpool merchants declared their concern at 'the sudden and unexpected removal', and those of Manchester opined that 'though there have been times when the Minds of Men were more captivated by the lustre of warlike transactions yet there never was a time when the Hearts of the People went along with an Administration more sincerely than with that in which your Lordship had a principal share.'[3] However these compliments were as nothing to the great chorus of approval which greeted Rockingham when he arrived in his own county. At York he was met 'by a great Number of Persons of Family and Fortune',[4] and a week later at the York races he was subjected to a stream of deputations and addresses. Wakefield, Leeds, Sheffield, Halifax, and Hull, proud that 'our county, in you, has produced an Example worthy of Imitation to all future Administrations',[5] showered him with testaments of their praise and admiration. Rockingham of course was delighted at such

---

[1] *Walpole Correspondence*, x. 222: Walpole to Montagu, 10 July 1766.
[2] The following addresses were received: to Rockingham: Bristol, Halifax, Hull, Lancaster, Leeds, Leicester, Liverpool, London, Manchester, Sheffield, Wakefield, York; (WWM.R59); to Dartmouth: Liverpool, London, Manchester; (H.M.C. *Dartmouth MSS.*, ii. 44, 46–8); to Burke: Lancaster; (*Correspondence of the Right Honourable Edmund Burke: 1744-97*, ed. Earl Fitzwilliam and Sir R. Bourke (London, 1844), i. 104.)
[3] WWM.R59–22: 4 Aug. 1766; R59–20: 28 Aug. 1766; R59–28: 15 Aug. 1766.
[4] Add.MS. 38205, f. 77: ? to Jenkinson, 22 Aug. 1766.
[5] WWM.R59–8: Halifax to Rockingham, Aug. 1766.

manifestations of his prestige and standing in the public eye. 'I never', he wrote to Newcastle from Wentworth, 'saw more good Humour nor more Appearance of thorough Approbation, than was kindly expressed to me by all Ranks and denominations of the Gentlemen of this Country—so that in Truth in what Regards myself in the last Events, I would not wish an Iota alter'd.'[6] His pleasure was doubtless not diminished by the sensational change of fortune which his successor's stock suffered at this time. The consequence of Pitt's blunder in taking a peerage was particularly marked in London; 'the city as an Alderman told me consider him as dead', Sir James Porter reported.[7] This dramatic fall from grace certainly threw Rockingham's popularity into high relief. 'You are really beating the late Great C[ommone]r at his own Weapons', Hardwicke assured Rockingham, 'and receiving those Eulogiums w[hi]ch his *Puffs* have hitherto supposed, that No-body was *entitled* to but himself.'[8]

Something of this mood of general admiration for a 'short but wise and virtuous Administration' was exploited by Edmund Burke in a pamphlet published in August 1766. The *Short Account of a Late Short Administration*, though less celebrated by posterity than his *Thoughts on the Cause of the Present Discontents*, *American Speeches*, and *Reflections on the Revolution in France*, is, for all its brevity, equally impressive, a flawless piece of political propaganda, unburdened by rhetorical passages or philosophical reflections. Setting out to describe 'plain facts; of a clear and public nature; neither extended by elaborate reasoning, nor heightened by the colouring of eloquence',[9] Burke made three basic claims for Rockingham and his friends—the wisdom and efficacy of their measures, the novelty and importance of their alliance with commercial and manufacturing interests, and the unwavering propriety and integrity of their political conduct. Though his brush was by no means impartial, Burke's picture was so skilful, its distortions so

---

[6] Add.MS. 32976, ff. 488–9: 29 Aug. 1766.

[7] H.M.C. *Weston Underwood MSS.*, p. 401: Sir J. Porter to E. Weston, 29 Aug. 1766.

[8] WWM.R1–679: 24 Aug. 1766; the version printed in *Rockingham Memoirs*, ii. 10, is slightly inaccurate.

[9] *Burke's Works*, i. 184.

subtle, that it was not easily rebutted.[10] In the nineteenth century, of course, what had been written (like much else of Burke's) in the heat of political strife, and with the most partisan of intentions, came to be accepted as an authentic historical record. Yet in retrospect there is little to sustain the veracity of Burke's account of the year which he and his masters spent in power.

No doubt the achievements listed by Burke, the Repeal of the Stamp Act and the Declaratory Act, the two statutes relating to colonial trade, the Repeal of the Cider Excise, the General Warrants Resolutions, the Russian Commercial Treaty and the Canada Bills Convention, all seemed to provide impressive testimony to the vigour and wisdom of the Rockingham Ministry. Yet a realistic appraisal might reveal two essential facts about these measures; they were largely negative, and they had little long-term importance. Virtually every act of Rockingham and his colleagues in 1765-6 was in some sense a concession to external pressures rather than a product of independent and constructive thought. The Stamp Act was repealed because Rockingham took the line of least resistance towards the clamour of the merchants and manufacturers, though he deserved some credit for adopting the saving expedient of the Declaratory Act. The Repeal of the Cider Excise, despite Dowdeswell's labours at the Treasury, was little more than a surrender to the demands of the West Country, while the commercial bills of the 1766 session were less the work of the Ministers than of the joint merchants' committees. The General Warrants Resolutions, if inaugurated by the Government, were all but taken over by Pitt and Grenville; the Russian trading agreement had been initiated and designed by the Grenville Administration; and the Canada Bills Convention was merely an inevitable compromise with the French Court. It remains one of the great paradoxes of the Rockingham Ministry, that while its achievements were manifold and beneficent, they owed relatively little to the industry or ingenuity of Rockingham and his fellow-Ministers. At least one nineteenth-century historian appreciated this.

All these measures were well and kindly meant. For the most part they were salutary and judicious. Yet still if we consider how decrepit was

[10] Grenville's hack pamphleteer, Charles Lloyd, wrote a rather pedestrian rejoinder, *A True History of a Late Short Administration* (London, 1766).

the state of the Government, and how naturally every feeble Government leans towards the easier course of concession, and shrinks from the more rugged duty of resistance, we shall, I think, ascribe these measures in part to its weakness, and not solely, as Burke would persuade us, to its wisdom.[11]

They were also measures of very limited significance in the long run, though the Ministers themselves could hardly be blamed entirely for this. The great advantage and benefit genuinely achieved by the Repeal and Declaratory Acts were wilfully squandered by the misguided strategy of Charles Townshend. The commercial legislation of 1766, bold though it was, was neutralized by the growing conflict with the American Colonies. The General Warrants Resolutions were quite meaningless exertions of Parliamentary energy—so much wasted breath on matters already settled by the Courts. The new cider tax represented an arguably useful reform, though hardly one of momentous importance. Very little of the legislative structure erected by the Rockingham Administration in 1766 had any practical significance a decade later.

In purely political terms Rockingham and his friends had still less on which to congratulate themselves. Though Burke made much of their record in this respect as in others, less partial observers were apt to consider that they had distinguished themselves by a long succession of misconceptions and blunders. Their last months in office, for example, had been marked by two mistakes, either of them quite sufficient to have brought about their downfall—Rockingham's insistence on the appointment of Richmond as Secretary of State and the furore over the Princes' Provision. However such errors sank into insignificance compared with the fundamental misapprehensions of the Ministry in its policy of espousing 'Pitt and popularity' at the cost of 'King and Court'. The consistent failure of Rockingham and his colleagues to conciliate or mollify the King's Friends, and their refusal to take the measures essential for the confidence and favour of the King combined with their futile and humiliating courtship of Pitt, to achieve their ruin. 'The state', Lord Holland fairly remarked, 'had neither fallen to Lord C[hat]h[am]s or Earl T[emple]'s share, if the preceeding Administration had Acted

---

[11] Lord Mahon, *History of England from the Peace of Utrecht to the Peace of Versailles* (London, 1853), v. 146.

with Common sense.'[12] Chatham, of course, who pursued
with alacrity precisely the tactics which Rockingham had
disdained to adopt, had no doubt that the priorities in the
politics of power lay at Court. His sudden unpopularity
apparently left him unmoved, declaring as he did,

> That He was very Sensible of The Run There was against Him; But, That
> It did not affect Him, nor should alter His Conduct; That If his Majesty
> was pleased, (which He did not seem in The least to doubt,) To continue
> His Confidence to Him, He would never desert The King; But support
> Him, in all Events, broke, and Old as He was;—That he has not the least
> Doubt of Success; And That His Administration would be a permanent
> One.[13]

All of Chatham's actions were designed to monopolize the
confidence of the Crown and restore the disciplined unity of
the Court and Treasury bloc, 'to shew, That He had The
absolute Sole Power, both in The Closet, and in The Administration'.[14] Almost his first act in office was to reinstate
Mackenzie at the Scottish Privy Seal, and within six months
of the inauguration of Chatham's Ministry, almost all those
numbered among the King's Friends had been taken in.
Northumberland was given a dukedom, Hillsborough was
restored to the Board of Trade and Despenser to the Post
Office. North was placed at the Pay Office, Stanley received
a diplomatic appointment to the Prussian and Russian Courts,
and Jenkinson and Nugent were established at the Boards of
Admiralty and Trade repectively. These were the men who
had declined to tie themselves to the Rockingham Ministry,
though as Newcastle complained, 'Their Accession might
have prevented any farther Alteration'.[15] It was not surprising
that the general view entertained 'no doubt of the strength
of the new administration',[16] nor that something like an air
of normality returned to the governmental scene after the
extraordinary developments of the previous year.

> Most of those who have been driven out of the King's service by different
> administrations [Barrington informed Mitchell,] are now restored to it;
> and I think it more for the honour and dignity of government first to
> do acts of justice, than to begin by gaining enemies . . . You must have

---

[12] Add.MS. 51421, f. 153: Holland to Ilchester, 13 Aug. 1766.
[13] Add.MS. 32977, f. 41: 'Substance of a late Conversation held by the E[arl] of
Ch[atha]m', 7 Sept. 1766.
[14] Add.MS. 32977, f. 42.
[15] Add.MS. 32976, f. 426: Newcastle to F. Montagu, 19 Aug. 1766.
[16] *Walpole Correspondence*, xxx. 234: Walpole to Holland, 2 Aug. 1766.

observed, that Lord Bute's friends have not been forgotten . . . My conclusion from the whole is that the present state of things is likely to continue, or rather to improve.[17]

The kind of ordinary eighteenth-century administration, which the 'Old Whigs' had appeared so reluctant to build, based securely on the totally committed support of the Crown and buttressed by a disciplined and united corps of Court and Treasury men, was once again in the making.

It is difficult to believe that in the normal course of events Rockingham and his followers would have had any political future at all after their dismissal in 1766. Most of the old Ministry had been absorbed into the new one. 'In the summer this year there was a partial change of ministry', Lord Palmerston noted in his diary,[18] and indeed the extent of the change was slight. Moreover, Rockingham and his friends carried their avowed intention of supporting the new Ministry into practice. Newcastle personally attended a meeting of the Privy Council which promulgated the contentious embargo on grain exports, Rockingham and his followers were present at the Government meetings which preceded the opening of Parliament, and on the first day of the new session (11 November) the whole body of 'Old Whigs' strongly supported the Administration in both Lords and Commons. Only the Grenville and Bedford groups were left to oppose. 'There is no standard of opposition set up', Gilly Williams wrote to George Selwyn on 18 November, 'nor will there, I believe, be above forty very important people left to decide on any questions in the house for the rest of the session.'[19] The stage seemed set for the permanent establishment of a 'Whig' Administration under Chatham, and the gradual obliteration or isolation of the little knot of Rockingham's friends who were not in place.

This prospect was shattered and the significance of the Rockingham Ministry thrown into a new light by the unexpected developments, largely of Chatham's creating, which drove Rockingham and his friends into overt opposition. It had long been the intention of Chatham to 'pick and cull from all quarters, and break all parties, as much as possible'.[20] What was made clear in the summer and autumn

[17] *Chatham Correspondence*, iii. 138–9: 14 Dec. 1766.
[18] B. Connell, *Portrait of a Whig Peer* (London, 1957), p. 65.
[19] J.H. Jesse, *George Selwyn and His Contemporaries*, ii. 73.
[20] *Walpole Correspondence*, x. 222: Walpole to Montagu, 10 July 1766.

of 1766 was that the 'Old Whigs' were not to be excepted
from this scheme. A series of manoeuvres involving Lords
Monson, Scarborough, and Grantham, and culminating in
the dismissal of Lord Edgcumbe from his office of
Treasurer of the Household, evinced Chatham's determination
to 'weed out', as Newcastle expressed it, 'all The True Friends
of the Party'.[21] Rockingham and his colleagues, 'fully convinced that L[or]d Chatham's Plan and Proceedings mean't
the destruction—or would have the Consequence of breaking
all our Friends',[22] were intent on breaking off relations with
the Government, and Chatham was not inclined to climb
down. Despite the frantic efforts of Conway and Bessborough
to arrange a compromise, the result was a string of resignations
which finally destroyed all possibility of cooperation between
Rockingham and Chatham. The resignations took place in the
last fortnight of November, and on the 25th the Rockingham
group went into open opposition. 'L[or]d Rockingham's
friends', it was reported three days later, 'divided on Tuesday
ag[ains]t the ministry and now the whole corps will be united
again in opposition. viz. Pelham and Rockingham—God
protect us.'[23] Thanks largely to Chatham's perverse desire to
humiliate the Whig lords, there was once again something like
a unified 'Old Whig' party to oppose the Court.

Chatham's blunder, in enabling the Rockingham connection
to retire into opposition with a semblance of order and a pretence of strength, gave the events of the preceding year a new
significance. It is true that members of the Rockingham group
of 1766 and thereafter have tended to be seen as the representatives of a continuous tradition linking the old corps of
George II's reign, the Minority during the Bute and Grenville
Administrations, the First Rockingham Ministry, and the
Whig Opposition of the late sixties and seventies. In such a
scheme of things the period in office in 1765 and 1766 was a
minor and much overrated incident in a long saga, the really
important development being the initial migration from office
in 1762. 'The establishment of a regular "dining club" on
23rd December 1762', it has been claimed, 'marks the formal

[21] Add.MS. 32977, f. 209: Newcastle to Onslow, 7 Oct. 1766. This is not the
place for a detailed account of the events which led to the breakdown of
relations between Chatham and the 'Old Whigs'; see J. Brooke, *The Chatham
Administration, 1766-68* (London, 1956), pp. 46–62.
[22] Add.MS. 35430, ff. 61–2: Rockingham to Yorke, 27 Nov. 1766.
[23] Strutt MSS., Gascoyne to Strutt, 28 Nov. 1766.

beginning of the Rockinghamite party.'[24] However the
validity of such a view and its implications may be questioned.
There is a strong case for arguing that the year of power in
the middle of the decade had a decisive and lasting influence
on the fortunes and future of the 'Old Whigs'. Of course it
must be conceded that many of those who followed
Rockingham into open opposition in November 1766 were
the authentic representatives of the earlier old corps. Indeed
an apparently irreducible rump of aristocratic clans and
connections was the strongest element in the continuity of
the Whig tradition. A hard core of peers and their clients
provided the basic voting power of the Rockingham party in
both Houses, and gave the structure of the party a superficial
similarity to that of other factions of the day, notably the
Bedfords.[25] Such were Rockingham himself, with his friends
in the Lords, Scarborough and Monson, and in the Commons,
Nathaniel Cholmley, James Scawen, Sir George Armytage, and
Savile Finch; such were Albemarle, his two brothers General
Keppel and Admiral Keppel, with the latter's naval associate
Sir Charles Saunders, and the Duke of Portland, a young and
vigorous recruit who commanded the votes of Lord Charles
Bentinck, Captain John Bentinck, and Lord Grey in the
Commons; such too were the Devonshire interest, comprising
the three Cavendish brothers and Robert Walsingham in the
Lower House, and Bessborough in the Upper, and the Yorke
interest which included Hardwicke, two of his brothers
(Charles and John) and Charles Cocks. Finally Newcastle
could boast a much reduced following of personal friends
and advisers—notably John White, John Offley, James West,
and the Archer family, and a few Sussex connections—John
Page, John Butler, John Norris, and Sir Matthew Fetherstonhaugh.
With the addition of Sir George Savile and two old friends, Sir
William Baker and Sir George Colebrooke, these men formed
the nucleus of consistent supporters on whom the 'Old Whig'
leaders could always rely.

Unfortunately their utility to the party was limited;
dependable for their votes at Westminster, they were not well
fitted to participate in debate, counsel, or even place and

---

[24] A. Foord, *His Majesty's Opposition*, p. 311.
[25] For a comparison between the two parties which contests Macaulay's judgement concerning the distinction between the Bedfords and Rockinghams, see
J. Brooke, *The Chatham Administration*, pp. 275–7.

profit. Lord John Cavendish held office in both Rockingham Ministries, spoke frequently in Parliament and was prominent in party conclaves, though Lady Holland obviously exaggerated when she claimed that he 'not only govern'd my brother [the Duke of Richmond] but Lord Rockingham'.[26] The two admirals Keppel and Saunders were experienced and useful professional men, and Savile, Baker and Colebrooke could all be helpful in debate. Otherwise there was little of ability or ambition among the unfailing supporters of the Newcastle-Rockingham group. None of the personal associates of Rockingham and Portland had any importance as politicians; Newcastle's little group contained only such capabilities as were nullified by apathy and lack of interest. Both Page and White were anxious to retire from Parliament, and neither West nor Offley was intent on a very active political career. Even some of the peers who led the party were less than enthusiastic. Albemarle was rapidly losing all interest in politics and quickly faded from the scene of action; Hardwicke remained rather detached from the Rockinghams, like his brother Charles Yorke, who 'always hung back as to personalities and political appeals to the public';[27] the new Duke of Devonshire was a nonentity, the old Duke of Newcastle almost entirely unconsulted by this time. All in all the 'old Whig families' and their dependents were not such as to inspire much confidence in the future of their party.

If there were those 'true Whigs' who declined to be moved by the vagaries of political life, one very large section of their friends was in a quite different situation. At the time of the resignations which followed the Edgcumbe affair it quickly became apparent that a considerable number of 'our own Old Friends', as Newcastle called them,[28] were no longer prepared to maintain their loyalty to the Cavendish-Pelham group. All but a handful of those who resigned in July and November—Lord John Cavendish, the Yorke brothers, Dowdeswell, Meredith, Saunders, and Keppel—were peers. The great majority of the more ambitious and more useful commoners were lost to the Government. These were, in Rockingham's words, the 'half Chathamites', rechristened by

[26] *Correspondence of Emily, Duchess of Leinster*, ed. B. Fitzgerald (Dublin, 1949-57), i. 467.
[27] Add.MS. 35428, f. 12: Hardwicke, 'A Memorial of Family Occurrences'.
[28] Add.MS. 32978, f. 80: Newcastle to White, 26 Nov. 1766.

Newcastle, *'whole Chathamites'*,[29] mostly young careerists who had provided the backbone of the Opposition to the Bute and Grenville Ministries, and who now saw no reason to re-enter the political wilderness. Even in July it had been transparently clear that if the need arose those prepared to resign merely because Rockingham was to give way to Chatham, 'would not appear very Numerous'.[30] Thus on 8 August Lord Harcourt noted that Newcastle's 'friends who followed him when he resigned about three years ago dont seem disposed to pay him the same compliment if one is to guess from some appearances, that are not apt to deceive one'.[31] When the moment of truth came in November this diagnosis was entirely borne out.

> The Resignations [Newcastle declared] will not be received by The Party, in The Manner, It was imagined, nor be generally, or at all follow'd by Those in Employment in The House of Commons . . . When My Lord Rockingham has lived long enough, To be deserted by Friends and Relations, as I have been, He will not always depend so much, upon Them *all*.[32]

The 'young men', 'our *Old* Friends, now *New Placemen*', had no hesitation in announcing that they were *'determined not to quit'*.[33] When Conway, an intimate friend of the Cavendish family and close confidant of Rockingham, refused to desert Chatham, it was not to be expected that lesser connections would do so. Place and profit were not to be surrendered to satisfy the whim of a handful of ruffled Lords. Thus Newcastle learned from Gage that 'He would go immediately to St. James's; But He would say afterwards, The D[uke] of N[ewcastle] had made him do a *damned Silly Thing*.'[34] Even Thomas Pelham, who was closely related to the Duke, felt justified in remaining in office; 'since I cou'd not Drown my seven Children, I was obliged to take care of them'.[35] Colonel George Onslow had ample reason to assure Chatham of the fidelity of 'a sett mostly of young men of good principles who by a little care may be preserv'd to your Lordship, and

[29] Ibid., f. 222: Rockingham to Newcastle, 8 Dec. 1766; f. 237: Newcastle to Rockingham, 9 Dec. 1766.

[30] Add.MS. 32976, f. 255: Newcastle to Rockingham, 26 July 1766.

[31] *Jenkinson Papers*, p. 422: Harcourt to Jenkinson.

[32] Add.MS. 32978, ff. 52, 54: Newcastle to Portland, 24 Nov. 1766.

[33] Ibid., f. 469: Newcastle to Rockingham, 24 Dec. 1766; f. 64: Newcastle to Portland, 25 Nov. 1766.

[34] Ibid., f. 186: Newcastle to Rockingham, 5 Dec. 1766.

[35] Ibid., f. 174: T. Pelham to Newcastle, 4 Dec. 1766.

whom your Lordships opposers have been using much industry to gain in the short time they have declared themselves'.[36]

Most of those who thus defaulted to the Court in 1766 were lost for good; returned to office by the singular chance of the King's loathing for Grenville in 1765, they were evidently resolved not to repeat their error of 1762-3 and go into a futile and uncongenial opposition. Thus not the least of the functions of the First Rockingham Ministry was to restore to their natural allegiance many of the old corps Whigs who in the confused political situation of the early sixties had been injudicious enough to abandon their normal viewpoint, and who in the seventies were to become an important element in North's reconstructed Court and Treasury party. Many indeed remained with North to the end and actually had to be dismissed by the Rockinghams on their return in 1782. John Buller, George Brudenell, and William Ashburnham all regained office with Rockingham in 1765 and were given places from which they had to be ejected seventeen years later. Others died in office before the establishment of the Second Rockingham Ministry. John Roberts, once Henry Pelham's Secretary to the Treasury, returned in 1765 to the seat at the Board of Trade which he had reluctantly sacrificed in 1762, and Andrew Wilkinson, Chief Storekeeper of the Ordnance under Pelham and Newcastle, was restored to his post at the same time. Both died in office in the seventies and both were typical instances of the old corps Whigs driven into opposition by the exceptional circumstances of the new reign, and only too glad to resume their traditional allegiance in 1765.

These deserters were not only characteristic politicians and civil servants of the Pelhamite establishment. They were also among the most active and vociferous of the Minority during the Bute and Grenville Administrations. The two George Onslows received places in the First Rockingham Ministry which they were to retain under North, and both had been prominent among the 'warm young men' who had caused Newcastle so much anxiety by the violence of their opposition between 1762 and 1765. William Fitzherbert, the friend of Wilkes and founder of Wildman's Club, who with 'indefatigable

unconquerable Zeal and friendship'[37] was responsible for the
recommendation of the Burkes to Rockingham, remained a
supporter of Government until his death in 1772. 'Spanish'
Charles Townshend, who was important enough to warrant
inclusion in the group which met at Claremont on 30 June
1765 to discuss the possibility of forming an Administration,
became a loyal and valuable supporter of North, eventually
to be dismissed as such in 1782. All the evidence points to
the migration of a substantial number of the most useful and
in many ways most typical members of the old Minority to
Court in 1765-6. In 1764 for example Wildman's Club had
included all those committed to the Opposition led nominally
by Newcastle. Yet by 1767 a larger proportion of its old
members (45 per cent) voted with the Chatham Administration
than with the Rockinghams in Opposition (42 per cent).[38]
Even eight years later when Grafton, as well as Chatham, was
again out of office, the percentage of members supporting
North (40) was only slightly less than that following
Rockingham (46). Again, of the eighteen of Newcastle's
closest and most considerable associates who had attended
the critical meeting at Claremont on 30 June 1765, only nine
(significantly, all but one of them were peers) remained with
Rockingham eighteen months later. The rest—eight commoners
and one peer—all went over to the Court in 1766.

From the Court's vantage-point these facts signified the
return to the fold of the most valuable of those who had left
it in 1762-3. When it is remembered that the vast majority of
the political establishment bequeathed to George III had
never seriously considered following their aristocratic leaders
in opposition, it is clear how comparatively slight and short-
lived was the break in continuity in the 1760s. The antagonisms
sparked off by the immaturity of the young George III, and
sustained by the personalities and attitudes of Pitt, Bute, and
Grenville, wrecked the forefront of the political stage in the
decade following the death of George II. But when the dust
had settled in the early seventies, North was firmly in control
with a Court and Treasury party which had a great deal in
common with that of Newcastle. From the point of view

---

[37] *Burke Correspondence*, i. 210: Burke to O'Hara, 9 July 1765.
[38] For the lists of Wildman's on which these and the following figures are based,
see Add.MS. 33000, ff. 360–1; Add.MS. 33035, f. 90; J. Almon, *History of
the Late Minority* (London, 1766), pp. 298–300.

of the Opposition, of course, the permanent loss of so many
supporters of the preceding three years was no less significant,
leading as it did to the final definition of the Rockingham
party in highly personal and aristocratic terms. 'I never did
believe', Onslow wrote to Newcastle on 26 November, 'I
should have it to tell you of a Division in the House of
Commons with myself on one Side, and the Cavendish family
on the other.'[39] In an important sense, 1766 saw the parting
of the ways for the two principal constituent parts of the
Whig Opposition after 1762, the old Whig families on the one
hand, the old corps careerists on the other. An important link
in the chain which connected the Whig traditions of the two
reigns was broken, and such a crucial development could not
but affect the character of the Rockingham party in the
succeeding years.

However the effect of the events of 1765-6 on the evolution
of the party was not entirely negative. Burke, comparing the
Minority of the early sixties with the Rockingham faction of
the late sixties, and as ever generalizing from the experience of
the intervening period, declared that under George III's
system of Government, 'it is soon found necessary to get rid
of the heads of administration; but it is of their heads only . . .
the party goes out much thinner than it came in; and is only
reduced in strength by its temporary possession of power'.[40]
Yet that critical year in power, while resulting in the loss of
an important section of the party—if party it was at that
stage—also added a new and no less significant element, and
Rockingham retired into opposition with a number of
followers who had had no previous connection with the 'Old
Whigs'. The newcomers were of course a very mixed group.
Some of them were merely accessions to the aristocratic
nucleus of the party. Richmond's junction with the men who
had made him Ambassador to the French Court and Secretary
of State also added his brother Lord George Lennox and
Thomas Conolly, formerly an adherent of Fox's who was
connected with Richmond by marriage. Aubrey Beauclerk,
hitherto a supporter of the Court, apparently transferred his
loyalties to Rockingham as a result of his marrying into
Bessborough's family. Two Irish peers, Downe and Verney,
who had regularly voted with the Government under Bute and

[39] Add.MS. 32978, f. 86.   [40] *Burke's Works*, i. 325.

Grenville, joined Rockingham in Opposition to the Chatham, Grafton, and North Ministries. Downe had initially been treated as an opponent by Rockingham in July 1765, but was suggested for a peerage in 1766 and by the end of the year was firmly attached to the party, an association doubtless strengthened by his estates and standing in Yorkshire. Verney's course was at this time dictated by the Burkes, whose benefactor he was; he also had his own reasons for gratitude to Rockingham, who in 1765 had awarded him a Privy Councillorship, an honour rarely accorded to those not holding office.

There were others who had once taken a view favourable to the Court of George III, and who yet found the Rockingham party to their taste in 1766 and after. George Dempster, a wealthy Scot who was given the office of Secretary to the Order of the Thistle in 1765 had followed his own inclinations since entering Parliament in 1761. After a fleeting connection with Bute he had become sufficiently intimate with Shelburne to consult him before accepting favours from Rockingham in 1765. In the event he conceived a new and lasting attachment to Rockingham, begging him to be allowed to 'regulate my parliamentary conduct in whatever shape is agreeable to you' in November 1766.[41] Frederick Montagu, who joined the Rockingham group at about the same time, had been connected with his cousin the Earl of Halifax before quarrelling violently with him in 1764. Both Dempster and Montagu were among the most vigorous and respected leaders of the Rockinghams in the seventies. Neither had an obvious personal interest in following Rockingham into Opposition and their accession to the party clearly demonstrated its capacity to attract recruits for whom the traditions represented by the great Whig lords meant little or nothing.

The most celebrated of the newcomers in historical perspective was naturally Edmund Burke. How near he came to deserting his new patron in 1766 is not altogether certain. His 'cousin' William Burke remained in office at least for the moment, and certainly there were those in the new Ministry— notably Grafton, Conway, and Shelburne—who were aware that Burke was worth winning, 'the readiest man upon all points perhaps in the whole House', Grafton called him, 'a

[41] WWM.R1–701: Dempster to Rockingham, 8 Nov. 1766.

most material man to gain, and one on whom the thoroughest dependence may be given, where an obligation is owned'.[42] But Chatham did not respond and Burke himself, though evidently anxious for a post in the Administration, apparently made it clear to Conway that he could not alter his allegiance.

The substance of my resolution [he wrote to O'Hara] was, and I explain it to him in Terms strong and precise; That I had begun with this party. That it was now divided in situation, though I hoped not in opinions or inclinations; that the point of honour lay with that division which was out of power and that if the place which should be offerd, should prove in itself never so acceptable, I could take it only on condition that, in accepting it, and in holding it, I must be understood to belong not to the administration, but to those who were out; and that therefore if ever they should set up a standard, though spread for direct and personal opposition, I must be revocable into their party, and join it. But would act fairly and give due notice. He told me, he feard that this condition might frustrate the whole.[43]

Quite clearly Burke, who could never in any degree separate his emotional and public lives, felt a strong commitment to his benefactors of 1765, a commitment of the utmost significance for the future of the 'Old Whigs'. No man had less in common with the old corps Whig tradition of the Pelham-Cavendish block than Burke; no man was to play a bigger part in the evolution of the party under Rockingham.

Scarcely less significant were Rockingham's Tory converts. With the general dispersal of the old Tory party in the sixties, the 'Old Whigs' rather surprisingly picked up no less than five in the middle of the decade. One, Henry Curwen, had local connections with Portland in Cumberland; another, Sir William Meredith, who had been accounted a Jacobite ten years earlier and who was to transfer his loyalties to the Court at the beginning of the American War of Independence, resigned with Saunders and Keppel from the Admiralty Board in November 1766. More interesting was the little group formed by coinciding territorial and personal interests in the West Country, consisting of Charles Barrow, Sir William Codrington, and William Dowdeswell. Dowdeswell had been particularly anxious to retain his position as Chancellor of the Exchequer in July, and was furious when only offered the Board of Trade by Chatham. Had he been permitted to stay in office, it is conceivable that he would have been a

---

[42] *Chatham Correspondence*, iii. 110–11: Grafton to Chatham, 17 Oct. 1766.
[43] *Burke Correspondence*, i. 279: [post 11 Nov. 1766].

little less ready to accompany Rockingham into Opposition than Burke was, though certainty is impossible. As it was, it may well be the case that Rockingham had Chatham to thank, at least in part, for the assistance in Opposition of his most trusted and respected lieutenant.

In terms of personnel, the First Rockingham Ministry was of crucial importance to the future development of the 'Old Whig' party. On the one hand the additions and losses for which it was largely responsible confirmed that basic division between the 'great Whigs' and the Chathamites which had long been implicit, but which many had declined to recognize. On the other hand it excised the careerist old corps element in the party and replaced it with a mixed group of newcomers who had little or no connection with the old Whiggism of the previous reign. Moreover it provided in Rockingham a leader not inappropriate for the future role of the 'Old Whigs'. There were still those who regarded Newcastle as the true or at least joint leader of the party,[44] and Newcastle himself was characteristically reluctant to surrender all authority. 'The Duke of Newcastle', Onslow informed West, is 'just now acting very like himself in the calm Sunset of his various Day.'[45] As ever he reacted bitterly to Rockingham's failure to consult him; 'I am persuaded', he told Grantham in August, 'His Lordship's Intention is, To shew the same Reservedness towards Me, Now we are Both out of Court, As He had, when We were in.'[46] Yet Newcastle knew well enough that Rockingham, 'who', in his own words 'takes upon Himself To be The Head of the Party', was now the master.[47] In some ways he was also, however humble his abilities, better qualified to lead a party of Opposition. Though both had 'the same Zeal for our party',[48] Newcastle placed a far higher premium on obtaining office for his friends than did his younger and less inhibited colleague. 'The only thing I fear is a real disunion amongst those *with whom I had the honour to be called into Administration*', Rockingham declared in August,[49] and throughout his career he was to give the party, and of course

[44] See for example, *Bedford Correspondence*, iii. 353; Strutt MSS., Gascoyne to Strutt, 15 Nov. 1766.

[45] Add.MS. 34728, f. 119: 6 Oct. 1766.

[46] Add.MS. 32976, f. 434: 21 Aug. 1766.

[47] Add.MS. 32977, f. 184: Newcastle to Portland, 1 Oct. 1766.

[48] Add.MS. 32976, f. 217: Newcastle to Rockingham, 24 July 1766.

[49] *Rockingham Memoirs*, ii. 13: Rockingham to Albemarle, 29 Aug. 1766.

its leadership, a priority which Newcastle, for all his professions
could scarcely maintain. Moreover, Rockingham's most prominent characteristic—'indolence of Temper'[50]—mainfested in a
marked disinclination to stir himself for prolonged periods
in public affairs, and combined with a thoroughly easy-going
disposition, gave him a degree of protection against the
frustrations and failures inseparable from a forlorn opposition
such as that adopted by the 'Old Whigs'. Such a temperament
was of course not without its disadvantages. Burke, whose
misfortune it was to be man of business for a party which
had limited interest and faith in business, was to spend much
of his time vainly urging his leaders to action. His first, mild
admonition to Rockingham was delivered as early as August
1766. 'I begin almost to fear', he wrote, 'that your Lordship
left Town a little too early. I think your friends must since
then have wanted your advice on more than one occasion.'[51]
This note, with less reserve and more vigour, was to be heard
a good deal in the succeeding years.

The 'Old Whigs' acquired more than a new set of friends
and a new leader as a result of their year in power; scarcely
less significant was the wealth of political experience on
which Burke particularly, as the party's exponent of ideas,
drew in later years. Though he naturally appealed to a long
tradition of Whig constitutionalism, it is no exaggeration to
claim that almost every political principle and prejudice
adumbrated by Burke was derived in some sense from the
events of the years 1765 and 1766. Pre-eminent of course
was the question of Bute and the King's Friends.[52] During
their Administration Rockingham and his colleagues had
operated on the basis that Bute and his associates must be
unceasingly proscribed and victimized, and once in Opposition
they professed to see every Government subordinated to the
influence of the 'Favourite' and his friends. Henceforth
the extirpation of this influence was to be their most consistent
rallying cry, though ironically it was at this very moment that
the actual influence of Bute and the King's Friends was
terminated. Bute had played no part in the change of Ministry
in July 1766, claiming quite truthfully 'I know as little, save

[50] Add.MS. 32977, f. 39: White to Newcastle, 6 Sept. 1766.
[51] *Burke Correspondence*, i. 266: 21 Aug. 1766.
[52] For a recent discussion of this, see I.R. Christie, *Myth and Reality in Late
Eighteenth Century British Politics and Other Papers* (London, 1970),
pp. 27–54.

from the newspapers, of the present busy scene, as I do of transactions in Russia.'[53] Moreover he quarrelled violently and irreversibly with George III in August, apparently because Pitt, instead of approaching him personally, had made direct overtures to his friends.

Is it possible [he asked his master] you should not see the total difference between men setting up to be leaders of a party, for seditious or ambitious purposes, and men, who since I was out of office, have uniformly held the language I did in it; look to the King, not to me, I want no men to attach themselves to me, 'tis to him and him alone you should pay regard; why, Sir, they are yours not mine, and always looked on themselves as such; now then what is Pitt's language, I will not take men that look up to the King himself, they must be mine and come as individuals; the Kings friends are Lord Butes; I know he has no party views, but I will implicate his friends under that general name; and thus I shall put an end to that unconstitutional attachment of men to the King and not directly to the Minister, which Lord Bute has been labouring at in this reign.[54]

Henceforth Bute's importance as an active force in politics was over, and the complete readiness of successive Ministers, Chatham, Grafton, and North, to conciliate and cooperate with those who had been particularly associated with the King and the King's Favourite, ensured that the King's Friends were for the future little more than a figment of the 'Old Whig' imagination.

Rockingham and his colleagues persisted in attributing their difficulties and eventual fall in 1766 to the conspiracies of these men. 'As to Lord Bute and *the Lady*,' Rockingham declared in August, 'I give them the Credit of being the secret spring of the late Events and continue on this subject the Calm Contempt, by which It is said I gave Offence when in office.'[55] Like many politicians before and after them, the 'Old Whigs' made the mistake of assuming that their failure was the result not of pursuing a particular strategy but of pursuing that strategy with insufficient thoroughness. Their universal panacea in the years of opposition was a double dose of the prescription adopted in 1765-6, and the result was a growing obsession with extraordinary notions of secret corruption, double cabinets, and so on, which bore little

---

[53] Add.MS. 35607, f. 286: Bute to Hardwicke, 26 July 1766; the version printed at *Rockingham Memoirs*, i. 360, is inaccurate.

[54] *Letters from George III to Lord Bute*, p. 257.

[55] Portland MSS., PwF. 8984: Rockingham to Portland, 28 Aug. 1766.

relation to reality. The lesson of 1766—the wrong lesson, wrongly learned and wrongly applied—was never forgotten by the Rockinghams.

> Government may in great measure be restored, [Burke was to insist] if any considerable bodies of men have honesty and resolution enough never to accept administration, unless this garrison of *king's men*, which is stationed, as in a citadel, to control and enslave it, be entirely broken and disbanded, and every work they have thrown up be levelled with the ground. The disposition of public men to keep this corps together, and to act under it, or to cooperate with it, is a touchstone by which every administration might in future be tried.[56]

If Bute and the King's Friends were not to be laid to rest, neither was the iniquity of the King himself. It remained a fundamental article of faith for Burke and his colleagues that the Rockingham Ministry had been weakened, and its downfall accelerated by the treachery of George III, who having accepted the 'Old Whigs' in July 1765 out of sheer necessity, had repeatedly betrayed them during the ensuing months. Even had their charges been justified it would have been both logical and judicious to concentrate on cultivating the Court and Closet more assiduously for the future. Instead it was their unshakable determination to find means to bind the King by force. As William Knox was to write over twenty years later, 'The old Whigs, as they call themselves, it is said, have been uniform in the pursuit of their plan of lowering the King's authority, by depriving the Crown of its influence, ever since their expulsion from Ministry by the Earl of Bute.'[57] Just as party was to be justified on the grounds that it presented the only secure means of combating Bute and his works, so it was to be employed to restrict the dangerous powers of the Crown, a doctrine which was ultimately to lead to Fox's claim that it was for the chief minister to select his colleagues and for them to select his successor. Nor were these prejudices against Bute and George III any stronger than that which the 'Old Whigs' had by 1766 conceived against Chatham. Throughout the early years of the new reign Newcastle and his connections had done their best to win Pitt's approval and leadership; his consistent rejection of their overtures in 1765-6 and his undisguised contempt for them once he had established his own Ministry, shattered all hope of an amicable

---

[56] *Burke's Works*, i. 371.   [57] W. Knox, *Extra Official State Papers*, p. 2.

union between the two branches of the old Opposition to the Bute and Grenville regimes. Though there were moments, notably in 1770 and 1775, when they were prepared to cooperate in Parliament, the division between Chathams and Rockinghams was irreversible by 1766, and was indeed to be perpetuated after the death of their leaders, in the bitter enmity of Shelburne and Fox.

In terms of detailed measures, too, the experience of 1765-6 influenced the future attitude of Rockingham and his colleagues. For example the colonial policy adopted by the Rockingham Ministry merely as a matter of expediency became an important weapon in the armoury of the 'Old Whigs'. The strategy for Anglo-American relations advocated by Burke in his great speeches of 1774-5 amounted to little more than an elaboration of that employed in 1766. Trade too came to play a significant part in the views of Rockingham and his friends. Burke made sweeping claims on this score.

That administration [he argued] was the first which proposed and encouraged public meetings and free consultations of merchants from all parts of the kingdom; by which means the truest lights have been received; great benefits have been already derived to manufactures and commerce; and the most extensive prospects are opened for further improvement.[58]

Such pretensions were most important for the future; henceforth the Rockinghams were assiduous—though not always with complete success—in courting mercantile, manufacturing, and financial interests. Of course their vigour in this respect tied in with their general concern, both in and out of office, to win the approval of 'popular', 'out of doors', and 'independent' elements, tactics which had not a little to do with Rockingham's fall in 1766 and which led more realistic politicans to despair of their sanity. Rockingham had wooed the Independents at Westminster and beyond while in power, and continued to do so during the years in Opposition. In this he was to have some success. Despite the obvious connection of the 'Old Whigs' with the Court and Treasury party of George II's reign, Rockingham and his followers came to acquire something of a 'Country' complexion not wholly dissimilar to that of the old Tory party.

[58] *Burke's Works*, i. 183.

In part this was the product of Rockingham's personal attitudes. In an important sense, Rockingham was and always had been a great Country Whig in a long and respected tradition.[59] The extraordinary determination with which he pursued policies scarcely compatible with the cultivation of the Court in 1765 and 1766 confirmed and strengthened this element in his political make-up. Rockingham was always able to attract the support of independent country gentlemen, whether old friends like Sir George Savile and John Hewitt, knights of the shire for Yorkshire and Nottinghamshire respectively, or relatively new adherents like Harbord Harbord M.P. for Norwich, and Sir Gilbert Heathcote, M.P. for Shaftesbury. Old Velters Cornewall, a Tory squire from the Welsh marches, assured him in August 1766,

> You are the only Marquiss from That of Winchester, whom I knew well, to That of Tavistock unknown, that I cared A Grey Groat for, and I care A million for you. The king (whom I love as my own Child) can never have A better or more generous or more diligent Servant, or the Parliament and All his Subjects A more popular, Trade-loving and Excise-hateing Minister than My Lord Rockingham. . . . We Country Squires, my Lord, often and boldly say that Modern Ministers are Jockeys, but you are called A good and high-bred Racer.[60]

These were unusual terms to apply to a great Whig aristocrat, and convey something of the position which Rockingham was carving out for himself and his party. This process was obviously materially assisted by the developments of 1766 in personnel. The loss of the younger old corps section of the party, the Onslows and Townshends and their friends, together with the assimilation of new elements, notably Burke and the Dowdeswell Tories, naturally facilitated the transmogrification of the 'Old Whigs' from an undistinguished political faction into something like a great Country party.

In its various ways the First Rockingham Administration created a party which for all its links with the past, was essentially new. At the time of its emergence, all that was clear was that it was likely for some time to remain in the wilderness. No doubt, like all politicians, the 'Old Whigs' were intent on returning to power—'everything came round

---

[59] On this theme, see C. Collyer, 'The Rockingham Connection and Country Opinion in the Early Years of George III', *Proceedings of Leeds Philosophical Soc.*, vii (1952-5), 251–75; 'The Rockinghams and Yorkshire Politics: 1742-61', *Pubs. of Thoresby Soc.*, xli, *Thoresby Miscellany*, xii (1954), 352–82.

[60] WWM.R1–678: 3 Aug. 1766.

in this country', Rockingham was said to have remarked.[61]
But everything about the men who composed the party and
the attitudes and ideas which activated it suggested that it
was better suited to Opposition than to Government. There
were admittedly those who felt that strong measures were
needed to ensure a speedy resumption of office. Thus
Bessborough pointed out to Newcastle at the end of November
1766, that as things stood at present 'you certainly have no
plan at all, no System, nor do we know one another's minds,
all is a float, excepting in a very small set of men, who can
make but a very small appearance in any division.'[62]
Bessborough considered that a working alliance with the
Bedford party and a request for aid to Mansfield, a powerful
and respected speaker in the Lords, would do much to ginger
up the rather negative attitude of his colleagues. 'I don't like
the doctrine,' he declared, 'that I hear from some of our
young friends. "Give Him (Chatham) rope enough and He
will do the business for us". perhaps that may happen but it
may likewise happen that it may be a very long Rope, and
difficult to find an end to it.'[63] Though this view was not
without its force, it was quickly made clear to Bessborough,
as also to Newcastle, who rather sympathized with him, that
there were some expedients to which the party could by no
means resort even to regain power. Portland, the type of the
Rockingham peer, strongly objected to the idea of an alliance
of convenience with the Bedfords. 'Will it not shew an anxiety
of acquiring power at any rate?' he asked.[64] Nor was he
inclined to approach Mansfield for assistance. 'Subserviency
to The Crown is a maxim which can not make me desirous
of seeing its teacher at the head of The Whigs.'[65] Rockingham
too, though much pressed by Charles Yorke to join with the
other factions in Opposition, was determined to remain
independent, and avoid all complications.

I am clear that by acting on such a Plan, [he assured Newcastle] we
shall always feel happy and justified in our Minds and I think it will
ensure us the Continuance of the Publick Good Opinion. Perhaps
adhering to such a Plan will not accelerate Success, but if it ever does
succeed, It will be a Foundation which will not afterwards be easily
shaken.[66]

[61] *Walpole's Memoirs*, ii. 271.   [62] Add.MS. 32978, ff. 488–9: 27 Nov. 1766.
[63] Add.MS. 32978, f. 282: 13 Dec. 1766.
[64] Ibid., f. 378: Portland to Newcastle, 17 Dec. 1766.   [65] Ibid., f. 379.
[66] Ibid., ff. 418–19: 19 Dec. 1766. See too Add.MS. 35428, ff. 114–15: Yorke,
'Minute of what I said to M[arquess] of R[ockingham] 20 Dec. 1766'.

This attitude, so characteristic of Rockingham himself and his party, was scarcely a recipe for a quick return to the pleasures of place and power; nothing separates the Rockingham party so clearly from the other parties of the day than its curious ambivalence about the desirability of office, its temperamental unsuitability for the task of governing, a far cry from the Whiggism of earlier years. In the last analysis Rockingham and his friends did not care sufficiently about the attractions of power to find their way back to office. They spent sixteen years in Opposition largely because they were fundamentally content with such a role. Though they naturally contined to regard themselves as future Ministers, it was sheer chance—the chance of disaster in war—which was ultimately to make them so once again. As early as December 1766 Burke, in a most perceptive mood, showed how well he understood the principles and persuasions which animated the party he had joined. Discussing the proposal for an alliance with the other groups in Opposition, he remarked to O'Hara,

The Bedfords and Grenvilles, as a set of people at once more bold and more tractable than our party will be preferred to us, and will run their Course as others have done theirs. It may possibly, in the revolution of this Political Plantonick year, come again to our turn. But I see this Event, (if I see it at all) at the End of a very long Visto. The View is dim and remote; and we do nothing in the world to bring it nearer, or to make it more certain. This disposition, which is become the principle of our party, I confess, from constitution and opinion, I like: Not that I am enamourd of adversity, or that I love opposition. On the contrary it would be convenient enough to get into office; and opposition never was to me a desirable thing; because I like to see some effect of what I am doing, and this method however pleasant is barren and unproductive, and at best, but preventive of mischief; but then the walk is certain; there are no contradictions to reconcile; no cross points of honour or interest to adjust; all is clear and open; and the wear and tear of mind, which is saved by keeping aloof from crooked politics, is a consideration absolutely inestimable. Believe me, I who lived with *your friend* [W.G. Hamilton] so many years feel it so; and bless Providence every day and every hour to find myself delivered from thoughts and from Characters of that kind.[67]

It could not be claimed that Burke, the great exponent of the politics of party, had either illusions or doubts about the cause to whose service he was now to devote himself.

---

[67] *Burke Correspondence*, i. 285: 23 Dec. [1766].

How this nascent party is to be viewed is matter for debate. Chatham, for example, was contemptuous of what he termed 'the remnant of the late Duke of Cumberland's party',[68] though he was to discover in the 1770s that this remnant was a good deal stronger than the following he could personally command. Today the Rockingham group has come to be regarded as but one more of the personal factions thrown up in the instability of the mid-eighteenth century.[69] In their own eyes of course they were 'Whigs', indeed the only true Whigs, and while the claim must be carefully qualified it is not to be dismissed out of hand. By the 1760s the old Whiggism and the old Toryism were either dead or dying. As Burke asserted in 1769, 'The great parties which formerly divided and agitated the kingdom are known to be in a manner entirely dissolved.'[70] The old Tory party dispersed completely in the early years of George III's reign, and a new one, despite the propensity of the Rockinghams themselves to discern Tories in every Government, was not to emerge for several decades.[71] As for the Whigs, the term had come to mean almost nothing by this time. 'It appears to me Impossible', Kinnoull insisted to Newcastle, 'in the present State of Things, to keep together any considerable Body of Whigs, as a distinct and respectable Party or Body of Men'.[72] This was perfectly fair comment. By the 1760s there were few politicians indeed who did not regard themselves as Whigs. Thus Bedford and Grenville, for example, were generally so labelled, while those who deserted Rockingham and Newcastle in November 1766 considered that they had 'as good right as any to be esteemed whigs' by remaining in office under Chatham.[73] Nor did Rockingham and his friends have a wholly indisputable basis for their assertions. Thus Grenville pointed out to his friend Buckinghamshire in June 1766 that Rockingham, Conway, Grafton and Richmond, Winchilsea and Dartmouth were all

[68] *Walpole's Memoirs*, ii. 398.
[69] See for example, J. Brooke, *The Chatham Administration*, pp. 275–7.
[70] *Burke's Works*, i. 308.
[71] For an interesting example of the view that George III's regime was a Tory one, see *A Parallel; drawn between the Administration in the Four Last Years of Queen Anne, and the Four First of George the Third* (London, 1766); for a conclusive rebuttal of the view, see I.R. Christie, 'Was there a "New Toryism" in the Earlier Part of George III's Reign?', *Journal of British Studies*, vol. v. (1965-6), no. i, pp. 60–76.
[72] Add.MS. 33070, f. 366: 8 Oct. 1766.
[73] Chatham MSS., lxvi. f. 82: T. Walpole to Pitt, 15 July 1766.

descended from great seventeenth-century royalists and even Kings,

with that *true Whig* the Chancellor of the Exchequer, and for their men of busyness and of confidence in the two great Offices of the Treasury and Secretary of State, the two Mr. Burkes, whose Whig pedigree, history and qualifications for this unlimited trust, may be learnt from those who have been lately to Ireland. I should not have mention'd nor judg'd of any man by the Party merit or demerit of his ancestors if the *Whig Families* had not been impudently urg'd to make up for their notorious deficiency in all other circumstances.[74]

But inconvenient as such facts were for Rockingham and his fellows, there is something to be said on their side of the question. With names like Pelham, Cavendish, Watson-Wentworth, Yorke, Keppel, Bentinck, and Legge, they had every right to be seen as the authentic representatives of the 'ancient Whig families'[75] of the two previous reigns, a fact which provided a far more real connection with the old Whig tradition than that to which some of their rivals could lay claim. Moreover it cannot be denied that no other politicians of the period bothered to call themselves Whigs so consistently so vociferously and so sincerely, as did the Rockingham party, and this itself constituted a not inconsiderable argument in their favour. Many contemporaries saw no objection to describing them simply and for all practical purposes exclusively as 'Whigs' and it is perhaps a little perverse of the historian to do otherwise. This is not to concede that their brand of Whiggism was related very closely to that of an earlier age; on the contrary almost everything about its men and measures combined to give it a new and paradoxical flavour. Indeed the historical significance of the First Rockingham Administration lies principally in the way it remodelled and redefined the party of the 'Old Whigs'. 'This new, honest, Whig administration', as Newcastle called it,[76] had a decisive impact on the future development of the party, substantially altering its composition, and redirecting its energies. Rockingham and his friends ever stressed their personal heritage, the continuity of the tradition which they claimed to uphold; they were not perhaps to know that they were also

---

[74] H.M.C. *Lothian MSS.*, p. 261: 23 June 1766.
[75] *Grafton Autobiography*, p. 104: C. Townshend to Grafton, [21 Nov. 1766], wrongly dated 25 Nov. 1766.
[76] *Newcastle's Narrative*, p. 31.

constructing a new tradition, and a new Whig party, of immense significance for the future.

APPENDIX A

SOURCES FOR PARLIAMENTARY DEBATES ON THE AMERICAN STAMP ACT IN 1766

The following is a list of the principal sources for proceedings in Parliament on the Stamp Act in 1766. It covers the dates 14 and 27 January, 3, 5, 7, 21, and 24 February, and 3 and 4 March in the Commons; 14 January, 3, 4, and 6 February, and 7, 10, and 11 March in the Lords. Sources for evidence given in the Commons' American Committee are to be found at page 179.

Commons

    Burke Correspondence, i. 231—2.
    Caldwell Papers, Part ii, vol. ii, 60—1, 70, 73—9.
    Chatham Correspondence, ii. 364—73, 394—5.
    Commerce of Rhode Island, i. 141—2.
    Cust Records, edd. Lady E., L., and Sir J. Cust, iii. 95—8.
    Elliot, G.F.S., *Border Elliots*, pp. 397—8.
    Correspondence of George III, i. 224—6, 246—7, 254—5, 266—8, 273—7.
    Grenville Papers, iii. 358—9.
    H.M.C. *Polwarth MSS.*, v. 363; *Round MSS.*, pp. 315—16; *Stopford-Sackville MSS.*, i. 107—9.
    Parliamentary History, xvi. 95—110.
    Rockingham Memoirs, i. 309—10.
    Walpole's Memoirs, ii. 184—204, 210—18.
    'Debates on the Declaratory Act, etc.', *Am. Hist. Rev.* xvii. 565—74.
    'Ryder Diaries', *Camden Miscellany*, xxiii. 261—91, 302—20.
    'Stamp Act Papers', *Maryland Hist. Mag.*, vi. 283—6, 291—302.
    South Carolina Hist. and Genealogical Mag., xxvi, 69—71.
    'William Baker's Account of the Debate on the Repeal of the Stamp Act', ed. D.H. Watson, *William and Mary Quarterly*, 3rd Ser., xxvi. 259—65.
    Add.MS. 22930, f. 12: Charlemont to Flood, 28 Jan. 1766.
    Add.MSS. 32973, ff. 133—5, 359, 361—2, 363, 373, 375, 377; 32974, ff. 45—51, 77, 79, 135—42: letters of West and Onslow to Newcastle.
    Add.MS. 35374, ff. 278, 284—5: letters of James Harris to Hardwicke
    Add.MS. 51406, ff. 128, 130, 134—5: Holland's letters to J. Campbell
    Braybrooke (Berkshire) MSS., 034/24, 23: Richard Neville's Notes, [3, 5, 21 Feb. 1766].
    Newdigate MSS., A.7: Newdigate's Diary; B2546/3, 4, 12—15, 16, 18: Newdigate's Notes.
    Strutt MSS., Gascoyne to Strutt, 16 Jan., 4, 6, 8 Feb. 1766.

Lords

   Caldwell Papers, Part ii, vol. ii, pp. 59, 68—9, 70—1, 81—2.

   Chatham Correspondence, ii. 283—5.

   Cust Records, edd. Lady E., L., and Sir J. Cust, iii. 98—100.

   Correspondence of George III, i. 226—7, 253—4, 255, 256, 261, 278—9, 280—1.

   Grenville Papers, iii. 357, 358—9.

   Parliamentary History, xvi. 165—81.

   Rockingham Memoirs, i. 313—14.

   Letters of Walpole, ed. P. Toynbee, Suppl. ii, 135—6.

   'Debates on the Declaratory Act, etc.', *Am. Hist. Rev.* xvii. 577—86.

   Add.MS. 22930, ff. 15—16: Charlemont to Flood, 13 Mar. 1766.

   Add.MSS. 33001, ff. 83—4; 33078, f. 93: Newcastle's accounts.

   Add.MS. 51406, ff. 131, 136: Holland's accounts.

   WWM.R53—14: a paper of Rockingham's.

Two sources not included here are Charles Gray's Notebook of Parliamentary Debates, which has disappeared in recent years, leaving only a brief extract in H.M.C. *Round MSS.*, pp. 315—16, and James Harris's notes of debates in the Malmesbury MSS., which have not proved accessible.

APPENDIX B

DIVISION LISTS ON THE AMERICAN STAMP ACT IN 1766

There were eight Parliamentary divisions relating to the problem of the American Stamp Act in 1766, four in the Lower House, four in the Upper. The following are the surviving lists of the voting.

Commons

On the division of 7 February upon a motion by Charles Yorke in Committee for the chairman to leave his chair (by implication rejecting Grenville's motion for an address to enforce the Stamp Act), which was carried 274 to 234.

1. Sir William Meredith's list of the Minority; 134 names. Add.MS. 32974, f. 167.
2. A list drawn up for Rockingham, also of the Minority; 131 names. WWM.R54−1.
3. Sir Alexander Gilmour's list of Scottish M.P.s voting for, against, and absent; 45 names. Add.MS. 32974, f. 25; WWM.R54−6.

On the division of 22 February upon a motion by Conway in Committee in favour of a resolution repealing the Stamp Act, which was carried 275 to 167.

1. A list of the Minority published under a Paris imprint to evade prosecution under the laws of Parliamentary privilege; 168 names.
2. Sir William Meredith's list of the Minority; 168 names. Add.MS. 32974, f. 169.
3. A list of the Minority drawn up for Rockingham; 167 names. WWM.R54−11.
4. Newcastle's list of the placemen voting in the Minority; 52 names. Add.MS. 33001, ff. 200−1.
5. Sir Alexander Gilmour's list of Scottish M.P.s voting for and against; 39 names. WWM.R54−5.

On the division of 24 February upon a motion by James Oswald to recommit the resolution repealing the Stamp Act, which was rejected 240 to 133.

No known lists are extant.

On the division of 4 March upon a motion to pass the bill repealing the Stamp Act, which was carried 150 to 122.

No known lists are extant.

Though most of these lists relate to the Minority, there can be no certainty even as to those voting against repeal, since the various lists differ in detail. For the division of 22 February, at least one list, that of Newcastle, is of doubtful value. Namier used it to endorse the validity of the Paris list as against that of Meredith's. However there is a strong possibility that Newcastle's list was actually based upon the published one, in which case it can hardly be treated as an independent source.

Altogether the various lists for the key division of 22 February yield a total of 189 names on the Opposition side. In addition Namier drew attention to evidence in the Newcastle Papers and the Harris Debates that two M.P.s not included in these lists, namely Sir Charles Hardy and George Selwyn, voted in the Minority. In fact one of these must be discounted, for when Newcastle told Rockingham of Selwyn's vote, Rockingham replied, 'Selwyn certainly voted with us' (Add.MS. 32974, f. 65: 22 February 1766). But if Hardy is included the total is 190. The lists agree on the names of 142 only; for the rest, the other 26 must be selected from the remaining 48 names.

Unfortunately there is no evidence as to the identity of those in the Majority, apart from Gilmour's lists of Scottish votes. If nothing else, the latter demonstrate how dangerous it is to speculate. Namier worked on the assumption that the proportion of those absent within any particular group of M.P.s was the same as the percentage absent in the House as a whole. On this basis he calculated that 9 Scottish representatives were absent and that, by implication, 9 voted for repeal. In fact Gilmour's list, with which Namier was not acquainted, makes it clear that only 5 Scots were absent; that is, Namier's calculation was in error by nearly fifty per cent. If this was the case with the Scots, there can be no surety that it was not so with other groups. (See Sir L. Namier, *The Structure of Politics at the Accession of George III* (2nd edn., London, 1957), pp. 154–5.)

Lords

> On the division of 3 February upon Grafton's motion in Committee in favour of the resolution later to be enshrined in the Declaratory Act, which was carried 125 to 5.

> > For the names of those in the Minority, which were common knowledge, see for example, *Correspondence of George III*, i. 253.

> On the division of 4 February upon Suffolk's motion in Committee substituting the word 'require' for 'recommend' in the resolution advocating compensation for sufferers by the Stamp Act riots, which was carried 63 to 60.

> 1. A list probably made out by Newcastle; 59 names voting in the Minority, 63 in the Majority; also 6 'absent'—those who were present in the House on the day but failed to vote. Add.MS. 33035, ff. 276–7.

> 2. A list partially annotated by Rockingham, giving 59 names 'for' and 63 'against'. The annotations seem to relate to the division of 6 February. WWM.R53–26.

On the division of 6 February upon Temple's motion in Committee to alter the words 'act of legislation' to 'stamp act' in a resolution requiring indemnity for those in the colonies failing to employ stamps, which was carried 59 to 55.

A list of 7 February made out by Newcastle and giving the names of the friends of Bute and Bedford in the Lords (66 in all with 9 erased) may conceivably relate to this division. Add.MS. 33001, ff. 89—90.

On the division of 11 March upon Grafton's motion to commit the bill repealing the Stamp Act, which was carried 73 to 61, 105 to 71 including proxies.

1. A list of the Minority published under a Paris imprint with 'Correct Copies of Two Protests' in 1766; 71 names.
2. A list of peers with places in the Minority; 19 names. Add.MS. 33001, f. 204.
3. A list of 'Lords, For and *against* The Repeal of The Stamp Act'; For: 105 names; Against: 71 names; also 17 names 'absent'. Add.MS. 33035, ff. 385—7; ff. 389—91 is a slightly earlier, corrected list.
4. An incomplete list of peers in the Majority, in Rockingham's hand; 26 names. WWM.R53—23.

BIBLIOGRAPHY

One of the difficulties of a study of this kind is that it commands a potentially vast bibliography. Though there is no definitive history of the First Rockingham Administration, a very large number of works on English and American history in the eighteenth century make some reference to it. However, most of them contribute nothing of importance or originality to this subject, and since what follows is not a bibliography of the political history of England in the years 1765 to 1766, but a select list of sources found particularly useful in the composition of a thesis, many which have been examined but found unhelpful are deliberately excluded. Some indication of specific types of material thus omitted is given at appropriate points.

The arrangement is as follows.

A. Manuscript Sources
  1. British Museum
  2. Public Record Office
  3. Other Record Offices
  4. Others

B. Primary Printed Sources
  1. Periodicals
  2. Pamphlets
  3. Other contemporary materials
  4. Published correspondence, documents, etc.

C. Secondary Sources
  1. Printed works
  2. Unpublished Theses

The standard works of reference and bibliography are not included.

A. MANUSCRIPT SOURCES

The manuscript materials for the history of the First Rockingham Administration are, on the whole, reasonably good. The papers of Rockingham at Sheffield, and of Newcastle in the British Museum, are of course particularly valuable, but there are also useful collections relating to the activities of many politicians, both on the Government side (for example Grafton, Egmont, Charles Yorke, Dowdeswell, and Burke) and in the Opposition (for example Grenville, Bedford, and Sandwich). Though many of the papers in these collections have been printed, the manuscripts are useful both for checking the authenticity and accuracy of the published versions, and for documents neglected by the nineteenth-century editors. Thus Albemarle's *Rockingham Memoirs* are unreliable for the reproduction of papers in the Fitzwilliam and Hardwicke collections, while Smith's *Grenville Papers*, on the whole a thoroughly scholarly work, contain only a proportion of the correspondence of George Grenville still extant today.

There are certain obvious lacunae in the manuscript sources. The papers of Cumberland are known to have been largely destroyed; the extant papers of Northington and Bute, two most important correspondents of the King, plainly represent only a fragment of the whole; finally, the great majority of the papers of Henry Conway, which certainly survived into the twentieth century, seem to have disappeared since. All these losses are serious.

1. *British Museum*

Almon Papers.	Add.MS. 2073.
Astle Papers.	Add.MS. 34711 to 34713.
Buckinghamshire Papers.	Add.MSS. 22358, 22359.
Egmont Papers.	Add.MSS. 47012, 47069. (This collection is in course of rearrangement.)
Flood Papers.	Add.MS. 22930.
Grenville Papers.	Add.MS. 42084.
Haldimand Papers.	Add.MS. 21668.
Hamilton Papers.	Add.MS. 41197.
Hardwicke Papers.	Add.MSS. 35361, 35362, 35367, 35368, 35374, 35385, 35424, 35425, 35428, 35429, 35430, 35451, 35607, 35630, 35631, 35637, 35638, 35870, 35879, 35881, 35911, 35912, 35914, 35915.
Holland House Papers.	Add.MSS. 51324, 51338, 51341, 51350, 51375, 51379, 51385 to 51389, 51398, 51402, 51405 to 51408, 51416, 51421, 51423 to 51426, 51432 to 51434, 51447.
Liverpool Papers.	Add.MSS. 38204, 38304, 38305, 38339, 38373, 38455, 38469.
Martin Papers.	Add.MSS. 41354, 41355.
Mitchell Papers.	Add.MSS. 6831, 6834, 6843.
Moore Papers.	Add.MS. 12440.
Newcastle Papers.	Add.MSS. 32965 to 32978, 30000 to 30003, 33030, 33035, 33036, 33041, 33069 to 33071, 33077, 33078.
Pelham Papers.	Add.MS. 33095.
Steven Transcripts.	Add.MS. 42258.
West Papers.	Add.MS. 34728.
Wilkes Papers.	Add.MSS. 30868, 30869, 30877.
Woodfall Papers.	Add.MS. 22780.

Also

Stamp Act Papers.	Stowe MSS. 264—5.

Various scattered papers probably once in the possession of the Seymour-Conway family: official letters of Henry Conway, letters from Lord Hertford to Horace Walpole, and letters from George III to Conway.

Add.MSS. 17497, 17498, 21501 to 21503, 23218, 23219; Egerton MS. 982.

2. *Public Record Office*
Papers examined fall into the following categories:
Colonial Office Papers   (C.O.)
State Papers Foreign   (S.P.)
Treasury Papers   (T.)
Admiralty Papers   (ADM.)
Papers Deposited, etc.   (P.R.O.)

C.O. 5/43, 66, 83, 84, 310, 378, 390, 404, 548, 574, 649, 658, 755,
    891, 920, 928, 934, 978, 987, 999, 1072, 1097, 1098, 1280,
    1331, 1345, 1368; C.O. 42/25, 26; C.O. 43/1; C.O. 217/21, 44.
Despite their designation as Colonial Office Papers, the above are of
course the correspondence of the Board of Trade, and Secretaries of
State, with colonial Governors and other Government departments
on colonial matters.

S.P. 75/118, 119; S.P. 78/267 to 270; S.P. 80/202, 203; S.P. 81/117;
S.P. 84/510; S.P. 90/84, 85; S.P. 91/76, 77; S.P. 94/171 to 174;
S.P. 95/107, 109.
These files contain correspondence relating to the following powers:
Denmark, France, the Hapsburg Empire, Brunswick, Holland, Prussia,
Russia, Spain, Sweden.

T. 1/437 to 443, 445 to 449, 451 to 455; T. 11/28; T. 27/29;
T. 29/37, 38: Treasury letters and papers in general, out-letters, and
minute-books.

ADM. 1/4126: Admiralty correspondence with Secretaries of State.

P.R.O. 30/8: Chatham Papers.
P.R.O. 30/29: Granville Papers.

3. *Other Record Offices*
Berkshire Record Office
    Braybrooke Papers
    Hartley Papers

Bury St. Edmunds and West Suffolk Record Office
    Grafton Papers
    Hervey Papers

Essex Record Office
    Braybrooke Papers
    Charles Gray Papers

Hertfordshire Record Office
    Baker Papers

House of Lords Record Office
    Lords' Sessional Papers
    Lords' Minute Books

Ipswich and East Suffolk Record Office
    Albemarle Papers

Northamptonshire Record Office
  Fitzwilliam Papers
  Northington Papers

Staffordshire Record Office
  Dartmouth Papers

Warwickshire Record Office
  Newdigate Papers

Wigan Record Office
  Gilbert Folliot Diary

4. *Others*

Bedford Estate Office
  Bedford Papers

Bodleian Library
  Clarendon Papers
  Dashwood Papers
  North Papers

History of Parliament Trust, Transcripts (Owners of originals in brackets)
  Buccleuch Papers (Duke of Buccleuch)
  Bute Papers (Marquess of Bute)
  Dowdeswell Papers (William L. Clements Library)
  Grenville Papers (Sir John Murray, Publishers)
  Grenville Letter Book (Huntington Library)
  Sandwich Papers (V. Montagu, Esq.)
  Strutt Papers (Lord Rayleigh)

Nottingham University Library
  Newcastle (Clumber) Papers
  Portland Papers

Sheffield City Library
  Wentworth Woodhouse Muniments: Rockingham and Burke Papers

B. PRIMARY PRINTED SOURCES

1. *Periodicals*

Provincial and colonial newspapers are not included; all the following
were published at London and are to be found in the British Museum,
though in some cases the files of newspapers there are very defective.

> *The Annual Register, or a View of the History, Politicks, and
> Literature of the Year . . .*
> *The Critical Review: or, Annals of Literature*
> *Daily Advertiser*
> *Gazetteer and New Daily Advertiser*
> *General Evening Post*
> *The Gentleman's Magazine and Historical Chronicle*
> *Lloyd's Evening Post and British Chronicle*

London Chronicle
London Evening Post
London Gazette
The London Magazine
The Monthly Review; or, Literary Journal
Owen's Weekly Chronicle; and Westminster Journal
Public Advertiser
Public Ledger
St. James's Chronicle, or the British Evening Post
The Universal Magazine of Knowledge and Pleasure
Westminster Journal and London Political Miscellany
Whitehall Evening Post, or, London Intelligencer

2. Pamphlets

The following list is highly selective, including mainly British pamphlets.
Only a few American tracts of particular interest for English politics
are listed. The more important colonial pamphlets are to be found
reprinted in *Pamphlets of the American Revolution*, ed. B. Bailyn
(Cambridge, Mass., 1965–) and an excellent bibliographical study of
tracts published in North America is the rather inaptly titled *American
Independence, The Growth of an Idea*, by T.R. Adams, (Providence,
1965).
Sub-titles, often very long, are not generally given in the following list.
The pamphlets were examined in the British Museum, except where
another location is indicated.

Almon, J., *The History of the Late Minority* (London, 1766).
—— *A Review of Mr. Pitt's Administration* (5th edn., London, 1766).
The Answer at Large to Mr. P-tt's Speech (London, 1766).
Appleton, N., *A Thanksgiving Sermon on the Total Repeal of the Stamp-
Act* (Boston, 1766).
*An Application of some General Political Rules, to the Present State of
Great-Britain, Ireland and America* (London, 1766).
*Authentic Account of the Proceedings of the Congress held at New York,
in 1765, on the subject of the American Stamp Act* (London, 1767).
*A Candid Refutation of the Charges brought against the Present Ministers
in a late Pamphlet, entitled the Principles of the Late Changes
Impartially Examined* (London, 1765) [Bodleian Library].
The Celebrated Speech of a Celebrated Commoner (London, 1766).
The Charters of the Following Provinces of North America; etc.
(London, 1766).
Chauncy, C., *A Discourse on "the Good News from a far Country"*
(Boston, 1766).
Cooper, G., *The Merits of the New Administration Truly Stated*
(London, 1765).
—— *A Candid Answer to a Late Pamphlet, entitled an Honest Man's
Reasons for declining to take any part in the new Administration*
(London, 1765) [apparently first published as *A Pair of Spectacles
for Short-Sighted Politicians*].

*Correct Copies of the Two Protests against the Bill to Repeal the
    American Stamp Act of last Session with Lists of the Speakers and
    Votes* (Paris, 1766).
Dickinson, J., *The Late Regulations respecting the British Colonies on
    the Continent of America Considered* (Philadelphia, 1765).
*Colonel Draper's Answer to the Spanish Arguments Claiming the Galeon,
    and Refusing Payment of the Ransom Bills, for preserving Manila
    from Pillage and Destruction* (London, 1764).
Drummer, J., *A Defence of the New England Charters* (London, 1765)
    [reprinted].
An Examination of the Rights of the Colonies upon Principles of Law
    (London, 1766).
Fothergill, J., *Considerations Relative to the North American Colonies*
    (London, 1765).
Free and Candid Remarks on a late Celebrated Oration (London, 1766).
Jenyns, S., *The Objections to the Taxation of our American Colonies
    by the Legislature of Great Britain, Briefly Consider'd* (London, 1765)
The Justice and Necessity of Taxing the American Colonies Demonstrated
    (London, 1766).
Knox, W., *The Claim of the Colonies to an Exemption from Internal
    Taxes imposed by Authority of Parliament, examined* (London, 1765)
—— *A Letter to a Member of Parliament, Wherein the Power of the
    British Legislature, and the Case of the Colonists, are briefly and
    impartially considered* (London, 1765).
*The late Occurrences in North America, and Policy of Great Britain
    considered* (London, 1766).
*A Letter to the Common-Council of London, on their late very extra-
    ordinary Address to His Majesty* (2nd edn., London, 1765).
*A List of the Minority in the House of Commons, who voted against
    the Bill to Repeal the American Stamp Act* (Paris, 1766).
Lloyd, C., *An Honest Man's Reasons for Declining to take any Part in
    the New Administration, in a Letter to the Marquis of ———*
    (London, 1765).
—— *A Critical Review of the New Administration* (London, 1765).
—— *A True History of a Late Short Administration* (London, 1766).
—— *The Conduct of the Late Administration Examined, Relative to
    the American Stamp-Act* (2nd edn., London, 1767).
Mayhew, J., *The Snare Broken* (Boston, 1766), reprinted London.
The Necessity of Repealing the American Stamp-Act demonstrated
    (London, 1766).
*A Parallel; drawn between the Administration in the Four Last Years
    of Queen Anne, and the Four First of George the Third* (London,
    1766).
The Principles of the Late Changes Impartially Examined (2nd edn.,
    London, 1765).
*Reasons why the British Colonies, In America, should not be charged
    with Internal Taxes* (New Haven, 1764).
The Secret Springs of the Late Changes in the Ministry Fairly Explained
    (London, 1766).

A Short History of the Conduct of the Present Ministry, with Regard to the American Stamp Act (London, 1766).

The Speech of Mr. P––––– and several others, in a certain August Assembly On a Late important Debate (London, 1766).

Thoughts on the Dismission of Officers, Civil or Military for their Conduct in Parliament (London, 1765) [Bodleian Library].

The True Interest of Great Britain with Respect to her American Colonies Stated and Impartially Considered (London, 1766).

Tucker, J., *A Letter from a Merchant in London to his Nephew in North America* (London, 1766).

–– *A Review of Lord Vis. Clare's Conduct as Representative of Bristol* (Gloucester, 1775).

A View of the Several Changes made in the Administration of Government since the Accession of his Present Majesty (London, 1767)

Whately, T., *The Regulations lately made concerning the Colonies, and the Taxes imposed upon Them, considered* (London, 1765).

–– *Considerations on the Trade and Finances of this Kingdom, and the Measures of Administration with Respect to those great National Objects since the Conclusion of the Peace* (London, 1766).

3. *Other Contemporary Materials*

Almon, J., *Memoirs of a Late Eminent Bookseller* (London, 1790).

–– *Biographical, Literary, and Political Anecdotes of several of the Most Eminent Persons of the Present Age* (London, 1797).

–– *Anecdotes of the Life of the Right Hon. William Pitt, Earl of Chatham* (7th edn., London, 1810) vol. ii.

Anderson, A., *An Historical and Chronological Deduction of the Origin of Commerce, from the Earliest Accounts* (London, 1787-9).

Bernard, F., *Select Letters on the Trade and Government of America* (London, 1774).

A Collection of Interesting, Authentic Papers, Relative to the Dispute between Great Britain and America; shewing the Causes and Progress of that Misunderstanding, from 1764 to 1775; Prior Documents (London, 1777).

A Collection of Tracts, on the subjects of Taxing the British Colonies in America, and regulating their Trade (London, 1773).

Gee, J., *The Trade and Navigation of Great Britain Considered* (new edn., Glasgow, 1767).

Henderson, A., *The Life of William Augustus, Duke of Cumberland* (London, 1766).

The History, Debates, and Proceedings of Both Houses of Parliament of Great Britain, From the Year 1743 to the Year 1774 (London, 1792).

Knox, W., *Extra Official State Papers* (London, 1789).

Maseres, F., *Occasional Essays on various subjects, chiefly political and historical* (London, 1809).

Mitchell, J., *The Present State of Great Britain and North America, with Regard to Agriculture, Population, Trade and Manufactures* (London, 1767).

Postlethwayt, M., *The Universal Dictionary of Trade and Commerce* (3rd edn., London, 1766).

Pownall, T., *The Administration of the Colonies* (4th edn., London, 1768

Rolt, R., *Memoirs of William Augustus, Duke of Cumberland* (London, 1766).

Whitworth, Sir C., *State of the Trade of Great Britain in its Imports and Exports; progressively from the Year 1697* (London, 1776).

The Controversial Letters of John Wilkes, Esq., the Rev. John Horne and their Principal Adherents, with a Supplement containing material Anonymous Pieces (London, 1771).

4. *Published Correspondence, Documents, etc.*

The following list includes some secondary works which happen to contain primary material of importance to this study. These are listed under subject rather than author. Excluded from the list are many primary sources, particularly on the American side, which duplicate other readily obtainable materials, or provide documents of peripheral importance.

Acts of the Privy Council of England, Colonial Series, ed. J. Munro (London, 1911), vols. iv (1745-66) and vi (Unbound Papers).

Diary and Autobiography of John Adams, ed. L.H. Butterfield (Cambridge, Mass., 1961), vol. i.

The American Correspondence of a Bristol Merchant: 1766-76, ed. G.H. Guttridge, University of California Publications in History, xxii (1934), 1–72.

The Arniston Memoirs, ed. G.W.T. Ormond (Edinburgh, 1887).

'William Baker's Account of the Debate on the Repeal of the Stamp Act', ed. D.H. Watson, *William and Mary Quarterly*, 3rd series, xxvi (1969), 259–65.

The Barrington-Bernard Correspondence and Illustrative Matter 1760-1770, edd. E. Channing and A.C. Coolidge (Cambridge, Mass., 1912).

Barrow, J., *Some Account of the Public Life, and a Selection from the unpublished Writings, of the Earl of Macartney* (London, 1807).

The Correspondence of John, Fourth Duke of Bedford, ed. Lord J. Russell (London, 1846), vol. iii.

Bowdoin and Temple Papers, Collections of the Massachusetts Historical Society, 6th series, ix (1897).

Brown, A.E., *John Hancock His Book* (Boston, 1898).

The Burd Papers, ed. L.B. Walker (1897-99).

The Correspondence of Edmund Burke, ed. T.W. Copeland (Cambridge, 1958-), vol. i.

Correspondence of the Right Honourable Edmund Burke; 1744-97, edd. Earl Fitzwilliam and Sir R. Bourke (London, 1844), vol. i.

The Works of the Right Honourable Edmund Burke (London, 1886), vol. i.

Edmund Burke, New York Agent, R.J.S. Hoffman (Philadelphia, 1956).

Selection from the Family Papers preserved at Caldwell (Glasgow, 1854), Part ii, vol. ii.

Calendar of Home Office Papers of the Reign of George III, 1760-65 and 1766-69, ed. J. Redington (London, 1878-9).

Sir Henry Cavendish's Debates of the House of Commons in the Thirteenth Parliament of Great Britain, 1768-74, ed. J. Wrighte (London, 1840-3).

The Letters of Philip Dormer Stanhope, Fourth Earl of Chesterfield, ed. B. Dobrée (1932), vol. vi.

Cochrane, J.A., *Dr. Johnson's Printer* (London, 1964).

The Letters and Papers of Cadwallader Colden, Collections of the New York Historical Society, vii (1923).

Commerce of Rhode Island: 1726-1800, Collections of the Massachusetts Historical Society, 7th series, ix and x (1914-15); see vol. ix.

Companion to the Newspaper and Journal of Facts in Politics, Statistics, and Public Economy: 1833-36 (London, 1834-7); see vol. for 1835.

Connell, B., *Portrait of a Whig Peer* (London, 1957).

The Correspondence of the Colonial Governors of Rhode Island 1723-1775, ed. G.S. Kimball (Boston and New York, 1902-3), vol. ii.

Records of the Cust Family, edd. Lady E., L., and Sir J. Cust (London, 1898, 1909, 1927), vol. iii.

'Debates on the Declaratory Act and the Repeal of the Stamp Act, 1766', edd. C. Hull and H.V. Temperley, *American Historical Review*, xvii (1911-12), 563—86.

'Letters of Dennys de Berdt, 1757-70', ed. A. Matthews, *Publications of the Colonial Society of Massachusetts*, xiii, Transactions (1910-11), 293—461.

Letters of George Dempster to Sir Adam Fergusson, 1756-1813, ed. J. Fergusson (London, 1934).

An Eighteenth-Century Correspondence, edd. L. Dickens and M. Stanton (London, 1910).

Elliot, G.F.S., *The Border Elliots and the Family of Minto* (London, 1897).

The Fitch Papers, Collections of the Connecticut Historical Society, vols. xvii and xviii (1918, 1920); see vol. xviii.

Fitzmaurice, Lord E., *Life of William, Earl of Shelburne* (London, 1875-6), vol. i.

Letters to Henry Fox, Lord Holland, ed. Earl of Ilchester (London, 1915).

Henry Fox, First Lord Holland: His Family and Relations, ed. Earl of Ilchester (London, 1920).

The Francis Letters, edd. B. Francis and E. Keary (London, 1901) vol. i.

Benjamin Franklin's Letters to the Press, 1758-1775, ed. V.W. Crane (Williamsburg, 1950).

The Autobiography of Benjamin Franklin, ed. L.W. Labaree (New Haven, 1964).

The Papers of Benjamin Franklin, ed. L.W. Labaree (New Haven, 1964 -) vols. xii, xiii.

The Correspondence of General Thomas Gage with the Secretaries of State, and with the War Office and the Treasury, 1763-1775, ed. C.E. Carter (New Haven, 1931, 1933).

'Hon. Charles Garth, M.P., the last colonial agent of South Carolina, and some of his work', ed. J.W. Barnwell, *South Carolina Historical and Genealogical Magazine*, xxvi (1925), et seq.

'Charles Garth and His Connexions', L.B. Namier, *English Historical Review*, liv (1939), 443—70, 632—52.

The Correspondence of King George the Third from 1760 to December 1783, ed. Sir J. Fortesque (London, 1927), vol. i.

Namier, L.B., *Additions and Corrections to Sir John Fortesque's Edition of the Correspondence of King George III (Volume I)* (Manchester, 1937).

Letters from George III to Lord Bute: 1756-65, ed. R. Sedgwick (London, 1939).

The Letters of Edward Gibbon, ed. J.E. Norton (London, 1956), vol. i.

Autobiography and Political Correspondence of Augustus Henry, Third Duke of Grafton, K.G., ed. W.R. Anson (London, 1898).

The Grenville Papers, ed. W.J. Smith (London, 1852), vol. iii.

Additional Grenville Papers, 1763-1765, ed. J.R.G. Tomlinson (Manchester, 1962).

The Harcourt Papers, ed. E.W. Harcourt (Oxford, 1876-1905), vols. vii, viii.

Hardy, F., *Memoirs of the Political and Private Life of James Caulfield, Earl of Charlemont* (2nd edn., London, 1812).

Harris, G., *The Life of Lord Chancellor Hardwicke* (London, 1847), vol. iii.

Historical Manuscripts Commission (Serial numbers in brackets).

Buccleuch MSS.	(45)
Dartmouth MSS.	(20)
Denbigh MSS.	(68)
Donoughmore MSS.	(27)
Hastings MSS.	(78)
Laing MSS.	(72)
Lothian MSS.	(62)
Polwarth MSS.	(67)
Round MSS.	(38)
Rutland MSS.	(24)
Stopford-Sackville MSS.	(49)
Various Collections (vi)	(55) (Knox)
(viii)	(55) (Wood)
Weston Underwood MSS.	(10)

The Letters of David Hume, ed. J.Y.T. Greig (Oxford, 1932), vols. i, ii.

The History of the Colony and Province of Massachusetts-Bay by Thomas Hutchinson, ed. L.W. Mayo (Cambridge, Mass., 1936).

'A Section from the Correspondence and Miscellaneous Papers of Jared Ingersoll', ed. F.B. Dexter, *Papers of the New Haven Colony History Society*, ix (1918), 201–472.

Journal of the Commissioners of Trade and Plantations, from January 1764 to December 1767 (London, 1936).

Journals of the House of Commons, xxx (London, 1803).

Journals of the House of Lords, xxxi.

The Letters of Junius, ed. C.W. Everett (London, 1927).

The Law and Working of the Constitution: Documents 1660-1914, edd. W.C. Costin and J.S. Watson (London, 1961), vol. i.

Correspondence of Emily, Duchess of Leinster, ed. B. Fitzgerald (Dublin, 1949-57), vol. i.

The Life and Letters of Lady Sarah Lennox, 1754-1826, Countess of
 Ilchester and Lord Stavordale (London, 1901), vol. i.
'London Merchants on the Stamp Act Repeal', *Massachusetts Historical
 Society Proceedings*, lv (1923), 215—23.
*A Series of Letters from the First Earl of Malmesbury, His Family and
 Friends from 1745 to 1820*, ed. Earl of Malmesbury (London, 1870).
'Extracts from the Letter-Book of Benjamin Marshall, 1763-1766',
 ed. T. Stewardson, *Pennsylvania Magazine of History and Biography*,
 xx (1896), 204—12.
The Maseres Letters, 1766-1768, ed. W.S. Wallace (Toronto, 1919).
Newcastle, Duke of, *A Narrative of the Changes in the Ministry, 1765-
 67*, ed. M. Bateson (London, 1898).
'New Materials on the Stamp Act in New Jersey', ed. D.L. Kemmerer,
 Proceedings of the New Jersey Historical Society, lvi (1938), 220—5.
The New Regime, 1765-67, edd. C.W. Alvord and C.E. Carter,
 Collections of the Illinois Historical State Library, xi (1916).
John Norton and Sons, Merchants of London and Virginia, ed. F.N.
 Mason (2nd edn., Newton Abbot, 1968).
Olson, A.G., *The Radical Duke* (Oxford, 1961).
Letters of Sarah Byng Osborne: 1721-1773, ed. J. McClelland
 (Stanford University, 1930).
*Memorials of the Publick Life and Character of the Right Hon. James
 Oswald of Dunnikier* (Edinburgh, 1825).
*The Parliamentary History of England from the Earliest Period to the
 Year, 1803*, xvi (London, 1803).
Phillimore, R., *The Memoirs and Correspondence of George, Lord
 Lyttelton* (London, 1845).
The Pitkin Papers, Collections of the Connecticut Historical Society,
 xix (1921).
Correspondence of William Pitt, Earl of Chatham, edd. W.S. Taylor and
 J.H. Pringle (London, 1839), vols. ii, iii.
'Extracts from the Letter-Book of Samuel Rhoads, jr. of Philadephia',
 ed. H.D. Biddle, *Pennsylvania Magazine of History and Biography*,
 xiv (1890), 421—6.
'The Duke of Richmond's Memorandum, 1-7 July 1766', ed. A.G.
 Olson, *English Historical Review*, lxxv (1960), 475—82.
Memoirs of the Marquis of Rockingham and his Contemporaries,
 ed. Earl of Albemarle (London, 1852).
'Parliamentary Diaries of Nathaniel Ryder, 1764-67', ed. P.D.G. Thomas,
 Camden Miscellany, xxiii, Camden Society, 4th series, vii (1969),
 229—351.
The Fourth Earl of Sandwich, Diplomatic Correspondence 1763-1765,
 ed. F. Spencer (Manchester, 1961).
Select Statutes, Cases and Documents, ed. C.G. Robertson (8th edn.,
 London, 1947).
George Selwyn and his Contemporaries, J.H. Jesse, (London, 1843).
'Stamp Act Papers', *Maryland Historical Magazine*, vi (1911), 282—305.
The Statutes at Large (London, 1786), vols. v, vii.
'Correspondence between William Strahan and David Hall, 1763-1777',
 Pennsylvania Magazine of History and Biography, x (1886), 86—99
 et seq.

306 BIBLIOGRAPHY

Tyler, J.E., 'John Roberts and the First Rockingham Administration',
  English Historical Review, lxvii (1952), 259–65.
Horace Walpole's *Memoirs of the Reign of King George III*, ed.
  G.F.R. Barker (London, 1894), vol. ii.
Letters of Horace Walpole, ed. P. Toynbee (Oxford, 1904, 1918, 1925),
  vols. vi, vii, supplements i, ii, iii.
John Wentworth, Governor of New Hampshire, 1767-1775, L.S. Mayo
  (Cambridge, Mass., 1921).
Memorials of the Family of Wemyss, ed. Sir W. Fraser (Edinburgh, 1888)
The Correspondence of the Late John Wilkes with his Friends, etc.,
  ed. J. Almon (London, 1805).
Wilkes and the City, W.P. Treloar (London, 1917).

C. SECONDARY SOURCES

1. *Printed Works*

Inevitably there is a very heavy bias towards American works and subjects in the following list. While there are very few monographs of
interest on the political side of the First Rockingham Administration,
the question of the Stamp Act has attracted an understandably large
number of writers. For the most part, only works of the most direct
interest are listed below. This of course includes some highly specialized
pieces on colonial history where they are of importance for imperial
policy. On the other hand, the older and more general studies of Anglo-
American relations in this period are listed only when they have a
particular contribution to make.

Adair, D., 'The Stamp Act in Contemporary English Cartoons', *William
  and Mary Quarterly*, 3rd series, x (1953), 538–42.
Adams, T.R., *American Independence. The Growth of an Idea*
  (Providence, 1965).
Alden, J.R., *General Gage in America* (Baton Rouge, 1948).
Alvord, C.W., *The Mississippi Valley in British Politics* (New York, 1916)
  vol. i.
Andrews, C.M., 'The Boston Merchants and the Non-Importation Move-
  ment', *Publications of the Colonial Society of Massachusetts*, xix,
  Transactions (1916-17), 159–69.
Armytage, F., *The Free Port System in the British West Indies* (London,
  1953).
Ashton, T.S., *Economic Fluctuations in England: 1700-1800* (Oxford,
  1959).
Bargar, B.D., *Lord Dartmouth and the American Revolution* (Columbia,
  1965).
Barrington, S., *Political Life of William Wildman, Viscount Barrington*
  (London, 1814).
Basye, A.H., *The Lords Commissioners of Trade and Plantations
  commonly known as the Board of Trade, 1748-82* (New Haven, 1925)
Baxter, W.T., *The House of Hancock* (Cambridge, Mass., 1945).
Bleackley, H., *Life of John Wilkes* (London, 1917).
Brooke, J., *The Chatham Administration, 1766-68* (London, 1956).

Burt, A.L., 'Governor Murray and the British Government', *Proceedings and Transactions of the Royal Society of Canada*, 3rd series, vol. xxii, Sect. ii, (1928), pp. 49—56.

—— 'The Mystery of Walker's Ear', *Canadian Historical Review*, iii (1922), 233—55.

Christelow, A., 'Contraband Trade between Jamaica and the Spanish Main, and the Free Port Act of 1766', *Hispanic American Historical Review*, xxii (1942), 309—43.

Christie, I.R., 'Was there a "New Toryism" in the Earlier Part of George III's Reign?', *Journal of British Studies*, v (1965-6), 60—71.

—— *Crisis of Empire* (London, 1966).

—— *Myth and Reality in Late-Eighteenth Century British Politics and Other Papers* (London, 1970).

Clark, V.S., *History of Manufactures in the United States* (New York, 1929), vol. i.

Collyer, C., 'The Rockingham Connection and Country Opinion in the Early Years of George III', *Proceedings of Leeds Philosophical and Literary Society*, vii (1952-5), 251—75.

—— 'The Rockinghams and Yorkshire Politics, 1742-61', *Publications of Thoresby Society*, xli, *Thoresby Miscellany*, xii (1954), 352—82.

Cone, C.B., *Burke and the Nature of Politics. The Age of the American Revolution* (University of Kentucky, 1957).

Copeland, T.W., 'Burke's First Patron', *History Today*, ii (1952), 394—9.

Coupland, R., *The Quebec Act* (Oxford, 1925).

Crane, V.W., 'Benjamin Franklin and the Stamp Act', *Publications of the Colonial Society of Massachusetts*, xxxii (1933-7), 56—77.

Davies, R., 'English Foreign Trade, 1700-74', *Economic History Review*, xv (1962-3), 285—303.

Dickerson, O.M., *The Navigation Acts and the American Revolution* (Philadelphia, 1957).

Donoghue, B., *British Politics and the American Revolution* (London, 1964).

Edwards, B., *The History, Civil and Commercial, of the British Colonies in the West Indies* (London, 1793), vol. i.

Evans, E.G., 'Planter Indebtedness and the Coming of the Revolution in Virginia', *William and Mary Quarterly*, 3rd series, xix (1962) 511—33.

Ericson, F.J., 'The Contemporary British Opposition to the Stamp Act, 1764-65', *Papers of Michigan Academy of Science, Arts and Letters*, xxix (1943) 489—505.

Foord, A.S., *His Majesty's Opposition: 1714-1830* (Oxford, 1964).

George, M.D., 'America in English Satirical Prints', *William and Mary Quarterly*, 3rd series, x, (1953) 511—37.

Gipson, L.H., *The British Empire before the American Revolution* (Caldwell and New York, 1937), vols. ix, x, xi.

—— *The Coming of the Revolution: 1763-75* (New York, 1962).

Greene, J.P. and Jellison, R.M., 'The Currency Act of 1764 in Imperial-Colonial Relations, 1764-76', *William and Mary Quarterly*, 3rd series, xviii (1961), 484—518.

Guttridge, G.H., *The Early Career of Lord Rockingham: 1730-65*, University of California Publications in History, xliv (1952).
—— *English Whiggism and the American Revolution* (Berkeley and Los Angeles, 1963).
Henley, Lord R., *A Memoir of the Life of Robert Henley, Earl of Northington, Lord High Chancellor of Great Britain* (London, 1831).
Hinkhouse, F.J., *The Preliminaries of the American Revolution as seen in the English Press, 1763-1775* (New York, 1926).
Hodge, H.H., 'The Repeal of the Stamp Act', *Political Science Quarterly*, xix (1904), 252—76.
Horn, D.B., *Great Britain and Europe in the Eighteenth Century* (Oxford, 1967).
Humphries, R. and Scott, S.M., 'Lord Northington and the Laws of Canada', *Canadian Historical Review*, xiv (1933) 42—63.
Imlach, G.M., 'Earl Temple and the Ministry of 1765', *English Historical Historical Review*, xxx (1915) 317—21.
Jarrett, D., 'The Regency Crisis of 1765', *English Historical Review*, lxxxv (1970) 282—316.
Jervey, T.D., 'Barlow Trecothick', *South Carolina Historical and Genealogical Magazine*, xxxii (1931) 317—21.
Johnson, A.S., 'British Politics and the Repeal of the Stamp Act', *South Atlantic Quarterly*, lxii (1963) 169—86.
Kammen, M.G., *A Rope of Sand* (New York, 1968).
Kelly, B.W., *The Conqueror of Culloden* (London, 1903).
Kemp, B., *King and Commons, 1660-1832* (London, 1957).
Kingsford, W., *The History of Canada* (London, 1888-98), vol. v.
Laprade, W.T., 'The Stamp Act in British Politics', *American Historical Review*, xxxv (1930), 735—57.
Lecky, W.E.H., *A History of England in the Eighteenth Century* (London, 1878-90), vol. iii.
Macalpine, I. and Hunter, R., *George III and the Mad Business* (London, 1969).
Macaulay, Lord, *Essay on the Earl of Chatham* (London, 1887).
MacPherson, D., *Annals of Commerce, Fisheries and Navigation, with brief notices of the arts and sciences connected with them, etc.* (London, 1805).
Mahon, Lord, *History of England from the Peace of Utrecht to the Peace of Versailles, 1713-83* (3rd edn., London, 1853), vol. v.
Mahon, R.H., *The Life of General the Hon. James Murray* (London, 1921).
Mahoney, T.H.D., 'Edmund Burke and the American Revolution: The Repeal of the Stamp Act', in *Edmund Burke: The Enlightenment and the Modern World* (Detroit, 1967), pp. 1—20.
Minchinton, W.E., 'The Stamp Act Crisis: Bristol and Virginia', *Virginia Magazine of History and Biography*, lxxiii (1965), 145—55.
—— *The Growth of English Overseas Trade in the 17th and 18th Centuries* (London, 1969).
Mitchell, B.R., and Deane, P., *Abstract of British Historical Statistics* (Cambridge, 1962).

Morgan, E.S., 'Colonial Ideas of Parliamentary Power', *William and Mary Quarterly*, 3rd series, v (1948), 311–41.
— and Morgan, H.M., *The Stamp Act Crisis* (rev. edn., New York, 1963).
Namier, Sir L., *The Structure of Politics at the Accession of George III* (2nd edn., London, 1957).
— *England in the Age of the American Revolution* (2nd edn., London, 1961).
— *Crossroads of Power* (London, 1962).
— and Brooke, J., *Charles Townshend* (London, 1964).
——— *History of Parliament: House of Commons: 1754 to 1790* (London, 1964).
Neatby, H., *Quebec: The Revolutionary Age: 1760-1791* (London, 1966).
Owen, J.B., *The Rise of the Pelhams* (London, 1957).
Pares, R., *King George III and the Politicians* (Oxford, 1953).
— *Yankees and Creoles* (London, 1956).
Penson, L.M., 'The London West India Interest in the Eighteenth Century', *English Historical Review*, xxxvi (1921), 373–92.
— *The Colonial Agents of the British West Indies* (London, 1924).
Pitman, F.W., *The Development of the British West Indies: 1700-1763* (New Haven, 1917).
Postgate, R., *That Devil Wilkes* (rev. edn., London, 1956).
Ramsay, J.F., *Anglo-French Relations: 1763-70*, University of California Publications in History, xvii, No. 3 (1939), 143–264.
Rea, R., *The English Press in Politics: 1760-1774* (Lincoln, Neb., 1962).
Reddaway, W.F., 'Macartney in Russia, 1765-67', *Cambridge Historical Journal*, iii (1931), 260–84.
Ritcheson, C.R., *British Politics and the American Revolution* (Norman, 1954).
Roberts, M., *Splendid Isolation, 1763-1780.* (Stenton Lecture, 1969) (Reading, 1969).
— 'Great Britain, Denmark and Russia, 1763-70' in R. Hatton and M.S. Anderson (edd.), *Studies in Diplomatic History in memory of D.B. Horn* (London, 1970).
Robertson, M.L., 'Scottish Commerce and the American War of Independence', *Economic History Review*, 2nd series, ix (1956-7), 123–31.
Schlesinger, A.M., *The Colonial Merchants and the American Revolution 1763-83* (New York, 1917).
— 'The Colonial Newspapers and the Stamp Act', *New England Quarterly*, viii (1935) 63–83.
Schumpeter, E.B., *English Overseas Trade Statistics: 1697-1808* (Oxford, 1960).
Sherrard, O.A., *A Life of John Wilkes* (London, 1930).
— *Lord Chatham and America* (London, 1958).
Sosin, J.M., *Whitehall and the Wilderness* (Lincoln, Neb., 1961).
— 'Imperial Regulation of Colonial Paper Money, 1764-1773', *Pennsylvania Magazine of History and Biography*, lxxxviii (1964), 174–98.
— *Agents and Merchants* (Lincoln, Neb., 1965).

Stephens, F.G. and Hawkins, E., *Catalogue of Prints and Drawings in the British Museum, 1. Political and Personal Satires*, iv, 1761-1771 (London, 1883).

Sutherland, L.S. 'Edmund Burke and the First Rockingham Ministry', *English Historical Review*, xlvii (1932) 46–72.

Sykes, N., 'The Duke of Newcastle as Ecclesiastical Minister', *English Historical Review*, lxvii (1942) 59–84.

Wallace, W.S., 'The Beginnings of British Rule in Canada', *Canadian Historical Review*, vi (1925) 208–21.

Wickwire, F.B., *British Subministers and Colonial America. 1763-1783* (Princeton, 1961).

Williams, B., *The Life of William Pitt, Earl of Chatham* (London, 1913).

Winstanley, D.A., *Personal and Party Government* (Cambridge, 1910).

Wolf, E., 'Benjamin Franklin's Stamp Act Cartoon', *Proceedings of American Philosophical Society*, xcix (1955), 388–96.

2. *Unpublished Theses.*

Gilbert, A., 'The Political Correspondence of Charles Lennox, Third Duke of Richmond: 1765-84', Oxford University D. Phil. Thesis 1956 (published in part; see p.305 above, under Olson, A.G., *The Radical Duke*).

Hardy, A., 'The Duke of Newcastle and his Friends in Opposition, 1762-5', Manchester University M.A. Thesis 1956.

Savadge, W.R., 'The West Country and the American Mainland Colonies, 1763-1783, with special reference to the merchants of Bristol', Oxford University B. Litt. Thesis 1951.

Smith, B.R., 'The Committee of the Whole House to Consider the American Papers (January and February 1766)', Sheffield University M.A. Thesis 1957.

Watson, D.H., 'Barlow Trecothick and other Associates of Lord Rockingham during the Stamp Act Crisis', Sheffield University M.A. Thesis 1958.

INDEX

NOTE: This index includes brief biographical details, where relevant. In the case of M.P.s and officeholders the information given relates only to the period covered by this study.

Peers are to be found under their title, not family name.

ortland, William Cavendish Bentinck, Duke of, 1738-1809, Privy Councillor, Ld. Chamberlain of Hshld. Jul. 1765-Nov. 1766, 13, 38, 160, 271, 285.

'rincess Dowager of Wales, 8, 52, 57, 281.

'russia, 10, 65, 84, 87, 88-90.

Quebec, 253-7.

Regency Bill, 8, 9, 41, 43, 55, 56, 60, 240.

Richmond, Charles Lennox, Duke of, 1735-1806, Ambassador to France Jul. 1765-May 1766, Sec. of State, (S. Dept.) May-Jul. 1766, 12, 19, 193, 244-5, 247, 249, 257; as Ambassador, 85, 86; and King's Friends, 227, 228, 243; appointment as Secretary, 238, 239; dismissal, 259; and Rockingham party, 276.

Rigby, Richard, 1722-88, M.P. Tavistock, Jt. Vice-Treasurer of Ireland to Jul. 1765, 5, 10, 46, 48, 212, 229, 243.

Roberts, John, c.1711-72, M.P. Harwich, Ld. of Trade from Jul. 1765, 22, 38, 49, 51, 94, 274.

Rockingham, Charles Watson-Wentworth, Marquess of, 1730-82, 1st Ld. of Treasury, Jul. 1765-Jul. 1766, and formation of Ministry, 4, 11, 15, 28-9, 49; career and character, 16-20, 244-9; and Cumberland, 16, 17-8, 31, 70, 73-4, 100, 101; and Burke, 22-3; and Newcastle, 35-6, 37, 93, 99; in Parliament, 19-20, 133, 222, 246; and Parliamentary situation, 93, 94-7, 132, 133, 162; and Yorkshire, 112, 249, 264-5; and trade, 111-6, 202; and American policy, Chap. iv passim, 149-53, 198, 208-12; and Pitt, 67, 105, 136, 138, 143-4, 145, 147, 232-3, 248, 262-3; and King's Friends, 226, 228-9, 237, 238, 243-4, 280, 281-2; and Strange affair, 163, 167, 168; resignation threats, 160, 239, 246, 252, 257; and Wilkes, 217; and Bedfords, 229; and public opinion, 116, 173, 241, 264-5, 283-4, 285; dismissal, 258-9; and party, 229, 247-9, 271, 279-80; and Chatham Ministry, 260-3, 269, 270.

Rockingham, Marchioness of, (nee Mary Bright), d. 1804, 20-1, 105.

Russia, 84, 87, 88, 90, 91, 99, 128-9, 266.

Sackville, Lord George, 1716-85, M.P. Hythe, Privy Councillor, Jt. Vice-Treasurer of Ireland Dec. 1765-Jul. 1766, 28, 103-4, 137, 162, 170, 201, 234, 240, 259.

Sandwich, John Montagu, Earl of, 1718-92, 1st Ld. of Admiralty to Jul. 1765, 4, 5, 47, 48, 87, 140, 162n, 193.

Saunders, Sir Charles, 1713-75, M.P. Hedon, Ld. of Admiralty Jul. 1765-Jul. 1766, Privy Councillor, 1st Ld. of Admiralty Aug.-Nov. 1766, 67, 271, 272.

Savile, Sir George, 1726-84, M.P. Yorkshire, 38-9, 109-10, 112, 129, 178, 195, 198, 215, 271, 272.

Scawen, James, 1734-1801, M.P. Mitchell, 271.

Scarborough, Richard Lumley-Saunderson, Earl of, 1725-82, Privy Councillor, Cofferer of Hshld. Jul. 1765-Nov. 1766, 270, 271.

Secker, Thomas, 1693-1768, Archbishop of Canterbury, 34, 152-3, 193.

Sheffield, 264 and n.

Shelburne, William Petty, Earl of (I), 1737-1805, Sec. of State (S. Dept.) from Jul. 1766, 49, 66, 108, 137, 142, 222, 277.

Spain, 84, 87, 92.

Spanish Trade, 113-7, 182, 188, 200-1, 203, 204, 205, 207.

Spencer, Lord Charles, 1740-1820, M.P. Oxfordshire, Comptr. of Hshld. to Jul. 1765, 47.

Stamp Act, see America, North.

Stanley, Hans, 1721-80, M.P. Southampton, Ld. of Admiralty to Jul. 1765, Special Envoy Aug.-Dec. 1766, 5, 47, 62, 101-2, 159, 268.

Strahan, William, 1715-85, 131, 135, 177, 180, 232.

Strange, James Smith Stanley, Lord, 1717-71, M.P. Lancashire, Chancellor of Duchy of Lancaster, 54, 64n, 163-8, 171, 191, 205.

Suffolk, Henry Howard, 1739-79, 47, 64n, 133.

$$\frac{\begin{array}{r} 1797 \\ -1725 \end{array}}{0072}$$